Autonomous Vehicles Opportunities, Strategies, and Disruptions

Second Edition

Updated July 24, 2021

Michael E. McGrath

Dedicated to:
My Amazing Family

Table of Contents

Introduction to July 14, 2021
Updated Second Edition

I published the first edition of this book in 2018. Because this fast-developing emerging industry changes rapidly, I released a significantly revised second edition in November 2019. Since then, I have continued to update that edition, first in June 2020 and now again in July 2021.

There are several significant updates in this Jul 2021 edition. Autonomous ride services (ARS) continues to be the first new industry for autonomous vehicles. However, the creation of this new market is delayed by a year because of the COVID-19 pandemic. ARS road testing was suspended during most of 2020, and that slowed overall testing progress. More importantly, the ridesharing industry was hit hard during the pandemic as people stopped traveling, and ARS is the modern version of ridesharing.

Despite this, ARS developed continued aggressively. In November 2020, there was a major milestone, Waymo initiated the first paid autonomous rides without any drive or safety person in the vehicle. ARS companies continued to raise billions for the development and launch of their services, and many clarified their strategies, which are updated in this update. ARS is inevitable. It will just launch in 2022/23 instead of 2021/22.

One of the more significant development is the progress made in autonomous long-haul trucking. At least three companies came public in the first half of 2021, raising billions of dollars and gaining more than $20 billion in combined market value. These companies publicly disclosed their strategies along with aggressive projections. It now seems that autonomous trucking from and to terminals located just off major highways will be the common strategy. This makes autonomous driving requirements much more manageable while providing most of the advantages.

Autonomous vehicles for individuals purchased through retail at dealers will continue to be a later market opportunity. New cars, particularly high-end models, will progressively get more autonomous capabilities. Sufficiently-autonomous vehicles will be available for purchase by individuals in what I refer to as Stage 2 (post-2025). These will still have driver controls for those limited cases where human driving is needed, but most driving will be done autonomously.

The development of autonomous vehicles outside of the U.S. has continued, especially in China. This update includes expanded coverage of autonomous vehicle development in China.

It looks at what is happening globally as companies in other countries are developing AVs. The impact on the auto industry was a significant focus of the first edition, and here I go into even more depth on it. For a better understanding of AVs, I added a chapter on how AVs think and act. I also included the new SAE definitions for autonomous driving, which are closer to my original descriptions.

The essential business models and forecasts are updated in this version, but they are directionally comparable. It has become apparent that autonomous ride services (ARS) will be the initial market for autonomous vehicles. In the first edition, I needed to explain why I thought that it would be. Now, this is generally recognized, and most companies have refocused their strategies to emphasize ARS.

A lot is written about autonomous vehicles. Some of it has been very insightful. But there have also been many articles written by people who are so ill-informed that I can say that they are expressing naïve opinions on something that they don't understand at all. I'm surprised by how many people claim to be experts when they haven't done any research or spent the time trying to understand autonomous vehicles, how they work, and the real issues. My intention in writing this book is to help more people understand.

Many critics pay lip service to acknowledge that autonomous vehicles may eventually transform transportation, but then they go on to look at AVs only as fully-autonomous for individuals. They ignore the transformation. The transformation is: autonomous ride services replace ridesharing and individual car ownership, autonomous long-haul trucking automating freight transportation using terminals located off highways, and autonomous home delivery replacing delivery where people are at home to receive goods. Autonomous vehicles don't need to do things the way they are today. They do things differently.

The benefits of autonomous vehicles (AVs) are mind-boggling. To start with, they will avoid more than 90% of all auto accidents, saving almost 40,000 lives annually and preventing severe injuries to millions of people in the United States alone. This is more than just a statistic. Here is a more personal way of looking at it. More than 3 million people will be killed in automobile accidents in the U.S. That's almost 1% of the population in the average person's lifetime. Everyone will be personally touched by at least one auto fatality that could be avoided.

AVs will reduce transportation costs by as much as 80% and save families thousands of dollars annually. The average person will do things other than driving, giving them nearly 300 hours of "found time" annually. That equates to more than 250 million hours of additional time in the United States alone. AVs will provide mobility to millions of people who cannot drive, improving their lives in ways that most of us take for granted. These benefits are unprecedented, and it makes the advent of autonomous vehicles inevitable.

Some people claim that an autonomous vehicle may never be able to drive every place in the world in every condition. That may be true, but it isn't relevant to autonomous vehicles replacing most of the miles driven by humans. This will be accomplished in the next ten years.

Autonomous vehicles are not only feasible; they are being tested in millions of miles of actual driving. Waymo is already providing autonomous rides without a safety driver in the vehicle. Some people criticize that it is taking a long time for AVs to start providing autonomous rides. Taking a long time for testing is not a failure to develop them; it's a conservative strategy of putting safety first and being careful to test them even more than the minimum required. This extended testing time is intentional, not a sign of failure.

The market opportunity for autonomous vehicles is enormous. Many estimates show it exceeding $1 trillion per year in the U.S. This opportunity is not a single market; autonomous vehicles will create several large markets and multiple market segments. The first significant market to emerge will be autonomous ride services. You will see why later in this book.

Let's look at a quick overview of what's in this edition. Part I introduces autonomous vehicles, starting with an entertaining view of how lifestyles will change. It then describes the benefits of AVs in detail, providing convincing arguments of why the move to AVs is inevitable. The savings in lives, time, and cost of transportation are so overwhelming they can't be ignored. Chapter 3 provides an overview of autonomous driving, starting by explaining the categories of autonomous driving, the SAE definitions, and alternative approaches to autonomous driving. This will define the practical categories for autonomous driving, including the definition that provides a critical strategic perspective. While it will take time for autonomous vehicles to master everything, the point that most people miss is that autonomous vehicles only need to be what I refer to as, *sufficiently-autonomous*. A similar classification has since been added to the recent SAE definitions. Part I also includes a new chapter that provides interesting insights into how an AV thinks and acts. Then for those who are interested, it goes into more detail on the technologies enabling autonomous vehicles.

Part II is the heart of the book. It discusses the opportunities and markets for AVs and the strategies being pursued to capture these opportunities. It starts with the first and most crucial market opportunity: Autonomous Ride

Services (ARS). ARS will be the first meaningful use of AVs because sufficiently-autonomous vehicles can provide complete services within geofenced areas. I explain the economic and business models that show how ARS businesses will work. They will deploy fleets of autonomous vehicles to provide these ride services in major metropolitan areas. The exceptional economics of ARS enables extraordinary profitability at a much lower price than ridesharing, which ARS will ultimately displace. In this chapter, I also describe the strategies for each significant ARS competitor in the U.S. Part II, then describes the other major AV markets. Sales of AVs at retail will wait until they are first proven and accepted in ARS. However, the real challenge for auto manufacturers and related industries will be the decline in new car sales. The increased use of ridesharing and then ARS will cannibalize auto ownership. An ARS vehicle will have 45%-50% utilization compared to the 5% utilization of a typical individually-owned vehicle. Each ARS AV will eventually displace 8-10 individually-owned cars.

Autonomous long-haul trucking has accelerated. Companies developing these technologies have determined a new model using terminals located just off highways. This simplifies the autonomous driving problem and creates most of the benefits. Autonomous long-haul trucks will be hauling freight without drivers by 2023.

Autonomous home delivery has been proliferating; even though, like ridesharing, it is losing money for most involved. The rationale for this is the same: autonomous home delivery will replace driver-based home delivery, making it a larger and more profitable business. COVID-19 has highlighted the potential importance of home delivery, and home delivery without a driver could be more attractive. Part II concludes by looking at the opportunity for autonomous trucks, shuttles, and buses. This second edition also looks at global opportunities for AVs.

Part III clarifies the disruptions expected from AVs as well as government regulations and support. There are some worrisome disruptions anticipated from the advent of autonomous vehicles. The enormous benefits discussed previously come at a cost. The emergence of autonomous ride services will decrease personal car ownership. Many auto-related industries also will be disrupted, including car dealers, gas stations, auto repair shops, car rental companies, non-autonomous ridesharing, taxis, public transportation, insurance companies, and many others. Ridesharing and delivery drivers will be particularly vulnerable to job losses early on. Autonomous trucking isn't expected to decrease truck driver jobs for some time since the trucking industry can't keep up with the increasing demand for drivers. Collectively, the advent of autonomous vehicles, particularly ARS, eventually will result in the loss of millions of jobs in the United States alone. I expect that a disruption of this magnitude will cause some to question if autonomous vehicles are a good thing. In the end, though, it's difficult to argue that it's not worth the

4

savings in lives, injuries, time, and economic benefits. I believe that society, at least in developed countries, may need to rethink the nature of work.

Government regulation in the United States has three levels: national (federal), state, and local (municipal). Each level of government has a different focus on the regulation and support of autonomous vehicles. At a national level, regulation focuses on making AVs legal to produce and sell. The state and municipal levels regulate the use of vehicles in that state or municipality. Focusing initially on ARS, little is needed from the federal government besides some clarifications on regulations. At the state level, different states have adopted various rules and support for AVs. So, ARS will start in the friendliest environments.

Part IV wraps up the book with projections of the timing for the launch of autonomous vehicles, using a stages-of-adoption model. It presents overall forecasts for adoption in each market by stage and then goes into more detailed descriptions for each market within each stage.

I am even more convinced that autonomous vehicles will change our fundamental lifestyles, and in doing so, create what may be the most significant opportunities of this century. Ford executive chairman Bill Ford agreed with this after reading the first edition of my book, saying, "You are right. The advent of autonomous vehicles will have a huge impact on our everyday lives due to the centrality of transportation to both society and business."

The benefits are unprecedented. The challenges are sizable but manageable. The new market opportunities are enormous. Several companies are following exciting strategies, while others are lagging. The disruptions still appear to be worrisome.

I decided to update the second edition of my book *Autonomous Vehicles: Opportunities, Strategies, and Disruptions for all these reasons.* I hope you enjoy it!

Michael E. McGrath
July 14, 2021

About the Author

Michael E. McGrath is an experienced technology consultant, executive, and author. He is a founder of PRTM, one of the most successful global consulting firms on technology development and strategy. At PRTM he created the firm's consulting practice in product development and strategy with the well-known PACE process.

He is a former CEO or Chairman of four publicly-traded technology companies. He led the turnaround of software company i2 (ITWO) Technologies in 2005 and later served as chairman of Entrust (ENTU). He currently serves as the chairman of the board of directors for National Instruments (NATI).

He authored seven books on strategy and decision making. His best-selling book, *Product Strategy for High-Technology Companies*, introduced new strategic concepts such as platform strategy and core strategic vision, which were successfully applied by hundreds of large companies over the last 25 years. His decision-making books include *Business Decisions, Decide Better for a Better Life,* and *The Wit and Wisdom of Decision Making*. His books on product development include *Product And Cycle-time Excellence* and *Next-Generation Product Development*.

In 2018, he started research on autonomous vehicles, specifically trying to understand how this technology would redefine transportation and the strategies companies would follow. *Autonomous Vehicles: Opportunities, Strategies, and Disruptions*, originally published in 2018 was the result of thousands of hours of research. Since then, he has continued to update this book to reflect technical advancements and strategy shifts. This 2021 update to the second edition incorporates many changes to bring readers most current.

To contact the author: michael_e_mcgrath@msn.com

Part I
Introduction to Autonomous Vehicles

Chapter 1
New Lifestyles

Autonomous vehicles offer the prospects of an exciting future, although most people can't fully envision it yet. Perhaps the best way to appreciate how autonomous vehicles, termed AVs, will change the ways we go about our lives and how we work is to imagine the new lifestyle models that they will create. AVs will change the way we commute to work, giving us new-found time. They will change the way we get to and from restaurants, activities, places, and events. They will enable significant lifestyle improvements by providing mobility for those who cannot drive. They will also change the ways food and packages are delivered. They will sometimes even make ground travel less expensive and more convenient than air travel.

Even more significantly than individually-owned AVs, autonomous ride services (also termed ARS), essentially Uber without a driver, will change the nature of transportation. I discuss this in detail in Chapter 7 but introduce some examples here.

Here, in this first chapter, I describe whimsical, but expected, ways autonomous vehicles could create new lifestyles. I hope these portrayals generate interest in learning more about autonomous vehicles.

Commuting

For most people, commuting to and from work is tiresome. It is non-productive time, often considered wasted. AVs will completely transform commuting as we know it today. Commuting by AV will be a more productive experience. Instead of driving or being stuck in traffic, people will work, enjoy entertainment, sleep, or socialize. Using commuting time more productively will provide an incentive for more people to live farther from where they work. It may also reduce the need to own a car for commuting or even use public transportation. Here are some examples.

Individually-Owned AV Commuting

Many individuals will use their own AVs for commuting to and from work, enabling them to replace their commuting time with more productive work or leisure activities. Here is an example:

Joan and her husband Mark use their AV primarily for their long commute to and from work. Even though they both work in the city, they decided to buy a more affordable home farther outside the city and then purchased a new AV to use the additional commuting time more productively.

They usually leave for work at 8 AM and use their 60-minute commute to have coffee and muffins and read the morning papers on their iPads. They purchased the mobile kitchen option in their AV that includes a coffee maker and a small refrigerator. They usually drop Mark off at work first, and then Joan last because her company offers a free AV parking lot a few miles from her office. The AV drops her off at her office and then drives itself to the AV parking lot. They usually leave work at 6 PM and watch the news on the way home, sometimes having a glass of wine together on the trip. They are pleased to afford a much nicer home farther from the city while not having to waste more time commuting. They have the house of their dreams for less than they would have paid for a smaller home closer to the city.

Shared AV Commuting

Shared AV commuting can replace carpooling as we know it, eliminating the need for someone to drive and provide a car. Here is a typical example:

Anthony shares an AV commuting vehicle with three co-workers. Autonomous Commuting Corp. provides this AV for a monthly fee. They each pay $20 per day ($400 per month) for the 30-mile (60-mile round-trip) commute. At the cost of $0.33 per mile each, this costs about half of their previous carpooling and parking expenses. In addition, they don't need to take turns driving or compensate one of them for driving, and the interior is much more comfortable. The spacious AV is designed primarily for commuting with comfortable individual seating and high-speed internet. The AV reliably picks them up at the same time every day. They each have their routine in the morning and the evening commute. They read, watch videos or TV, drink their coffee, or sleep. One of them is using her time to learn a new language. If they work late, they merely request an alternative ride from Autonomous Commuting. Autonomous Commuting uses the AV throughout the day to transport others, enabling it to provide low-cost commuting.

City Commuting

Many people who work in a city will use an autonomous ride service to get back and forth to work instead of owning a car or using public transportation. They might not have a scheduled pick-up time or monthly contract. Instead, they will use an autonomous ride service (ARS) the same way people use Uber ridesharing today, only it will be less expensive and more convenient, as is seen in this example:

Carrie lives and works in Atlanta but doesn't own a car. She merely requests an ARS when she leaves for her three-mile trip to work, and the ARS vehicle usually arrives within five minutes. The cost is $3.50, less than it previously cost to take a taxi or Uber, and just a bit more than the $2.50 price of MARTA, Atlanta's transportation system. It also takes her only 5-7 minutes to get to work, compared to the 15-25 minutes it takes by public transportation. Most importantly, she doesn't need to walk five minutes each way to and from the bus stop. After work, she frequently requests an AV to take her to meet friends for dinner. Overall, Carrie estimates that she spends about $125 per month commuting and saves at least a half-hour a day compared to MARTA. The benefits are evident: it costs her $10 more per week and saves two-and-a-half hours. She estimates that she spends $200-$250 per month for all transportation, which is only 7% of what she earns. If she owned a car, it would cost her more than $1,000 per month, including parking at her apartment and office, and would consume more than 25% of what she made.

Free AV Rides

Autonomous ride services (ARS) will become so inexpensive that it will sometimes be free. For example, retail stores and restaurants will use free ARS to attract more customers, as is seen in these examples.

Complimentary Restaurant Transportation

Once ARS becomes available, there will be a rush to use these services to gain an advantage in attracting customers. Restaurants provide an exciting example. Many high-end restaurants offer valet parking as a service to their customers. Complimentary ARS will offer a unique competitive advantage for restaurants and probably won't cost more than valet parking.

Valet parking is typically $25-$35 per hour for each valet attendant, not including tips or the cost to rent parking spaces. An ARS will cost $8-$15 per customer round-trip for a typical local trip. So, the costs can be reasonably similar, depending on volume. Initially, there may even be a substantial competitive advantage for restaurants that provide a free autonomous ride service to pick up and return their customers, potentially fueling a rush to use these services.

Sam made a dinner reservation for 7 PM on Open Table at Chez Duncan, a restaurant that provides complimentary ARS transportation to and from dinner. The app knows where he is, relative to the restaurant, and it offers free ARS. He clicks to accept, and the restaurant's ARS picks him up at 6:30. Sam usually only goes to restaurants that provide this complimentary service; otherwise, he pays for the ARS himself. He never drives to restaurants anymore, so that he doesn't need to worry about parking or drinking. When he and his guests finish their dinners, their waiter notifies the ARS, and the complimentary AV will be waiting to take him home. Chez Duncan negotiated an excellent deal to provide ARS to its customers and found that its business increased 15% from more customers and increased wine sales.

Free ARS as a Promotional Incentive

Free ARS may also be an incentive for people to shop at a particular location or attend an event. For example, a shopping mall may provide free ARS to attract more shoppers. A fundraiser could offer complimentary ARS to get people to participate in its event. Here is an example:

A local shopping mall provides free AV transportation on Tuesdays to attract more shoppers. It gets 1,000 more shoppers every Tuesday, and the stores in the mall each pay from $20-$60 to fund this promotion. The mall is working with its ARS provider to include paid advertising in the AVs as an additional way to pay for the service.

Airport and Hotel Shuttles

Airport travel provides some unique opportunities for AVs. Millions of people traveling by air need to commute to/from and park at the airport. Parking is costly. Driving to and from the airport can be stressful. Also, many travelers stay at hotels near airports that provide shuttle service to and from the terminals and the hotel. AV shuttle services will completely change these.

ARS to and from the Airport

Getting to and from an airport can be very expensive. Airport parking can cost $15 to $30 per day. A car service can be less costly for longer trips but still costs $75-$150 each way. ARS customized for airport transportation will dramatically reduce this cost, as is seen in this example:

Like many road warriors, Peter flies almost every week. It typically costs him $75 for airport parking, plus the cost of driving to and from the airport. A car service is $100 each way. He often leaves early in the morning, arrives late at night, and dislikes having to drive when he is tired. Now, he uses an ARS designed for travel to that airport. He provides his flight information, how much buffer time he wants, and the ARS automatically picks him up in the morning. When he arrives home, he doesn't need to do anything; the ARS monitors the arrival time and waits for him when he arrives. The ARS trip costs him less than half of the car service and even less than parking.

Airport Shuttles

Airport hotels can use AVs to replace shuttle buses to provide more individual service at a lower cost, as can be seen in the following example:

A major hotel chain has 50 hotels at major airports throughout the U.S. It previously used a shuttle bus that ran every 30 minutes at each hotel and employed five drivers to provide the service 20 hours per day. While customers appreciated the shuttle service, it was not very convenient since they frequently had to wait until the next shuttle, and the trip took longer because of stops at other terminals. The hotel chain replaced the shuttles with several AVs at each hotel. Now, customers have their own ride directly to their terminal whenever they are ready, and on top of that, it costs the hotel much less than the shuttle service. The hotel decided to purchase a small fleet of AVs identifying the hotel for advertising and promotional purposes. Even though the investment in AVs was $10 million for its 50 hotels, the return on investment was impressive, and that's not even counting the increase in revenue from guests who now stay at their hotels because of this convenience.

Transportation for Those Unable to Drive

There are more than 50 million people in the United States who can't or don't drive. This estimate includes children, those who are disabled, and the elderly who prefer not to drive. The availability of ARS will enrich their lives and remove a burden from those who now need to drive them around.

Children

There will be some debate about the minimum age for ARS passengers. Those who are close to driving age in their early teens will probably be able to, but probably not young children. I envision an ARS geared toward transporting children with an adequately controlled environment and continuous video monitoring so parents can watch their children. Here is an example of how it might benefit a typical family:

Jose and Brandy have three children, ages 9, 12, and 14, who are all very active in sports and school activities. In a typical school week, they estimate that they have 8-12 events that their children attend. Before using ARS for their children, they felt as though they ran a bus service. Now their oldest always uses the Uber ARS to get to and from sports and music practices, frequently traveling with one or two close friends.

He is also very comfortable traveling alone, and he prefers it to have his mom or dad drive him because that is embarrassing socially. The two youngest children frequently go together using the Apple Children's ARS, which requires an authorized adult when the kids get in and out of the car, biometric identification of the child, and continuous monitoring of the children during travel. The 12-year-old can't wait to turn 13 to be eligible to use regular services, and the parents can't wait for the youngest to become 10 so she can travel alone in the Children's ARS. The parents estimate that they save each week from not having to drive

the kids. They use this time for work and shopping, enabling them to spend more quality time with the children with the time saved.

The Elderly

There are 16 million people older than 75 in the United States, and while many of these can drive, some of them will prefer to use ARS when it's available. For those who cannot drive any longer, ARS provides them with the freedom to come and go as they want, as can be seen in this example:

Tom and Mary are in their late 70s. Tom drove until two years ago when he had a minor accident. After that, they stayed home most of the time, except when their daughter could take them to the store or the doctor. Then, their daughter convinced them to try the new ARS recently initiated in their community. Now, they are out and about continually, more active than they were in many years. Mary goes shopping 4-5 times a week, while before that she could only arrange to go once a week. She also takes the ARS to church activities and knitting twice a week with her friends. Tom uses the ARS for his weekly doctor's appointments, breakfast three times a week with friends, and his regular Thursday night card game. On Thursday night, he typically shares an autonomous ride with two friends. Tom and Mary are so happy with the new lifestyle enabled by ARS that they convinced two friends to relocate to their community because of the availability of autonomous ride services. One of their doctors claims that it could add years to their lives because they are more active.

The Disabled

ARS will provide flexible transportation for the millions of people who are disabled. Sometimes, the ARS service will provide customized AVs for those who are disabled, or the person will own a customized AV. Here is an example of someone who owns a personalized AV:

Bart cannot walk and requires a wheelchair, which he is very capable of using alone. Ironically, he was disabled in an automobile accident a decade ago. Bart has a customized AV van. Whenever he wants to go somewhere, he remotely opens the garage door, pushes a button to open the vehicle's back, and the ramp extends to the ground. He then moves his wheelchair into position and pushes another button to lift him into the van. He then tells the autonomous van where he wants to go. Previously, Bart owned a van that accommodated him, but he still needed a driver.

Midrange and Long Drives

AVs will also change the way people take long drives. Sometimes, traveling by AV can be less expensive and more convenient than airline travel. Here are a few examples.

Using an Individually-Owned AV

Some people may find that it's more cost-effective to use their AV to drive long-distance:

Donna and Sam travel 1,500 miles every year from Boston to Miami, Florida. They usually drive down in October and drive back in May to have their car at each location. Sometimes they would fly and pay to have their car transported. Sam looked at the economics of using an AV. He figured that they drive the 1,500 in three days, including two overnight stops at hotels. If they used an AV, they could do the trip in a single long day, probably 24-28 hours without stopping, except to refuel and take breaks for food. They could watch movies together on the trip and sleep along the way. They save about $500-$600, plus two days, and eliminate the stress of driving. The savings offset the extra cost for an AV. Sam also compared the cost of flying home for the holidays. Flying each way cost them about $750-$900, including the cost of airport parking, plus they needed to spend another $300-$500 to rent a car. Sam figured it was about the same cost to take a day and have their AV drive them back and forth for the holidays. And they could fill the car with all their holiday gifts.

Family Member Medium-Distance Transportation

Here is an example of how an AV helps in a specific situation involving a family member:

Martha's mother lives 120 miles away and doesn't like to drive. So, to get her mother to visit, she and her husband need to drive four hours round-trip to get her and then another four hours to bring her back. This trip is challenging on holidays since they are already busy with their kids. Therefore, they don't see her mother as frequently as they would like. Now, they have an AV, and they send it to pick up their mother. They usually put a snack in the car and set up one of her favorite movies to watch on the two-hour trip. It took only two visits for her mother to get comfortable with the AV, but now she loves it. On the first trip, Martha accompanied her mother in the AV. Now Martha sees her mother more frequently.

Medium-Distance ARS from Rental Car Companies

Rental car companies will suffer from ARS replacing much of the need for rental cars. However, there may be opportunities for rental car companies to use AVs for medium-distance travel. Travel between two cities may be an opportunity for rental car companies, which is different from municipal ARS fleets:

A formerly successful car rental company struggled to survive because of the success of ARS. In 2023, it introduced an AV long-distance rental program. For less than $1 per mile, a customer could rent an AV for a minimum of $250. This program became an instant success, diverting passengers away from the airlines. Boston-to-New York, New York-to-DC, or LA-to-San Francisco costs only $250 – door to door. Even trips from New York or Boston to Chicago were cost-effective. Frequently, the travel time was less than the flight time plus the time it took to get to and from the airport. And it was more comfortable and convenient, as is seen in this example:

Jim and Sue live in the Boston suburbs and now travel to New York several times a year for weekends. The long-distance ARS picks them up at their home on Friday afternoon and drops them at their hotel in New York in time for a late dinner. They usually have a bottle of wine on the way to get in the mood for their weekend. On Sunday after brunch, the ARS picks them up at the hotel, and they are home by late afternoon. The round-trip costs them $500, much less than the $1,000 it would cost to fly, park, and take a taxi from the airport in New York and back. Plus, it is faster and more convenient.

Business Travel

Business travelers need to endure travel to meetings and to visit clients; frequently, these trips are too long to drive but inconvenient and expensive to fly. With AVs, they can now travel productively by car instead of flying. They will also find creative uses for AVs. Here are some examples.

Travel to Business Meetings

Executives and managers frequently travel to business meetings in small groups. Some companies will purchase a few specialized AVs to transport people to and from these meetings. These AVs will lower travel costs and significantly improve productivity and convenience:

Advanced Equity Investors is based in Boston, but its executives and managers frequently travel to New York. These trips were expensive, inconvenient, and the travel time wasn't productive. So, the company acquired three four-passenger AVs designed for business. Its executives merely schedule the vehicle for a trip to New York, and the car picks up each of the executives at home in the morning. On the trip to New York, they review their presentation and make changes as needed. Each of the business AVs has a printer so the executives can print a client copy before arriving. The AV drops them off directly at the client's office and

17

then goes to the nearest AV parking lot to wait. When the meeting is over, they summon the vehicle to pick them up and drive them home. The company even provides some wine and cheese in the AV for the ride back.

Salespeople

Salespeople typically travel several days a week to visit the businesses that they serve. With AVs, they can significantly increase productivity:

Brian services 400 accounts from Maine to New Jersey, and he is on the road 3-4 days a week. His company just provided him with an AV specifically designed to enable him to work while traveling from account to account. He can now do his preparation and follow-up work instead of driving, allowing him to be more productive. He estimates that he can visit 25%-30% more accounts each week, and he is not fatigued from driving, especially in traffic. His sales have increased significantly, and the company has gotten a fantastic return on its investment in three AVs for its salespeople.

Business Promotion

Some businesses will offer free AV trips for clients travel to meetings as a convenience to promote their services:

The Estate Planning law firm does estate and wills for wealthy clients. It acquired two luxury AVs to use for its clients. When it schedules a meeting with its clients, it offers to have them picked up and taken to the office using one of these AVs. The clients love it. They feel special and don't need to drive or find a place to park. Its clients tell all their friends, and business is up 30% since they started providing this service. It also saves the Estate Planning partners from having to travel to their clients to be more productive.

18

Home Delivery

Package and food delivery will be revolutionized with the advent of AVs specialized for delivery. As I will discuss later, food delivery will benefit more than package delivery. Here are what I think will be a couple of typical examples.

Pizza Delivery

Pizza delivery will be one of the first new markets to adopt delivery by AVs. There are 70,000 pizzerias in the United States, and most offer delivery. More than 1 billion pizzas are delivered every year in the United States. There are 16,000 Pizza Hut locations and 13,000 Domino's locations. Let's use Domino's as our fictitious example:

> *Domino's was one of the first to use AV delivery vehicles for pizza delivery. Marco ordered pizza at least twice a week from Domino's. With his two friends, Max and Becky, visiting, he ordered two pizzas from his Domino's app. They had never ordered pizza from an AV delivery vehicle, so they were intrigued by how it works. About 25 minutes later, the app notified him that the delivery was 3 minutes away from his apartment. (He set the notification time for 3 minutes because that's how long it took him to go downstairs.)*

> *He confirmed the delivery, and the app sent him the "pizza passcode." They all went downstairs to see the process. The unique Domino's Delivery vehicle pulled up at the front door, the compartment with his pizza flashed, and he entered the pizza passcode. The door opened to*

the heated storage tray, he removed the two pizzas, and they went back upstairs to their apartment. "It saves me $6 for delivery because of the lower delivery charge and no tip. It makes the pizza 30% cheaper!" Marco told them.

Meal Delivery

Food delivery is not limited to pizzas. Higher-end restaurants will also offer more home delivery. Some meal delivery services are doing this already with drivers, but it becomes more cost-effective with AV delivery, as can be seen in this example:

Chuck and Amy regularly order meals from about a dozen local restaurants that offer complimentary AV delivery. Today, they had another couple over for dinner. They talked about the different restaurant options and picked a restaurant, then they went online to the menu and ordered on their account. They had cocktails, and in about 40 minutes, they got a notice that their meals were waiting outside. They just went out their front door, put in their account code, and removed their meals from the warming drawers. The frozen desserts were in the cooler. They prefer the convenience of dining at home more often without having to cook, and they figure that they save money because there is no delivery charge, they don't have to pay a tip, or pay the markup for wine with dinner.

Major Event Travel

Massive parking lots and incredible traffic jams are taken for granted at significant events such as concerts, football games, major golf tournaments, and other sporting events. AVs may provide solutions to mitigate these problems and make these events more attractive to attend in person. Here is an example.

Big Football Games

Let's take a big football game, for instance. As many as 80,000 people, sometimes more, attend a big game, creating severe logistics problems. More important, those attending these games get frustrated sitting in traffic, sometimes after having too much to drink. AVs, particularly ARS, can help solve these problems:

The NFL team introduced an AV program for its games to alleviate congestion and frustration. It uses several different types of autonomous transportation. Individuals with their own AVs are dropped off in an exclusive drop-off zone; then, their cars drive away to an off-site parking area. After the game, the AVs return on a rotating schedule to pick up the passengers. ARS passenger vans bring groups of 5-8 fans from their homes to the game together. They can mingle and have drinks on the way

20

and after the game since nobody is driving. They rent the ARS passenger vans for the day and use the same van each way. And the driver doesn't need to get frustrated by the traffic. These vehicles also drop off and return on a rotating basis. Finally, conventional ARS vehicles drop off and pick up passengers from the game at a lower cost than parking fees. The vehicle drops them off and then picks up a new group of passengers for the game. There is some wait time for these rides, but there is a lower price for those who agree to wait longer. This program significantly reduced congestion and eliminated the frustration of driving in traffic. To accommodate the increased need for vehicles, the ARS companies dispatch additional AVs in groups that they call AV flocks to the event. Some go from one major event to another around the region.

Chapter 2
Benefits of Autonomous Driving

The economic and social benefits of autonomous driving are so significant that autonomous vehicles are inevitable. While this seems like a bold statement, understanding these benefits makes it more evident. Autonomous driving will save as many as 36,000 lives annually in the United States alone (and eventually half a million annually worldwide), and it will help avoid millions of serious injuries. Autonomous driving will save typical drivers approximately 300 hours annually of driving time, enabling them to do something more productive or enjoyable than driving. Transportation is the second-highest cost to families, and autonomous vehicles (AVs) along with autonomous ride services (ARS) will reduce this cost considerably for all families. Also, AVs will enable children, older people, and those with disabilities to have the freedom to travel that they are missing today. Let's look at these benefits by category and try to estimate the magnitude of each.

Almost Eliminate Auto Accidents

Although we take auto accidents for granted, they are not inevitable. Based on recent data, there were more than 6.4 million auto accidents in the U.S. in 2017.[i] The cost of these accidents in terms of human lives, injuries, and financial impact is enormous. However, autonomous vehicles can change this. Autonomous vehicles will significantly reduce the number of auto accidents and eventually eliminate them. Some people think that AVs are more dangerous than human drivers, but the opposite is true: human drivers are risky.

How AVs Reduce Auto Accidents

Driver errors cause more than 90% of all automobile accidents. The National Highway Traffic Safety Administration estimated that in 2017 there were:

- 2,189,000 automobile crashes, with 4,031,000 vehicles, 3,945,000 drivers, and 1,982,000 passengers involved in these crashes.

- The causes of these accidents were blamed on the driver in 94% of the crashes. The remaining reasons were vehicle failure or bad weather.
- Among an estimated 2,046,000 drivers who caused accidents, recognition errors accounted for about 41%, decision errors 33%, and performance errors 11%.

Much of this "human error" comes from reckless driving. The National Highway Traffic Safety Administration (NHTSA) analysis of causes for fatal accidents[ii] in 2015 illustrates the significance of human recklessness in causing accidents.

- **Speeding:** Excessive speed was a contributing factor in 28% of the fatal accidents, causing the loss of 9,557 lives.
- **Drunken Driving:** 10,265 people were killed in alcohol-impaired driving crashes. These alcohol-impaired driving fatalities accounted for 29% of all motor vehicle traffic fatalities in the United States.
- **Distracted Driving:** Distracted driving is an increasing problem. Activities that take drivers' attention off the road, including talking or texting on cell phones, eating, conversing with passengers, and other distractions, constitute a significant safety threat. 3,477

people were killed in distraction-caused crashes. This was 9.6% of all fatal accidents.

- **Running Red Lights**: More than 900 people die annually, and more than 100,000 are severely injured from vehicles running red lights. About half of those deaths were pedestrians and occupants of other vehicles who are hit by red-light runners.

- **Falling Asleep**: A study from the AAA Traffic Safety Foundation found that 37% of all drivers fall asleep behind the wheel at some point in their lives. An estimated 2% of fatal crashes, 13% of accidents resulting in severe injury, and 6% of all crashes involve a drowsy driver.

These five reckless behaviors of human drivers cause almost all fatal traffic accidents. AVs will follow traffic regulations, not excessively speed, not drive drunk, not get distracted, not run traffic lights, nor can they fall asleep.

Many accidents happen when a driver fails to see an oncoming or turning car or fails to see a pedestrian. Autonomous vehicles are safer because they won't make these errors. With an extensive array of sensors continuously monitoring everything happening around the vehicle, autonomous vehicles can anticipate and respond faster to almost any situation.

Semi-autonomous driving systems are already showing some benefits. A 2016 study by the Insurance Institute for Highway Safety found:

- Automatic-braking systems reduced rear-end collisions by about 40% on average, while collision-warning systems cut them down by 23%.

- Blind-spot detection systems lowered the rate of all lane-change crashes by 14% and the rate of such accidents with injuries by 23%.

- Lane-keeping systems lowered rates of single-vehicle, sideswipe, and head-on crashes of all severities by 11%. Accidents of those types in which there were injuries were reduced by 21%.

Saving Lives

The most significant benefit of AVs is that they will save tens of thousands of lives each year. Data from the National Safety Council show that as many as 42,060 people are estimated to have died in motor vehicle crashes in 2020. That was an 8% increase over 2019, even though people drove fewer miles in 2020 because of the pandemic. The rise in death rate was the highest year-over-year jump that the NSC has calculated in 96 years.

Almost everyone in the U.S. knows a friend or relative killed in an automobile accident. It's so prevalent that it's all too often taken for granted. Just think about this for a moment. More than 3 million people will be killed in the U.S. from auto accidents during the average person's lifetime. That's almost 1% of the population over a lifetime. Auto accident fatalities do not affect everyone equally. For example, it is the leading cause of death for younger people from 15-29 years old. Most of these are alcohol-related.

The NHTSA reports an average of 6,000 pedestrians killed annually. 73% of these occur outside intersections with crosswalks, and 75% of them happen in the dark. Drivers have difficulty seeing pedestrians in these conditions; however, AVs have advantages. They use their sensors to monitor all the surroundings continuously and can see in the dark.

On a global level, these numbers are even more staggering. Nearly 1.3 million people die in road crashes each year, on average 3,287 deaths a day. Road traffic crashes rank as the ninth leading cause of death and accounts for 2.2% globally. Globally, I expect that autonomous driving will have less of an initial impact, as traffic accidents are more predominant in underdeveloped countries, where it will take much longer for autonomous vehicles to come into widespread use.

If autonomous vehicles can prevent auto fatalities and will, then this benefit far outweighs almost any disruption. A 90% reduction in auto accidents will save 36,000 American lives annually and more than 350,000 in a decade. To put this in perspective, this is almost as many as American lives lost in all wars in the 20th century.

Currently, the press focuses on accidents involving autonomous vehicles. These are more attention-getting because they are rare. Fatalities from auto accidents are so commonplace and taken for granted that they are hardly newsworthy. If they are reported at all, they are only reported in local papers in brief articles.

However, once autonomous driving becomes a substantial percentage of driving, the press will begin to compare autonomous driving accidents to those caused by humans. "This accident would not have occurred if the other car was autonomous" will be reported with increasing frequency. Victims, or families of victims, will be outraged that the accident could have been prevented with AVs.

Preventing Injuries

The NSC estimated that 4.8 million people were seriously injured in auto crashes in 2020. Auto accidents cause serious injuries, some of which may lead to permanent disabilities and impairments. Many of those critically injured don't return to normal for many years, and some never do.

To bring this point beyond statistics, let's look at the types of injuries from auto accidents. The most common permanent conditions associated with these accidents are:

- **Partial or total paralysis.** Damage to the spinal cord can affect how the nerves transmit signals between the brain and various parts of the body, resulting in paralysis.

- **Vision or hearing loss.** Damage to the eyes caused by glass or shrapnel, or a severe blow to the head, can cause permanent sensory impairments such as losing the ability to see or hear.

- **Crushed limbs and amputations.** When bones in an extremity are crushed, the limb may require amputation.

- **Traumatic brain injuries.** Mild head trauma can lead to a concussion, while a solid blow to the head or jolt to the body can leave crash victims with a moderate or severe brain injury. These injuries can cause significant physical, mental, or behavioral deficits that can affect nearly every aspect of their daily life.

- **Ongoing psychological trauma.** The mental and emotional effects of a car accident can be long-lasting. Some victims may develop debilitating or disabling anxiety, depression, or post-traumatic stress disorder.

In addition to the savings in lives, a 90% reduction in auto accidents will keep more than two million American people from being severely injured every year.

Saving Accident Costs

Car accidents are costly. The NSC estimated that cost of auto accidents to society was $474 billion in 2020. These costs are not just paid by those involved in accidents. Those not directly involved in crashes pay for more than three-quarters of all accident costs, primarily through insurance premiums, taxes, and congestion-related costs such as travel delays, excess fuel consumption, and increased environmental impacts.

Auto insurance costs almost $200 billion in the United States. Property damage from accidents is more than $75 billion, and there are also other related costs. Legal costs from auto accidents are more than $10 billion. Emergency services cost about $1 billion, and the total estimated public spending costs on auto accidents are $18 billion.

An eventual 90% reduction in traffic accidents would materially reduce healthcare costs in the United States. More than 2 million Americans—nearly 7,000 people per day—enter the emergency room with injuries from motor vehicle collisions. Many of these were hospitalized.

Incentives for Accident Reduction

The reduction of car accidents with the resulting decrease in deaths, injuries, and costs benefit society. However, as we learned with the reluctance of millions of people to get a simple COVID-19 vaccination, many people will not take action to benefit society. Passengers in an autonomous vehicle will benefit from avoiding an accident that would have been caused by their vehicle, but they can still get hit by a drunk driver. Eventually, we will need incentives for using autonomous vehicles because they are safer. Lower insurance, steeper penalties for causing accidents, and more restrictions are possible examples.

In addition, while a reduction in accidents benefits most of society, it is not such good news for the "accident industry.". Many companies, organizations, and people benefit from auto accidents. This includes many law firms and trial lawyers, insurance companies, courts, auto repair businesses, etc. A significant reduction in accidents will affect them. While it's disappointing, their organizations are lobbying to postpone autonomous vehicles to delay this benefit to society and keep auto accidents higher.

While this is the most significant benefit of autonomous vehicles, initial adoption will rely on other incentives. Fortunately, cost savings and increased convenience are substantial.

Significantly Reduce Transportation Costs

Transportation is the second-highest expense for American families. The U.S. Bureau of Labor Statistics estimates that transportation costs are approximately $9,000 annually or 14% of the average expenditure for families. Transportation expense is second to housing, which is roughly $10,000 or 16%. In contrast, food is 10% of the total cost of living.

It's expensive to own a car, especially one that sits idle 95% of the time, and most families on average own more than one. In the United States, car ownership averages almost two cars per household. However, recent studies show a trend toward fewer cars and lower miles driven per person, driver, and household.

There are several ways that AVs will significantly reduce the cost of transportation. Autonomous ride services (ARS) will provide a much lower-cost alternative to the high expense of owning a car, especially for those living in cities and families with more than one car. Ridesharing is already having an impact, but the cost advantages of ARS will accelerate it. For those already using ridesharing, the lower cost of ARS will provide immediate savings.

The reduction in the cost of transportation will be so significant that it will benefit all families and benefit society. One area to note is that lower transportation costs will significantly help lower-income families.

In the following sections, I'll attempt to project some of the benefits of reduced transportation costs. Again, this is not intended to be precise, only to provide a directional magnitude to illustrate the significant potential benefits.

Reduction in Car Ownership

For many people, autonomous ride services will be more convenient than owning, maintaining, and parking a car. More than 15% of the people don't own a car in urban areas, and this percentage is expected to rise with lower-cost ARS. Surprisingly, more than 50% of the households in urban areas own more than one car, some owning three or more. Likely, some of these will reduce the number of cars they own as ARS becomes a viable alternative for some travel needs.

While most suburban households own a car, almost 2/3 own more than one. In most cases, this is because members of the household need to travel to different places at different times, so using a single car is inconvenient. When ARS is available for a low cost in a suburban region, many households may reconsider how many cars they need to own. The cost savings can be very significant, and the ARS can eliminate the inconvenience.

Figure 2-1 -- Cost of Car Ownership to Ridesharing and ARS

Miles Driven	Monthly Parking	Cost of Owning	Ridesharing $2.25/Mile	ARS $1.25/Mile	ARS $0.75/Mile	ARS $0.50/Mile
			Cost Per Year			
18,000	$600	$18,500	$40,500	$22,500	$13,500	$9,000
18,000	$300	$14,900	$40,500	$22,500	$13,500	$9,000
18,000	$0	$11,300	$40,500	$22,500	$13,500	$9,000
12,000	$600	$17,600	$27,000	$15,000	$9,000	$6,000
12,000	$300	$14,000	$27,000	$15,000	$9,000	$6,000
12,000	$0	$10,400	$27,000	$15,000	$9,000	$6,000
9,000	$600	$17,150	$20,250	$11,250	$6,750	$4,500
9,000	$300	$13,550	$20,250	$11,250	$6,750	$4,500
9,000	$0	$9,950	$20,250	$11,250	$6,750	$4,500
6,000	$600	$16,700	$13,500	$7,500	$4,500	$3,000
6,000	$300	$13,100	$13,500	$7,500	$4,500	$3,000
6,000	$0	$9,500	$13,500	$7,500	$4,500	$3,000
3,000	$600	$16,250	$6,750	$3,750	$2,250	$1,500
3,000	$300	$12,650	$6,750	$3,750	$2,250	$1,500
3,000	$0	$9,050	$6,750	$3,750	$2,250	$1,500

Source: Author Estimates

Let's look more closely at the potential cost savings. When is ARS less expensive than owning a car? Figure 2-1 estimates this based on two primary factors: annual miles driven and monthly parking cost. The cost per mile driven for a personally owned car depends on the number of miles driven since the yearly ownership cost is fixed. Using AAA car ownership estimates as the fixed cost, it costs a little more than $3 per mile for a car driven only 3,000 miles per year. On the other hand, at 18,000 miles driven annually, the cost per mile is only $0.63.

Parking can include the cost of parking a car at work, downtown, and at paid parking for apartments or condos. $600 monthly parking equals $20 per day, and $300 is $10 per day. The comparison chart illustrates three levels of parking costs. Figure 2-1 demonstrates that ridesharing and ARS are more economical at fewer miles and higher parking costs. These characteristics are most notable in urban environments.

The estimated cost per mile for ridesharing is $2.25. At this price, ridesharing is a better economic alternative for those who would only travel 3,000 miles per year or are in cities with very high parking expenses.

The cost per mile for ARS is estimated to be $1.25, but over time, it could be $0.75 or even $0.50. This chart progressively shows the impact of cheaper ARS. The shaded cells in the chart indicate where ridesharing or ARS is less expensive than owning a car. At the initial cost of $1.25 per mile, ARS is less expensive, starting at 9,000 miles per year, except in rural areas with no parking costs. At a lower cost of $0.75 per mile, ARS is less expensive than owning a car in all cases, again except where there is always free parking and even then, only at 18,000 miles or more. Average savings would be $9,000 to $12,000 per year. Let's try to project how considerable these savings would be across the country. Assume that 15 million households, or 15%, trade in one of their cars for ARS. This would result in a saving of more than $150 billion. Uber and Lyft combined have about 3 million drivers with 3 million cars. When ARS displaces ridesharing with fleets of autonomous vehicles, there will be a reduction of car ownership by many of these drivers as well.

ARS Costs Less Than Ridesharing

Based on my estimates, ARS will eventually cost almost half as much as ridesharing, primarily because there won't be any cost for a driver. Most of these cost savings will be passed on to those using transportation. As ARS displaces ridesharing, there will be significant costs savings for people currently using ridesharing.

The ridesharing market in the U.S. was estimated to be more than $65 billion in 2019 and forecasted to be more than $100 billion by 2022. At estimated growth rates, the ridesharing market could reach more than $200 billion by 2025, if not for ARS. ARS could be very profitable at $1.25 per mile, or less, compared to more than $2.25 per mile for ridesharing. This is approximately 45% less. If ARS takes 20% of the ridesharing market by 2025, the cost savings could be projected to be $18 billion. By 2030, I expect ARS to have the majority share of the combined ridesharing/ARS market and the price of ARS to be even lower.

For someone using ridesharing regularly, the savings can be significant. For example, for someone who spends $75/week on ridesharing to get to work and recreational travel, the savings could be more than $1,500 per year.

Eliminate Parking Expense

In the U.S., there are more than 40,000 garages and parking lots. Overall, parking in the United States is estimated to be a $100 billion industry with the equivalent cost passed on to drivers. Autonomous vehicles will reduce this cost significantly.

For individual drivers, the cost of parking can be prohibitive, particularly in some large cities. It can be $40-$50 for short-term (2 hours) parking and $400-$700 per month. For this reason, autonomous vehicles could have an earlier impact in cities with high parking rates.

The reduced need for parking can also transform many urban areas. Interestingly, in the United States, there are three non-residential parking spaces for every car. The number of parking spaces required is usually set by local zoning to be sufficient for peak demand. The reduced need for parking lots and garages could transform cities. Buildings could be designed to use less land because of a lower need for adjacent parking. Parking lots could become green spaces and parks. City planners are already beginning to imagine the positive ways to use this additional space.

Benefits to Low-Income Families

Increased opportunities for low-income families are one of the benefits of the lower cost of ARS that has recently been gaining attention. Many low-income families cannot afford to buy and maintain a car, so they are forced to live near their work or school. This limits their opportunities and forces them to live in generally more expensive urban housing.

With the advent of lower-priced and more convenient ARS, low-income families will have more options. They won't need to buy a car to have flexibility. They will have more opportunities for work and school. They will be able to move outside of urban areas to areas with better housing for the price they pay.

Create More Productive Time

Time is a precious commodity. Almost nobody has enough of it. Most people wish they had more. Moreover, most driving time, especially time stuck in traffic, is wasted. Those who spend so much time commuting to work, school, or other places, will be able to replace their wasted time with more productive time.

Let's look at the overall opportunity to replace driving time and time savings from traffic jams and parking.

Reduce Driver Time

Americans spend a lot of time driving. A U.S. Census Bureau 2021 report shows the average one-way commute in the United States increased to a new high of 27.6 minutes in 2019. In 2019, the average one-way commute in the United States rose to a new high of 27.6 minutes.

A 2016 survey from the AAA Foundation for Traffic Safety found that American drivers typically spend an average of almost 300 hours behind the wheel annually. During this time, a typical American driver traveled nearly 10,900 miles.

Autonomous vehicles will enable drivers, particularly during commutes, to increase productive time. This benefit of gaining 300 hours in more valuable time translates to:

- *The equivalent of seven 40-hour workweeks per year. If people can use the commuting time for work, would this translate into more weeks of vacation?*

- *Approximately 5% of a person's waking hours of their adult life. What would you do with 5% more time?*

- *The equivalent of adding 3-4 years to their useful life.*

While this is the average time savings per driver, some people will save even more time, and AVs will be more critical. The average American worker spent about 225 hours just commuting to and from work in 2018, according to the U.S. Census Bureau. This equates to nine days per year. There were 4.3 million workers with commutes of 90 minutes or more. What is this time savings worth? At $20 per hour, 225 hours would be worth $4,500 per year, but it would be priceless for many. Imagine how valuable an additional hour and a half or more per day would be to 4.3 million people?

What will drivers do with all this free time when they no longer need to drive a car, and everyone becomes a passenger. They will be able to replace wasted driving time with increased productive working time or increase leisure or social activities:

- *They could work on their computers while commuting, participate in conference calls, or make business calls without being distracted drivers.*

- *They could use their time to get an online degree or take specialized courses.*

- *They could learn a foreign language.*

- *They could sleep or eat breakfast.*

- *They could watch a movie or read.*

- *They could play video games.*

- *Several people in a vehicle could have a meeting while being transported by the autonomous vehicle.*

- *Families could have family time together instead of the driver needing to pay attention to driving.*

- Friends could use the time to talk or have cocktails (since there isn't a need for a designated driver).

It will be interesting to see if people use this saved time to do other necessary activities. For example, could someone use the commuting time for work and then only need to be in the office for 6.5 hours, or better yet, work only four days a week? Alternatively, will they use this time freed up from driving in an AV to increase leisure time by watching movies, reading, sleeping, or relaxing.

It's still too early to predict how recovering this driving time will change working habits, society, and culture. And after the pandemic, working practices may change. Will companies allow employees to count this more productive work time as working hours, giving them shorter workweeks or increased vacation time? Will people use this time more for productive pursuits such as education or use it for increased leisure? Regardless, the increase in time available – 300 hours a year, 5% of waking time, the equivalent of 3-4 additional years – will be an unprecedented benefit for many people!

Reduce Congestion and Traffic Jams

Congestion and traffic jams waste driver time. Autonomous driving can reduce traffic congestion in several ways. It will increase throughput on road systems with better synchronizing traffic. Think of how traffic congestion occurs on highways when a car slows for some reason, causing all the following vehicles to slow until congestion occurs. If all vehicles are coordinated, traveling simultaneously, say 70 miles-per-hour, there would be more throughput with less congestion. Autonomously coordinated traffic passing through intersections will eventually allow even more efficient use of roads. Fewer cars will be stopped at traffic lights with no traffic passing through

The reduction in traffic accidents will also decrease congestion. Accidents are a significant cause of traffic congestion, and congestion, especially sudden congestion, is likewise a cause of traffic accidents.

One of the leading causes of traffic jams is selfish driver behavior. When drivers space out and allow each other to move freely between lanes on the highway, traffic flows smoothly, regardless of the number of cars on the road. However, there is another benefit to vehicles traveling down the highway at regularly spaced intervals and communicating with one another. More cars could be on the highway simultaneously because they would need to occupy less space. The results of a Columbia University study showed that highway capacity, measured in vehicles per hour per lane, could be increased to nearly

12,000 from 3,000, given a scenario in which 100 percent of the cars on the highway were autonomous and communicating with one another at 75 mph. The improvement comes because the safe vehicle distance could shrink to about 16 feet for AVs going 75 mph, compared to the over 115 feet necessary for safe stopping by human-operated vehicles at the same speed.

What is the estimated saving of reduced congestion? The cost of congestion is estimated to be $123 billion per year, considering: time wasted in congested traffic, fuel consumed, and the effect of traffic congestion on the environment. It also considers indirect costs, given that it is more expensive and time-consuming to transport goods or attend meetings in traffic-congested cities. This estimate is based on the INRIX index that collects data using satellite navigation systems from more than 180 million vehicles and devices on the road every day.

Traffic jams are particularly acute in certain cities. Inrix estimates that through 2026, traffic jam hotspots will cost Los Angeles commuters $90.9 billion, New York commuters $63.9 billion, and Boston commuters $18.9 billion. The estimates mainly consider the value of drivers' time based on median household income and other factors. The U.S. Department of Transportation estimates a value of $12.81 per hour for a commuter and $25.19 per hour for a business traveler. Non-business travel, like running errands, is worth $9.51 per hour. Inrix also factored in 57 cents per minute for the fuel cost and the health and environmental cost of increased carbon emissions.

Reduce the Need for Parking

Autonomous vehicles will reduce the time needed for finding parking. Autonomous vehicles can return to the starting or alternative location instead of parking and waiting. They will be able to drop off passengers at the front door of their destinations, park themselves somewhere less costly or return home, and come back to pick up their passengers when summoned. Drivers won't have the frustration and wasted time of looking for a parking space. With an AV, it doesn't matter how far away that parking space is.

In addition to the cost savings, looking for parking spots can be stressful. Almost two-thirds of America's drivers (61%) reported they felt stressed trying to find a parking spot, nearly half (42%) missed an appointment, one-in-three (34%) abandoned a trip due to parking problems, and one-quarter (23%) experienced road rage.

Finding a parking spot can be frustrating and expensive. In the first-ever study to estimate the economic impact of parking pain, INRIX leveraged its parking database of more than 35 million spaces in 8,700 cities across 100 countries and combined this with a large-scale study of 17,986 drivers' parking behavior and experience across 30 cities in the U.S., U.K., and Germany.[iii] It estimated that searching for parking imposes a significant economic burden on drivers. In the U.S., U.K. and Germany, drivers wasted an estimated 17,

44 and 41 hours a year respectively at an estimated cost of $72.7 billion, £23.3 billion, and €40.4 billion a year in these countries.

Provide More Convenient Travel Alternatives

Lower-cost ARS will not only reduce the cost of ridesharing; it will also provide more convenient alternatives. For example, it will offer an affordable option for people currently using public transportation. I realize that those responsible for public transit, and those who advocate for it, won't see this as a benefit, but those who use public transportation may. Disruptions like this to public transit are legitimate concerns discussed in a later chapter.

Many people in urban environments who use public transportation must walk several blocks to get to the subway or bus stop and wait for the train or bus. Then they need to do the same when they arrive, and then again on their return. This can add a half-hour to more than an hour to their trip. It is wasted time and can be miserable in bad weather. They either can't afford to own a car, or the cost of parking their car is too expensive. A taxi, and maybe even ridesharing, is too costly for them. They don't have any alternative.

With lower-cost ARS, they will have a new alternative of going directly from their home to work, school, or whatever their destination. The cost will be much lower than a taxi or ridesharing. It may be a little more expensive than public transportation, but it will be worth the savings in time. Getting back an hour or more every day can be invaluable.

AVs and ARS will provide more convenient alternatives in other situations as well. We looked at some examples in the first chapter. People will be able to take an AV door to door directly for medium-distance trips instead of the hassle of getting to an airport, parking, going through security, flying, and then getting from the airport. AVs and ARS will make more convenient alternatives economically feasible, such as eliminating driving to airports or sporting events.

Enable Mobility for Children, the Elderly, and the Disabled

AVs will provide new independence of travel for the millions of people who are disabled and unable to drive, older adults who cannot or will not drive, and children who are too young to get a driver's license. Ridesharing provides some alternatives for these, but ARS will lower the cost and expand the opportunity.

Mobility for Those with Disabilities

There are more than 40 million people in the U.S. with disabilities. Twenty million people have ambulatory disabilities, 7.5 million have vision disabilities, 11 million have hearing disabilities. [iv] Some of these are still able to drive, although many do not.

While autonomous vehicles do not solve the mobility problem entirely for those with disabilities, they will enable mobility for many of them. This can provide significantly increased quality of life and allow many to get better jobs. Currently, earnings for those with disabilities are much lower.

AVs can also be used to lower the cost of providing public transportation for those with disabilities. Under the Americans with Disabilities Act of 1990, all public transit agencies must offer transportation services to people with physical handicaps, visual or mental conditions, or injuries that prevent them from driving on their own. In most cities, this type of transport, typically called "paratransit," is sort of like an extra-helpful taxi service run by public transit. Riders make reservations in advance for rides, such as to grocery stores or medical appointments.

This service can be costly to municipalities. For example, The Massachusetts Bay Transportation Authority's paratransit program for people with physical, mental, or cognitive disabilities is provided for people where it is difficult or impossible to ride the MBTA's fixed-route bus, train, and ferry services. Called The Ride, it satisfies requirements under the 1990 Americans With Disabilities Act for transit systems to provide services for those who cannot ride the fixed-route system. The Ride has an operating cost of over $65 per rider per trip; passengers only pay between $2 and $3.50 per trip. The cost to the city of Boston was almost $100 million in 2015. For many disabled, autonomous vehicles can provide this service at a much lower cost. The savings to large cities alone can be in the tens of millions of dollars per year.

In addition to those permanently disabled, AVs can provide a means of transportation to millions of people recovering from an injury or surgery and unable to drive. They will continue to work and won't be a burden on family and friends to drive them during this time.

Mobility for Children

Autonomous vehicles have the potential to provide mobility for those too young to drive. It could give parents an option for getting their kids to school in the morning, picking them up in the afternoon, driving them to soccer practice, or dropping them off at the movies on the weekend. I expect that it will take some time for most parents to be comfortable with this, especially for younger children. There will be some debate about the appropriate age for children to use autonomous vehicles.

The logistics of parenting are challenging today. Overbooked children and overworked parents scramble to get children where they need to be. Driven mad by the child-chauffeuring dilemma, parents are naturally looking to outsource the job to ridesharing services. Unfortunately, Uber and Lyft forbid drivers from picking up any unaccompanied riders under 18. Accountholders who allow their children to access their accounts risk losing access to Uber. Many parents go ahead anyway, in open defiance of the rules.

There is currently a discussion about how old teenagers need to be to use ridesharing. Uber has a minimum age of 18, but some parents let their younger children use it because of the convenience. They monitor the ride using iPhone tracking apps to make sure their kids are traveling to the correct location. Some also let their younger teenagers use ridesharing when they travel as a group.

Others are turning to specialty ridesharing services to provide transportation for their children. There are several regional ridesharing services geared toward children. They use specifically qualified drivers, such as off-duty police, first responders, licensed child-care providers, or veterans. All drivers receive in-depth background checks. The minimum age requirement for children varies but is usually five to six years old.

The general concern with ridesharing for children is the risk of an unknown driver. Several questions will be debated. Is a child safer in a vehicle with no driver than an unknown driver? Will child-safe AVs provide autonomous ride services that are perceived to be safe enough for parents? Will the convenience of not having to drive children around outweigh other considerations? Are there limited conditions that will be considered safe, such as an ARS taking two 15-year-olds a few miles from home to practice? What will be a reasonable age for younger teenagers and even younger children to use these services? Will parents consider the autonomous family car safer for their children to use than an autonomous ride service? Will parents think an autonomous vehicle is safer than having their children travel with 16- or 17-year-old drivers? Parents will resolve these questions differently, but eventually, AVs will provide some mobility for children.

Special child-safe AVs will provide that service. A parent or authorized adult will be able to make sure the child gets into the vehicle. A video feed will enable parents to watch their child in the car, and the vehicle will notify the parent when the child reaches the destination.

There is a significant potential for providing transportation for children. Even if you consider just 13- to 16-year-olds, approximately 16 million children could become mobile with autonomous vehicles.

Mobility for Older People

Autonomous vehicles can provide mobility on the other side of the age spectrum as well. Millions of elderly people can't drive, won't drive, or shouldn't drive. There is no magic age when people are no longer permitted to drive, and many older people continue to drive when they shouldn't because they have no viable alternative.

In 2016, an estimated 13 million people 80 and older lived in the U.S. Older drivers will be an increasingly larger population share. The U.S. Census Bureau estimates that the population 80 and older is projected to increase to almost 20 million in 2030.

There is some debate about increased dangers presented by older drivers. Many older drivers have impairments that affect their driving, such as memory loss, eyesight problems, slower reactions rates, etc. Many older people tend to drive less because they know their limitations. They tend to avoid driving at night, during rush hours, and in bad weather conditions.

Nevertheless, AVs and ARS will provide much better and safer mobility options for older people. If we take 80 years old as a cut-off where many people would stop or reduce driving if they have a viable option, then there will be almost 20 million people over 80 in the U.S. who would benefit from using autonomous vehicles in 2030.

Reduce Shipping Costs

Autonomous long-haul trucking will produce significant shipping cost savings. Autonomous long-haul trucks will drive almost all the trip from one terminal just off the highway to another. When they arrive at a terminal, the autonomous semi will detach from the trailer, and a human-driven semi will connect and take the trailer to the destination. This will eliminate most of the cost for a driver, which is about 40% of the total cost.

There are additional cost savings as well. Autonomous trucks will use less fuel by driving more efficiently, and eventually, with lower accident rates, the insurance cost will reduce. They will also make deliveries much faster on long trips. A typical 2,600-mile truck shipment takes about four days to complete – approximately 90 hours, including four required 8-hour stops for the driver to sleep and for bathroom and refueling stops. Autonomous trucking will reduce the total 2,600-mile trip from 90 hours to 58 hours, improving 35%. A fleet of approximately 35% fewer trucks will be needed to haul the same loads.

These benefits of 40%+ lower cost and 35% faster deliveries will most likely be passed on to consumers with lower prices.

Make Same-Day Home Delivery Cost-Effective

Autonomous home delivery will revolutionize same-day home delivery of food, groceries, and related items. Some segments of food delivery, particularly pizza delivery, work well today with delivery drivers. New segments, such as those by Uber Eats and DoorDash, are making inroads into the delivery of meals and groceries. However, these are still unprofitable for both the delivery service and the restaurants.

Autonomous home delivery will enable home delivery to become economically feasible. Eliminating the cost of the driver will cut delivery costs by two-thirds. While it will require investment in a new fleet of autonomous delivery vehicles, these vehicles will be less expensive than the cars used today for delivery. They can be smaller, have less sophisticated autonomous driving capabilities, and be made of cheaper materials because they won't need to worry about the risk to occupants.

During the COVID-19 pandemic, home delivery of meals and groceries increased significantly. More people became comfortable with this as an alternative, and more restaurants and grocery stores created processes for doing this. At the same time, it demonstrated increased concerns over human interaction. Leaving food on the doorstep became popular. In addition to making home delivery much less expensive, autonomous home delivery will also remove human interaction.

More Efficiently Use Energy

Will AVs reduce energy use? There are two parts to answering that question. First, will AVs be more efficient in providing transportation, resulting in fewer miles driven by vehicles? Second, will AVs drive the adoption of electric vehicles, and will that reduce energy consumption?

Fewer Miles Driven?

Autonomous driving could significantly reduce energy usage – or increase it, depending on your assumptions. These estimates are currently a matter of debate and uncertainty. Here are some of the arguments on each side of the issue.

The Energy Information Administration estimates that by 2050, autonomous vehicles could reduce fuel consumption by 44% for passenger vehicles and 18% for trucks. This is based on the ability of AVs to provide more efficient transportation and reduce the number of miles driven. That may happen.

However, those gains could be offset if autonomous vehicles make travel more convenient and cheaper for everyone and liberate shut-in populations, such as the elderly, disabled, and people too young to drive, the study says. Boosting the total vehicle miles traveled could slightly worsen fuel consumption.

The most significant potential downside of driverless cars for the environment is that AVs could increase the total number of miles traveled because it would make travel more accessible and less expensive. Commuters might not mind living a few more miles, or even a few dozen more miles, further away from work if they could do something else while the car did the driving. In already crowded cities like New York, where parking is expensive, it might be cheaper for car owners to send their vehicle continually driving around the block rather than pay for a pricey urban parking space. Moreover, AVs could safely travel faster than human-driven vehicles, which matters because fuel economy typically decreases at speeds over 50 miles per hour.

On the other hand, more appropriate-sized vehicles could reduce energy consumption. People could order a much smaller and lighter vehicle for a single-passenger commute than the current case where those same people might own an SUV so it can manage the occasional need for extra space. Also, once AVs avoid accidents, they might be redesigned with lighter-weight materials, reducing energy needs.

Accelerated Adoption of Electric Vehicles

AVs will undoubtedly accelerate the adoption rate of electric vehicles (EVs). Most autonomous vehicles will be electric; the rest will be hybrids. The automated controls in an AV are much more compatible with electric vehicles. Also, the companies designing AVs tend to be more conscious of the need to reduce emissions.

Will the faster adoption rate for EVs save energy? The EPA claims that EVs use energy more efficiently than gas engines. EVs convert about 59%–62% of the electrical energy from the grid to power at the wheels. Conventional gasoline vehicles only convert about 17%–21% of the energy stored in gasoline to power at the wheels. EVs are also more environmentally friendly. They emit no tailpipe pollutants, although the power plant producing the electricity may emit them.

My educated guess is that AVs will positively affect the environment and energy usage, but not a lot.

Chapter 3
Introduction to Autonomous Vehicles

There is a lot of confusion about what autonomous driving is and what it isn't. Most people don't know how an autonomous vehicle works. In discussions, people ask about control wires buried in the roads, satellites sending signals to direct each car, and radio signals required from one vehicle to another. There are multiple definitions, as well as different expectations and forecasts for autonomous driving. There are several autonomous driving alternatives, and each of these has different expectations and timing. There are out-and-out critics, and then there are those who see the potential of AVs. In doing my research, I've found that a lack of understanding doesn't stop many people from having strong opinions

There is inconsistent terminology, and some terms are used differently. Historically, a lack of clarity in terminology is a characteristic of innovative technologies and embryonic markets. New vocabulary needs to be defined, used consistently, and eventually established. It takes a while for everyone to agree on what words to use. For autonomous driving, we struggle for common vocabulary to describe and understand the new concepts. Hopefully, this book will add some clarity.

In this chapter, I'll provide a basic introduction to autonomous vehicles. I'll start by breaking down autonomous driving into three simple categories that follow Advanced Driver Assistance Systems (ADAS): semi-autonomous, sufficiently-autonomous, and fully-autonomous driving. The importance of these categories will become more apparent as you progress through this book. I'll also show how autonomous driving will evolve using these categories. In the next chapter, I'll go into more detail, describing the individual functions of autonomous driving by category.

Currently, the most accepted autonomous driving definitions were created by the industry association, Society for Automotive Engineering (SAE), which defines six levels for autonomous driving (Level 0 – Level 5). The SAE updated these definitions in 2019 and 2021, making them more practical. I'll explain the classifications and relate them to my straightforward categories.

Finally, we will look at the three alternative methods for autonomous driving. This will help explain some of the differences when people discuss autonomous driving.

Categories of Autonomous Driving

Tare three primary categories of autonomous driving: semi-autonomous, sufficiently-autonomous, and fully-autonomous. Of these categories, sufficiently-autonomous will be the one that will have the most significant impact. Below these categories are cars with nothing autonomous (what I'll call "dumb cars") and advanced driver assistance systems (ADAS).

Basic Driver-Assistance Functions and ADAS

Basic driver-assistance functions make vehicles more intelligent and provide valuable driver support. This includes functions such as lane-departure warning, blind-spot detection, navigation, backup cameras, and cruise control. These are now standard features in most new cars.

Advanced Driver Assistance Systems (ADAS) were the next evolution of automation, providing more driver assistance and safety. Cruise control improved to be adaptive cruise control, enabling a vehicle to regulate its speed based on the distance behind the car ahead. Lane-departure warning advanced into automatic steering control to keep the vehicle within its lane. Collision warning progressed into automatic stopping without driver intervention. Generally, these ADAS are subsystems in a vehicle instead of a central control system.

Semi-Autonomous Driving

Advanced Driver Assistance Systems (ADAS) provided the path to semi-autonomous driving by combining some critical systems. The minimum functionality for a semi-autonomous vehicle combines adaptive cruise control with lane-keeping and automatic stopping. Adaptive cruise control automatically adjusts the car's speed to that set by the driver, accelerating and slowing the vehicle based on a predetermined safe distance behind the vehicle ahead of it. Lane-keeping or lane-centering systems control the steering of the vehicle within painted lane markings on the road. While this keeps the car within the lines, it doesn't turn the car around corners. Automatic stopping comes in variations by different manufacturers, but most of these perform well enough to stop the vehicle automatically when needed.

These three capabilities enable a car to drive comfortably on its own for long distances, primarily on interstate and state highways but also on many secondary roads. Semi-autonomous driving is autonomous in certain situations but cannot turn corners, stop at traffic lights, etc. It requires the driver to take control of the vehicle quickly when it cannot handle the driving situation.

Semi-autonomous vehicles require the driver to be attentive, and it usually monitors drivers to ensure that they have their hands on the steering wheel. Some vehicles use cameras facing drivers to make sure they are paying attention. These restrictions are primarily to minimize the risk for manufacturers of semi-autonomous vehicles until more experience is gained. Semi-autonomous vehicles can go for long distances, especially on highways, without driver intervention.

I've driven three Mercedes cars and a Tesla with semi-autonomous functions for thousands of highway miles, and I've also driven them semi-autonomously on regular roads, without doing much other than touching the steering wheel and making lane changes. I found that I drive very differently and more safely with these semi-autonomous capabilities. I put the car into the Mercedes Distronic Plus or Tesla Autopilot mode, set the speed I want, and then let the car do the driving while still staying aware of the situation. I'm comfortable maintaining that speed or an adjusted slower speed based on the speed of the car ahead, even if other cars are speeding by and cutting in lanes. Previously, I drove like many other drivers, at a speed that was more in relation to other cars (usually a little too fast) and frequently moving from one lane to another.

Semi-autonomous vehicles are much safer. They maintain a regular speed and aren't tempted to go faster based on other traffic. They keep a safe distance behind the car ahead, and they can stop more quickly than a human driver when traffic ahead abruptly stops. Semi-autonomous vehicles apply the 80/20 rule. They accomplish 80% of the driving with 20% of the capabilities.

In the semi-autonomous category, new capabilities are progressively introduced. These features include the ability to park the car automatically, retrieve the car from a garage, avoid pedestrians or obstacles on the road, drive autonomously in traffic jams, turn the car onto an exit ramp, automatically change lanes to pass cars on highways, etc. Tesla autopilot enables the vehicle to automatically change lanes on the highway and exit from the highway when in Navigate on Autopilot mode. The vehicle can also be summoned by its owner in parking lots.

Vehicles become progressively autonomous as more features are added. Some of these features require new sensor hardware, but software upgrades may enable most of them. The next category, sufficiently-autonomous vehicles, requires more advanced capabilities.

Sufficiently-Autonomous Driving

Some people get hung up thinking that autonomous vehicles won't be able to do everything and go everywhere (that is, be fully-autonomous) for a long time. They erroneously conclude that autonomous driving is a long way off. While fully-autonomous driving is a ways off, that's irrelevant. Sufficiently-autonomous driving requires an AV to drive only a predetermined route from Point A to Point B. In its simplest form, this could be a limited route, such as taking passengers from a hotel to an airport, but it can include almost all locations and road systems in a metropolitan area. The essential pragmatic point in this definition is that autonomous driving can be successful without being able to drive on all dirt roads, maneuver through a complex road construction site (instead, the car will avoid it), drive during a blizzard, complete the trip by driving down a narrow alley, maneuver through a complicated intersection, etc.

Sufficiently-autonomous vehicles will be able to negotiate almost all turns, stop at traffic lights and stop signs, avoid obstacles, park themselves, etc. They will accomplish 95% - 98% of most driving requirements but will achieve 100% of what is required for defined routes.

Sufficiently-autonomous vehicles are now viable, well ahead of fully-autonomous driving. All too often now, autonomous vehicles are held to the unrealistic standard of 100% autonomy. This is like predicting that nobody would buy a boat unless it could travel in the high seas, maneuver down narrow rivers and work well in low-tide on tidal rivers. People buy boats that work sufficiently in the conditions they intend to use them for.

This sufficiently-autonomous distinction is critical because, as I'll explain later, this will enable the first wave of autonomous ride services vehicles and start the autonomous driving revolution. All the primary streets and routes in a city can be mapped to the level necessary for autonomous driving. The essential street infrastructure can be implemented to enable seamless driving throughout the city. Passengers can request an autonomous ride service with a *from* and *to* location, and if that is a feasible predefined route, the vehicle will provide the trip.

There are two subcategories of sufficiently-autonomous vehicles. Those designed exclusively for autonomous ride services will not have a driver, and the interior will be designed for the comfort of passengers. Passengers will order a ride through an app for a feasible route, and a driverless car will pick them up. AVs designed for private use will need to accommodate a driver when necessary. Usually, a driver will still be required to be in the car, but the car will also drive autonomously on approved routes, both with and without passengers.

Sufficiently-autonomous vehicles require some significant capabilities beyond semi-autonomous functionality. They need to be able to turn the vehicle at corners and intersections. They must be able to read stop signs and traffic signals, and then act accordingly. They need to detect other vehicles and pedestrians. They need to translate a navigation route into precise turns.

This increased level of functionality requires more sensors, particularly lidar. The vehicle needs to access very detailed maps accurate to a centimeter and position itself precisely on that map. This also means a significant system architectural change from mostly independent ADAS subsystems to a single tightly integrated autonomous system where all data are processed together and all control signals directing the car come from the same source. This massive data processing requires very powerful onboard computing.

Fully-Autonomous Driving

Fully-autonomous driving will accomplish all, or virtually all, driving requirements. Licensed drivers will not be necessary. The autonomous vehicle (AV) will be in complete control of all driving. Everyone in the car will become passengers. It will take some time for everyone to get comfortable with AVs, so it will take some time for fully-autonomous AVs to replace most cars in the United States.

I expect that fully-autonomous driving in individually-owned vehicles will take some time to perfect and be accepted. Therefore, the initial focus on autonomous driving will be sufficiently-autonomous vehicles providing autonomous ride services.

Evolution of Autonomous Driving

It is now clearer how autonomous driving will evolve, as Figure 3-1 illustrates. It shows the level of autonomous driving on the vertical axis and the approximate time of introduction on the horizontal axis. There is a definite dividing line and increase in capabilities between semi-autonomous and sufficiently-autonomous. The evolution from sufficiently-autonomous to fully-autonomous will take more time but will not require a significant increase in capabilities. I realize that this distinction may not be entirely consistent with other current views on the evolution, but this will become clearer.

Basic DAS (Driver Assistance Systems) included capabilities such as the early versions of cruise control that controlled the speed of the car without the driver needing to use the gas pedal. This was followed by more advanced ADAS (Advanced Driver Assistance Systems) capabilities such as adaptive cruise control that adjusted the car's speed based on the distance of the car ahead of it. These ADAS capabilities required the addition of radar and camera sensors.

Generally, these systems were somewhat independent of each other, using their own microprocessors and embedded software. ADAS capabilities were combined to enable semi-autonomous autonomous driving where a car could drive autonomously on highways and other roads by adjusting the speed based on the car ahead, keeping the car centered in a lane, and automatically stopping when needed. More capabilities are being added to semi-autonomous vehicles, such as changing lanes and self-parking.

The distinction between semi-autonomous and sufficiently-autonomous vehicles is significant. While it seems like an evolution, sufficiently-autonomous vehicles require a different autonomous driving platform. This platform requires additional sensors, particularly lidar. It functions very differently by locating the vehicle within highly detailed maps instead of locating the vehicle between lane markers. This platform requires a centralized computing system on the vehicle that integrates all sensor data and does the positioning. These capabilities, as well as redundancies for safety purposes, make sufficiently-autonomous vehicles more expensive.

Figure 3-1
Evolution of Autonomous Vehicles

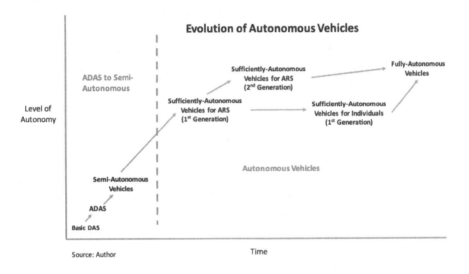

One of the key points illustrated in Figure 3-1 is that sufficiently-autonomous vehicles will be introduced first for autonomous ride services. The reasons for this are cost and the ability to function only on defined routes.

I expect that it will take much longer for sufficiently-autonomous vehicles to be made broadly available to individual ownership. They will still be more expensive and have limited autonomous driving routes. Over time, the cost will come down, and the routes available for autonomous driving will increase, making sufficiently-autonomous vehicles cost-effective for individual ownership. This a shift in thinking from previous perspectives, but most companies developing autonomous vehicles recognize this now.

Fully-autonomous driving does not require much more autonomy than sufficiently-autonomous driving. It mainly requires increased coverage of the detailed high-definition maps, some improvements in road system infrastructure, and other accommodations. Fully-autonomous by the definition that a vehicle can drive everywhere without exception may be a far-reaching goal.

SAE Levels of Autonomous Driving

Originally issued in January 2014 but updated several times, SAE International's J3016 provides a standard taxonomy and definitions for automated driving. The six levels of driving automation span from no automation to full automation. They claimed not to imply an order of market introduction, but the order described is logical. Elements indicate minimum instead of maximum system capabilities for each level. A vehicle may have multiple driving automation features such that it could operate at different levels depending on the feature(s) that are engaged.

SAE J3016™ LEVELS OF DRIVING AUTOMATION™
Learn more here: sae.org/standards/content/j3016_202104

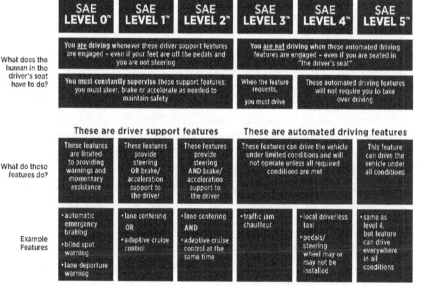

	SAE LEVEL 0™	SAE LEVEL 1™	SAE LEVEL 2™	SAE LEVEL 3™	SAE LEVEL 4™	SAE LEVEL 5™
What does the human in the driver's seat have to do?	You *are* driving whenever these driver support features are engaged – even if your feet are off the pedals and you are not steering			You *are not* driving when these automated driving features are engaged – even if you are seated in "the driver's seat"		
	You must constantly supervise these support features; you must steer, brake or accelerate as needed to maintain safety			When the feature requests, you must drive	These automated driving features will not require you to take over driving	
	These are driver support features			These are automated driving features		
What do these features do?	These features are limited to providing warnings and momentary assistance	These features provide steering OR brake/ acceleration support to the driver	These features provide steering AND brake/ acceleration support to the driver	These features can drive the vehicle under limited conditions and will not operate unless all required conditions are met		This feature can drive the vehicle under all conditions
Example Features	• automatic emergency braking • blind spot warning • lane departure warning	• lane centering OR • adaptive cruise control	• lane centering AND • adaptive cruise control at the same time	• traffic jam chauffeur	• local driverless taxi • pedals/ steering wheel may or may not be installed	• same as level 4, but feature can drive everywhere in all conditions

While widely accepted, as autonomous technology evolved, there were some practical problems with these definitions. For example, there wasn't a way to separate autonomous capabilities that were sufficiently autonomous for the tasks they were expected to do; specifically, it didn't define autonomous ride services limited to restricted areas. Fully-autonomous driving occurs at Levels 4-5. There was some debate about the meaning and intent of SAE Level 4 as being sufficiently-autonomous. There were also differing opinions regarding the need for a driver to intervene in an emergency such as an unanticipated highway situation, in an unexpected non-critical situation such as a disabled car blocking traffic, or in an anticipated situation such as driving on an uncharted dirt road.

So, in 2021, SAE announced a new chart for its J3016 Levels of Driving Automation standard that redefined the six levels, also from no automation to full automation. This used more consumer-friendly terms and definitions for each level and dropped a descriptive term for each level. The new chart helped eliminate confusion by providing clarity and using terms more commonly used by consumers. It also clarified Level 4 as being consistent with sufficiently-autonomous.

SAE Level 0 through Level 2

The driver must constantly supervise all driving in these three levels, even if the steering wheel and pedals aren't being used.

- *SAE Level 0: At this level, features are limited to providing warnings to the driver, such as blind spot or lane departure warnings.*

- *SAE Level 1: Individual features, such as lane centering or adaptive cruise control, are introduced at this level.*

- *SAE Level 2: This is the level that I refer to as semi-autonomous driving. It must include lane centering, adaptive cruise control, and automatic braking. As previously described in semi-autonomous driving, the vehicle can function on its own for highway driving, as well as some secondary roads. Still, the systems require that the driver be attentive to take over control immediately when needed. A driver must always be in the driver's seat and prepared to take control when autonomous driving cannot handle the situation. An example is a vehicle driving on a highway in a semi-autonomous mode that automatically exits the highway but requires the driver to retake control from that point.*

SAE Level 3 through Level 5

The following three levels introduce autonomous driving. The driver isn't necessary when the vehicle is operating at these levels. More importantly, the driver doesn't need to be paying attention to driving at these levels.

- *SAE Level 3: In Level 3 and Level 4, a vehicle can drive itself under defined conditions such as geofencing and will not operate unless all requirements are met. Conditions can mean precisely mapped roads that are approved for autonomous vehicles or pre-defined weather conditions. The differences between these two levels are minor. When requested, a driver needs to take control of the vehicle, but there is no need to take immediate control. An example of this is a traffic jam pilot, which operates in traffic conditions. This will also be the level used to distinguish privately-owned vehicles where a driver may want to drive the vehicle outside the defined conditions.*

- *SAE Level 4: This is the most crucial level, which I refer to as sufficiently-autonomous driving. The vehicle can drive itself under limited conditions such as geofencing without the expectation that a driver would need to take control. This is the level required for autonomous ride services, autonomous long-haul trucking, and autonomous home delivery. SAE indicated accurately that driver controls such as a steering wheel or pedals might not be installed in Level 4 vehicles.*

- *SAE Level 5: At this level, the vehicle can drive itself under all conditions. This is what I refer to as fully-autonomous driving. It is like Level 4 autonomous driving, except that the vehicle will drive everywhere in all conditions. Level 5 is frequently incorrectly cited as the requirement for autonomous vehicles. It will be a long time for an AV to drive in back alleys in New York city, narrow cobblestone roads in Eastern Europe, or on long forest trails in Maine.*

Also, these clarified levels now better match the simplified definitions that I used in the first edition of this book.

Three Alternative Approaches to Autonomous Driving

There are three different approaches to autonomous driving. This shouldn't be surprising. It's typical of new technologies. The battle between George Westinghouse and Thomas Edison over AC vs. DC electrical systems is an excellent historical example.

These three alternative approaches are different primarily in the method they use to position an AV in its surroundings. Each of these autonomous driving methods has its advantages and disadvantages. I'll explain each of them and provide my opinion.

Camera-Based Autonomous Driving

A camera-based system is the primary methodology used for semi-autonomous driving, and it is the approach that Tesla uniquely uses in its attempt to achieve fully-autonomous driving. This system relies primarily on cameras to determine the specific location of a vehicle. In semi-autonomous driving, the system locates the vehicle within the lanes of a road. This can be a single-lane road with painted lines or a multi-lane highway. Lane-centering software keeps the vehicle in its lane and gradually turns it as the lines curve. Radar-based adaptive cruise control sets the speed.

However, the vehicle only knows that it is centered within painted lines and guides it as the lines curve. It has no idea where it is. It could be on a highway in Texas or a city street in Manhattan. Tesla improves on this a little with Navigation on Autopilot that guides the vehicle to exit the highway. It does this using GPS to identify generally where the vehicle is on its route and determines that it is approaching an exit. The vehicle then automatically initiates turning off the exit (directional lights, slowing speed, and turning) when it sees the painted exit lines. However, exiting this way is a little uncomfortable and illustrates the problem with this approach. The vehicle doesn't slow down until it sees the exit lines, so it could go 70 MPH right until it slows quickly at the exit. In normal driving, most people will begin to slow as they are approaching the exit.

Camera-based autonomous driving needs simultaneously to identify where the vehicle is and build a map of its surrounding. In software terms, this is referred to as simultaneous localization and mapping, or SLAM. In a general sense, a vehicle uses simultaneous localization and mapping software to estimate its position and orientation while creating a map of its environment. It doesn't use a pre-defined map (as is used in the following method) but only uses GPS for general positioning.

There are several problems using this system beyond semi-autonomous driving. The first is turning corners without a detailed map. Unlike highway driving, there may not be painted lines at an intersection for the vehicle to follow to make a turn. It may know from GPS that it is at an intersection, but that is only accurate to a few yards. It needs to build a more detailed map of the intersection while it is there to make the turn, and that may not be reliable. The second problem is a lack of boundaries. This system is unconstrained and allowed to operate on any road in the world, and I don't think it is feasible. Finally, this system may be too risky. By relying entirely on cameras, it may not detect critical objects such as stop signs. If a stop sign is blocked by a truck or something else, the vehicle could keep going through the intersection, although it would avoid a collision.

Most importantly, the camera-based approach to autonomous driving has never been proven to work. Semi-autonomous vehicles have driven hundreds of millions of highway and similar miles. Still, this has not been tested sufficiently on routes requiring turning a corner or stopping at traffic signals. Tesla has done a limited demonstrations. Beyond that, there have not been any extensive trials.

Nevertheless, if it works, there are two significant benefits to the camera-based approach. First, it is much less expensive than the following approach because it doesn't require costly lidar. This makes it more feasible for autonomous vehicles sold at retail. The second is that it would be unconstrained and not restricted to geofenced areas. It would enable the leap from semi-autonomous directly to fully-autonomous Level-5 driving.

Tesla is virtually alone in proving this approach to autonomous driving. Elon Musk promised that Tesla vehicles would be fully autonomous by 2020, but they weren't. In my opinion, even though I own and drive a Tesla with the Fully Autonomous option, I don't think the camera-based system will work beyond advanced semi-autonomous driving. However, I will stop short of saying with certainty that it will never happen.

Lidar and HD-Maps Based Autonomous Driving

This second approach is fundamentally different from the previous one. It uses predefined high-definition maps on each AV. These maps very precisely locate (within inches) everything around the vehicle. The vehicle knows that it is stopped at a stop sign, six inches from a curb that turns 18 inches with a specific radius. The map identifies the stop sign, bike lanes, trees, crosswalks, intersection dimensions, etc. The vehicle knows precisely where it is. AVs applying this approach also use cameras and radar to identify moving objects, but positioning is done with lidar and detailed HD maps.

An AV developer needs to drive all the routes with map-creating software using lidar (Light Detection and Ranging) sensors to create detailed HD maps. AVs also use lidar to identify where they are and position themselves in the HD map. As they move, they continuously reposition themselves on the map. This enables them to turn precisely around corners, stop at stop signs, move exactly, etc. Going back to the previous example, with this approach, the AV will know that a stop sign is blocked from view because it knows exactly where the stop sign is supposed to be.

There are a few significant drawbacks to this approach. First, the AV is restricted to driving autonomously in areas previously mapped. It won't be permitted to travel autonomously outside of these boundaries. The second is that the maps must always be current. If there is a physical change, the map needs to be updated. Finally, it is more expensive. I expect these costs will drop significantly in the future, however. There is also a significant expense for creating and updating digital HD maps.

The Cadillac Super Cruise uses a variation of this approach. Cadillac uses lidar to create high-resolution maps of specific areas, particularly highways, for its Super Cruise. However, instead of using lidar to position every vehicle within the digital maps, it uses cameras for positioning.

The lidar and HD-maps approach has been proven to work. Hundreds of AVs from as many as a dozen developers have driven tens of millions of miles successfully using lidar and HD maps. It is proven, extensively tested, and it works safely.

Autonomous ride services (ARS) are the primary application of this approach because the drawbacks are not significant. ARS will be offered in selected metropolitan areas, so restricting the AVs is not a problem. The ARS service creates detailed HD maps of that area and then permits its AVs to drive only on those roads. This is referred to as geofencing. And the higher cost is not a problem either. Unlike individually-owned vehicles, the AV used in ARS will have much higher utilization, so cost is not a factor.

For these reasons, all major companies (other than Tesla) are pursuing the ARS market as the first AV opportunity and using the lidar and HD-maps approach. I describe this more extensively throughout this book.

The Connected Car Autonomous Driving

As will be described in a later chapter, the connected car means a vehicle communicates with other vehicles and the surrounding infrastructure such as traffic lights, stop signs, stationary objects, etc. These communications are used to position the vehicle by interpolating its distance from multiple objects sending out signals. It is also used to place the vehicle relative to other vehicles and direct the vehicle in coordination with other vehicles.

In this approach, it's the infrastructure that provides the intelligence instead of the vehicle. It requires fast and reliable data communications, such as 5G. This was the approach envisioned by some experts many years ago, and some still hold on to this approach for AVs. I still hear people talking about how 5G is necessary for autonomous vehicles to work.

The connected car approach is not practical for several reasons. First, it requires an enormous investment in infrastructure throughout the country. Every stop sign, traffic light, corner, etc., would need an intelligent transmitter. Second, it requires complete and reliable 5G communications everywhere, and this will take at least a decade. Finally, it requires that all cars must be connected. Otherwise, there would be accidents because those not connected would not coordinate with those that are connected.

Few companies are now following this connected car approach. One of them is Volkswagen. It is trying to be a pioneer in vehicle-to-everything (V2X), announcing that all its vehicles will be capable of communicating with other vehicles and infrastructure.

There are also efforts in China to develop and implement this approach for a couple of reasons. First, the centralized Chinese government can more easily control infrastructure changes. Second, Chinese companies have strengths in 5G technologies but not AV technologies. Third, major Chinese companies such as China Mobile and Huawei have vested interests in the revenue from this approach, if successful.

Nevertheless, I don't believe that a connected car is a practical approach to autonomous vehicles in the next 10-15 years, especially outside China. Eventually, it will be a way of taking AVs to the next level of performance, such as enabling AVs to travel at more than 100 MPH a few meters behind the AVs in front because they are all synchronized.

Chapter 4
Autonomous Driving Functions

erhaps the best way to understand autonomous driving is to consider the driving functions that autonomous vehicles perform. I'll review these progressively, from basic driver-assistance functions that most people are already familiar with to those typically included in semi-autonomous driving to those necessary for sufficiently-autonomous driving. I describe these here from a functional or user viewpoint, not a technical one. In a later chapter, I'll review the enabling technologies.

Driver Assistance Functions

The first set of basic driver-assistance functions sets the stage for autonomous driving but is not part of the semi-autonomous driving functions.

Automotive Navigation Systems

Most people are already familiar with navigation systems used to position a vehicle on a visual map. It uses GPS (Global Positioning System) to establish its location in the world, which correlates to a specific location on a digital map stored in the vehicle's navigation system. GPS was initially developed and maintained by the U.S. Department of Defense. It uses the transmission of microwave signals from a network of 24 satellites orbiting 12,000 miles above Earth to pinpoint a vehicle's location, as well as its speed and direction of travel. Initially restricted to military use, President Reagan authorized the civilian use of GPS in 1983 after 269 passengers and crew died on a Korean airliner shot down when it strayed off-course into Russian airspace. GPS quickly became a widely-used navigation aid throughout the world. The early versions of GPS navigation systems cost between $35,000-$70,000. Compared to their early predecessors, today's GPS devices are compact, inexpensive, and highly accurate.

By combining the use of signals from the satellites with interactive computerized maps in the vehicle, GPS car navigation systems can plot travel routes to a given destination. Some GPS car navigation systems are interconnected with traffic information sources, enabling them to automatically account for construction and congestion when determining the best route. If a driver misses a turn, GPS car navigation systems can quickly correct the error with updated routing. They can also help drivers find the nearest gas station or their favorite restaurant.

Besides navigation systems installed in cars, many people use Apple or Google Maps on their phones or iPads to provide directions. Navigation systems are extremely useful in helping drivers identify alternative routes, show upcoming turns, and estimate arrival time. Still, they are not accurate enough to determine how to initiate a turn. Currently, standard GPS is only accurate within approximately 5 meters or so of an object's actual location. Autonomous vehicles need road accuracy, which lets the car know which road it's on, and lane accuracy with precision down to a meter or several feet.

Backup Cameras

A backup camera is a type of video camera designed for aiding in backing up. It provides the driver with a view behind the car. The design of a backup camera is unique because it flips the image horizontally so that the output is a mirror image. This mirror image enables the camera and the driver to face the opposite direction. Otherwise, the camera's right would be on the driver's left and vice versa. This reduces the camera's ability to see faraway objects, but it allows the camera to see a continuous horizontal path from one rear corner to the other.

Almost 75% of the cars in 2015 model-year new vehicles include backup cameras, and all new vehicles must now have a backup camera. According to NHTSA, standard backup cameras will go a long way toward preventing injury and death, especially among children. Almost 200 people were killed each year, and another 14,000 were injured in back-over accidents when drivers reverse over another person without noticing them. Most of the victims were children because they are smaller and more difficult to see from the driver's seat.

Telematics

Telematics is an onboard system that receives wireless information and does something useful with it. Telematics doesn't have to include two-way communication, but most do. Usually, there's an embedded cellular modem, as with GM's OnStar. Some of the telematics work can be handled by your connected smartphone, as happens with Ford Sync.

The best way to explain telematics is to describe OnStar, the original passenger car telematics system, first announced by General Motors in 1995. It uses a cellular data modem, GPS, a backup battery, and connections to sensors. The box is in the back of the car, shielded from most crashes. It connects to a roof-mounted antenna that has more range than a mobile phone. The best-known feature is automatic crash notification. When a vehicle sensor reports a significant accident, OnStar sends that information to an OnStar call center, which then makes a voice call reporting the accident and location to a public-safety answering point, virtually a 911 service. Simultaneously, OnStar opens a voice link to the car to get more information from the occupants to inform them that help is on the way. OnStar is also used for navigation, sending a destination to the vehicle from a smartphone or web browser, or having it looked up and sent to the car by the call center. Over time, OnStar and other services added low-overhead, high-perceived-value features such as monthly vehicle diagnostics reports. OnStar also includes data services such as weather, sports scores, stocks, movie times, and traffic information.

Blind-Spot Detection

Traditional mirrors can help remove blind spots behind a driver, but they typically leave large dead areas on both sides of a vehicle. Blind-spot detection systems use various sensors and cameras to provide drivers with information about objects outside their range of vision. Cameras can provide views from either side of a vehicle that allows drivers to verify that their blind spot is clear.

Other systems use sensors to detect the presence of objects like cars and people. Some blind-spot detection systems can tell the difference between a large object like a car and smaller objects like a person, and they will alert the driver that there is a car or pedestrian located in one of the blind spots. Some systems will display a simple warning in the corner of the rear-view mirror if there is a vehicle in the blind spot.

Surround-View Cameras

Although this is a relatively new technology, surround-view cameras are a driver-assistance function since it explicitly helps a driver instead of providing a function for semi-autonomous driving. A surround-view camera system offers a birds-eye view of the car from overhead and shows the car as a moving image on the car's LCD display, along with parking lot lane markings, curbs, adjacent cars, garage walls, etc.

For example, when a car backs down a driveway, it shows where the car is centered. When backing out of a garage, it shows the car moving inside the garage to avoid bumping into objects. When parking in a parallel or perpendicular parking space, the driver can correctly center the car in the middle using the surround-camera view. On most cars, the parking view comes on automatically when the car is in reverse. Or it can be activated manually to show the view when moving forward. The camera typically only works at low speeds, generally below 5 to 7 mph.

Surround-view uses multiple cameras, typically four, with software blending these into a single video. Typically, one camera is in the middle of the front grille. Two more ultra-wide-angle cameras look down from the side view mirrors along the side of the car. A fourth is placed just above the license plate. Software blends (stitches) the four images together and inserts an image of the vehicle in the middle, making it look like there is a camera hovering above the car.

Lane-Departure Warning

Lane-departure warning (LDW) systems monitor the lane markings on the roadway and notify the driver with an alarm or vibrate the steering wheel whenever a vehicle starts to deviate from its lane. The driver can then take corrective action by steering the car back to the middle of the lane. It only works on roads with good lane markings and may not work if the lane markings are faded. Lane-departure warning systems are designed not to alert when the turn signal is on, or the brakes have been applied.

According to the National Highway Transportation Administration, 70% of all single-vehicle highway fatalities in the United States occur in run-off-road accidents. Since run-off-road accidents happen when a vehicle leaves its lane and drives off the roadway, lane-departure warning systems can prevent many fatal accidents. AAA says lane-departure warning systems could eliminate half of all head-on collisions.

Lane-departure warning systems have advanced to lane-keeping and lane-centering functions, but lane-warning continues to be necessary. These systems use several different technologies: (1) video sensors mounted behind the windshield (typically integrated beside the rear-view mirror), (2) laser sensors (installed on the front of the vehicle), or (3) infrared sensors (mounted either behind the windshield or under the vehicle).

Adaptive Headlights

Each adaptive headlight system works a little differently since they don't all perform the same functions. Some use sensor inputs to determine when the vehicle is turning. The headlights rotate with the turn, which illuminates the road in front of the car, instead of illuminating the side of the road when cornering or shining off the road entirely, which can lead to unsafe conditions.

Others use sensors to determine when the brightness should be adjusted. This automatic adjustment saves the driver from operating the high beams manually, allowing for a maximum sight distance. Additionally, some can determine how far away other vehicles are and adjust the brightness of the headlamps so that light reaches them without creating glare.

Semi-Autonomous Driving Functions

These functions enable semi-autonomous driving under certain conditions, such as highway driving. Many of these functions are categorized as ADAS (Advanced Driver Assistance Systems), but a minimum set is required for semi-autonomous driving. In my definition, the minimum functions for semi-autonomous driving are adaptive cruise control, lane-keeping or lane-centering systems, and some form of automatic braking system.

Adaptive Cruise Control

Adaptive cruise control (ACC), sometimes called autonomous cruise control, was the beginning of semi-autonomous driving. It automatically adjusts a vehicle's speed to maintain a safe distance from vehicles ahead. Initially introduced as cruise control, which enabled a car to maintain a set speed without the driver using the accelerator, it didn't reduce the speed when approaching too close to a car in front. With adaptive cruise control, the driver sets a speed then the vehicle automatically slows the vehicle when it is approaching another vehicle ahead. Then it accelerates when the distance separation increases.

Adaptive cruise control has already improved driver safety by maintaining optimal separation between vehicles and reducing driver errors. It also increases driving convenience. It is an essential component of autonomous vehicles.

Lane-Keeping Systems

Lane-keeping systems (LKS) monitor lane markings like lane departure warning systems, but they can take corrective action. Lane-keeping systems act to keep the vehicle from drifting. The methods that these systems use to provide corrective actions differ from one system to another. Some of the first lane-keeping systems used electronic stability control systems to keep a vehicle in its lane. This was accomplished by applying slight braking pressure to the appropriate wheels. Modern systems can tap into power steering controls to provide a gentle steering correction.

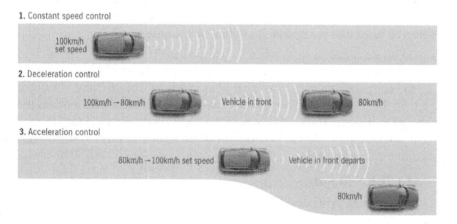

1. Constant speed control

100km/h set speed

2. Deceleration control

100km/h → 80km/h   Vehicle in front   80km/h

3. Acceleration control

80km/h → 100km/h set speed   Vehicle in front departs

80km/h

Automatic Lane-Centering

Automatic lane-centering (ALC) always tries to keep the car centered in the current lane. It provides continuous control across the lane, while lane-keeping systems provide control only near lane boundaries. Controlled steering is primarily implemented through shared braking and steering control services with longitudinal control systems.

Unlike an LKS, which gently steers the vehicle back into its lane by braking the inside wheels while vibrating the steering wheel as a warning, ALC uses adaptive cruise control in conjunction with cameras and steering control electronics to keep the car centered in its lane.

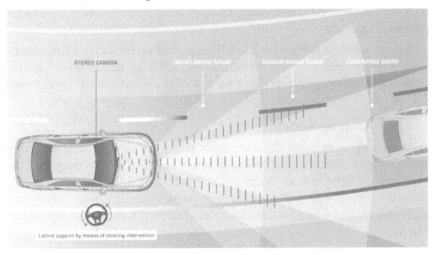

While it's not entirely autonomous, this function makes significant progress in that direction, especially considering its cameras are robust enough to perceive lanes that are nearly 1,640 feet or 1/3 mile away.

ALC is designed to work when the car senses drivers have their hands at least lightly on the steering wheel. For example, in the Mercedes version of ALC, the car notifies you if you have your hands off the steering wheel for more than 20 seconds. The Mercedes also uses a steering wheel icon on the dashboard to indicate if its ALC is engaged. ALC is an essential step toward vehicle automation when integrated with other vehicle control systems such as adaptive cruise control.

ALC/LKS in Snow

As discussed, ALC and LKS use various sensors to read lane markers, but that's a problem when snow is covering the lane markers. That makes current ALC/LKS systems unable to function correctly. When driving in snow, human drivers who cannot see the lane markers typically make their best guess to determine road positioning based on other visible markers like curbs, signs, and other cars. Ford is teaching its autonomous vehicles to do something similar by creating high-fidelity, 3D maps of roads. Those maps include details like the exact position of the curbs and lane lines, trees, and signs, along with local speed limits and other relevant rules. The car can use them to figure out, within a centimeter, where it is at any given moment. If the car can't see the lane lines but can see a nearby stop sign, which is on the map, its lidar scanner tells it exactly how far it is from the sign and, therefore, from the lane lines.

A relatively new possibility uses ground-penetrating radar when the AV is driving on a snowy road to figure out its precise location.

Automatic-Braking Systems

Automatic braking systems (ABS) combine sensors and brake controls to prevent high-speed collisions. Some automatic-braking systems can prevent collisions altogether; others are designed just to reduce the speed of a vehicle before it hits something. Automatic-braking systems can save lives and reduce the amount of property damage that occurs during an accident.

Some of these systems notify the driver with an alarm, while others activate the brakes with no driver input. Semi-autonomous driving requires automatic braking. These systems rely on sensor input, such as lasers, radar, or video data. If the sensor detects an object in the vehicle's path, then the system determines if the speed of the vehicle is higher than the speed of the object in front of it. A significant speed differential may indicate a likely collision, in which case the system automatically activates the brakes.

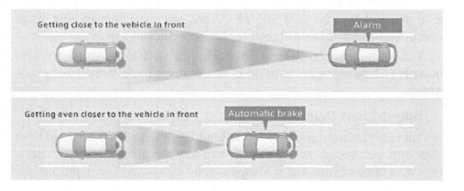

For example, Mercedes offers what it calls an Active Brake Assist with extended functionality. It warns drivers of imminent crash situations to assist them during emergency braking and, if necessary, initiates automatic, autonomous braking. Active Brake Assist uses the radar sensors installed in the vehicle as well as the multi-purpose stereo camera. These enable it to detect whether the vehicle in front is slowing down, stopping or is stationary. If the system detects a risk of collision, and the driver fails to respond to a collision warning, or is late responding, the system automatically initiates autonomous braking. The Cross-Traffic Function of Active Brake Assist also detects crossing traffic and pedestrians in the danger area in front of the vehicle.

Tesla's automatic braking is initiated instantaneously when it detects that the speed of the vehicle ahead is slowing while the Tesla is accelerating. This avoids accidents where the car ahead slows unexpectedly for some reason, just as you are starting to accelerate. I've experienced this several times in my Tesla.

Traffic-Jam Pilot

Audi was the first to introduce specific traffic-jam functionality for autonomous driving in its A8 Traffic-Jam Pilot. When the car is in traffic and the speed falls below 37 mph, the dash display shows a vehicle within white markings, signaling that the system is ready to take over. By pressing the Auto AI button, the car starts to drive itself. Currently, Traffic-Jam Pilot only engages the system if the vehicle is on a limited-access divided highway, has a vehicle directly in front and a line of slow-moving vehicles in adjacent lanes, and the system can identify lane markings and the edge of the roadway (with a barrier or guardrails, for instance).

In some European countries, once the system is engaged, the driver can watch TV, respond to text messages, or have a face-to-face conversation with a passenger. The entertainment and productivity features are fully integrated with the vehicle's interface to warn the driver if needed.

The Traffic-Jam Assist feature, available on the 2017 Audi A4 and Q7, allows for 15-second intervals of hands-off driving at slower speeds. The driver must always be alert and aware and intervene immediately when needed. Traffic-Jam Pilot will require some government approvals.

Other semi-autonomous cars may not have a specific traffic-jam function but enable adaptive cruise control with lane-keeping to perform in those conditions.

Speed-Limit Detection

Currently, some cars have speed-limit detection (SLD) to inform the driver of posted speed limits. There are two ways to do this. One uses a camera system that identifies and reads speed-limit signs using image processing. A windshield-mounted camera monitors the area in front of the car, looking for road signs. A computer scans the camera image for round-shaped surfaces typical of speed-limit signs, but algorithms filter out all round-shaped objects that do not resemble traffic signs. The symbols are sent to the cockpit display so that the driver is always aware of the current speed limit and can adjust the car's speed accordingly.

I recently drove behind a truck with a large speed limit 75 MPH sign painted on the back in the exact image of a speed-limit sign. They did this to celebrate their 75th anniversary. Objects like this could cause accidents in the future and need to be policed in some way.

Speed-limit identification in other cars, such as those made by General Motors and Mercedes, uses a roadway database in the vehicle's navigation system. The speed limit from the database is displayed in the instrument cluster. Drivers need to be careful as this is not always accurate. For example, on a recent 1,500-mile trip, I noticed a half dozen occasions when the SLD reading was incorrect. For example, it was reduced from 55 to 45 in a 20-mile construction zone and increased from 65 to 70 but not correct in the database.

Currently, SLD is used only to provide information to the driver and is not an autonomous function, but this will be essential to autonomous vehicles. In autonomous vehicles, speed-limit detection will determine the speed a vehicle can travel, so the speed-limit database needs to be continuously updated.

There is some discussion on whether to use SLD to set the maximum speed a vehicle can travel. It also can provide data in the car that identifies when the speed limit was exceeded since it has the actual speed and the posted speed limit. This won't be popular with drivers, but law enforcement officials, accident investigators, and insurance companies would find it helpful.

Collision Avoidance

Automobile collision avoidance systems operate under the guiding principle that even if an impending collision is unavoidable, the proper corrective measures can reduce the severity of an accident. By reducing the severity of an accident, any incidental damages to property and injuries or loss of life are similarly reduced. Collision avoidance systems use a variety of sensors that can detect unavoidable obstructions in front of a moving vehicle. Depending on the system, it may issue a warning to the driver or take any direct, corrective actions.

Most automobile collision avoidance systems draw on existing technologies. Since these systems require front-facing sensors, they often use data from the same sensors used by an adaptive cruise control system. Depending on the system, those sensors may use radar, lasers, or other techniques to determine the physical space in front of a vehicle. When it receives data from front-facing sensors, a collision-avoidance system performs calculations to determine any potential obstructions present. If the speed differential between the vehicle and an object in front of it is too high, then the system may perform several different tasks to avoid an accident.

Evasive Steering

Evasive steering helps an AV steer around an imminent crash. It uses a front-mounted camera and radar detector to monitor the surrounding traffic. If a collision is imminent, the vehicle applies the brakes. Evasive steering turns the car the exact right amount to avoid the obstacle while also preventing the car from crashing.

Evasive steering comes into play, avoiding pedestrians or other objects in the roadway. The cameras detect the pedestrian as well as oncoming traffic. The AV then instantly computes the evasive maneuver and initiates evasive action faster than can be done by a human.

On-Ramp and Off-Ramp Turning

Once on the highway, an autonomous vehicle needs to exit the highway at the appropriate time safely. The Tesla on-ramp and off-ramp function when in Navigate on Autopilot mode is an example of this. Once on the freeway, the Tesla will determine which lane it needs to be in and when to exit correctly. In addition to ensuring it reaches its intended exit, Autopilot will watch for opportunities to move to a faster lane when the car is behind slower traffic. When it arrives at the exit, it will depart the freeway, slow down, and transition control back to the driver.

Automatic-Parking Systems

There are different types of automatic-parking systems (APS), although they are designed to perform similar tasks. Some automatic parking systems offer hands-free parallel parking, and others only provide some helpful assistance.

Automatic parallel parking is easier for a car's computer than it is for a human. It follows a simple formula, and computers are better at that:

- Pull alongside the front parked car, allowing a 3-foot gap to that car,
- Align the back tires with the front parked car's rear bumper,
- Go into reverse and start turning the wheels hard-right,
- Then start backing up slowly until reaching a 45-degree angle, then stop,
- Turn the wheels hard-left,
- Then slowly continue to back up parallel with the curb,
- If needed, go backward or forward to even out space ahead and behind.

Automatic parallel-parking systems use various sensors to determine the approximate size of the space between two parked vehicles. Then the onboard computer calculates the necessary steering angles and velocities to navigate into the parking spot safely. Early automatic parallel-parking systems had difficulty working in tight quarters.

Some automatic parking systems are also capable of backing into traditional parking spaces in addition to parallel parking. Those systems use the same technology to allow a computer to calculate the proper steering angles and velocities to park perpendicularly between two other vehicles.

Some cars require the driver to change gears from forward to reverse, etc. Other cars, like Tesla, can park themselves in a garage and back out of the garage at the owner's request. Sufficiently-autonomous vehicles will require automatic parking without a driver.

Over-the-Air Updates

Autonomous vehicles (AVs) are basically computers using a lot of software. Software updates are essential to AVs so that new improvements and software fixes can be rapidly and efficiently transmitted to vehicles. Over-the-air (OTA) updating is already the common way to update cell phones and iPads, but it is not easy for cars.

When Tesla introduced the Model S, it had an electronic architecture that enabled every line of code to change remotely. Tesla has some unique advantages in this. The cost of transmitting a lot of software over cellular systems to millions of vehicles can be prohibitive. To overcome this, Tesla uses a process for over-the-air update of its Autopilot driver-assist system that replaces only the changed code rather than the entire file, making it much more efficient.

But there is a more significant impediment restricting many car manufacturers. By some state laws, auto manufacturers can't offer existing customers new features for their vehicles without the car dealerships getting their cut. So, software updates need to be made at the dealership. This restriction contrasts with Tesla, which has done much to highlight the utility of OTA updates. Because Tesla doesn't have dealers, it isn't restricted by laws that prevent it from rolling out new features to customers without having a dealership as a mandatory middle step. Tesla frequently does OTA software updates. These can correct minor issues and introduce new features. One, for example, added advanced summon and Netflix.

Security is also a significant issue with OTA updates, which will continue to get a lot of attention. There are many controls in place to provide security, but this will require continued diligence.

Sufficiently-Autonomous Driving Functions

Sufficiently-autonomous driving requires a significant upgrade from semi-autonomous capabilities. A vehicle needs to plan and initiate turns, read traffic signs and lights, and avoid obstacles and pedestrians. It needs to drive anywhere without a driver or even a passenger, but it needs to do this only in a limited, defined area.

Sufficiently-autonomous vehicles need to have a more comprehensive sensor package than semi-autonomous vehicles. These sensors, particularly lidar, are necessary for improved object identification and interpretation, more precise positioning within a detailed map, and increased awareness of surroundings.

They will use detailed high-definition maps that are not needed for semi-autonomous driving. These maps enable the vehicle to identify precisely where it is relative to the edge of the road, a corner, a curb, or an intersection. This is a significant change from the way semi-autonomous vehicles work.

Sufficiently-autonomous vehicles will use much more powerful computer systems. These systems will combine the data from all sensors, precisely position the vehicle, identify the path it needs to follow, and guide the vehicle.

It is now likely that sufficiently-autonomous vehicles will initially be used for autonomous ride services. This enables them to confine their operation to a limited set of predefined routes for which these detailed high-definition maps have been created and where the road conditions and traffic conditions are safe for AVs.

The following are some of the additional functions for sufficiently-autonomous driving.

Enhanced Perception and Localization

Semi-autonomous driving requires the vehicle to perceive lane markings and similar boundaries. Sufficiently-autonomous driving requires much-enhanced perception. The more advanced sensors combine data with high-definition maps to localize the vehicle. Perception detects and classifies objects, determines their location, and provides their speed and direction. It builds a three-dimensional model of the world that keeps track of important objects. Perception also predicts these objects' anticipated motion — pedestrians and trucks have different predicted movements.

Using the three-dimensional model and map data, perception determines the drivable space around the vehicle and identifies other environmental uncertainties. It knows where it must look for moving objects. This allows prudent decision-making and operation based upon both what the sensors "see" and what may be hidden from view.

Path Planning

Path planning uses the information captured in the vehicle's detailed maps to safely direct the vehicle to its destination while avoiding obstacles and following the rules of the road. Although path-planning algorithms will vary in different systems, the following describes a general path-planning algorithm:

The algorithm determines a rough long-range plan for the vehicle to follow while continuously refining a short-range plan (e.g., change lanes, drive forward 10m, turn right). It starts from a set of short-range paths that the vehicle would be dynamically capable of completing given its speed, direction, and angular position and removes all those that would either cross an obstacle or come too close to the predicted path of a moving one.

For example, a vehicle traveling at 50 mph would not safely complete a right turn five meters ahead. Therefore, that path would be eliminated from the feasible set. The remaining paths are evaluated based on safety, speed, and any time requirements. Once it identifies the best path, a set of throttle, brake, and steering commands are passed to the vehicle's onboard processors and actuators. Altogether, this process takes, on average, 50 milliseconds. However, it can be longer or shorter depending on the amount of collected data, available processing power, and complexity of the path-planning algorithm.

Vehicle Control

Vehicle control implements the final path from planning, converting its commands for the actuators that control the steering, throttle, brake, and drive unit. Since there is no human driver to intervene, vehicle control must be capable of the full range of driving commands. This is how the vehicle turns corners and avoids obstacles.

Turning Corners

Turing corners reliably and accurately is an essential function that AVs need to master. Currently, this can't be done in semi-autonomous vehicles using only GPS-based navigation, since it's not accurate enough. More precise positioning with detailed HD mapping enables a vehicle to know that it is 6 inches or less from a corner and can maneuver the turn.

Turns can have many variations and complexities. For example, Uber admitted that its autonomous vehicles had a "problem" with the way they handle bike lanes and that the company was working to fix a programming flaw with cars making unsafe turns in cycling lanes. Rather than merging into bike lanes early to make right-hand turns, as per California state law, the Uber vehicle reportedly pulled across the bike lanes, risking collisions with oncoming cyclists.

Right Turn on Red

At busy intersections, a right on red requires a human driver to simultaneously track multiple moving objects in different directions, from fast-moving cars on the left who have the green light to pedestrians crossing in front. There are also rules specific to each state; cars in California are required to enter the bike lane before and during a right turn, but in Texas, cars must leave the bike lane clear.

AVs can identify situations where making a right turn on red is permissible, and the sensors provide good visibility of left-hand traffic. After coming to a complete stop, the AV nudges forward to get a better view (for example, if there's a truck or bus blocking the line of sight). Software and sensors are good at tracking multiple objects and calculating the speed of oncoming vehicles, enabling the AV to judge when there's a big enough gap to safely make the turn. And because the sensors are designed to see 360 degrees, the AV is always looking for pedestrians stepping off curbs or cyclists approaching from behind.

Turning Left

Instructing an autonomous vehicle to turn left is one of the more formidable problems. It's also a difficult problem for humans. Accidents are more than ten times likely to involve left-hand turns than right-hand turns. A right-hand turn is a consistent maneuver, while the left-hand turn involves many variables.

Unprotected left turns are particularly challenging for humans as well as AVs. An unprotected left turn occurs at an intersection where there is no traffic light to signal the turn and give the vehicle turning left preference over other vehicles. The driver or AV needs to yield to oncoming traffic and pedestrians. This can create dangerous situations, which is why the accident rate is higher. Many road systems are being modified to use left-turn signals or prohibit left turns in response to this risk. In addition to lowering accident rates for drivers, it will enable AVs to operate more efficiently.

For left-hand turns, AVs need to estimate the speed, distance, and timing of oncoming cars. They can do that part more efficiently than humans can. Humans, though, will sometimes make judgments on when to risk cutting off an oncoming car based on intangible factors: how long the line is of cars coming toward them, how many cars are waiting behind them, driving characteristics of the oncoming car, and how long before the light turns red again.

Even protected left-hand turns can be tricky for drivers. For example, intersections in Florida frequently use a left-turn arrow to give priority to those turning left. Then it changes to a solid green light, meaning that those turning left then need to defer to cars proceeding through the intersection. Essentially, this changes the turn from protected to unprotected. Too many drivers get confused and continue to think they have the priority to turn left, causing dangerous accidents. An example of this was the fatal accident of a van carrying a college rowing team that turned left, thinking it still had the priority after the light switched from green arrow to solid green. AVs will be 100% reliable in avoiding these types of accidents.

GM Cruise has been testing its AVs in San Francisco, and in 2019 it was safely making more than 1,400 left-hand turns per day. Cruise AVs were not only making these turns safely; they were also making them smoothly.

Maybe AVs will adopt the "UPS rule," which routes its 100,000 trucks in a way to avoid left-hand turns whenever possible. AVs will soon have sufficient intelligence to make these left-hand turns. It is also possible that AV-compatible communities will implement more left-hand turn traffic signals at major intersections.

Obstacle Avoidance

An AV identifies the current and predicted location of all static and moving obstacles in its vicinity with obstacle avoidance. This is a continuous process of detection and identification. Obstacles are categorized in a library of pre-determined shape and motion descriptors. The AV rapidly matches obstacles to objects in this library to identify them. It then predicts the future path of moving objects based on their shape and prior trajectory. For example, if a two-wheeled object is traveling at 40 mph versus ten mph, it is most likely a motorcycle and not a bicycle, and the vehicle will categorize it as such. The internal map incorporates the previous, current, and predicted future locations of all obstacles in the vehicle's vicinity. The vehicle then uses to plan its path to avoid the obstacle safely.

Traffic-Light Detection

Traffic lights pose a unique perception problem for AVs. A previously established map can indicate when and where a vehicle should be able to see a traffic light, but vision is the only way to detect the state of that light, which may include detecting which sub-elements of the light are illuminated. This process includes distinguishing colors (red, yellow, green) and identifying and colored arrows for turning. Although any vision task may be challenging due to the variety of outdoor conditions, traffic lights have been engineered to be highly visible, emissive light sources that eliminate or substantially reduce illumination-based appearance variations. A camera with fixed gain, exposure, and aperture can be calibrated to traffic-light color levels.

The most common failure conditions in a traffic light detection (TLD) system are either visual obstructions or false positives such as those induced by the brake lights of other vehicles. Using a map of traffic lights, the vehicle can predict when it should see traffic lights and take actions, such as braking gradually to a stop when it is unable to observe any lights. In addition to detecting the traffic light or stop sign, the AV needs to detect the stop line on the roadway and bring the vehicle to a stop there if it is the first vehicle stopping.

TLD is a requirement for even sufficiently-autonomous vehicles. Any road will contain traffic lights, and the vehicle needs to stop reliably at a red light and proceed when it turns green. It's one of the autonomous driving functions that must be 100% accurate and reliable.

Eventually, traffic lights will emit an electronic signal that autonomous vehicles can interpret without seeing the light. These will also provide more information, such as the time before a light change, to help the vehicle pace itself better. However, reliable TLD will be needed until then.

Traffic-Sign Recognition

Traffic-Sign Recognition (TSR) is a technology that enables a vehicle to recognize traffic signs, e.g., "speed limit" or "children" or "turn ahead." The technology is being developed by several automotive suppliers, including Continental and Delphi. It uses image-processing techniques to detect traffic signs based on color, shape, etc. The Vienna Convention on Road Signs and Signals signed in 1968 standardizes traffic signs across different countries. The convention broadly classifies road signs into seven categories designated with letters A-H. This standardization has been essential for the development of a traffic-sign recognition system for global use.

These first TSR systems, which recognize speed limits, were developed in cooperation by Mobileye and Continental AG in late 2008 on the redesigned BMW 7-Series, and the following year on the Mercedes-Benz S-Class.

Modern traffic-sign recognition systems use convolutional neural networks, mainly driven by the requirements of autonomous vehicles where the detection system needs to identify a variety of traffic signs and not just speed limits. This is where the Vienna Convention on Road Signs and Signals helps. A convolutional Traffic-Sign Recognition (TSR) is a technology that enables a vehicle to recognize traffic signs.

Traffic-sign recognition can fail to work in certain situations. In Naples, Florida, a month after Hurricane Irma, hundreds of street signs, including stop signs, were down or bent over and would not be recognized by an autonomous vehicle. In the age of autonomous vehicles, repairing traffic signs will be a high priority; otherwise, autonomous vehicles will not function safely. A neural network can be trained to "learn" these predefined traffic signs and use this to determine the meaning of signs.

Emergency Vehicle Identification

Awareness and identification of approaching emergency vehicles is a specific function that must be managed by autonomous vehicles. The identification usually begins with sound detection of approaching sirens, from which the distance and then the approaching path are determined. This alert makes the car's camera sensors aware of looking for and identifying emergency vehicles. The software guidance systems control the car appropriately, such as pulling over to the side of the road.

Eventually, all emergency vehicles will have vehicle-to-vehicle communications that will notify other vehicles of their approach and request actions from those other vehicles.

Recognition of Police Hand-Signals

AVs need to function in unique situations such as construction zones, manual traffic control, and power outages where a policeman uses hand signals to direct traffic. Waymo's AVs can distinguish between civilians and police standing in the roadway and can follow hand signals. They will yield and respond based on the recognition that it is a police officer. It provided this interesting example:

A Chrysler Pacifica minivan in Waymo's automated ride-hailing fleet rolled up to a darkened stoplight in Tempe, Arizona. The power had gone out, and a police officer stood in the roadway directing traffic. In dash-cam footage, the minivan stops at the intersection, waits for the cross-traffic and a left-turning car coming the other way, then proceeds when waved through by the officer.

Passenger Communications

Sufficiently-autonomous vehicles will need a way to communicate with passengers and take direction from them. For example, passengers may want to instruct the car to stop at the next rest area or market. They may want the car to change the destination or stop along the way. Passengers may also want to make inquiries about the car, such as how long it will take to reach the destination. The car may also need to notify passengers about relevant information, such as an upcoming stop for refueling.

Most likely, most passenger communications will be voice-based but expect that there also will be a high-quality display in the autonomous vehicle for maps and entertainment selection. Most likely, there will also be an onboard integrated entertainment system.

There will most likely be communications with a customer support center for that service in autonomous ride services cars. This communication network would respond to passenger problems or requests and allow the center to contact passengers.

Fully-Autonomous Driving Functions

Fully-autonomous driving contains all the sufficiently-autonomous functions, but in addition, it also encompasses the ability to drive autonomously without any constraints. The fully-autonomous AV can drive in any location, including unmapped roads, private driveways, off-road trails, etc. To do this, the AV will need some other capabilities.

SLAM

SLAM is the ability to locate and map where a vehicle is simultaneously. The AV needs to build a unique map of its surroundings and locate where it is on the map. From there, it needs to determine what direction to proceed on its own, even if there are no road markings.

User-Defined Maps

People who own their AVs will need some way of updating maps for their individual needs. This could be to add a map of their driveway or courtyard, so the AV can pull in correctly and park in a proper position, such as the correct garage bay. Conversely, it could be a unique map of work locations where they prefer their AV to park.

This will require some type of user-friendly custom-mapping function, most likely on a smartphone app. The AV could show a map of the area around it, and the user could specify the preferred path and positioning.

Off-Road Capabilities

For an AV to drive off-road, it will need unique capabilities for positioning itself and identifying a path that is appropriate to drive. It will need to avoid obstacles by driving off the path through acceptable terrain. It will also need to remember how it got to where it is to turn around and return the same route.

Chapter 5
How an AV Thinks and Acts

Many people want to know how an autonomous vehicle (AV) thinks. How does it know what to do? What is its thought process? How does it learn? Is it similar or different from human drivers?

Autonomous vehicles (AVs) mimic the thinking of human drivers, but they are much different. In this chapter, we look at how an AV thinks and acts and explore some unique issues. Then we will look at how AVs cope with pedestrians and communications between AVs and humans.

Early AV pilot testing has shown AVs safer and more careful than human drivers, but this can be frustrating for other drivers who expect a little more aggressive driving behavior. Will AVs have different personalities? Will they follow speed limits and safe driving practices, or will there be some flexibility? We will also consider the ethical issues of how AVs will make decisions and look at some unique circumstances that may be difficult for AVs.

Let's start by looking at how an AV sees the world.

How an Autonomous Vehicle Sees the World

An AV sees the world similarly to humans, but it does it more broadly and faster. At the most basic level, human drivers need to answer four questions in sequence: "Where am I?" (perceiving where they are), "What's around me?" (identifying and classifying other vehicles, pedestrians, etc.), "What will happen next?" (predicting how these others will behave), and "What should I do?" (making driving decisions based on that information). AVs answer those questions, too.

As outlined in their safety reports, almost all companies developing AVs use a similar sequential process. In its safety report, Waymo explained and illustrated its approach.

1. Where Am I?

Waymo starts by building detailed three-dimensional (high-definition) maps highlighting relevant information such as road profiles, curbs, sidewalks, lane markers, crosswalks, traffic lights, stop signs, and other road features. Instead of relying on GPS, Waymo's vehicles cross-reference these three-dimensional maps with real-time sensor data to precisely determine their location on the road. The AV finds the correct detailed map from its database and verifies it by comparing it to actual surroundings.

The photo illustrates this. The AV is shown as an image in the center of the picture. It is at an intersection in the second lane from the left. The far-left lane is a left-turn lane. The turn lanes for the crossroads are also on the map. Note that the picture shows only fixed objects around the vehicle in this first step, and it doesn't show anything else that may be around it. Those are added in the next step.

2. What's Around Me?

The sensors constantly scan for objects around the vehicle—pedestrians, cyclists, vehicles, road work, and obstructions. They continuously read traffic controls, such as traffic light colors, railroad crossing gates, and temporary stop signs. Its vehicles can see up to 300 meters away (nearly three football fields) in every direction.

All the data from these various sensors are "fused" together, meaning the computer on the vehicle creates a single set of images based on multiple inputs. The computer software may select one sensor's data over another, depending on which is more accurate. The AV's computer software then characterizes these images into objects by comparing them to objects in its vast database. This characterization doesn't just use an object's size and shape; it also uses other information such as an object's speed.

The illustration shows the computer image used by the AV in the upper half and a photo of the same scene at the bottom for comparison. The AV has identified other vehicles, pedestrians, and cyclists at the intersection. These are called dynamic objects because they move in comparison with stationary objects like street signs.

The large box outline to the left front of the AV is the object for a bus, as seen in the comparison photo at the bottom. The green object in front of the AV is a pickup truck. The other boxes are stationary vehicles. The two objects next to the AV are trucks because they are larger shapes than the AV. The three to the right are cars stopped at the intersection.

Pedestrians are crossing the road to the right. The cyclist is crossing the same intersection. There is also a cyclist up ahead on the right in the AV's direction of travel. It's crucial to distinguish pedestrians from cyclists since they have different behaviors, travel in different paths (sidewalks and roads), and move at differing speeds.

Though it is not illustrated, the AV also knows the state of the traffic light. As can be seen in the photo at the bottom of the illustration, it's green so that the AV can proceed

3. What Will Happen Next?

The next step is to predict what each of the vehicles, pedestrians, and cyclists will do so that the AV can proceed safely.

The software predicts expected movements for each dynamic object based on current speed and trajectory. It understands that a vehicle will move differently than a cyclist or pedestrian. The software then uses that information to predict the many possible paths that other road users may take. It also considers how changing road conditions (such as a blocked lane up ahead) may affect the behavior of others around it. The numbers superimposed on the objects demonstrate how the software assigns predictions to each object surrounding the AV—other vehicles, cyclists, pedestrians, and more.

Now, the system uses its mathematical software to predict the timing in the movements of all dynamic objects using pre-defined formulas. This is like how humans make assumptions and intelligent guesses on how each dynamic object will move, but the computer does it much faster and watches more objects simultaneously.

The system assumes the truck on the left of the AV will turn left because it is a left-turn only lane. It also predicts that the truck to its right will proceed straight, along with the estimated speed it will take, which determines where the truck is likely to be at each split-second ahead. If that truck begins to turn left and cut off the AV, it will immediately react how a human driver would, but maybe much faster.

The AV also assumes that the pedestrians and cyclists on the right crosswalk will continue to cross without dashing across its lanes. If the pedestrian makes an unexpected movement, the AV will immediately recalculate new possible movements.

4. What Should I Do?

The next step is to determine the path that the AV should take. This is called path planning. The AV knows its overall route from its navigation system. In this step, it identifies exactly how to proceed precisely through the intersection.

The software considers all this information and examines many different alternative routes, some just slightly different in speed and trajectory. It then selects the best specific path for the vehicle to take. The Waymo software determines the exact trajectory, speed, lane, and steering maneuvers needed to safely navigate this route. The vehicles are constantly monitoring the environment and predicting the expected behavior of other road users in 360 degrees around them. They can respond quickly and safely to any changes.

In the image, the path indicates the trajectory through which the AV can proceed ahead. It shows that the AV can proceed and that it has identified the vehicles ahead and understands it must maintain a certain headway.

How Do AVs Learn to Drive?

In general, AVs learn to drive in a similar way that humans do. However, the learning experience is much faster, more comprehensive, and more extensive. Artificial intelligence software enables AVs to learn from experience. The experience comes in several ways: simulation, closed-course testing, and real-world driving.

Simulation creates unusual driving scenarios an AV may encounter and rapidly iterates alternatives and outcomes until it learns the best one. It also recreates the most challenging AV situations on public roads and turns them into virtual scenarios for the simulation software. It then rigorously tests any changes or updates to the software before it's deployed. Waymo has run more than 6 billion miles of simulated driving, running 10 million driving miles of simulation per day, the equivalent of 25,000 cars driving for 24 hours.

Initially, new AVs are tested on a closed course that simulates a real-world driving environment. Once AV software is working as intended, it is tested with real-world driving on public roads. The more miles traveled on public roads, the more opportunities to monitor and assess the performance of the software. Waymo announced in 2018 that its vehicles completed more than 10 million test miles of driving since 2009.

AVs also have other essential learning mechanisms. They have crash avoidance capabilities, safety 'force fields", and are programmed to come to a safe stop. The first AVs, autonomous ride services vehicles, will drive just in a pre-defined area with restricted routes, so they only need to learn how to drive autonomously in those areas.

Perhaps the most essential aspect of AV learning is that its learning is broad-based and continuous. Whatever one AV learns will be used to update the learning of all other AVs or at least those from the same AV developer. Imagine how much better all human drivers would be if everyone immediately learned from the experience of all other drivers.

Let's look at the AV learning process in more detail.

Artificial Intelligence and Machine Learning

To some extent, AVs use driving algorithms to instruct them how to drive, but more importantly, they use artificial intelligence to "learn" how to drive. Artificial intelligence is the ability of a computer program to think and learn. It works on its own without complex instructions or algorithms. In a sense, it mimics the human mind.

For example, with image recognition, an AV examines images and characterizes the objects in each image. Initially, most of its guesses will be wrong, but the algorithm modifies internal parameters or parts of its structure and tries again. This process continues, discarding changes that reduce the algorithm's accuracy, keeping modifications that increase the accuracy until it correctly classifies all images.

Later, when given a new object to interpret, the software algorithm it developed will classify it accurately. For example, it will recognize someone on a bicycle as that object and then associate the characteristics it learned about how a bike might move.

Artificial intelligence is also used for actions and evaluations. Instead of supplying the vehicle with a fixed evaluation scheme from which the right move for each situation can be deduced, programmers feed the artificial intelligence software with many traffic situations and specify the correct action for each. The program then searches by itself for the best configuration of internal parameters and internal decision logic, which allow it to act correctly in these cases. Like human drivers, it may be difficult to explain why an AV exhibits a specific behavior in a new situation. Explicit rules are not necessary. The behavior decision results from the many traffic situations to which the algorithm was exposed beforehand. That's why AV software developers are "training" the systems with millions of cases through simulation.

Another characteristic of AV software is its use of probabilistic outcomes. It maintains a distribution of outcomes with specific probabilities and selects the best one.

Apple filed a patent application for an autonomous navigation system that learns from human driving routes. The Apple system gets trained initially by driving the vehicle along a particular route. As the vehicle drives along the route, sensors develop a characterization of that route. The system progressively updates the route as it repeatedly drives it. Once certain confidence thresholds are reached, then the autonomous navigation will turn on.

Simulation

Simulation software is used to educate and train autonomous vehicles at an accelerated rate. It simulates "real world" situations that a vehicle may encounter, tests its response, and then modifies it if necessary. Simulation software primarily runs outside of the vehicle in development labs. What it learns from the simulation is then transferred to the AV software on each vehicle.

There are several advantages to simulation. First, a simulation can "drive" a lot more miles than would be possible to do physically. It can test millions of miles per day. Imagine a new driver having to simulate a million miles of driving before getting a license. Second, simulations can focus on the more challenging situations drivers encounter rather than the standard boring miles. Third, the development time for software is much faster. And fourth, all the simulated conditions can be saved and then used to test future releases of the AV software.

All companies developing autonomous systems use driving simulation software, but they tend to keep their efforts secret. Waymo first discussed its autonomous simulation software with Atlantic Magazine for an article by Alexis Madrigal on August 23, 2017. The software, called Carcraft (named after the software game World of Warcraft), simulates eight million miles of virtual driving per day. Here are some of the highlights:

- *At any time, 25,000 virtual self-driving cars are making their way through fully modeled versions of Austin, Mountain View, and Phoenix, as well as test-track scenarios. Waymo might simulate driving down a particularly tricky road hundreds of thousands of times in a single day. In 2016, the simulations logged 2.5 billion virtual miles compared to a little over 3 million miles by Waymo's real-life self-driving cars that run on public roads. And crucially, the virtual miles focus on what Waymo people call "interesting" miles where they might learn something new. These are not dull highway commuter miles.*

- *The software has a model of the city of Phoenix. It shows where all the lanes are, which lanes lead into other lanes, where stop signs are, where traffic lights are, where curbs are, where the center of the lane is, etc. It is everything you need to know. To demonstrate it, they zoom in on a single four-way stop somewhere near Phoenix and start dropping in synthetic cars and pedestrians and cyclists. Then the objects on the screen begin to move. Cars act like cars, driving in their lanes, and turning. Cyclists act like cyclists. Their logic is modeled from the millions of miles of public-road driving Waymo has done. Underneath it all, there is that hyper-detailed map and models for the physics of the different objects in the scene. In this case, there are 800 scenarios generated by this four-way stop.*

- *Not surprisingly, the hardest thing to simulate is the behavior of other people. It's like the old parental concern: "I'm not worried about you driving. I'm worried about the other people on the road."*

- *There is one fundamental difference between this and the real world. In the real world, they must take in fresh, real-time data about the environment and convert it into an understanding of the scene, but most simulations skip that object-recognition step. Instead of feeding raw data to identify as a pedestrian, they merely tell the car: a pedestrian is here.*

Closed-Track Testing

A closed track is used to recreate real-world driving in a secure environment that is safer. Closed-track testing is used to subject test vehicles to edge cases and difficult situations. Some AV companies have their own closed-track testing facilities.

Florida is building a $42 million closed test track as a partnership between the Florida Department of Transportation, Florida's Turnpike Enterprise, and Florida Polytechnic University. The Florida track will be designed for unmanned car testing, slated to be complete by spring 2021. Companies testing their AVs on the site will be able to choose from various environments on the 200-acre infield area, including:

- *An urban area that simulates intersection configurations and complex lighting, signing, and signal conditions,*

- *A roadway geometry track made up of complex horizontal and vertical curves, plus irregular grade changes, and*

- *A pick-up/drop-off area to replicate various multi-modal passenger transfers, such as transit centers.*

Using a closed-testing facility, a company can create system failure cases to see how the vehicle reacts.

Testing on Public Roads

Real-world testing on public roads enables AVs to validate and improve their performance. After all, driving on real roads is what AVs are being developed to do. AV developers can monitor their systems to ensure they demonstrate expected reactions and build on the experience to enable smoother driving. Real-world testing provides a continuous feedback loop to refine AV systems. This iterative approach to testing with public-road validation safely helps AVs scale capabilities.

AVs testing on public roads include safety drivers in each vehicle. Many companies use two people: one as a safety driver and the other to log essential information about what is happening.

California requires that all companies testing AVs in the state file what are called disengagement reports. This specifies the number of AVs tested on California roads by each AV company, the miles driven in autonomous mode, and the number of disengagements. A disengagement occurs when the human driver takes control from the autonomous system. These reports shed some interesting light on the extent of testing.

- *In 2019, 60 companies had permits with 37 active. This is an increase from 48 permitted and 28 active in 2018.*

- *547 AVs were tested in 2019, compared to 467 in 2018 and 230 in 2017.*

- *These AVs drove almost 3 million miles in 2019, 50% more than the 2 million miles in 2018, with 500,000 miles in 2017.*

- *The two leading companies testing were Waymo with 109 AVs driven 1.45 million miles and GM Cruise with 224 AVs driven 831,000 miles*

These statistics represent only a portion of the actual testing of AVs on public roads since much of it is done in other states. Testing on public roads in selected states across the country will continue to increase in the number of companies, vehicles, and miles driven. This helps to improve AV technology and prove safety.

Testing Crash Avoidance Capabilities

In addition to testing core behavioral competencies, engineers also conduct crash-avoidance testing across a variety of scenarios. Waymo has completed thousands of crash-avoidance tests at its private test track. Each of these individual tests recreates a distinct driving scenario and allows them to analyze vehicle response. They then use a simulator to test these scenarios further and improve software capabilities.

They draw from a variety of sources to learn which collisions to test against, including its analysis of sources such as NHTSA's fatal crash database and use of extensive experience operating self-driving vehicles. It also tests situations in which other road users create potentially dangerous situations, such as vehicles suddenly pulling out of driveways, large vehicles cutting across target lanes, motorcyclists weaving through traffic, and pedestrians jaywalking. Just four crash categories accounted for 84% of all crashes: rear-end crashes, vehicles turning or crossing at an intersection, vehicles running off the edge of the road, and vehicles changing lanes. For example, here is how Waymo tests one category.

Crash Avoidance Category	Example Test Scenario
Rear-end Demonstrate ability to avoid or mitigate crashes with lead vehicles.	Fully self-driving vehicle approaches stopped lead vehicle
	Fully self-driving vehicle approaches a disabled vehicle
	Fully self-driving vehicle approaches lead vehicle traveling at a lower constant speed
	Fully self-driving vehicle approaches lead vehicle traveling at a slower speed and initiating strong braking
	Fully self-driving vehicle approaches lead vehicle accelerating
	Fully self-driving vehicle following a lead vehicle making a maneuver (e.g., cutting into a lane or pulling out of a driveway)
	Fully self-driving vehicle approaches lead vehicle decelerating
	Fully self-driving vehicle approaches another vehicle(s) reversing
	Fully self-driving vehicle approaches another vehicle(s) parking

Restricted Driving Areas

Autonomous ride services (ARS) are designed, so an AV does not operate outside of its approved operational design domain. For example, passengers cannot select a destination outside of approved geography, and the software will not create a route that travels outside of a "geo-fenced" area, which has been mapped in detail.

Vehicles can comply with federal, state, and local laws within their geographic area of operations. Legal requirements, and any changes in those requirements, are identified and built into systems as safety requirements, including applicable speed limits, traffic signs, and signals. Before vehicles drive in a new location, they are trained to understand any unique road rules or driving customs, with software updated so the vehicles can respond safely. For example, California and Texas (home to two of Waymo's test cities) have differing rules for how to make right turns in the presence of a bike lane.

The operational domain includes the streets in the cities where the vehicle will operate, at all times of day and night, and in light-to-moderate inclement weather (e.g., fog or rain). The vehicle's computers treat these mapped areas as a strict boundary for the vehicle. Thus, the vehicle will choose only routes that fall entirely within the mapped area. Within the mapped areas, the vehicles will be capable of complying with all applicable traffic laws.

When the vehicle detects rapid or abnormal changes in weather conditions, it will adjust how it operates to accommodate the weather and how other road users are behaving, such as when traffic slows during heavy rain. At all times, the AV fleet will communicate with a centralized fleet operations center.

Coming to a Safe Stop

Cars rely on a human driver's control if a situation on the road becomes too complex. AVs need to handle similar situations automatically. If an AV can no longer proceed on a planned trip, it must be capable of performing a safe stop or fallback. This might include situations when the AV system experiences a problem, when the vehicle is involved in a collision, or when environmental conditions change in a way that would affect safe driving within an operational design domain.

AVs are designed to detect each one of these scenarios automatically. In addition, vehicles run thousands of checks on their systems every second, looking for faults. Systems are equipped with a series of redundancies for critical functions, such as sensors, computing, and braking. How the vehicle responds varies with the type of roadway on which a situation occurs, the current traffic conditions, and the extent of the technology failure. Depending on these factors, the system will determine an appropriate response to keep the vehicle and its passengers safe, including pulling over or coming to a safe stop.

Continuous Learning

Waymo has a robust system for collecting and analyzing data from its encounters. Anything learned from the experience of one vehicle is applied to its entire fleet. Waymo's system can detect when it has been involved in a collision and will notify Waymo's operations center automatically. Trained specialists can initiate post-crash procedures, including procedures for interacting with law enforcement and first responders to the location.

ARS fleets will monitor their vehicles and collect data on their performance. As this data identifies opportunities for improvements, the ARS fleet will update the software in all the vehicle, so the entire fleet will continue to get better. When one AV experiences something new, that data is sent back to the operations center, and every other vehicle in the fleet learns from it.

Waymo's AVs have two data-recording features: a conventional Event Data Recorder (EDR) and a second robust data-logging system. The data-logging system is highly reliable, has self-diagnostics, and stores data securely, protecting it against loss. The data-logging system is designed to keep data intact even in the event of a crash. If a collision occurs, the data-logging system stores predefined data from the vehicle. The collected data includes information on sensors, vehicle actions, degraded behavior, malfunctions, and other helpful information for event reconstruction.

In addition to collisions, a robust data recording capability provides information on vehicle performance during everyday driving and avoided crash situations. This retrieved data can evaluate the design and driving performance during vehicle development and deployment and for continuous improvement for future self-driving vehicles.

Safety Force Field

Some autonomous vehicles aim to create a "safety force field" to avoid accidents. An example is Nvidia's Safety Force built into Nvidia's Drive autonomous vehicle software suite. It's a decision-making policy that monitors unsafe actions by analyzing real-time sensor data and makes predictions to minimize harm. The framework ensures that the measures it recommends never create, escalate, or contribute to unsafe situations.

Safety Force Field is an open-source collision avoidance algorithm for autonomous vehicles that uses computational predictions to guess where nearby cars, pedestrians, and other obstructions will be in the immediate future and then shield autonomous vehicles from a collision with a combination of emergency braking and intelligent steering around obstacles. Nvidia makes the Safety Force Field algorithm available for other developers when building their autonomous platforms.

It uses robust mathematical calculations backed by physics-based "zero-collisions" verifications that follow a single core principle — collision avoidance. The calculations are performed on-vehicle and frame-by-frame. They have been validated using both real-world and simulated synthetic data entailing high-risk highway and urban driving scenarios.

Safety Force Field can consider both braking and steering constraints, enabling it to identify and eliminate "anomalies" arising from both. Mathematically, it intends to operate like magnets that repel each other, keep themselves out of harm's way and not contribute to unsafe situations.

Similarly, Intel's Mobileye self-driving car division announced its mathematical collision avoidance model — Responsibility-Sensitive Safety (RSS) — in October 2017. It is described as a deterministic formula-based system with "logically provable" rules of the road. It's intended to provide a "common sense" approach to on-the-road decision-making that codifies good habits, like maintaining a safe following distance and giving other cars the right of way.

Will AVs Be Overly Cautious?

Generally, everyone broadly agrees that "safety first" is critical for AVs. Almost everyone believes that they need to be more cautious than the average driver, at least initially. While cautious driving is necessary for AVs, as it should also be necessary for human drivers, this cautious driving may irritate many human drivers and may lead to minor accidents.

Early Complaints About Cautious Waymo AVs

Early reports in 2018 of Waymo's AV testing in Arizona, show some frustration with their AVs cautious driving. Residents in areas around Phoenix said its AVs seem to have difficulty in certain traffic situations, such as making left turns across lanes with fast-moving traffic and merging onto highways in heavy traffic. The cars also stop and brake abruptly when encountering unusual situations.

This problem stems from Waymo's AVs being more cautious than the human drivers they share the road with. Its AVs stop for a full three seconds at every stop sign (the legal requirement) and try to maintain a wide berth when making turns. Most human drivers aren't so conservative. "Safety remains our highest priority as we test and deploy our technology," Waymo states, and that's the way it should be, but human drivers need to recognize this.

Frustrated drivers are even taking videos of these cautious AVs. In one example, a video shows the Waymo AV hesitating for 7-8 seconds to take a right-hand turn on a green light because two women were at the corner poised to walk across the road at the crosswalk. After that pause, the vehicle slowly made the turn. The vehicle was deferring to the pedestrians out of caution, but in the video, they were talking to each other and probably not intending to cross. They didn't even notice the vehicle. There weren't any cars behind the AV, but if there were, the other drivers would have honked their horns in frustration. The Waymo AV proceeded in the turn just before the traffic light turned red.

A human driver may have read the body language of the women and assumed they weren't crossing, which in some cases might not have been correct. Maybe a driver would have honked the horn to alert the women to either cross or stay. These questions will arise with the advent of AVs. Will others accept more cautious driving? Do AVs need to be less cautious? Will we need to implement more pedestrian crossing signals at intersections and enforce their use?

Accidents from Cautious Driving

The more cautious behavior of AVs can also cause minor accidents because human drivers sometimes expect other drivers to be more aggressive. Most AV accidents in the early trials have been the rear-ending of the AV by a human driver. An August 24, 2018, accident involving one of Apple's test AVs is a case in point. The accident report reads:

> On August 24th at 2:58 PM, an Apple test vehicle in autonomous mode was rear-ended while preparing to merge onto Lawrence Expressway South from Kifer Road. The Apple test vehicle was traveling at less than one mph, waiting for a safe gap to complete the merge when a 2016 Nissan Leaf contacted the Apple test vehicle at approximately 15 mph. Both vehicles sustained damage, and no injuries were reported by either party.

This rear-ending accident is typical of differences in driving behavior between an AV and a human driver and between two human drivers. You are behind another car waiting to enter a road by merging into traffic. You think that the car ahead will merge when there is at least a minor gap, as you would do. Maybe you can even follow that car and merge at the same interval in oncoming traffic. You see a small opening, and then the car ahead starts to move, so you assume that it will begin to merge, so you accelerate a little and look at the oncoming traffic to see if the gap is big enough for you to merge too. Then BANG! The car ahead of you didn't merge; it stopped when you turned to look at the oncoming traffic. You rear-ended it. (I know how this works because I've done it myself, but not to an AV.) The more cautious behavior of an AV is not what other drivers are expecting. Maybe human drivers need to start recognizing that AVs are more cautious and act accordingly.

Slower ARS Driving

As I've stated, AVs will first become popular in autonomous ride services (ARS); cautious driving will have some implications. Initially, ARS will be slower and "more pokey" than ridesharing drivers. ARS passengers will appreciate the focus on safety and caution but will not like taking longer to get where they are going.

I expect that early critics will complain that ARS is too slow. This may reduce acceptance a little at first, but eventually, the software in ARS AVs will mature a little and get more confident. This will enable them to drive more like humans, although still more cautious than the average driver. Drivers have different driving personalities. Some are cautious. They don't exceed speed limits, and they obey all driving rules. They willingly defer to other drivers. Yet, other drivers are what could be called "aggressive." They consistently exceed the speed limits. They drive aggressively, cutting off other cars and taking risks.

Will AVs Have Different Personalities?

Will each type of AV have its unique personality, will they be all the same, or will owners (or even passengers) choose the AVs personality? Will Waymo's AVs be more aggressive than Ford's or GMs? Will Apple be noted for the most cautious AV? These are rhetorical questions for now, but soon publications will have fun classifying the personality types of different AVs.

Let's look at some of the possibilities.

Speed Limits

Most drivers today drive at speeds exceeding speed limits but stay within reasonable boundaries of the speed limits. For example, 5-10 miles over the speed limit is usually considered acceptable by many drivers. Most drivers feel comfortable going with the speed of traffic even though traffic may be going above the speed limit. In many situations, other drivers will frequently get angry at drivers going too slow even when they are going the speed limit.

Practices for giving speeding tickets vary by state, municipality, and by individual police officers. However, in general, there is some flexibility. For example, a study of speeding tickets in New Hampshire showed that the average speeding ticket was given 16 MPH above the speed limit. In 50-55 MPH zones, only 1% of the speeding tickets were issued for speeds of less than 10 MPH over the limit.

With semi-autonomous cruise control, the driver sets the desired maximum speed, and the vehicle stays within that maximum speed, adjusting the speed only based on the car in front. Some vehicles now indicate the posted speed limit when the driver sets the speed, but the driver decides how much to set it.

With advances toward autonomous driving, the AV needs to set the speed based on the posted speed limit. It determines the posted limit either from a camera reading the speed limit sign or from a database indicating the speed limit at that point on the road.

Will AVs precisely follow speed limits? This is an interesting question. If the AV is programmed to go above the speed limit, will the manufacturer be fined automatically? Unlike human drivers, AV speeds are programmed and accurately measured. There is no "wiggle room" of uncertainty. If they precisely follow speed limits, they will suffer the scourge of other drivers who are going about the speed limit and will see the AVs as a problem slowing the other vehicles.

Tesla has been trying to find the right speed limit balance with autopilot. Generally, it adjusts the speed to 5 MPH above the posted speed limit. Still, it regularly gets owner complaints that it is forcing the car to go too fast or too slow, depending on the owner's preferences. There are also complaints that, in some cases, the speed limit database is incorrect.

Perhaps there will be differences in how AV manufacturers implement speed limits. One AV may stay at the speed limit while another may go up to 7 MPH faster in certain circumstances. Maybe this will even become a selling point. Or, possibly, an AV may provide passengers with options to set the speed limit above the posted level. ARS vehicles pose a unique condition in that they are unlikely to let passengers set the speed limit.

Eventually, AVs may be allowed to travel at speeds exceeding posted speed limits. Perhaps there will even be high-speed lanes for AVs on selected highways.

Aggressive Driving

In addition to speeding, aggressive driving is manifested in several other ways. Aggressive drivers will merge forcefully into a traffic lane, cutting off other drivers and forcing them to brake to let their car enter in front of them. Likewise, aggressive drivers on the road will not slow down to let other cars merge into traffic and may even accelerate to reduce the gap for a car to merge.

Aggressive drivers also weave in and out of traffic on highways to keep getting ahead of other cars. Frequently, this causes other drivers to slow down to avoid an accident, but they don't care. Tailgating is another form of aggressive driving. Aggressive drivers drive too close to the car ahead, making the distance between the two cars insufficient for stopping safely. In addition to doing this because of impatience, they do it to intimate the driver ahead to get out of their way or to provide too small a gap to let another aggressive driver try to cut in front of them. Running traffic lights that are turning red or not stopping at stop signs are other forms of aggressive driving.

I doubt that AVs will ever become very aggressive drivers like this, but they may become a little less cautious as they gain more experience.

AV Driving Personality Settings

Today, some cars have different drive settings, like sports mode or comfort mode, enabling the driver to adjust the way the car accelerates and feels. Will AVs have different personality settings like that?

Will AV owners be able to select different modes depending on their moods or needs? For example, an AV could have several personality settings:

- *Cautious Mode* – *The vehicle will follow all speed limits and drive with courtesy and respect for other drivers.*

- *Normal Driver Mode* – *Here, the AV will drive more like a typical human driver, traveling a little over the speed limit when possible and being slightly more aggressive in safer situations.*

- *More Aggressive Mode* – *This would be another level above the previous one.*

- *Angry Driver Mode* – *This is the aggressive driver mode, enabling the AV to do everything described for aggressive drivers. Not likely to be a mode available on AVs, but it may be a customizable hack from a third party.*

Driving Personality Automatically Adjusted to Passenger Comfort Level?

Another alternative is to adjust the type of driving to the comfort or stress level of the passengers. Apple filed for approval of a patent to do just that.

A sensor device located at the front of the vehicle's cabin could potentially monitor passengers in a vehicle, which could be used to identify individuals. While driving, the sensors could be used to ascertain an occupant's eye movements, body posture, gestures, pupil dilation, blinking, body temperature, heartbeat, perspiration, head position, and other factors of each passenger. This data, and previous experiences known about the passengers, could be used to create an occupant profile and enable the vehicle to select one of several comfort profiles.

A comfort profile would dictate how the vehicle drives, changing various settings, so the car moves with as much comfort for the user or users as possible. These driving control parameters can include adjusting the speed, straight-line acceleration, the turning rate, how fast the car can perform lane changes, the stiffness of the suspension, enabling or disabling traction control, and other elements that dictate how the vehicle ultimately moves.

As the system continues to take in live data, the comfort profile can be altered. For example, if it detects the stress level of a passenger rises during a fast turn, it could move to a different comfort profile that is slower and smoother to remove that stress.

Pedestrians and AVs

AVs encounter additional challenges with pedestrians, but so do human drivers. Pedestrians pose some unique challenges.

Uber Accident

The tragic death of a pedestrian hit by an Uber autonomous vehicle (AV) provides some insight. Elaine Herzberg, 49, was walking her bicycle far from the crosswalk on a four-lane road in the Phoenix suburb of Tempe about 10 PM on Sunday, March 18, 2018, when she was struck by an Uber autonomous vehicle traveling at 38 miles per hour, police said. "The pedestrian was outside the crosswalk. As soon as she had walked into the lane of traffic, she was struck," Tempe Police Sergeant Ronald Elcock told reporters at a news conference. The video footage shows the Uber vehicle was traveling in the rightmost of two lanes. Herzberg was moving from left to right, in the dark, crossing from the center median to the curb on the far right. She was looking away from the vehicle, and she never even turned slightly toward it when the lights shined on her.

This was not an example demonstrating that an autonomous vehicle is less safe than a human driver. "It's very clear it would have been difficult to avoid this collision in any kind of mode (autonomous or human-driven) based on how she came from the shadows into the roadway," stated the local police chief. Based on the AVs onboard video recorder, the pedestrian appeared suddenly from the dark and was visible for only 1 second before impact, and she didn't appear to notice the car even though the headlights were shining directly on her. It takes a human 2 seconds to react instantly to a situation like this.

However, this is a case where an AV should have outperformed a human driver. There was no other traffic around, and nothing to obstruct the other sensors in addition to the video from detecting Herzberg. When she came into view of the camera, she had crossed the left lane and was halfway across the right lane, having moved at least 20 feet from the median. She was also walking her bicycle across the road, not dashing out in front of traffic. That means she was out in clear space (although unseen in the dark) on the road for at least a couple of seconds. The Volvo XC90s that Uber is using for development was equipped with cameras, radar, and lidar sensors. Radar and lidar are capable of "seeing" their surroundings in complete darkness and should have detected Herzberg's presence in the roadway. The Volvo was traveling at 38 mph, a speed from which it could stop in no more than 60-70 feet, or steer around Herzberg, to the left, without hitting her.

Uber later disclosed that its lidar detected her crossing but couldn't interpret the data as a human. She was walking her bike with bags draped on it, so it didn't look like a person from images used to train the computer.

Pedestrian Behavior

In 2019, there were 6,590 pedestrian fatalities in the U.S., a 5% increase from 2018. Additionally, more than 120,000 pedestrians were treated in emergency rooms following accidents. Let's look at the causes for these to get some insight.

- *Jaywalking, or failure to cross at crosswalks is the primary factor in pedestrian fatalities. Between 80%-90% of pedestrian fatalities occur outside crosswalks.*

- *Distracted walking, not just distracted driving, is an increasing cause of pedestrians being hit by vehicles. Pedestrians are increasingly crossing roads while looking at their smartphones and not paying attention.*

- *Additional marijuana use may be increasing pedestrian accidents. States that legalized recreational marijuana had an increase of 16.4% in pedestrian accidents in the first six months of 2017.*

- *Alcohol was a cause of many pedestrian fatalities, but not just in the way you would expect. The Governors Highway Safety Association reported that 15% of the pedestrians killed in 2017 were hit by drunk drivers. Still, surprisingly more than a third of the pedestrians killed were legally drunk themselves.*

- *Age is also a factor. Pedestrians 65 and older account for 19% of all pedestrian fatalities. Children are also more likely to be victims.*

- *About 75% of the fatalities occur at night, making improved lighting more critical.*

Jaywalking, not crossing at designated crosswalks, is a problem for human drivers, and it is also a problem for AVs. According to the National Highway Transit Safety Association's 2010 study, 79% of pedestrian fatalities occurred at non-intersections versus at intersections. The term "Jaywalking" reportedly comes from the historical use of the word "Jay" as the generic term for someone who was an idiot. In the advent of cars, automobile-related companies popularly used this term in various anti-pedestrian campaigns. When pedestrians cross a street, they need to be alert and process much information. They need to identify vehicles, estimate distance and speed, and anticipate driver behavior. It's a lot to "compute," and this is jeopardized when the pedestrian is impaired by alcohol or drugs, or distracted by talking, texting, or listening to music on a smartphone. Crossing at an intersection with a pedestrian signal is much safer.

AV Precautions

When pedestrians are not using crosswalks, drivers need to determine if those on a sidewalk intend to cross the street or just stand on the sidewalk. Also, if a pedestrian is jaywalking, the car needs to yield to the pedestrian. Autonomous vehicles will be very good at stopping when a pedestrian is in the way, but it will be more challenging to determine a standing pedestrian's intentions. There are even more subtle variations of these situations. For example, it's well known in Boston that a pedestrian needs to avoid eye contact with the driver, or the driver won't stop. Conversely, the driver needs to pretend not to see the pedestrian so the pedestrian will defer to the pedestrian car.

In the early years, AVs will be extra cautious. They will probably stop if someone on a sidewalk steps into the road, whereas many drivers just blow their horns and give the pedestrian an angry gesture. While appropriate, and what human drivers should do, it will irritate other drivers, particularly those behind the AV. It will also encourage some, probably younger, less mature people, to play games with AVs, seeing whether they can get them to stop suddenly by pretending to jump in front of them.

All of this may lead to increased enforcement of pedestrian walkways to prevent jaywalking. Cities in some other countries have already done this by providing more crosswalks and using small fences on the side of roads to discourage jaywalking. Critics of AVs will use this as a reason not to permit them, but the fact is that it will also reduce the number of pedestrian fatalities by human drivers.

AV Communication with Human Drivers and Pedestrians

Eventually, all vehicles will be autonomous, but that will take a very long time. Until then, AVs and human drivers need to coexist on the same roads. Today, human drivers can communicate with other drivers and pedestrians in subtle ways. They can wave their hands for another driver to turn or go ahead. They can use eye contact and a slight nod to permit another driver to cut in ahead. Or they can nudge their car ahead a little to signal that the other driver shouldn't dare to cut in front. They can wave their hands to signal that it is OK for a pedestrian to cross the street. They can even use eye contact to acknowledge that they see the other vehicle or pedestrian. And they can use hand gestures to show their displeasure with someone else, but that's not relevant to AVs.

AVs will need some way of signaling human drivers too. Jaguar Land Rover is testing a vehicle with two large eyeballs in the front that can stare at and follow pedestrians to communicate that it sees them. I think that this is an unlikely solution, but it indicates an awareness of the issue. I expect that some sort of lights and sounds will be used to communicate with pedestrians and human drivers. For example, a beep to indicate that it sees a pedestrian and two beeps to signify it's OK to cross. Maybe a typical car horn sound will be used to alert pedestrians that it is proceeding, and they should let it pass. Visual signals will be used to communicate with drivers, but I don't know how they will simulate the wave of the hand or nod of the head.

The Volvo 360c concept vehicle illustrates some interesting solutions for communicating with humans. The fins at the back function as an information board, indicating a reservation number when the 360c is used for ARS. This will be necessary when multiple ARS vehicles arrive to pick up different passengers. There are also information readouts at the front of the car, fitted right next to the LED headlights, and integrated below them is a black bar with radar detectors, 3D cameras, and a laser sensor. That sensor bar is also mirrored on the back, and all around the car is a 360-degree strip of LED lights used to communicate the car's intent to pedestrians and human-driven cars.

Using a mix of sound and light, the Volvo 360c communicates (a) when it's on, and its autonomous mode is active, (b) when it intends to depart a stationary position and its direction, (c) when it senses a cyclist or pedestrian nearby, and (d) an alert targeted to anyone who might be in the car's path. The wing mirrors of the 360c are replaced by 3D cameras facing both the front and back, but they still extend out a little further, just to give more visibility and emphasis to the car's visual signals.

There are already pedestrian communications problems with electric vehicles. These are very quiet since they don't have any engine noise. People walking in the middle of a road may not realize there is an electric vehicle directly behind them. I experienced this problem frequently when driving my Tesla in a vacation location where people would always walk in the middle of the road. There is currently some debate about having electric vehicles use a recorded sound when traveling at a slow speed.

Eventually, I expect that sounds and lights for communicating with pedestrians will be standardized to avoid confusion.

How Do AVs Compare to Human Drivers?

Are AVs or human drivers better? There are several different aspects to determining this, and each is a little different.

Perception

Human drivers are limited to their perceptions of what is happening around them. They can see ahead or in their rearview mirrors. AVs can see all of this, plus much more. AVs can see in 360-degrees around the vehicle. They can accurately measure the speed and speed changes of the vehicles ahead, behind, and approaching from the side.

Human drivers may not see a car at a crossing failing to stop at a light until it is too late, but the AV will know before that. Human drivers may not realize when they stop quickly that the car behind won't stop and will rear-end them. Their complete attention is on the reason ahead of them that caused them to stop suddenly. The AV can see both what is ahead and the car behind, and it will compensate accordingly. Human drivers may not notice instantly that a car ahead is veering into their lane until it's too late, but the AV will see it instantly. Human drivers may not see a child or a dog in the dark running toward the road ahead. The AV will see and identify objects in the dark.

Interpretation

Humans tend to be very good at interpreting what they see. Some of this is instinctive. They can associate many factors in making a quick interpretation. Using the classic example, a playground is coming up in the right, and an object, maybe a ball, starts rolling toward the road. Most human drivers will instinctively make all the associations very rapidly that a child may be close behind, although there may not be one visible.

An AV may see the ball but not interpret it as more than a less important object. It doesn't have the same instincts. While a familiar example, it's not a good one because the programmers of every AV will have programmed the child chasing the ball case into the AV's logic.

AVs are getting better at interpretation. Through artificial intelligence and the experience gained by millions of miles of driving, as well as billions of miles of simulation, they may be better now than most humans at interpreting what they see, but not yet at instinctive recognition.

Reacting/Acting

Computers are better at computations. For example, if a car ahead slows from 60 MPH to 30 MPH, computing how to adjust the vehicle speed is a mathematical formula that computers can do much better than humans. But human drivers don't do that calculation in their heads. They don't compute the speed change of the slowing car and run the computations in their head. They use their instinct to slow their own car and then make braking adjustments instinctively. This works OK, but it is one of the reasons causing traffic jams because some car will over-adjust, causing all the cars behind it to compensate more. This is the accordion effect.

An AV can react faster than a human driver. If both recognize the need to stop, the AV can instruct the brakes to initiate stopping more quickly than humans can put their feet on the brake pedal and get it to react. This may only be 2-3 seconds faster, but that might be an essential difference.

Experience and Learning

One of the most significant differences between AV and human drivers is the ability to learn from experience. All AVs from the same developer/manufacturer use the same experience base. One hundred drivers have 100 different grounds of experience. If one learns a lesson from an accident or near accident, none of the others will learn anything about that experience. AVs, however, all learn together. If one learns a new experience, it is added to the common base of experience for the other 100,000 AVs made by the same company.

Besides this, before the first AV even goes on the road, it has already gone through millions of simulated driving experiences and tested the AV system on hundreds of thousands of hours of controlled driving. Imagine how much better a new 16-year-old driver would be with millions of miles of simulation and hundreds of thousands of controlled driving before getting a license.

When there is a notable incident such as the one involving the Uber AV pedestrian fatality, all AVs can be programmed to avoid that situation if it ever happened again. While a human driver involved in this type of accident may learn from it personally, the other hundreds of millions of drivers won't. This is a big difference between human drivers and AVs. Every AV will learn from this experience and be more cautious in the same conditions. This is because the software, which is the brains of the AV, will put this case in its memory to be called on in any similar circumstances. The sensors on AVs will be validated to detect and properly characterize similar objects.

This ability to distribute learning will make AVs exponentially safer over time. Within a few days after that accident, I expect that all companies developing AVs have verified this case situation and made sure they would have detected the pedestrian and taken corrective action. It is unlikely that a similar accident will occur with any AV in the future.

Distractions/Impairments

There are many ways human drivers get distracted: using smartphones, talking to children, eating food, listening to music, looking at the navigation system, etc. Most distractions don't matter because the driver doesn't need to do anything. But, sometimes, drivers get distracted at the wrong time, and they can't see what's happening, interpret it, or react in time.

AVs won't be distracted at all.

The Ethical Decisions

There has been much discussion on how AVs will react when there is a choice between a reaction that may increase the risk to the driver or increase the risk to someone else. These discussions tend to be intellectually interesting but irrelevant in the real world. It uses examples like this. A group of children is waiting for a bus on the sidewalk when the vehicle ahead stops suddenly. Does the AV veer toward the children to avoid slamming into the car ahead, risk a head-on collision by swerving into the oncoming lane, or simply smash into the car ahead? In other words, does the AV value the life of one driver above that of several children?

This ethical problem is a derivative of the famous "Trolley Problem." In this, you see a runaway trolley headed toward five workers on the track who don't see it coming, but you have a lever to switch the trolley to another track where there is only one worker. Do you do nothing and allow the trolley to kill five people, or do you switch the trolley to kill someone who wouldn't otherwise be killed. The debate weighs the argument of saving a net four people against the argument that distinguishes allowing from causing death. Most people tend to say they would pull the switch. But then the follow-up to this is that the one person to be killed is the person they love the most. Then, most people won't do it.

There is also a variation of this using a brilliant organ transplant surgeon with four patients in separate rooms requiring different organs who will die soon. Another healthy patient comes in for an exam in another room, and then he falls asleep. He has the compatible organs that the others need to live. Does the surgeon kill the sleeping patient to save the others?

Nobody knows how different drivers would react to the original situation posed. And AVs won't always be programmed to take a simple, specific course of action, such as avoid endangering the AV at the risk of others. They will very quickly compute the probabilities and potential outcomes of alternative actions and take the one deemed best. The actions will be more complex, such a blow the horn, put on the brakes, swerve a little to the other lane and see if the advancing car is stopping; if not then swerve back again, check, and see if the children have reacted to get out of the way, etc. And do this all in 2-3 seconds.

Chapter 6
Technologies Enabling
Autonomous Vehicles

S
ome exciting new technologies enable autonomous driving. Chapters 3, 4, and 5 introduced autonomous vehicles and provided insights into how they think and learn. In this chapter, I'll explain *how* AVs work and describe the technologies that make them possible. This includes describing the sensors used for autonomous driving, how the data from these sensors is processed, and how the vehicle responds.

A significant amount of money has been invested in the technologies that make AVs possible. I estimate that more than $100 billion has already been invested or committed to the development of AVs. This includes the R&D done by car manufacturers and the acquisitions they have made. As an example, based on a GM investor presentation, it planned to have 2,100 people working on AVs in 2018, which I estimate equates to a $400-$500 million annual investment. The overall investment in AVs includes the R&D investment that is not disclosed by major technology companies, specifically Apple and Google (Waymo). Based on a legal disclosure, Google invested more than $1 billion in AV development through 2015. The overall investment also includes the R&D investment by numerous companies developing the sensors, processors, and detailed maps, many of which are start-up companies with venture capital funding. Intel acquired Mobileye for $15 billion.

As you will see, some of the technologies already developed will become more affordable. Others are in the early stages of development, but they are proven feasible and just need to be completed and brought to market. There is not yet universal agreement about which technologies to use to solve specific problems in some cases. This is typical of most technological revolutions. The critical point is that all the technologies to make AVs are feasible.

An autonomous vehicle requires a variety of sensors to "see" and very quickly interpret its environment. The primary sensors use camera-based vision, lidar (Light Detection and Ranging), sonar, and radar technologies. The output from these sensors is processed and interpreted instantly by a high-powered microprocessor-based computer system onboard the AV, which is operated by sophisticated software using artificial intelligence. The computer system using detailed maps initiates the actions to "drive" the vehicle by braking, accelerating, and turning the vehicle.

Sensors

Sensors are essential to autonomous vehicles. They instantly enable AVs to sense and identify the characteristics of their surroundings. There are different configurations of sensors, depending on the sensor design approach of the AV manufacturer, but the diagram from Texas Instruments is a typical configuration.

This sensor diagram illustrates how the different types of sensors perform various functions. Long-range radar provides adaptive cruise control. Short-range radar provides cross-traffic alert and rear-collision warning. Cameras provide traffic signal recognition and surround view. Lidar provides mapping of the environment.

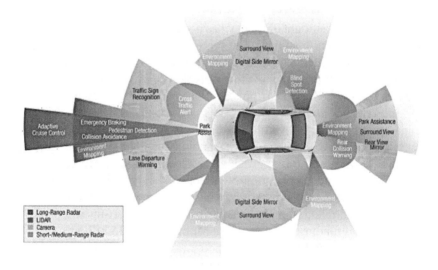

Also, you can see in the illustration that they overlap with each other. There are trade-offs among these sensor technologies. Cameras are effectively the autonomous replacement for a driver's eyes, letting the car 'see' what's happening in the world around. Still, they provide a full surround vision that drivers don't have. Radar can accurately measure an object's motion and speed. Lidar is the most powerful sensor. When it comes to cost, cameras are cheaper than radar or lidar, but the latest high-definition cameras require powerful processors to digitize and interpret the millions of pixels in every frame.

The safest approach is to use an array of sensors to build redundancy and offset the limitations of any one type of sensor. Each sensor solves a different part of the sensing challenge, and sensor-fusion software integrates all this varied input.

The cameras detect and track stationary and moving objects such as traffic lights and pedestrians. The articulating radar provides a broader field of view to detect turns, double-parked vehicles, and intersections. Lidar is used to provide detailed 3D mapping. The non-articulating radar detects vehicles and their velocities at a longer range. The ultra-short-range radar is a low-cost sensor for sensing objects close to the vehicle.

Let's look at the technology in each of these sensors.

Cameras

Video cameras are the primary sensors for autonomous vehicles. Cameras excel at classification and texture interpretation, and they are the cheapest and most available sensors. However, cameras use massive amounts of data (full HD video has millions of pixels in every frame), making processing video input computationally intense and algorithmically complex. Unlike both lidar and radar, cameras can see color, making them more useful for scene interpretation. Cameras are the cheapest sensor of the three, and they will likely remain important for the foreseeable future. However, the use cases will be dependent on the software algorithms and processing power for the massive amount of data generated.

There are also different cameras for various functions: narrow-focus cameras for longer distances, wider-focus cameras for shorter range, side-facing cameras, etc. Cameras can capture color or monochrome images. Color images can best interpret objects since color can be meaningful (traffic lights are the best example). Monochrome images require less processing power than color; so, there are some trade-offs.

Tesla has chosen to use cameras instead of lidar. This approach is much cheaper, and the cameras can be built into the car to make them almost invisible. As illustrated, Tesla uses eight surround cameras to provide 360-degrees of visibility around the car at up to 250 meters. Twelve ultrasonic sensors complement this vision system, allowing for the detection of both hard and soft objects at nearly twice the distance of the previous Tesla system. A forward-facing radar with enhanced processing provides additional data on a redundant wavelength that can see through heavy rain, fog, dust and even the car ahead because cameras struggle to see in these conditions.

Tesla uses monochrome cameras instead of color in its autopilot system to avoid overloading the car's processor, but color helps in object recognition.

Color images can be semantically segmented, such as identifying streetlamps, trees, and buildings. Color allows AVs to interpret better what they see. For example, color cameras can interpret a bright white truck in front of a bright blue sky. This limitation of monochrome cameras was the cause of a fatal full-speed accident in 2016 involving a Tesla, which I want to clarify was blamed on the driver and other circumstances, not the car's autopilot.

"Neither the autopilot nor the driver noticed the white side of the tractor-trailer against the brightly lit sky, so the brake was not applied," Tesla wrote on June 30, 2016. "The car was headed east on a sunny afternoon, and the driver was not paying attention. The car's forward-looking monochrome camera couldn't distinguish the color difference between the truck and the sky. The car's forward-looking radar was ignored because it could mistake over-head road signs for vehicles".

Cameras will be a primary sensor for all autonomous vehicles. The open questions are: (1) can they be used exclusively instead of lidar to reduce costs, (2) will monochrome versions work sufficiently to minimize processing requirements, or will color be necessary, and (3) how much processing power will be required to processes video images instantaneously?

Radar

Radar is an object-detection system that uses radio waves to determine the object's range, angle, and velocity. A radar system consists of a transmitter producing electromagnetic waves in the radio or microwave spectrum, a transmitting antenna, a receiving antenna (often the same antenna is used for transmitting and receiving), and a receiver and processor to determine the properties of objects. Radio waves (pulsed or continuous) from the transmitter

reflect off the object and then return to the receiver, giving information about the object's location and speed.

Their operating distance ranges can classify radar sensor range: (SRR) 0.2-30-meter range, medium-range radar (MRR) in the 30-80-meter range, and long-range radar (LRR) from 80-meters to more than 200-meters range. Long-range radar is the sensor used in adaptive cruise control and highway automatic braking systems, illustrated in this Audi cruise control image.

Radar is excellent for motion measurement. It requires less processing power than cameras and uses far less data than a lidar. While less angularly accurate than lidar, radar can work in every condition and even use reflection to see behind obstacles.

LRR radar sensors sometimes have limitations. They might not react correctly to certain conditions such as a car cutting in front of a vehicle, thin profile vehicles such as motorcycles being staggered in a lane, and determining distance based on the wrong vehicle due to the road's curvature. Radar also has lower resolution. To overcome the limitations in these situations, a radar sensor could be paired with a camera sensor to provide additional context to the detection. Many AVs use a combination of radar and lidar to "cross-validate" what they're seeing and to predict motion.

Even though radar may often pick up the same surrounding objects as other sensors, it doesn't need a line of sight because radio waves can be reflected, making it more efficient than cameras and lidar in poor weather conditions.

The FCC expanded the frequency allocations for vehicle radar. Initially limited to 76-77 GHz, the FCC extended the vehicle radar allocation to 76-81 GHz, taking over frequencies allocated to radiolocation and amateur radio operators.

Lidar

Lidar (an acronym for Light Detection and Ranging) is an active remote sensor that works on a similar principle to radar but uses light waves instead of radio waves. Lidar initially was invented in the 1960s, just after the development of the laser. The Apollo 15 mission in 1971 used lidar to map the surface of the moon, giving everyone the first glimpse of what it could do.

Lidar is the most powerful of the three sensors, and it's also by far the most expensive. Current lidar systems use 64 beams and sit on the roof of the vehicle, identifying all detail to the centimeter in all directions from 100 meters away. It can generate a comprehensive and precise high-definition 3D map of the immediate world around it. Unlike camera-generated images that require pattern recognition software to make the data useful to onboard computers, lidar systems create a stream of datapoint clouds that are immediately useful to computers. Lidar systems can render one million data points per second covering a 360-degree field of view with a range of 393 feet through low-visibility conditions. Both the level of detail and distance are critical to autonomous driving, especially at higher speeds. At 90 miles per hour, stopping distance is approximately 400 feet, so detecting an object that far out can be critical.

Lidar is a series of rotating, stacked lasers that shoot out at different angles. Two laser beams form what is called a channel. The signal from each channel creates one contour line and put together, those lines generate a 3-D image of the surrounding environment. The more lasers in each stack, the higher the resolution. Velodyne, for instance, manufactures lidar products with 16, 32 and 64 laser channels.

Fundamentally, a lidar sensor illuminates a target area with invisible light and measures the time it takes for this light to bounce back to its source. As light moves at a constant speed, it calculates the distance between the sensor and objects with high accuracy.

Today, most, but not all, experts agree that lidar is one of the critical sensing technologies required to enable fully and sufficiently autonomous driving. There is also general agreement that lidar technology is currently too expensive and not aesthetically acceptable as a big ugly system sitting on top of the vehicle's roof.

Solid-state versions of lidar are being developed. They are hardly visible in cars and are cheaper. Conversely, solid-state lidars, which are sold in higher volumes, are limited in scope to less than 90-degree optical scans and must be embedded in the front and back bumpers of cars to achieve a comprehensive view of the surroundings. In this way, there are four devices integrated into the car, with two on each bumper. Solid-state devices also require extra software to manage the four separate data streams from the four devices.

The cost and attractiveness of lidar may not matter as much initially because they are expected to be deployed in limited fleets of autonomous ride service vehicles, which can afford the investment. And as a rider, when you hail a car as part of an autonomous ride service, you don't care that much if there is a large lidar device on top of the car.

Waymo is focused on lidar as its primary distinguishing technology. CEO John Krafcik stated that Waymo built the entire sensor suite used by its self-driving Chrysler Pacifica Hybrid test vehicles. This was a significant accomplishment for the company, making Waymo no longer vulnerable to third-party suppliers. According to a Bloomberg article, the company worked on scalability, leading to a 90% decrease in the cost of the lidar sensor. Krafcik also told Bloomberg the new sensor package on the Waymo Chrysler

Pacifica is "highly effective in rain, fog, and snow," which have typically been trouble for lidar systems because of the reflective nature of water in the air.

Waymo later accused Uber of stealing its work, claiming a former Google employee downloaded 14,000 technical files from a company server, then used the information to launch the autonomous truck startup, Otto. Uber acquired Otto a few months later and appointed him to lead its AV program. This lawsuit was settled in Waymo's favor.

Lidar also has another important use. It can create detailed high-definition digital maps for autonomous driving (this will be discussed later). On mapping vehicles, the lidar units are usually mounted high, to get the necessary height for modeling, and tilted down. As the vehicle drives along the road, the lidar units capture a 3-D model of the road and its surroundings. It effectively builds the model by taking slices of the outside environment as the vehicle travels.

Ultrasonic Sensors

Ultrasonic proximity detectors measure the distance to nearby objects using sensors located in the front and/or rear bumper or visually minimized within grills or recesses. The sensors emit acoustic pulses, with a control unit measuring the return interval of each reflected signal to calculate object distances. In a semi-autonomous vehicle, the system can warn the driver with acoustic tones or visual warnings, such as LED or LCD readouts to indicate object distance. In an autonomous vehicle, ultrasonic sensors serve multiple purposes. A Tesla, for example, has 12 ultrasonic sensors providing the system with 360-degree vision at a range of about 5 meters. They are used by the auto parking system to identify parking spots and by the autopilot for changing lanes into traffic.

The theory behind the ultrasound sensor is based on echolocation (like SONAR, the same thing bats use to navigate). The sound frequency is so high that humans cannot detect it, so it is inconspicuous. As sound hits a solid object, it is reflected, creating an echo. Since the speed of sound is known and constant for similar conditions (such as wind or humidity), it is possible to determine the distance of the object from an echo by multiplying the speed of sound by half the time it takes to hear the echo.

As an ultrasonic system relies on the reflection of sound waves, the system may not detect flat objects or object insufficiently large to reflect sound, for example, a thin pole or a longitudinal object pointed directly at the vehicle or near an object. Objects with flat surfaces angled from the vertical may deflect return sound waves away from the sensors, hindering detection.

Electronic Control Systems

In autonomous vehicles, electronic control systems are embedded systems that control one or more of the electrical systems or subsystems, such as the throttle, brakes, steering, and braking. This is a needed shift from systems that required a human to change gears, step on the brakes or gas, etc.

Electronic Throttle Control

The electronic throttle control (ETC) system electronically connects the accelerator pedal to the throttle, replacing mechanical linkage. The system uses software to determine the required throttle position by calculations from data measured by other sensors, including the accelerator pedal position sensors, engine speed sensors, vehicle speed sensors, and cruise control switches. In AVs, the electronic control system eliminates the accelerator pedal position and uses the control signals from the primary computer system instead.

Although ETC is an enabling technology for AVs, it has been introduced in many cars already. It makes vehicle powertrain characteristics seamlessly consistent irrespective of prevailing conditions, such as engine temperature, altitude, and accessory loads. It also improves the ease with which the driver can execute gear changes and deals with the torque changes associated with rapid accelerations and decelerations. ETC facilitates the integration of features such as cruise control, traction control, stability control, and other functions that require torque management since the throttle can be moved irrespective of the position of the driver's accelerator pedal. ETC also provides some benefits in areas such as air-fuel ratio control, exhaust emissions, and fuel consumption reduction, and it also works in concert with other technologies such as gasoline direct injection.

Brake-by-Wire

Drive-by-wire technology replaces the conventional mechanical and hydraulic control systems with electronic control systems using electromechanical actuators and human-machine interfaces. Brake-by-wire is frequently used to describe the technology that controls brakes through an electrical system instead of a mechanical one. It can supplement conventional brakes or be a standalone brake system, as it will be in AVs. The technology replaces traditional pumps, hoses, fluids, belts, vacuum servos, and master cylinders with electronic sensors and actuators.

Brake-by-wire technology has been widely commercialized with the introduction of electric and hybrid vehicles.

Steer-by-Wire

Originally steering used a rack and pinion system to direct a car in the desired direction. Next came hydraulically-assisted steering, which became popular starting in the 1950s. Then hydraulics was replaced with electric motors. The motors are usually placed either at the base of the steering column or directly on the steering rack.

Steer-by-wire is frequently used to describe an electronic system used to steer a vehicle automatically. It replaces the traditional steering control of a car that uses components and linkages between the steering wheel and the front wheels. The control of the wheels' direction is established through electric motors, which are actuated by electronic control units monitoring the steering wheel inputs from the driver, or in the case of AVs, from a central computer system.

Unlike the two previous systems, automatic steering control is relatively new and not yet approved as an independent control system for many uses. Even in a Tesla, the steering wheel is still mechanically connected to the front wheel. However, if the promise of autopilot is real, then the steering system must operate automatically without any driver control. It will be one of the new requirements for AVs.

Shift-by-Wire

Shift-by-wire is a term typically used to describe the system by which the transmission modes are engaged and changed in a vehicle through electronic controls without any mechanical linkage between the gear shifting lever and the transmission. Transmission shifting was traditionally accomplished by mechanical links to put the vehicle in Park, Reverse, Neutral, and Drive positions through a lever mounted on the steering column or a gear shifter near the center console. A shift-by-wire transmission system enables a driver to select the next desired gear, and the system completes the shift automatically.

In more vehicles, mechanical linkages are disappearing in favor of shift-by-wire. Yet, in some semi-autonomous vehicles, such as Mercedes, the driver still needs to change gears for automatic parking. Shift-by-wire will be necessary for all AVs to shift gears.

Computer Processing

AVs will require enormous computing power, which is one of the reasons they haven't been feasible until now. Approximately a gigabyte (equal to roughly a billion bytes) of data must be processed each second by an AV's real-time operating system. This data will need to be analyzed instantly so the vehicle can react in less than a second. For example, it will need to figure out when, how hard, and how fast to brake based on analysis of a range of variables, from the vehicle's speed to the road conditions to surrounding traffic. It will need to successfully gauge the flow of traffic to merge onto a freeway and account for the unpredictable behavior of pedestrians, bicyclists, and other cars.

AVs require a new computer architecture. The primary processing functions will be more centralized. Today, a typical car can have between 25 and 50 processors, controlling blind-spot and pedestrian-collision warnings, automated braking and maintaining a safe distance via smart cruise control, and many others. Most of these functions have their computer software. This has spawned a distributed-computing approach that accommodates a growing ecosystem of embedded control units. But with each new addition, complexity, and cost increase, as do the challenges of integrating so many disparate systems. There are many benefits to a more centralized processing model for AVs.

The companies developing AVs disagree on the computing capacity needed to achieve autonomous driving, and this disagreement results in as many different computing solutions as there are autonomous vehicle programs. Tesla reached level 2 with 0.256 trillion of operations per second (TOPS) in Autopilot 1.0, but Level 3 to 5 are expected to need significantly greater capacity – anything from 2 to 20 TOPS. Nvidia's new processing platform provides 310 TOPS, which it believes is the requirement for autonomous driving. In my opinion, the highest level of computing power will be required.

However, while the processors in AVs must deliver increasing computing power, they also must do so as efficiently as possible, which means managing the amount of power and cooling needed.

Several computing companies are developing specialized processors for AVs. They combine experience in powerful processing, graphics processing, and complete systems. One of these, Nvidia, has created early momentum and provides a glimpse into the processing requirements with its Drive PX platform, particularly its Pegasus system. The Drive PX Pegasus computer platform was designed to control AVs. The platform must not only have sufficient computing power to process the data of an entire array of sensors in real time and derive driving decisions from it, but it also must meet the highest requirements for functional safety. To be resilient and fail-safe, it is equipped with multiple different processors that serve as a back-up for each other.

To achieve this computing power, the PX Pegasus is equipped with four processors – two SoCs (literally systems on a chip) and two next-generation GPUs, each designed specifically for deep learning and autonomous driving. The Pegasus has a computing power of 320 TOPS (this means trillions of operations per second), ten times as much as Nvidia's previous AI platform Drive PX 2. The platform is designed for updates via the over-the-air interface (OTA) to keep the software running on the computer up to date.

The high demands on reliability and redundancy mean that these computers require very high computing power. Compared to semi-autonomous vehicles, sufficiently-autonomous and fully-autonomous vehicles need overlapping surveillance. The vehicle itself must continuously know its position to the centimeter and immediately recognize other vehicles and people in the vicinity. Because of these requirements, sufficiently and fully-autonomous vehicles require 50 to 100 times more computing power than semi-autonomous vehicles.

Software

Software provides the intelligence for autonomous vehicles. AV software is extensive and complex, and it requires a tremendous investment. Most of the companies developing AVs create their own software because this will be the defining technology of their AV platforms. There are also some smaller companies specializing in developing AV software. Autonomous driving demands some of the most complex, real-time computing capabilities ever developed. The good thing about software is that while it has a high development cost, the cost to have it installed in each vehicle is negligible.

AV Software Architecture

The architecture, or overall structure of AV software, defines the different functions and how they work together. This architecture is critical for the development and maintenance of this sophisticated software. Major companies developing AV software keep their architecture proprietary since it provides a competitive advantage. So, to illustrate what AV software architecture looks like, I'll use an example from one of the successful entrants in the DARPA Urban Challenge (Figure 6-1). This is the software architecture used by Team Victor Tango's Odin from Virginia Polytechnic Institute and others. It was developed using the LabVIEW software platform from National Instruments.

At the left side of this architecture in Figure 6-1 is the data coming from the laser (lidar) and camera sensors, as well as GPS data. The first set of software modules address *Perception*. The *Localization* module takes input data from the sensors and GPS and uses perception software algorithms to position the vehicle where it is on the road. Vehicle localization requires accuracy and 6-degrees of freedom. This is the freedom of movement of a rigid body in three-dimensional space. Specifically, the body is free to change position as forward/backward, up/down, left/right translation in three perpendicular axes.

Road Detection localizes the road and identifies markings on the road. The *Object Classification* module uses sensor data to detect and interpret the characteristics of other objects, such as vehicles and pedestrians. There are two types of objects: static (fixed and unmovable) and dynamic (capable of and expected to move). The *Predict* module handles dynamic objects and predicts where the object will be in a second, few seconds, etc. The output of the Perception set of modules provides the vehicle position, roads, and objects to the *Planning* set of modules.

Figure 6-1
AV Software Architecture Example

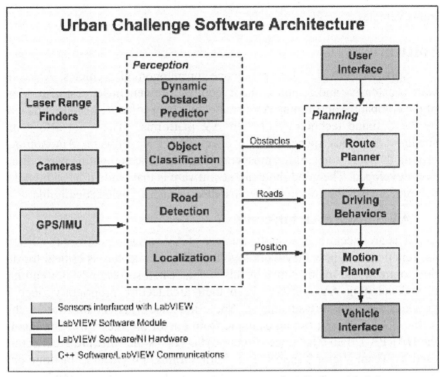

Source: National Instruments and Team Victor Tango's Odin from Virginia
Polytechnic Institute

The *Planning* modules plan the movement of the AV. The *Route Planner* module takes the vehicle location data (where it is) and adds the data on where it wants to go, and then it plans the route it needs to take to get there. For example, proceed 50 meters in the right lane and then make a right turn into the correct lane. The *Driving Behaviors* module adjusts the timing and possibly the planned movement based on how other objects might move. For example, there is a car ahead, and the AV needs to wait for that car to proceed. From that data, the *Motion Planner* module determines the specific operations the car needs to follow.

Finally, the *Vehicle Interface* software ties into the steering, throttle, brake, etc. It sends the appropriate instructions to these systems to initiate and continue the specific maneuvers.

Sensor Fusion

In simple terms, sensor fusion is the stitching together of data from various sensors, typically video, radar, lidar, and ultrasonic. Sensor fusion software captures raw images and allows an AV to build a 360-degree model of its surroundings.

Sensor fusion does much more than just reading sensor data. Each sensor type has shortcomings that cannot be overcome using the same sensor. For example, a camera working in the visible spectrum has trouble in dense fog, rain, sun glare, and the absence of light. Radar lacks the high- resolution of lidar sensors, but it is excellent for measuring distances through rain and fog. Cameras don't work well in these conditions or the absence of light, but they can see color and have a high resolution.

Sensor fusion takes the inputs of different sensors and sensor types and uses the combined information to perceive the environment more accurately. That results in a better and safer decision than independent systems could make.

An example of sensor fusion is combining the functions of a front camera with the front radar. The front radar can measure the speed and distance of objects up to 150 meters in all weather conditions, while the camera is excellent in detecting and differentiating objects, which includes reading street signs and street markings. Using multiple camera sensors with a different field of view and different optics, such things as pedestrians and bikes passing in front the car, as well as objects 150 meters and more ahead, can be identified.

Using different sensor types also offers a certain level of redundancy to environmental conditions that could make all sensors of one kind fail. Such a sensor-fused system could maintain some basic or emergency functionality, even if it lost a sensor.

Although the core concept underlying sensor fusion software algorithms seems simple, its implementation calls for various development tools and a broad spectrum of skill sets. The design requires software development platforms that enable the creation of sophisticated and customized algorithms to accommodate the unique requirements of these applications. Sensor fusion software must be capable of a high level of abstraction to support flexible integration, different kinds of sensors, and various algorithms. Developers must be careful to avoid data overload and latency – most sensor fusion processing must be done in real-time. And the algorithms themselves must be able to accurately react to every possible outcome of human behavior (including irrational behavior).

There are many different types of sensor technologies. Still, the critical issue is the fusion of these technologies into an integrated platform that enables the vehicle to assess the world around it and drive accordingly accurately.

Simultaneous Localization and Mapping

SLAM technology stands for simultaneous localization and mapping, a process where an AV can create a map of its surroundings and orient itself correctly within this map in real-time. This is no easy task, and it currently exists at the frontiers of technology research and design. A significant roadblock to successfully implementing SLAM technology is the chicken-and-egg problem introduced by the two required tasks. To successfully map an environment, the vehicle must know its orientation and position within that environment, and usually, this information comes from a pre-existing map of the environment.

SLAM technology typically overcomes this complex chicken-and-egg issue by building a pre-existing map of an environment using GPS data. This map is then iteratively refined as the AV moves through the environment. The real challenge of this technology is one of accuracy. Measurements must continuously be taken as the AV moves through space, and the technology must consider the "noise" that is introduced by both the movement of the AV and the inaccuracy of the measurement method. This makes SLAM technology primarily a matter of measurement and mathematics.

Machine Learning

It's easy to envision AV software as large programs consisting of millions of elaborate rules specifying how the car should act for every conceivable situation. The typical example is an If/Then case: "If a ball rolls across the road, then reduce the speed and watch for children that might come running after the ball." This example implies that there is a theory of driving implemented in the software, which there is not. It examines the images and guesses the object in each image.

Initially, most of its guesses will be wrong, but the algorithm modifies internal parameters or parts of its structure somewhat and tries again. This process continues, discarding changes that reduce the algorithm's accuracy, keeping modifications that increase the accuracy until it correctly classifies all images.

Then, when given a new object to interpret, the software algorithm it developed will classify it with high accuracy. For example, it will recognize someone on a bicycle as that object and then associate the characteristics it learned about how a bicycle might move.

Machine learning can also be used for actions and evaluations. Instead of supplying the vehicle with a fixed evaluation scheme from which the right move for each situation can be deduced, the programmers feed the machine learning software with many traffic situations and specify the correct action for each situation. The program then searches by itself for the best configuration of internal parameters and internal decision logic, which allow it to act correctly in these cases. Like human drivers, it is difficult to explain why the AV exhibits a specific behavior in a new situation. Explicit rules are not specified. The behavior decision results from the many traffic situations to which the algorithm had been exposed beforehand. That's why AV software developers are "training" the machine learning systems with millions, probably billions, of cases through simulation.

Another characteristic of AV software is its use of probabilistic outcomes. It maintains a distribution of outcomes with specific probabilities and decides with the highest likelihood.

Machine learning algorithms are classified into supervised algorithms and unsupervised algorithms. The difference between the two is how they learn. Supervised algorithms learn using a training dataset and keep on learning until the algorithms reach the desired level of confidence. Unsupervised algorithms try to make sense of the available data. That means an algorithm develops a relationship within the available dataset to identify patterns or divides the data set into subgroups based on the similarity between them.

HD Mapping (Localization)

Early developers hoped that autonomous vehicles might position themselves sufficiently using the standard definition maps like the ones most people use today, along with GPS-based turning. Sensors would do the rest. That hasn't worked adequately, and now most experts realize that more precision and accuracy are required.

To solve this problem, highly-detailed, three-dimensional, computerized maps, which pinpoint a car's location and understand its surroundings, appear necessary. Fundamentally, the problem is that the vehicle needs to locate itself on the correct road and in the proper lane for a turn, and even how close it is to the curb or side of the roadway. These highly detailed maps, called HD (high definition) maps, provide localization. They identify precisely (how many feet or inches) where the vehicle is and where it needs to be. I say "appears to be necessary" because some experts still believe that GPS accuracy can be improved sufficiently, and these detailed HD maps won't be necessary.

High-definition (HD) maps enable an AV to do two critical things. To localize itself (know where it is exactly) and more rapidly perceive its surroundings to identify anything transitory, such as pedestrians. They are considered high-definition because they have much richer and more precise data than what's on Google Maps or Apple Maps. In terms of detail, HD maps contain information like the height of a speed limit sign, the timing of a traffic light cycle, or the location of on-street parking spots. As to their precision, a meter or less detail is expected.

This illustration from Here Technologies illustrates the detailed measurements from HD mapping. Here, which was started by Nokia and then acquired by the German automakers BMW, Daimler' and Audi is also mapping roads in the United States and Europe. It is drawing on data from scanning systems that trucking companies have agreed to install on their vehicles. Here also has its fleet of cars collecting images, and it is working on algorithms to enable computers to annotate the maps.

Creating HD maps is a massive task. There are more than four million miles of roads in the United States and compared with the maps used by GPS and navigation systems, the level of precision must be much higher. Waymo is creating maps for roads around its headquarters in Mountain View, Calif., and other cities where it expects to launch its autonomous ride services. Waymo creates the maps using cars equipped with lidar units mounted on their roofs, creating images of the road and the surroundings. Engineers review the images and tag the objects that are found, like stop signs, buildings, stoplights, etc. The laser equipment needed to do this scanning is expensive. It can cost $100,000 or more to outfit just one vehicle to do this job.

HD mapping is done city-by-city or metropolitan area, so AVs, particularly ARS vehicles, can function in these locations once they are mapped.

China is using HD mapping to create roadblocks for U.S. automakers and tech companies to bring AVs to the world's largest auto market. Citing national security concerns, China is limiting the amount of mapping that can be done by foreign companies. Global carmakers already need to form a partnership with a local company to open factories in China, but some are skeptical they will find a way to operate their AV software in China because of the mapping restrictions.

Vehicle-to-X Communication

Vehicle-to-X communication is a term used to describe the connected vehicle, where X can be another vehicle or infrastructure such as traffic lights and street signs. Connected vehicle technology leverages advancements in wireless technologies to communicate with vehicles, infrastructure, and other portable devices. The connected car or vehicle-to-X communications is not necessary for AVs to be successful initially, although some simple communications on things like traffic light status would be helpful. Vehicle-to-X communications will enable the next stage of AV performance by coordinating the activities of all vehicles in a particular location.

Vehicle-to-Vehicle

Vehicle-to-vehicle (V2V) communications use a wireless network where vehicles send messages to each other with information about what they're doing or things that are important about traffic conditions. Instead of working independently, vehicles will be able to transmit vital information to other nearby vehicles to improve the overall efficiency and safety of the roadways. V2V systems can use dedicated short-range communications (DSRC), which are two-way wireless channels that enable V2V-equipped cars to communicate with each other roughly ten-times per second over short distances. On a busy highway, vehicles might send automated messages to each other communicating things like "Road is slippery," or "Ambulance coming!" or "Traveling 63 mph, road clear." It will give AVs situational awareness.

It can also be like the popular crowd-sourced application Waze, which warns drivers of accidents ahead, potholes, vehicles on the roadside, etc. It is unlikely that it will alert drivers of police ahead as Waze does. Some of the warnings communicated by other cars include forward-collision warning where the cars ahead have an impending collision, emergency braking by the car ahead, lane change warning that a nearby car is changing lanes, intersection movement alert that coordinates turns by all cars in an intersection, and a loss of control warning.

The U.S. Department of Transportation says car-to-car communication can help, as it has the potential "to significantly reduce many of the deadliest types of crashes through real-time advisories alerting drivers to imminent hazards." It could ease traffic congestion. Imagine if all the individual data points from thousands of cars went to a central hub. With so much real-time traffic data, transportation managers could adjust traffic light timing and redirect traffic to make rush hour flow more smoothly. Not only that, but each car could use the data to make individual adjustments.

It also presents privacy concerns. V2V data can reveal all kinds of things about you: where you're going and when, as well as your driving habits. Who has access to this data? And how might they use it? Liability could get complicated. V2V communications could be more vulnerable to hacking. The proliferation of V2V communication, whether in human-piloted or driverless cars, gives malicious hackers a new opportunity.

Vehicle-to-Infrastructure

Communications of AVs with traffic signals or other stationary devices is called V2I, or vehicle to infrastructure. The application for this and the expected benefits are still unclear. There are different focuses: is the information being transferred from the infrastructure to the vehicle, or is the vehicle communicating information to the infrastructure? There are also a few simple applications and much more complex applications.

I think the initial applications will be simple ones that communicate essential information to AVs. The most basic application is a traffic signal conveying its status to approaching vehicles: "Currently green for the next 60 seconds." This capability may lead to Signal Phase and Timing (SPaT). SPaT applications of V2I communications focus on the ability to coordinate driving speeds with traffic light patterns to maximize fuel economy and speed. SPaT patterns can provide the optimal traffic flow in high traffic areas.

Helpful information transmitted from the infrastructure to a vehicle includes traffic signal information, stop sign and stop location information, lane closures, recommended speed, hazards/construction sites, intersection maps, and updates. These seem affordable and reasonable, and I expect metropolitan areas will implement these to be compatible with AVs, especially autonomous ride services.

Another simple and needed V2I application will be the ability for an AV to transmit a signal to open a gate in gated communities. Autonomous ride services AVs won't have a driver to operate a call box and will need to open gates to pick up passengers. I see this as the earliest application of V2I.

The full extent of more complex V2I technologies' benefits and costs is unclear.

Intelligent Stickers on Street Signs

One of the easiest and low-cost alternatives to having signs communicate with AVs is being explored by 3M, the maker of Post-It-Notes and Scotch Tape. They are testing stickers that appear transparent to the naked eye but contain something like "barcodes" that autonomous vehicles can read.

In addition to defining the sign itself, these codes could contain GPS coordinates, traffic light warnings, distance to the curb, corner distances, etc. They are also testing this for work-zone signs and road-worker vests.

5G Communications

Simply put, 5G is the next "G" or "Generation" of wireless networks. Up until now, 3G and 4G have allowed users to connect to the internet via their phones, with each new generation up to 10 times faster than its predecessor. But the next step, 5G, will benefit communication between people and between machines, promising significant benefits for the energy, healthcare, and automotive industries.

It will let more data move at higher speeds with lower latency and ultra-reliability, and it will be essential in supporting the billions of connected devices. The big difference with 5G is that autonomy requires split-second connectivity, which 5-G can provide.

There are differing opinions on the importance of 5G for autonomous vehicles. Is 5G a requirement before AVs can be useful? Probably not. Dedicated short-range communications (DSRC), just discussed, can accommodate all necessary vehicle-to-vehicle and vehicle-to-infrastructure communications in modules that are already commercially available. To its credit, DSRC already boasts many desirable features for assisted and autonomous driving: it operates in fog or a snowstorm, can function at high speeds, and has a time delay of mere milliseconds. The wireless technology enables vehicles to send and receive short digital packets of information about their whereabouts, intentions, and speed within a short to medium range.

And as I previously mentioned, AVs can operate successfully without the connected car. So, I don't expect AVs to rely on 5G communications.

Where 5G becomes very important is in mobile entertainment. AVs will free everyone to be a passenger, and there will be an immediate demand for streaming video and related services that will require 5G communications. As mobile network operators begin to introduce 5G technology into their networks, they will focus on urban areas. 5G technology is expected to improve mobile wireless network capacity significantly and increase data speeds, allowing network providers to offer much more robust internet connections to devices.

Lidar vs. Video Cameras

Perhaps the primary technical debate for autonomous vehicles concerns the use of lidar. Lidar is an expensive technology that is fundamental to the operation of most autonomous vehicles. Lidar is used to position an AV precisely within a digital map of its surroundings. It is used in conjunction with other sensors such as video and radar.

But because lidar is currently very expensive, many AV developers built their autonomous systems without lidar, relying primarily on video instead. Tesla is the most notable of these. When it unveiled its autonomous driving system back in 2016, it didn't use the depth-sensing lidar system used by practically every other AV developer. Tesla claims that the eight included cameras were enough to support Level 5 autonomous rides – no bulky lidar shooting lasers required. Tesla Chief Executive Elon Musk called lidar "a fool's errand," berating the technology for being expensive and unnecessary.

Tesla uses eight cameras, augmented with radar and ultrasonic sensors, which detect objects a user may otherwise miss due to poor visibility or blocked view. Tesla has an A.I. chip capable of processing 2,000 frames per second to power it.

Nissan Motor Co Ltd said it is developing, at least for now, self-driving technology that uses radar sensors and cameras, avoiding lidar or light-based sensors because of its high cost. Nissan believes that lidar lacks the capabilities to exceed the latest technology capabilities in radar and cameras, stating that there is an imbalance between its cost and its capabilities.

Lidar is currently used by companies including General Motors Co, Ford Motor Co and Waymo. Lidar technology uses light-based sensors that fire roughly 1 million laser pulses a second as it collects measurements that are analyzed and processed into 3D models and maps. More than $1 billion in corporate and private investment has been pumped into some 50 lidar startups, based on a Reuters analysis of publicly available investment data.

Still, it is a technology in flux. Initially using bulky spinning devices placed on the roof of cars, lidar developers have transitioned to more compact solid-state devices that can be mounted on other parts of a car. These now sell for less than $10,000 in limited quantities. They and are widely expected to eventually sell for as little as $200 in mass production.

Lidar isn't necessary for semi-autonomous driving. Cameras and radar are sufficient to keep a vehicle centered in a lane, control acceleration a safe distance behind the car ahead, and initiate emergency braking. I do believe that lidar is necessary for sufficiently autonomous driving, particularly to enable an AV to turn corners. The implication of this is that Tesla vehicles may be excellent semi-autonomous vehicles but not sufficiently autonomous.

The cost of lidar is important for selling autonomous vehicles for individual ownership, and current lidar costs are prohibitively expensive. This is one reason why individually owned autonomous vehicles will not be popular for a while, probably not until the later-2020s. On the other hand, vehicle cost is not a factor for ARS AVs. The economics work well with a $100,000 AV. So, with most of the early AVs being used for ARS, lidar will be the standard.

Electric vs. Hybrid Vehicles

Electric vehicles (EVs), or battery-operated vehicles, are not the primary focus of this book, but this is an essential set of technologies for autonomous vehicles. There is a technology question on whether AVs will primarily be electric battery-operated or not.

Autonomous vehicles are technology-based platforms, and electrically powered cars are much more compatible than internal combustion engines (ICE) to being operated by software. Electric motors are more responsive to control and easier to integrate into an autonomous platform. In most cases, autonomous vehicles will be entirely new platforms built for the future. Since most experts expect electric to be the future drive system for cars, it makes sense to use electrically powered engines as the basis for the platform. Although some of the early AVs will modify existing vehicles.

Tesla set the stage for combining autonomous capabilities and electric vehicles. The technology companies expected to create autonomous vehicles are environmentally friendly, and they don't want to build an ICE. Autonomous EVs also will encourage governments to enable favorable regulations for autonomous vehicles.

However, there are several reasons why electric vehicle propulsion may not become the standard for early AVs. The first is the significant power consumption of the computers and sensors in an AV. This power consumption could quickly drain the batteries in electric AVs, limiting their driving range even further. An AV engineer in GM disclosed that the first-generation Cruise AVs consumed 3-4 kilowatts, which could significantly drain the 60kWh capacity of a Bolt. AV engineers are still wrestling with this issue, and power consumption is expected to improve. Power consumption is a definite concern for all the AV systems, starting with powering the computers in AVs.

The availability of charging stations may also be a limiting factor in the rapid growth of electric AVs. It will take some time for enough charging stations to replace gas stations before long-distance driving can be comfortable. There may also be concerns about raw material constraints to making enough EVs in high volumes.

As I stated previously, autonomous ride services (ARS) will be the first AV market, and it will grow rapidly. Ford is taking an interesting strategy for this market. It is developing an entirely new AV from the ground up, instead of retrofitting an existing model, and it is targeting this AV for initial use by its own service as well as for other ARS companies. This new AV targeted for release in 2022 will be a hybrid. Ford's reason for this is quite compelling: it wants to make this vehicle more profitable for ARS providers. A hybrid can drive much longer without refueling than an EV, and this can be very important to ARS providers where utilization is critical. Having a significant portion of its fleet down for an hour of recharging during peak periods could become a big problem.

Most likely, electric AVs will become the standard. Battery technology, AV systems' power consumption, raw material constraints, and charging station limitations may be short-term issues. In first-generation AVs, however, hybrid AVs may play a significant role.

Part II
Opportunities, Markets, and Strategies

Chapter 7
Autonomous Ride Services

In the 2018 first edition, I introduced autonomous ride services (ARS). I explained how it would be the first use of AVs, coming more than several years before individually-owned autonomous vehicles. Since then, almost all major autonomous vehicle companies have confirmed this by shifting their strategies to provide ARS first.

There are many different terms used to describe autonomous ride services: mobility, mobility as a service, transportation as a service, personal mobility, robo-taxies (I'm not too fond of that term because it envisions a robot at the steering wheel.), on-demand rides, the passenger economy, etc. I'll use the term *ridesharing* to refer to the current services provided by companies such as Uber and Lyft, where drivers use their own vehicles. I'll use the term *autonomous ride services* (*ARS*) to refer to the driverless version of this service.

In many ways, ridesharing is the precursor to autonomous ride services. Ridesharing is a service that arranges a ride on short notice, or scheduled, using a smartphone app. Three technological advances enabled ridesharing: GPS navigation, smartphones, and social networks. Smartphone apps allow passengers to schedule a ride and get paired with a driver. The app uses GPS to identify the passenger's location, and the passenger enters the desired destination. The app estimates the cost of the ride in advance for the passenger. Ridesharing drivers use their own vehicles to provide rides and get approximately 70% of the money from the ride. The passenger is billed on a credit card for the trip and can also charge a tip to the driver.

Ridesharing was a large and growing market until the COVID-19 pandemic. The two dominant players in ridesharing in the United States are Uber and Lyft. Uber's gross bookings in 2019 (prior to revenue shared with drivers) were $55 billion, providing 6.9 billion rides globally (not including approximately $10 billion for Uber Eats) and growing at more than 30% annually. Uber's estimated market share was 70%, so the U.S. ridesharing market for 2019 was approximately $65-$70 billion and was expected to grow to more than $90 billion by 2020 prior to COVID-19. However, due to the pandemic, the ridesharing market dropped precipitously.

By March 2020, COVID-19 hit the ridesharing market hard. Uber and Lyft reported 75%-80% declines in the number of trips. Almost nobody was traveling, and many people were working from home. While most people will return to work and travel will resume, neither is expected to return to previous levels for several years. In addition, many people are now concerned with the viral safety of riding with a driver they don't know in a car that may not be sufficiently sanitized.

Ridesharing started to recover in mid-2021, but then there was a driver shortage as drivers gave up on this as a way of making money. This shortage reduced the reliability of getting rides and significantly increased ridesharing prices. Both changes may help to make ARS a more attractive alternative. The new concerns over viral safety may provide another advantage to ARS. Some riders may prefer to use an autonomous vehicle with no exposure to a human driver. They may also trust the vehicle sterilization practices of large well-known companies more than the practices of unknown drivers.

ARS will create an incredible new market opportunity and change the very nature of transportation. As an example of projections for this new market, GM's executives believe that Cruise, its majority-owned ARS business, will be part of what could be an $8 trillion global market in the future.

In this chapter, we will look closely at the expected structure of the ARS industry, including the significant elements of the broader ARS platform. ARS is currently in the development and launch stages, so we will also consider the phases for launching these services.

Ridesharing is global, but the companies providing the service are different in each country. For example, Didi Chuxing is the dominant ridesharing provider in China. Differences by country will be valid for ARS as well. The focus of this chapter will be on the U.S. ARS market.

Because ARS presents an entirely new business model, we will look at what I believe will be the ARS model. ARS will replace ridesharing, so we will consider why this is inevitable. Finally, we will assess the ARS market, the expected significant competitors, and their strategies. But first, let's start by reviewing why ARS will be the first application for AVs.

Why ARS Will be First

In the first edition, I argued that ARS would be the initial market for autonomous vehicles. Here is a summary of the reasons why ARS will be the first market for AVs:

1. ARS will significantly lower the cost of transportation. People, particularly those who live in metropolitan areas, are increasingly seeing the advantages of using ridesharing instead of owning their cars. The primary benefit is the lower cost of ridesharing than owning a car, especially with the high cost of parking in major cities. Autonomous ride services will be even cheaper than ridesharing. Later in this chapter, I model the estimated cost of ARS to be almost half the cost of ridesharing. The lower cost of ARS enables many people to further reduce the cost of transportation by replacing both ridesharing and car ownership.

2. ARS will be more convenient. The first chapter provided some insight into the convenience of ARS. Even people who own a car will frequently use ARS to go to dinner or out with friends to avoid the risks of driving after drinking and the hassle of parking. They will use it to enable a trip to be more productive than driving. They will use it to replace taxis, ridesharing, and car services. They will use it to get to airports and to replace rental cars.

3. People will use ARS before buying an AV. It will take time for most buyers to be comfortable with owning fully-autonomous vehicles. They will be nervous about the technology. It is new, and people will need to learn how AVs work. Many will be reluctant to invest in AVs that quickly could become obsolete like other emerging technologies, such as cell phones. Also, the cost of sufficiently-autonomous or fully-autonomous vehicles will initially be high, pricing most people out of the market. In contrast, most people will readily use ARS. Many people will want to try it right from the start, and when they do, most will continue using it.

4. ARS vehicles only need to be *sufficiently* autonomous. As explained in previous chapters, the technology required for ARS is easier than fully autonomous. Autonomous ARS vehicles will use predefined HD maps. ARS routes can be geofenced, meaning that they can be limited to roads that a sufficiently-autonomous vehicle can maneuver. When a passenger requests an ARS trip, the app will identify if that is an approved route. If not, then it won't offer that trip. Over time, the number of roads and routes available to ARS will increase considerably.

5. ARS can be introduced by municipality. When you consider autonomous driving technologies, the ability to develop highly detailed digital maps will be an early challenge. A significant early advantage of ARS is that it can use very detailed mapping in a defined geographic area, specifically the city or municipal area where it provides the ride service. Additionally, autonomous driving will be embraced earlier by some municipalities that support autonomous driving. ARS will be offered by fleets that will oversee the service within that area.

6. ARS vehicles will be more comfortable. Early versions of privately-owned AVs will need to accommodate human drivers. However, second-generation autonomous vehicles for ARS will be custom designed for passengers only.

7. ARS is the fundamental strategy of ridesharing companies. The actual objective of ridesharing companies, like Uber and Lyft, is to provide autonomous ride services. Their strategy is to develop the market, gain customer loyalty, and then replace drivers with autonomous ride services. With the current ridesharing business model, they are losing a lot of money. It's unlikely that the business model of contractors/drivers using their own cars for ridesharing will ever be very profitable.

8. Technology companies, such as Google and Apple, will enter the ARS market. Waymo (Google), and possibly Apple, have their eyes set on this significant opportunity for AVs, but they have difficult distribution obstacles to enter the retail market selling cars to consumers. They don't have manufacturing capabilities, retail sales channels, or service capabilities. Putting this infrastructure in place would require significant time and enormous investments. Tesla struggled with this. So, instead, they will enter the ARS market.

9. Capturing ARS metropolitan markets will be like a new "land rush." I believe that companies will aggressively launch ARS in new metropolitan markets to capture those markets before competitors. Once a company establishes a presence in a local metropolitan market, it will discourage other companies from investing in the same market because the chances of success will be lower. This incentive will create a "land rush" effect. The major competitors will rush to new metropolitan markets to capture that market before others, accelerating the growth of ARS even faster.

ARS Will Be a Local Service

An essential characteristic of autonomous ride services is that it will be deployed by local metropolitan areas. An ARS company will deploy a fleet of autonomous ride services vehicles in a metropolitan area with a local fleet operations center to manage that fleet. Fleet sizes will vary in size from several hundred vehicles to many thousand.

Local fleet operations center management will be responsible for managing its municipal area. It will work with local government authorities to get all necessary approvals for its services and coordinate improvements to local road systems. For example, the local municipal area may improve traffic signals, set aside designated ARS drop-off spots, etc. The fleet operations center will also coordinate with local police and emergency services.

Local fleet operations management will be responsible for designating the roads and routes that it will serve, essentially geofencing that municipal area. It will be responsible for maintaining detailed HD maps and adjust them as needed. The routes serviced in a new municipal area will be limited initially, but they will progressively increase until the fleet can cover most of the metropolitan area.

Local fleet operations will manage the ride request and dispatch platform for that municipality. It will add new routes, adjust routes for traffic or construction, and may even set local pricing. There will be a capability for passengers to contact the local fleet dispatch center for questions, issues, and emergencies. Will dispatch roadside assistance when needed.

The fleet operations center will also maintain its autonomous vehicle fleet. This will include routine services such as cleaning, sanitizing, refueling/recharging, regular maintenance, etc. In addition, the fleet operations center may also regularly recalibrate the sensors and update computer software.

Each ARS company will launch its service in targeted metropolitan areas by placing a fleet of autonomous vehicles in those metropolitan areas to provide autonomous ride services within that metropolitan area. For example, Waymo may initiate its ARS in selected suburbs of Phoenix and then expand to the greater Phoenix area. It could then expand into southern Florida, Los Angeles, and cities in Texas. Cruise may start in San Francisco and then expand into Phoenix and Michigan. Argo/Ford may launch its ARS in Austin, Miami, and Washington DC. Motional may start its service in Las Vegas and then expand to a host of other cities.

Given the expected substantial profitability of ARS, this will become a "land rush" where the primary ARS competitors will invest to capture the most valuable metropolitan markets as fast as possible. The need to capture a local market before competitors will significantly accelerate the deployment of ARS. Once most of the best markets are served, there will be some consolidation and rationalization across the ARS industry.

Generations of ARS Vehicle Design

There will be three generations of ARS vehicles used over the next five years, and each generation will have very different interiors. First-generation ARS vehicles are retrofit versions of current cars with the sensors and computing added. They still have driver controls, even though they aren't used, and passengers sit primarily in the back seat. Second-generation will be custom designed around passengers but are practical designs looking like shuttles. Third-generation vehicles will be more luxurious and incorporate more entertainment technology. ARS vehicle strategies vary, as will be discussed in detail later in this chapter. Some early entrants to the ARS market are using first-generation retrofit vehicles. A couple of them have designed second-generation vehicles that they will use by 2023. Third-generation vehicles are still under development. Companies developing ARS vehicles need to get customer experience to create the vehicles that will be most popular.

First-Generation ARS Vehicles

First-generation ARS vehicles will be retrofitted versions of cars currently in production that were designed for drivers. For example, Waymo is

purchasing and retrofitting 20,000 Jaguar I-Pace SUVs and 60,000 Fiat Chrysler Pacifica hybrid minivans. Its new assembly facility in Michigan will retrofit these into ARS vehicles. This large-scale facility will modify tens of thousands of vehicles as it builds Waymo's fleet. The retrofitting includes the integration of high-powered computers, lasers, lidars, radars, and cameras. It will also include the addition of interior display panels and passenger amenities before they go into service. Magna is partnering with Waymo for this retrofitting.

Retrofitting existing production vehicles for the first generation makes sense. It avoids costly delays in getting ARS vehicles to market because it takes several years to design a new vehicle and set up new production lines. It enables the ARS company to focus on proving its autonomous driving technology. The ARS company can get some early experience that it can use to design next-generation vehicles. And it also reduces the investment for acquiring initial ARS vehicles since they are cars manufactured in high volumes.

Vehicles acquired in large quantities for retrofitting will most likely be built without any semi-autonomous capabilities since it would be a costly waste to include but not use them. I refer to these as "dumb" base vehicles for retrofitting of autonomous capabilities. Generally, providing these base vehicles will be a low-margin fleet sale business for car manufacturers.

First-generation retrofitted ARS vehicles will continue to have steering wheels and other driver controls, although they won't be used very often.

Passenger seat configurations will be similar to what they currently are today. An exception may be customizable vans that could have more flexible interiors.

Second-Generation ARS Vehicles

Ultimately, retrofitting current car models is not the best approach. It doesn't take advantage of the opportunities to design a more passenger-friendly vehicle, and there are wasted costs in all the unused driver controls and seating. Second-generation ARS vehicles are custom-designed for ride services around passengers, not drivers. Passengers will be able to sit comfortably and face each other. There may be a table or individual tabletops. Passengers will be able to have coffee, drink cocktails, review documents, or watch movies together.

Cruise and Zoox have demonstrated versions of their second-generation ARS vehicles. They look more like shuttles without a driver than an automobile. These are intended to be practical, transporting people from location to location. These ARS vehicles will be evident in their design and will stand out from ordinary cars. They will be easy to get in and out with sliding doors and an open interior. They are designed primarily for lower-speed urban transportation but will be able to drive on highways. From a cost standpoint, they will be much less expensive than first-generation ARS vehicles and can be more profitable at lower utilization.

Third-Generation ARS Vehicles

Third-generation vehicles will be much more luxurious with more interior technology. I expect there will be various interior designs for short commutes, longer trips, and particular purposes.

Eventually, third-generation ARS vehicle interiors will become a competitive differentiator. Most third-generation vehicles will have sophisticated video capabilities. Everyone could watch a movie together, or they could each manage their programs. When passengers get into an ARS vehicle, their video and audio programs will automatically be loaded for their access.

These attractive features of third-generation ARS vehicles will enable

providers to charge a premium and capture the market from first-generation ARS vehicles. There are not yet any third-generation ARS vehicles designed for production, although there are several concept vehicles. Most likely, Apple will enter the ARS market later than others, and it may enter with a third-generation vehicle.

Autonomous Ride Services Industry Structure

ARS will create an entirely new industry. There are different parts to this industry structure, and companies may participate in different ways. Using the concepts of product–platform management, Figure 7-1 illustrates the layers of the expected structure of the ARS industry.

There are three principal layers to the ARS industry platform structure. The top layer of the platform provides the basic ARS service to passengers, while the lower layer provides the autonomous vehicles to the ARS service providers. In-between is the layer of fleet ownership. Within each of these are different layers are the components of products and services necessary to provide autonomous ride services. Let's look at each of these layers in more detail.

Ride Request and Dispatch

Ride request and dispatch services are the top layer of the platform. This layer includes the ride-hailing app used by passengers to request a ride and the underlying computer services to dispatch vehicles, bill customers, and manage logistics. Ride request and dispatch may be the controlling point in the entire ARS market, as customers will initiate a ride based on their preferred service. The leading U.S. ridesharing companies, Uber and Lyft, have an established advantage to attract customers, but ARS will introduce other features to lure customers, including quality, safety ratings, pricing, and the availability of autonomous vehicles in an area.

A local ARS fleet operations center will complete ride request and dispatch. Each local fleet operation center will do the regional mapping and update the detailed maps and routes used by vehicles based on changing conditions such as detours, construction, traffic avoidance, etc. It will also include a local support center to communicate with passengers when needed and dispatch roadside assistance services, such as replacing a vehicle when there is a problem. Pricing and promotion may also be managed locally to optimize utilization and take advantage of surge pricing. For example, each municipal fleet operations center will make special service arrangements with restaurants, retail stores, performance venues, etc. The ride request and dispatch platform will be supported by artificial intelligence and analytics to predict rider travel demand levels and travel patterns.

Municipal Fleet Management

Fleet management will also be done locally for each fleet. This includes the ARS vehicle fleet parking, maintenance, update, cleaning, and refueling. Municipal fleet management will most likely subcontract some of these components to others. For example, fleet management will be an opportunity for car rental companies, such as Avis and Hertz, that have the experience and facilities to do vehicle parking, cleaning, and maintenance. It may also be an opportunity for some car dealers and entrepreneurs to perform these services.

Figure 7-1 Autonomous Ride Services Industry Structure

Ride Request and Dispatch							
Ride Request App	Dispatch and Routing	Billing	Local Pricing	Local Mapping	Route Adjustment	Customer Communications	Emergency Services

Fleet Management					
Fueling	Cleaning	Maintenance	Testing	Upgrades	Parking

Fleet Ownership/Leasing/Financing

Autonomous Ride Services Vehicles	
First Generation Vehicles	Second Generation Vehicles
System Integration of Base Vehicle and Autonomous Driving System	Final Assembly of ARS Vehicles

Basic (Dumb) Vehicle	Sensors				Custom Designed ARS Vehicle	Sensors			
	Radar	Lidar	Cameras	Sonar		Radar	Lidar	Cameras	Sonar
	AV Computer					AV Computer			
	AV Software					AV Software			
	Detailed Maps					Detailed Maps			

Source: author

Municipal fleet management will also include more advanced tasks. The ARS vehicles will need regular software and mapping updates. They will need regular testing and calibration. These companies will not risk an accident because a sensor was damaged or bumped and is no longer reliable. The maintenance of the sensor package, computers, and software most likely will be performed by the local fleet operations center and not subcontracted.

Fleet Ownership/Leasing/Financing

The next layer of this industry structure is the ownership of the autonomous vehicle fleet; essentially, this is who invests in the fleet. This investment will be very significant, probably in the hundreds of millions of dollars, or even a billion dollars, per municipal area. It isn't clear if this will be done by the primary fleet operator or another financial business. Some ARS companies may own and control their fleets – Waymo and Apple have sufficient capital to do this. Others may need external financing.

ARS Vehicles

Autonomous ride services (ARS) require autonomous vehicles. I consider this as a separate layer of the ARS industry structure. Some ARS competitors may not design and manufacture the vehicles themselves. Others may create their unique vehicles but subcontract manufacturing.

As discussed earlier, ARS vehicles will be introduced in several generations. The first generation will integrate AV systems (sensors, computers, and software) into a standard vehicle already in production. Second-generation and third-generation ARS autonomous vehicles will be custom-designed for ARS. Figure 7-1 illustrates the similarities and differences between these two generations. So, this layer is split into two parts.

First-Generation Vehicles

First-generation ARS vehicles will integrate a currently-in-production base vehicle with an autonomous driving package. This package includes sensors (lidar, radar, sonar, and cameras), a powerful AV computer, AV software, and detailed high-definition maps. The primary ARS company will provide this autonomous driving package. Autonomous driving technology is what I refer to as the "defining technology" for autonomous vehicles, and it's where AV companies have been investing billions of dollars. They will also provide their AV software and detailed maps for the software to use.

Lidar is a new critical technology, and most major ARS companies are building their lidar, frequently through acquisitions. They want to control this critical technology. The other sensors (radar, sonar, and cameras) are more commodities, and they will most likely be purchased. Many ARS companies are using powerful computers from Nvidia, but some may develop their own.

For first-generation vehicles, current auto manufactures will provide the base (dumb) vehicles. For example, Waymo is purchasing its base vehicles from Jaguar and Chrysler and doing the systems integration at its Michigan facility. The auto manufacturers entering the ARS market will be more vertically integrated. They will provide the base vehicle, the autonomous driving package, and do the integration themselves.

Second-Generation and Third-Generation Vehicles

Second-generation ARS vehicles, and third-generation vehicles, will be custom-designed for autonomous ride services. They will have a passenger-friendly interior without any driving controls. They won't have a driver's seat, steering wheel, or a brake.

Second-generation components are different from the first. It starts with a custom-designed vehicle instead of using an already-existing base vehicle. The vehicle design may be done by the primary ARS company with the manufacturing subcontracted, just like Apple does with its iPhones.

The autonomous-driving package will be similar to the first-generation vehicles, but instead of retrofitting the AV technology into the vehicle, it will be included directly in the final assembly of the vehicle. Here, again the auto manufacturers participating in the ARS industry will be more vertically integrated, and they will do the design and manufacturing themselves.

Phases for Development and Launch of ARS

Autonomous ride services are being launched carefully and deliberately in several phases. Each phase has a specific set of objectives that must be achieved before the next phase is initiated. As will be seen in the next section on ARS strategies, significant competitors are currently in different phases.

Phase 0 – Autonomous Vehicle Development

This is the first phase where autonomous driving technology is developed. The sensor package is configured with lidar development or acquisition. The most significant work in this phase is the development and testing of the AV software. During this phase, companies will do preliminary testing of their software in simulations, test tracks, and limited street driving. In this phase, street driving is done in controlled circumstances.

This phase takes several years and billions of dollars of investment. Most of the expected ARS competitors started this years ago, and many of these are sufficiently complete to move on to the next phase.

Phase 1 – Local Mapping

Autonomous vehicles require detailed high-definition local maps. And it takes some time to develop these local maps. In this phase, an ARS company will do local mapping for its initial pilot test locations. This involves vehicles equipped with lidar driving all the roads and routes expected to be used. Generally, they will need to drive these multiple times to get sufficient data.

To get a sense of this, let's look at Argo's plans for this phase as it first entered the Austin market:

Over the coming months, our vehicles will be manually driven through East Austin as well as downtown, mapping the city's main corridors in preparation for autonomous testing. Eventually, we will expand beyond these areas, but these initial mapping trips help us develop a comprehensive understanding of the environment around our vehicles. For example, we use sensors on our vehicles to create high-resolution 3D maps of streets, buildings, and all permanent static objects in areas where we plan to operate.

During our mapping process, we also get a sneak peek at what challenges may await us. Austin features heavy pedestrian activity, notably people riding bicycles and scooters. Scooters are especially interesting because they're essentially motorized pedestrians, with speedy and unique movement behavior that needs to be accounted for. Austin has more scooter activity than we've seen in other cities where we're currently testing.

In addition to helping ensure our vehicles can safely navigate the streets, we'll also concentrate on developing a self-driving system that drives as people expect it to. That requires developing a comprehensive understanding of local rules of the road and driving habits, which helps us better anticipate what others will do. These types of details go a long way towards developing a ride experience people feel comfortable with and find convenient.

This is a relatively short phase, taking a few months, but it needs to be done for each ARS location, unlike the previous phase.

Phase 2 – Initial Testing and Refinement

This phase is the extensive testing of autonomous vehicles in selected geographical areas such as Phoenix, San Francisco, Silicon Valley, Las Vegas, Pittsburg, and Detroit. Many companies are in this phase with their staff inside the AVs to take control if necessary. This testing requires a fleet of AVs to drive hundreds of thousands or millions of miles.

The initial testing of AVs in this phase takes some time, generally a year or more. However, this phase is much shorter in each new metropolitan area when the AV is sufficiently tested.

Phase 3 – Pilot Testing of ARS Service

This is the most crucial phase. This is when autonomous ride services prove they can work. Several companies are now in this phase, and others are planning to enter this phase in 2021.

The first group of passengers for the pilot testing will be carefully selected, and they may ride for free initially. There will also be a safety driver on board. Then the ARS service will begin to charge for these rides to test pricing and customer satisfaction.

Waymo launched its ARS ahead of others with its Early Rider program in the later part of 2018 in Arizona. Essentially, it was a pilot program that enabled selected passengers to go places they frequent every day, from work, to school, to the movies and more. Then, they share their thoughts and experiences to help shape Waymo's ARS. Early routes were in parts of the Phoenix metropolitan area, including Chandler, Tempe, Mesa and Gilbert.

Waymo started charging some of its Early Rider customers directly for rides in October 2018. Waymo also earned some revenue from retailers, like Walmart, which offered customers the option to order groceries online and then pick them up in a Waymo vehicle.

In November 2018, Waymo was issued a permit by the California Department of Motor Vehicles to begin testing its cars in an autonomous mode, which would not require a safety driver. The permit was the first issued by the state, allowing Waymo to use the vehicle's driverless capabilities in an area between Palo Alto and San Jose. Specifically, Waymo listed testing locations in Mountain View, Sunnyvale, Los Altos, Los Altos Hills, and Palo Alto. The permit allows Waymo to operate its AVs on the road during both the day and night, so long as weather conditions do not exceed fog and light rain. Vehicle speeds are limited to 65 miles per hour.

In late 2020 it launched its ARS, Waymo One, in the Phoenix area to paying passengers using autonomous vehicles with no safety drivers.

Aptiv also launched its pilot test for ARS at the end of 2018 in Las Vegas. Using 30 autonomously modified BMWs, it offered paid autonomous rides with a safety driver to 1,600 stops in Las Vegas. Many of the rides were offered in partnership with Lyft. Lyft claimed to have provided 55,000 rides in less than a year, and these riders gave it an excellent passenger rating of 4.97 stars. The pilot program operated the AVs for 20 hours per day within a 20-square-mile section of Las Vegas, which includes the busy Las Vegas strip area with more than 2,000 hotels, casinos, and restaurants. Passengers were charged the same as a standard fare for a driver-based Lyft ride.

Phase 4 – Initial ARS Launch

Once the pilot testing is completed and autonomous services are proven, ARS companies will launch their services in a few locations. The roads and routes will be geofenced and limited but will be broadened increasingly.

Waymo made its ARS available to members of Waymo One, the company's premium membership. Then on Oct. 8, 2020, it was made available to anyone in Chandler, Southeast Tempe, and Southwest Mesa through Waymo's app.

Phase 5 – Broad and Aggressive Rollout

Once a company successfully launches its autonomous ride services in one location, it will aggressively launch it in other areas through a multi-step process:

1. Identify potential municipal areas that meet the appropriate economic criteria and have a favorable road system.

2. Work with local government officials to get appropriate permits, support, and possible road system improvements, such as painting street lines. If a local municipal government is not supportive, the ARS company will simply skip that area for the time being and move on to another.

3. Complete the detailed high-definition mapping for each municipality and establish an ARS operations center.

4. Bring in a fleet of ARS autonomous vehicles for that municipal area.

5. Perform limited testing in that municipal area to ensure all the roads and routes in the geofenced area are safe and efficient. Local authorities such as fire and police will be involved in this step.

6. Promote and launch the service. This includes marketing and working with local businesses to promote the ARS.

This work is expected to take approximately six months for each metropolitan area. I anticipate that ARS companies will work with multiple metropolitan areas simultaneously. At this point, the ARS rollout will be aggressive. Whoever gets running in a new metropolitan area will have first-to-market advantages in capturing that market.

Autonomous Shuttle Services

Shuttle services transport people a short distance, typically along a predetermined route. Airport shuttle services taking arriving passengers from the airport to rental-car facilities, parking lots, or hotels are examples. Shuttles that transport students around a college campus are another example.

Types of Autonomous Shuttles

Shuttles provide short transportation in different situations. Autonomous shuttles will replace these with increased convenience and a much lower operating cost. Here are a range of examples.

Airports

Shuttles have a variety of uses at airports. They transfer passengers between terminals, to/from hotels, to/from car rental locations, to/from public transportation centers, and to/from parking locations. They are also used to transfer thousands of airport employees. These all operate over fixed routes and at lower speeds. Drivers are most of the cost of operating a shuttle. In order to manage costs, some shuttles only operate a few times each hour. Others, like rental-car shuttles tend to be very large in order to accommodate as many passengers as possible per driver.

Autonomous airport shuttles can provide lower-cost and more shuttle alternatives. Because they won't require drivers, operating costs could be reduced by 80%-90%. Even more importantly, there can be more shuttles operating more frequently on an as-needed basis.

Universities

College campuses are ideal for autonomous shuttles. Typically, campuses are contained in a large closed geographic area. Students and faculty need to move about the campus to classrooms, to parking, and from dormitories. The internal road systems are frequently closed to traffic, and slow-moving shuttles work effectively. The University of Michigan ran early trials of autonomous shuttles on campus.

Cities

Cities require a variety of public transportation alternatives, including rail and buses. Autonomous shuttles can provide another useful and cost-effective element in these transportation systems. Cities, including Detroit, Denver, Columbus, and Las Vegas have already piloted autonomous shuttles, which typically carry ten people or fewer on a fixed route through a section of their downtowns. For cities and their populations, and for operators, these new mobility solutions provide smooth, low-cost, and sustainable transportation that optimizes transportation performance over the first and last mile.

One early trial illustrates the potential. Providence RI is testing a fleet of six-passenger autonomous shuttles supplied by May Mobility along a 5.3-mile fixed route that connects the downtown area with nearby Olneyville Square. There are no public buses along most of the route, which mostly has empty factories but is attracting new businesses and residential buildings. The free shuttle will operate seven days a week between 6:30 am and 6:30 pm, helping those who live near Olneyville commute to work or shop at the Providence Place Mall. There will be 12 predetermined stops along the way.

Boston start-up Optimus Ride will run vehicles on private roads within the Brooklyn Navy Yard site located on New York's East River. The shuttle will help workers get around the large site. The City and County of Denver and the Regional Transportation District have launched their first on-road transit route that uses autonomous vehicles.

Theme Parks

If you have ever been to Disney World, you have seen its massive fleet of buses, taking guests from one park to another, and from hotels to the theme parks. There are many individual routes needed, and like most bus companies, Disney provides bus routes with numerous stops along the way. Autonomous shuttles can provide more individualized routes directly from one point to another, when requested by a guest. And can provide this flexibility at a lower cost.

135

Beyond the massive theme parks like Disney, there are many other amusement parks that can use autonomous shuttles to take guests to and from parking or public transit.

Large Retirement Communities

Large retirement communities offer unique opportunities for early implementation of autonomous vehicles. They have extensive internal roads systems with low-speed limits, large populations that needs to get around within the community, and many residents who prefer not to drive. Within these communities, AVs can operate at low speeds and within clearly defined routes.

In some cases, the vehicles are ordinary autonomous vehicles, not just shuttles with multiple pick-ups and drop-offs, but I classify them here as such because they are more limited. Eventually, they may operate more like shuttles.

Easier Implementation of Autonomous Shuttles

Autonomous shuttles have several advantages that make them easier for autonomous technology. Shuttles can provide immediate, small-scale transit improvements, helping solve the first-mile, last-mile challenge.

They travel along short, fixed routes, as compared to AVs that need to be prepared for a wider range of routes. This makes the route programming much simpler and easier to implement. Autonomous shuttles must be prepared to handle situations such as pedestrians and other traffic, but these can be contained along a fixed route.

Autonomous shuttles travel at lower speeds. This reduces risk and enables a lower cost for sensors and computing. They can be put into service earlier because the risk is lower. They travel on short routes. If there is a problem, passengers can more easily just get out and walk or find other alternatives. Autonomous shuttles also differ in that they transport larger groups of people. The combination of short routes, slow speeds, and other passengers will encourage more people to try autonomous shuttles as their first autonomous experience.

Benefits of Autonomous Shuttles

While convenient, driver-based shuttle services can be expensive. Some airports use large extended-length shuttle buses to and from car rental facilities to reduce labor costs. Hotels limit the number of trips to scheduled times and try to use employee drivers who do other work. Labor costs are what make shuttle services expensive.

Autonomous shuttle services will be an early use of AVs. There will be both significant benefits in the elimination of labor costs and increased convenience because autonomous shuttles can pick up passengers more frequently. Most of the cost of driver-based shuttles is the cost of the driver. They travel short distances, so fuel and maintenance costs are low. The cost of a shuttle bus is not that much, typically they can be leased for $600 - $900 per month. Whereas the costs of drivers can be $8,000 - $10,000 per month assuming 16-hours per day of operation every day a year.

The increased cost of adding autonomous capabilities to shuttles won't be that high because the operating requirements are simpler than other AVs. It may increase the monthly lease costs by $200-$300 per month. With the savings in the cost of drivers, the overall cost of autonomous shuttles could be as much as 90% lower.

Autonomous Shuttle Companies

Autonomous shuttles are not the primary focus of mainstream car manufacturers or big technology companies, because the volumes are not that large. Most of the companies working on these tend to be smaller start-ups.

Optimus Ride

Optimus Ride is a Boston company developing technologies for autonomous shuttles. The company doesn't build them; they are made by Polaris, the Canadian maker of snowmobiles and all-terrain vehicles. Optimus retrofits each shuttle with cameras and sensors, as wells as computing and software. The company raised more than $40 million in venture capital funding by 2019.

In 2019, Optimus started testing its autonomous shuttle at the Brooklyn Navy Yard, and in the first few weeks it had more than 1,000 riders. Optimus is primarily developing vehicles that will operate in geo-fenced areas, like university campuses or housing developments. The Brooklyn Navy Yard is one such contained environment, a 300-acre complex that is home to coffee roasters, sculptors, prototyping shops, and import businesses. The benefit of such environments is that they are far less challenging for AVs to navigate, and the routes are essentially pre-planned, like those of shuttle buses.

Navya

Navya, a French technology company, is developing a fully electric shuttle which has a capacity for up to 11 seated passengers and four standees. Maximum operating speed during its trials is 5-15 miles per hour, and the vehicle can operate for up to 13 hours on a single charge. Navigation and obstacle detection use a four-step process that combines radar, lidar, GPS and camera scanning, along with the algorithmic processing of geographical and geotechnical data. The company employs a "route scrubbing" method when the vehicles are initially deployed, allowing the primary camera and scanning data to be analyzed and refined by back-office teams before deploying the vehicles with passengers.

It works with partners to run the shuttle services using its autonomous shuttles. In 2019, it partnered with Beep to provide autonomous shuttle services to the Lake Nona (central Florida) community. The shuttles are monitored by Beep's control center.

EasyMile

EasyMile was founded in 2014. The company is headquartered in Toulouse France with offices in Singapore and Denver. It received approximately $30 million in investment as of 2019. EasyMile also operates through value-added resellers notably in Japan and the Middle East. It develops and deploys autonomous mobility solutions worldwide based on vehicles manufactured by its industrial partners. Its customers include transport operators, city authorities, airports, corporations, business parks, and universities.

The EasyMile EZ10 is an autonomous electric bus. It seats up to six people and allows four more passengers to ride standing or can accommodate a wheelchair. It aims to bridge the first mile/last mile of a trip. EasyMile says its autonomous shuttles have been used in 22 countries, carrying more than 320,000 passengers for greater than 200,000 miles without any collisions or injuries until early 2020.

A passenger in Columbus, Ohio fell from their seat after the EasyMile shuttle made an emergency stop. The vehicle was traveling at seven miles per hour. US vehicle safety regulators suspended operations for EasyMile. According to the National Highway Traffic Safety Administration (NHTSA), the battery-powered bus service will be halted in 10 US states while it investigates "safety issues related to both vehicle technology and operations." EasyMile, which has pods operating in various locations, says that the vehicles are still permitted on US roads, but won't be able to carry passengers while the NHTSA conducts its review. It's not the first time EasyMile has faced safety criticism. An elderly passenger was injured in a similar braking incident in Utah last year. EasyMile subsequently added seatbelts for passengers to resume operations.

Voyage

Voyage was spun-off from the online education company Udacity in 2017. In September 2019, it raised an additional $31 million, bringing its total investment to $52 million. In March 2021, it was acquired by Cruise, and it's not clear if it will continue to develop a shuttle.

The Economic and Business Model of Autonomous Ride Services

Although current ridesharing services and the future autonomous ride services (ARS) perform the same task, their economics and business models couldn't be more different. Ridesharing today is a labor-intensive contractor-based model with no investment in cars or most employees. The drivers are contractors using their own cars, although this may change in some states. The key to success is the app that people use to get a ride, along with a critical mass of contractors to provide enough coverage for reliable service. Ridesharing has yet to prove that it can be a profitable business model.

Ridesharing was a large and growing market until the COVID-19 pandemic, and then it declined significantly. As the nation began to recover from the pandemic, a shortage of drivers willing to return to work hindered ridesharing, increasing prices and diminishing service. It remains to be seen how fast it will recover.

Autonomous ride services are a very different business model. It is technology/capital-intensive. The ARS company needs to acquire its autonomous vehicle fleet or partner with someone else who invests in the fleet, and it must manage vehicle utilization efficiently. Unlike ridesharing, ARS will be a very profitable business.

Since the ARS business model is not yet established, we need to construct the expected model based on assumptions and estimates to grasp the potential for its success. The numbers are so large that rough estimates can provide a reasonable approximation of the potential. This will be done in four steps:

1. Estimate the expected revenue per ARS vehicle, using pricing and utilization assumptions.
2. Estimate the profit contribution per vehicle, using assumptions for the cost of operating each vehicle. These are the direct costs per vehicle, such as fuel, cleaning, maintenance, etc.
3. Since ARS will be delivered by fleets of vehicles managed by a fleet operations center, the cost of a typical operations center needs to be estimated. A gross margin can be computed after estimating these fleet management costs.

4. Finally, a projected income statement can be modeled based on an assumption of the total number of vehicles an ARS company may have in operation at a given point in time. There is no assumed date for the number of vehicles.

Revenue Per ARS Vehicle

There is a range of assumptions needed to estimate revenue per vehicle, but the two most critical ones are pricing and utilization (trips and miles per day). Figure 7-2 estimates revenue per vehicle as the average of a range of assumptions for these two variables. The base case business model assumes a 7-mile average ARS trip, which is a typical ridesharing trip.

Figure 7-2 -- Estimated Revenue Per ARS Vehicle

	Scenario A	Scenario B	Scenario C	Scenario D	Average
Trips per Day	30	30	40	40	
Miles per trip	7	7	7	7	
Miles per Day	210	210	280	280	2
Trips per Hour (12 Hrs.)	2.5	2.5	3.3	3.3	2
Average speed MPH	30	30	30	30	
Hours Used per Day	7.0	7.0	9.3	9.3	8
Utilization per day	29%	29%	39%	39%	34
Price per Mile	$2.25	$2.00	$1.75	$1.25	$1.8
Price per Trip	$15.75	$14.00	$12.25	$8.75	$12.6
Revenue per Day	$473	$420	$490	$350	$43
Days Used per Year	350	350	350	350	3
Miles per Year	73,500	73,500	98,000	98,000	85,75
Annual Revenue	**$165,375**	**$147,000**	**$171,500**	**$122,500**	**$151,59**

Source: Author Estimates

Pricing

Autonomous Ride Services (ARS) will offer various pricing plans and programs, enabling them to fit different market needs, manage capacity utilization, and achieve competitive advantage. Here are some potential pricing plans:

- **Basic Rates** – ARS rates will be set by miles traveled, by time, or by a combination of the two. Long-distance rides may offer lower prices.

- **Off-Peak and Surge Pricing** – Rates may vary to improve the utilization of the autonomous vehicles (AVs) in an ARS fleet. When demand is higher, prices will be higher. When demand is lower, rates will be lowered to encourage utilization during those periods.

- **Promotional Rates** – It's very likely that there will be price competition with many special promotional programs in some markets. I also expect that there will be aggressive promotional programs to get people to use ARS for their first few rides.

- **Wait-Time Charges** – Some ARS companies may offer a wait-time charge, particularly during off-peak hours. This will enable customers to pay a little extra to keep the same AV waiting for them while they run errands, have a doctor visit, etc.

- **Subscription Programs** – I expect several versions of subscription programs to be available. These will be monthly or annual programs that enable customers to get lower rates and preferred availability of services.

- **Pre-Scheduled Rides** – ARS can more easily pre-schedule passenger pickup than ridesharing. This is particularly useful for people who need a reliable ride to the airport early in the morning. Pre-scheduled trips may have a scheduling fee.

- **Cleaning Fees** - One of the challenges for ARS will be cleaning between rides. Most will have an additional cleaning fee associated with special cleaning that goes beyond typical usage.

Let's make some assumptions on pricing using ridesharing as the reference point. Ride Guru estimated the cost of a typical 8-mile, 19-minute ride in 2019 as follows[v]:

- Lyft and Uber X - $16
- Lyft Plus and Uber XL - $24
- Lyft Premier and Uber Select - $29

Surge pricing could increase these by 50%. Tips would be in addition to these costs. Pricing in major cities such as New York could be twice this cost. For comparison, the same trip by taxi is estimated at $26.

Including a 15% tip, a non-surge ridesharing standard ride would be approximately $2.30 per mile, and a Premier or Select ride in a better car would be more than $4 per mile. ARS pricing hasn't been set yet, but early Waymo pricing seems close to the ridesharing rates. ARS pricing could be close to ridesharing initially and then come down to increase market share after ARS is more accepted.

To determine estimated revenue in Figure 7-2, a range of prices per mile is used. Scenario A uses $2.25 per mile, which is close to the standard ridesharing price. Scenarios B through D then reduce this rate progressively to $1.25 per mile. This results in an average of $1.81 per mile.

Utilization

Unlike ridesharing, the usage of an ARS vehicle is not limited by driver availability. It can drive many more miles and complete many more trips. Uber drivers average about 2.5 trips per hour, although that varies widely. The models used in Figure 7-2 range from less than 30% utilization to almost 40%, increasing as the price is reduced. The utilization of individual vehicles will vary by different companies and different areas, and that difference will become competitively significant. Utilization metrics will become clearer as the ARS market become a reality.

Utilization will become one of the most critical variables for ARS vehicles. I expect that ARS companies will keep improving utilization through different pricing options, optimization models, and artificial intelligence. Ridesharing utilization is determined by individual drivers and their experience that determines when and where to work, in addition to surge pricing. ARS optimization can be perfected to a higher level by central fleet optimization.

Vehicle Operating Costs and Profit Contribution Per Vehicle

The next step is to estimate the costs of operating an ARS vehicle. These are costs such as fuel, maintenance, insurance, and taxes attributed to each vehicle. Figure 7-3 estimates the operating costs and profit contribution for a typical ARS AV.

The average revenue for an ARS vehicle determined in Figure 7-3 is $150,000, based on approximately 85,000 miles per year. 30% additional non-passenger miles are assumed for operating costs. Fuel costs of $6,000 equate to roughly $0.055 per mile, much more than the currently estimated $0.033 per mile estimate for electric vehicles.

Figure 7-3 -- Operating Costs Per ARS Vehicle

Revenue per Vehicle	**$150,000**
Passenger Miles	85,000
Non-Passenger Miles	25,000
Total Miles per Year	110,000
Operating Costs	
Fuel	$6,000
Insurance	$6,000
Cleaning & Maintenance	$25,000
Taxes	$3,000
Depreciation	$20,000
Total Operating Costs	**$60,000**
Contribution per Vehicle	**$90,000**
Source: Author Estimates	

Cleaning and maintenance costs will be relatively expensive since the car is being driven 110,000 miles annually. These are estimated at $25,000 per year per vehicle. Insurance costs should be reasonable since the autonomous vehicles should have very few accidents, but let's conservatively estimate $6,000 per vehicle, although this will go down over time. I expect that the companies running ARS will generally self-insure most of their insurance costs in the early years.

Also, there will most likely be city, state, and federal taxes on this new industry – let's assume $3,000 per vehicle per year. Vehicle depreciation will be a significant cost. This is estimated to be approximately $20,000 per year per vehicle, although this is expected to vary. Second-generation vehicles will be less expensive because they won't include all the driver controls, and they will be designed to be more durable. This equates to three years total depreciation for a $60,000 vehicle.

As seen in Figure 7-3, the total operating costs on average are estimated to be approximately $60,000 per vehicle per year. This would provide an estimated profit contribution of roughly $90,000 per vehicle per year before the costs for the fleet operations center and corporate expenses.

Typical Municipal ARS Fleet Operation Center Costs

ARS will be provided by fleets of AVs that serve designated metropolitan areas. Each of these ARS fleet operations centers will offer a range of services: oversee the dispatch of AVs in the fleet, intervene directly in customer problems and issues, and track the location of all vehicles 24/7. They will provide regular maintenance, manage the cleaning of all vehicles, upgrade AVs with new technology, manage the size of the fleet, work closely with local authorities to ensure the services work smoothly and follow regulations, and maintain the detailed mapping and geofencing of the municipal area. Some municipal fleet operations will manage marketing and promotion and set prices relative to competition.

Fleets will vary by size, depending on the metropolitan market. Initially, I envisioned smaller fleets

Figure 7-4 -- Fleet Operations Costs

Number of Vehicles In Fleet	1,000
Revenue Per vehicle	$150,000
Profit Contribution Per Vehicle	$90,000
Revenue Per Center (millions)	**$150.0**
Vehicle Contribution (millions)	$90.0
Fleet Operations Costs (millions):	
Operations Staff	$4.0
Facilities Rent	$1.0
Information Tech.	$0.8
Administration/Other	$0.5
Local Marketing & Promotion	$1.0
Total Operations Center Expense	$7.3
Fleet CenterGorss Profit	**$82.7**
Gross Margin	**55%**

Source: Author Estimates

143

of a few hundred vehicles, but now I see somewhat larger fleets given some initial deployments and market estimates. The minimum fleet size will probably be 500 vehicles, but some may be as large as 5,000. Annual revenue for a 500-vehicle fleet center would be approximately $75 million, and a 5,000-vehicle fleet would be more than $750 million.

Fleet operations costs would include the staff at the location, as well as typical facilities costs. There will also be local marketing and promotion costs as well. I estimate that a small fleet will have 30-40 employees, while a more extensive fleet could have as many as 200. Vehicle costs were already estimated in Figure 7-3, with the gross profit per vehicle carried over to Figure 7-4.

Each fleet is projected to be very profitable. A 1,000-vehicle fleet would have an estimated revenue of approximately $150 million per year and an incredible expected gross profit of more than $82 million, or 55%, annually. Remember, though, each fleet will require a significant capital investment. A 1,000-vehicle fleet will require an investment of $100-$120 million.

This exceptional return on an ARS fleet operation has two implications. First, prices may go much lower with competition, but this would also grow the market faster. The second implication is that this profitability will fuel the "land rush."

Once they have perfected autonomous technology, ARS companies will try to rush in and "own" as many municipal markets as they can. Fleet operations center profits would be aggregated by the company that owns the center, and this gross margin would be used to fund corporate marketing, R&D, and administration.

Projected ARS Business Income Statement

The final step in projecting the potential revenue and profitability of an ARS business is to estimate projected income based on the number of ARS vehicles it has across all its fleets. Figure 7-5 estimates the projected income statement at different ARS business volumes ranging from 200,000 ARS vehicles to 1 million ARS vehicles. The number of vehicles an ARS business operates depends on the overall size of the market and its market share.

The first two estimates – 200,000 and 400,000 are most likely for market leaders by the end of the first stage of the market in 2025 or 2026, when there will be an estimated 1 million or more ARS vehicles operating in the U.S. Estimated market growth by stage and the assumptions deriving it are covered in more detail in the final chapter. The estimated number of ARS vehicles of 750,000 and 1 million are more likely at the end of Stage 2 in 2030 or 2031, when there will be an estimated total of more than 5 million ARS vehicles in operation in the U.S. market.

Revenue at these estimated volumes is based on an estimated $150,000 revenue per vehicle. This should hold even if prices decline because it would be offset by increased vehicle utilization. Estimated ARS revenue ranges from $30 billion to $150 billion per year for the leading companies.

Figure 7-5 -- Projected Income Statement for ARS at Various Volumes

Number of ARS Vehicles	200,000	400,000	750,000	1,000,000
Revenue (millions)	**$30,000**	**$60,000**	**$112,500**	**$150,000**
Gross Profit (55%)	$16,500	$33,000	$61,875	$82,500
Operating Expenses				
R&D	$4,500	$7,200	$11,250	$15,000
Sales & Marketing	$4,500	$6,000	$9,000	$10,500
General & Administrative	$3,000	$6,000	$9,000	$10,500
Total Operating Expenses	$12,000	$19,200	$29,250	$36,000
Operating Income	**$4,500**	**$13,800**	**$32,625**	**$46,500**
	15%	23%	29%	31%

Source: Author Estimates

Operating expenses at the corporate level include R&D, Sales & Marketing, and General & Administrative expenses. Remember the costs of operating each vehicle and the costs of fleet operations were previously estimated to determine an estimated gross profit. R&D will continue to be a significant expense. It is estimated at 15% in the first two levels and then decreasing as a percentage of revenue at higher levels. The overall amount of R&D investment could be very substantial, ranging from $4.5 billion to more than $10 billion. Sales and marketing are estimated at 15% at the lower volumes and then decreasing as a percentage. This is in addition to the estimated local marketing and promotion expenses of approximately $1 million per 1,000 vehicle fleet. General & administrative expenses are estimated at levels typical for businesses of this size.

This proforma model illustrates the significant potential profitability of an ARS business with operating income potential in the first stage of $4.5 - $13 billion and longer-term profits of $32 - $46 billion. As a reference point, a business of that size and profitability could be worth almost a trillion dollars. Looking at models like this explains why large companies are investing billions in developing the ARS market.

ARS Will Displace Ridesharing

The business model of ARS is very different from the model for ridesharing. Ridesharing is a classic labor-intensive business model. ARS is a technology- and capital-intensive business model. The fundamental strategic difference in these business models is well-proven by examples throughout history. A technology-based capital-intensive business model will always displace a labor-intensive business model.

Figure 7-6 -- Comparison of Uber to ARS ($ millions)

	Uber	ARS
Uber Gross Bookings/ ARS Revenue	$49,800	$49,800
Driver Costs	$39,000	$0
Net Revenue	$10,800	$49,800
Cost of Revenue		
Uber Cost of Revenue	$5,600	
ARS Vehicle Costs		$19,920
Operations	$1,500	$2,400
Total Cost of Revenue	$7,100	$22,320
Gross Margin	$3,700	$27,480
Operating Expenses		
R&D	$1,500	$6,000
Sales & Marketing	$3,200	$5,000
General & Administrative	$2,100	$5,000
Total Operating Expenses	$6,800	$16,000
Net Income	($3,100)	$11,480

Source: Uber data from Uber S-1 IPO filing with 2018 data
ARS data is author estimate from prior models

Ridesharing is not yet profitable, and it cannot hope to be competitive with ARS in the long run. Ridesharing drivers are 70%, or more with a tip, of the cost of a trip, and they won't drive at a substantial cut in compensation. One can argue about the timeframe for ARS to displace ridesharing. Is it going to start in two years or four years? Will ARS take 20% of the ridesharing market by 2025? With ARS only available in certain areas, will ridesharing continue to grow in others? Regardless of the timeframe, the conclusion is inevitable: ARS will eventually displace ridesharing.

Figure 7-6 illustrates the stark difference between these two business models. The Uber data is its actual financial data for 2018 filed in its IPO document. Uber had almost $50 billion in bookings with a driver cost of $39 billion. The equivalent revenue for ARS would be the model previously described in Figure 7-5 with 332,000 ARS vehicles in service. This compares to an estimated number of Uber drivers in the U.S. of 1 to 1.5 million. The revenue comparison also demonstrates how realistic the estimated ARS revenues are. By the end of 2025, revenue would only need to be comparable to Uber in 2018.

The difference in net revenue is very significant. ARS net revenue is 5X greater on the same level of business because there are no driver costs. The cost of revenue is much higher for ARS because of ARS vehicle costs, derived from the estimated costs of $60,000 per vehicle from Figure 7-3 for 332,000 ARS vehicles. Fleet operations costs are also estimated to be higher for ARS. Nevertheless, the gross margin for ARS is much more significant: $27 billion compared to $3.7 billion.

Operating expenses are estimated to be higher for ARS in part because of conservative assumptions. R&D expense is more for the technology-intensive ARS business: $6 billion compared to $1.5 billion. Uber's R&D expense is expected to go down significantly since it sold its autonomous driving unit. Marketing and administrative expenses are also higher for the ARS business, primarily because of conservative assumptions.

In comparison, at the same business level ($49.8 billion), ARS is much more profitable. It will make an estimated net income of $11.4 billion compared to a loss of $3 billion for Uber. Uber is expected to reduce its loss through improving operations and disposing of its autonomous driving unit. Still, because of its basic labor-intensive business model, it is not likely to be very profitable, if at all. Making a profit will be even more difficult for Uber if it is forced to classify its drivers as employees and pay benefits and employment taxes.

Lyft explicitly recognized this difference between ridesharing and ARS in its 2019 IPO prospectus:

> *New and existing competitors may develop or utilize autonomous vehicle technologies for ridesharing, which are expected to have long-term advantages compared to traditional non-autonomous ridesharing offerings.*

The cost gap between ridesharing and ARS may grow even larger in the next few years. Coming out of the pandemic, ridesharing companies were forced to raise their prices significantly to get drivers back to work. Gridwise Inc, which tracks Uber and Lyft prices estimated that ridesharing fares increased 79% from Q2/19 to Q2/21. In addition, ridesharing companies are fighting legislation in many states that will force them to reclassify drivers as employees and pay full benefits.

ARS Routing Optimization

ARS also has another critical advantage over ridesharing, something I'll call route optimization. Ridesharing is fundamentally a driver-based optimization model. Drivers try to position themselves to get more frequent and better trips. They may cruise around a particular location such as a hotel, trying to be nearby to get assigned more or preferred trips. They work when they want, but some are motivated to drive when there is surge pricing. This self-organizing way of optimization works well for individual drivers, and it isn't bad for the overall ridesharing network, but it isn't an optimal use of resources. It wastes a lot of driving miles and creates more traffic congestion as drivers cruise around.

ARS will use fleet-based optimization. Centralized fleets can optimize the deployment of the correct number of vehicles to selected locations. They can deploy vehicles to parking locations based on projected demand. For example, fleet optimization systems will know how many trips vehicles made to drop off passengers at restaurants and can have the correct number of needed vehicles in the area for later pick up. While individual ridesharing drivers know this instinctively, they can't do overall fleet optimization, so there may be too many or too few vehicles in the area.

Fleets can also make advanced reservations more efficiently. For example, people going to a theater performance can make reservations for pick up after the show. ARS vehicles can queue up (ironically like a taxi queue) at the venue, picking up ARS passengers as they arrive at the queue. They can coordinate closely with public transportation, deploying vehicles for the arrival of a passenger train based on its actual arrival time.

The number of vehicles in an ARS fleet can also change based on an expected surge in demand. For example, the size of a fleet in a seasonal location may increase to be several times larger during the season. The fleet could increase temporarily for major events to cover increased demand in a metropolitan area. ARS vehicles can be deployed from one location to another, even if they are hundreds of miles away. This change in supply is challenging, if not impossible, for ridesharing. Most ridesharing drivers wouldn't move to or from a location seasonally.

This ability to optimize gives ARS another service and cost advantage over ridesharing, and perhaps, more importantly, it will enable ARS to reduce traffic congestion.

Company Strategies in the ARS Market

ARS will be a regional, not global, market. It is a services market, not a product market. Approximately a half-dozen major companies are expected to compete for that market in the U.S., rolling out their ARS services by metropolitan area. Waymo, a subsidiary of Google (Alphabet), is the first to market. Cruise Automation (GM) is expected to follow in late 2021 or early 2022. Ford Autonomous Vehicles LLC and Argo AI are planning on launching an ARS service in 2022. ARS is crucial for Uber and Lyft, because it will cannibalize their ridesharing business. Lyft is partnering with Motional, and Uber is partnering with Aurora. They will need to compete in this market or face extinction. Zoox was acquired by Amazon and now has the financial resources to compete in this market. Apple is the wildcard in the ARS market. It has yet to declare its intentions, but it is investing heavily in AV development and testing, and the ARS market is the only one that makes sense for it.

The capital requirements to compete in the ARS market are significant. As discussed, it is basically a technology and capital-intensive model replacing a labor-intensive market (ridesharing). This may even be the most significant industry transition of this type in history. Waymo plans to convert 80,000 vehicles for ARS by 2023 or 2024. Including the AV driving package, this will cost them approximately $8 billion. By the late 2020s, if it wants to have a significant share of the ARS market, another investment of $80-$100 billion may be necessary, assuming the cost of an ARS vehicle is reduced to approximately $80,000, and it wants to capture 20%-25% of the estimated 5 million vehicle market by 2030.

The capital investment required to compete in the ARS market will be a challenge. Cruise Automation (GM), Ford Autonomous Vehicles LLC, and Waymo have all formed subsidiaries with external investors to get the necessary capital. Most likely, they will all spinoff these subsidiaries to be independent businesses that can raise even more capital through public stock offerings and debt. Apple and Amazon have enough cash to invest in this market, but they may still spin off this business.

Let's look more closely at the strategies for each of the expected ARS competitors. The more comprehensive strategies of the auto manufacturers (GM, Ford, and Tesla) are covered in the next chapter.

Waymo

Google (Alphabet) is considered the pioneer in autonomous vehicles, starting its self-driving car project back in 2009. Google's massive cash flows and scattered innovation "strategy" enabled it to invest heavily in what was a speculative initiative at the time. It took advantage of this lead to get the most experience in autonomous driving, and it is currently the leader in AVs, particularly ARS.

In late 2020, Waymo launched its ARS, Waymo One, in the Phoenix area to paying passengers using autonomous vehicles with no safety drivers. The service was first made available to members of Waymo One, the company's premium membership. Then on Oct. 8, 2020, it was made available to anyone in Chandler, Southeast Tempe, and Southwest Mesa through Waymo's app. By the middle of 2021, Waymo claims to have provided thousands of ride-only trips.

Waymo LLC has more than 2,000 employees. It currently uses more than 600 autonomous vehicles and has 80,000 more on order from Fiat Chrysler and Jaguar. Waymo built a factory in Michigan to retrofit these for autonomous driving.

In December 2016, Google officially separated its self-driving research unit into a separate company called Waymo. That was a clear intention by Google that it expected Waymo to become viable as a stand-alone business, rather than a mere research project. It then spun-off Waymo as a separate business. In March 2020, Waymo raised outside investment for the first time. It received $2.25 billion from investors including: Silver Lake Partners, Andreessen Horowitz, Canada Pension Plan Investment Board, Mubadala Investment, Magna International, AutoNation, and Waymo's parent company, Alphabet. In May 2020, it raised another $750 million from Perry Creek Capital, T. Rowe Price, and Fidelity Investments. In June 2021, it raised another $2.5 billion from a dozen diversified investors. Most certainly, these sophisticated investors, particularly the private equity firms, did substantial due diligence before investing. In that process, they would have been given access to all Waymo's testing, technical data, and business forecasts.

The primary purpose of outside investments is to start making the company independent from Alphabet. The most significant impact of Waymo taking outside investment is that it is now functioning as a semi-independent business. It has a more independent governance structure with its own board of directors. This is a profound change in the way Waymo will be managed. It will no longer be under the complete control of Alphabet.

Forming an independent business with sophisticated outside investors validates that Waymo is a serious business with a significant business opportunity. Most likely, the new independent governance of Waymo played a role in the decision of its long-time CEO, John Krafcik, to depart. He was replaced by the promotion of two internal executives to become Co-CEOs. Although the announcement was the typical "leaving for personal reasons to pursue other opportunities," this is generally a code for the board being unhappy with progress. My interpretation is that there are continuing delays, and the board wants to be more aggressive in launching the Waymo ARS. So, there may be some delays in the further roll-out of Waymo One.

The latest round of $2.5 billion investment appears to be focused on expanding its fleet of ARS autonomous vehicles as it prepares for expansion of its service.

Waymo Autonomous Vehicles

Waymo's initial ARS strategy was to gain first-to-market advantages. So, it focused on using a first-generation ARS AV to introduce its service first and quickly expand its ARS market footprint. In the first stage of its ARS strategy, Waymo is retrofitting vehicles currently produced by two major car manufacturers. It started by using 600 Fiat Chrysler Pacifica hybrid minivans. In June 2018, it announced that it would acquire up to 62,000 more. Shortly before that announcement, Waymo also announced its intention to purchase up to 20,000 Jaguar I-Pace electric vehicles. If Waymo acquires and retrofits these vehicles, it would have an ARS fleet of more than 80,000 vehicles.

However, delays in launching its ARS may cause issues with this strategy. By being first, it could capture some key metropolitan markets before competitors. It could also refine its service offering faster as it gains more experience. However, it had to enter the market with a first-generation ARS vehicle, and some of these are hybrids and not all-electric. As it takes longer to enter the market, its competitors entering with second-generation vehicles are catching up. Second-generation vehicles will have some advantages.

The Pacifica is a hybrid, which was appropriate early on, but now most AVs will be fully electric. Waymo does have the Jaguar I-Pace to use instead if it chooses. More importantly, the delay enabled competitors, such as Cruise, to develop a second-generation autonomous vehicle explicitly designed for autonomous ride services without any driver controls. This may diminish Waymo's first-to-market advantage. There are no insights into Waymo's plans for a custom-designed second-generation ARS vehicle. This issue may also have been behind the leadership change.

Its first-to-market advantage gives Waymo the most self-driven miles of any AV company. It reported that its AVs drove more than 20 million miles by 2020, and these millions of autonomous driving miles were achieved in "25 different cities across the United States: in sunny California, dusty Arizona, and snowy Michigan, and from the high-speed roads around Phoenix to the dense urban streets of San Francisco." Waymo supplements actual autonomous driving with extensive simulation. By early 2020, it completed more than 10 billion miles of simulated driving, and it is running approximately 10 million miles of simulations for per day.

Lidar is the most critical sensor technology, and Waymo developed its own. Its Laser Bear Honeycomb system has several advantages over many other 3D lidar sensors. It has a vertical field of view of 95 degrees, instead of the standard 30 degrees, as well as a 360-degree horizontal view. When it sends out a pulse of light, it can see up to four objects in a laser beam's line of sight (for example, both the foliage in front of a tree branch and the tree branch itself).

Moreover, the lidar sensor has a minimum range of zero, meaning it's able to perceive objects immediately in front of it, enabling capabilities such as near-object detection and avoidance. In 2020, Waymo began selling its lidar to other companies, primarily those not in the autonomous vehicle market.

Waymo has stated that "we develop hardware and software in-house so that our self-driving technology works as a seamless, single system." A vital part of that process is integrating its self-driving system into the vehicles it purchases for its fleet. Waymo has a factory with Magna in southeast Michigan to retrofit vehicles into AVs. The first AVs produced will be autonomous versions of the Chrysler Pacifica Hybrid minivan and Jaguar's I-PACE electric SUV. All the AVs produced will be capable of sufficiently-autonomous, Level 4, driving. This enables a vehicle to drive itself without a human driver in certain limited conditions, operating within a specified geofenced area using extensive digital maps for that area. Waymo appears to be primarily using the I-Pace as its AV in San Francisco.

Waymo AV Testing Disclosure

Waymo provides some interesting insights into its testing. It disclosed detailed information on its AV operations in Phoenix, including the number of "contact events" with other road users. Between January and December

2019, Waymo's AVs with trained safety drivers drove 6.1 million miles with an additional 65,000 miles of driving by AV with no drivers in the vehicle.

Waymo reported that in these 6 million miles, its vehicles were involved in 47 "contact events" with other road users, which includes other vehicles, pedestrians, and cyclists. Eighteen of these events occurred, while the additional 29 were simulated outcomes from situations where the safety driver took control. Almost all these collisions were the fault of another human driver or pedestrian, and none resulted in any "severe or life-threatening injuries." Here is a summary:

- Rear-end collisions were the most common type of crash involving Waymo's vehicles. Waymo said it was involved in 14 actual and two simulated events, and in all but one, the other vehicle was the one rear-ending the Waymo AV. Waymo's vehicles often drive very cautiously in ways that can frustrate a human driver and can lead to fender-benders. Still, Waymo says its vehicles aren't rear-ended more frequently than the average driver.

- The one incident where Waymo rear-ended another vehicle was in simulation: the company determined that the AV would have rear-ended another car that swerved in front of it and then braked hard despite a lack of obstruction ahead, which the company says was "consistent with an antagonistic motive." The speed of impact, had it occurred in real life, would have been one mph.

- The only crash involving a fully driverless Waymo vehicle without a safety driver behind the wheel was also a rear-ending. The Waymo vehicle was slowing to stop at a red light when it was rear-ended by another vehicle traveling at 28 mph. An airbag was deployed in the vehicle that struck the Waymo vehicle.

- The company highlighted eight incidents that it considered more severe or potentially severe. Three of these crashes occurred in real life, and five only in simulation. Airbags were deployed in all eight incidents.

- Just one crash took place with a passenger in a Waymo vehicle. The crash occurred when a Waymo vehicle with a safety driver behind the wheel was rear-ended by a vehicle traveling around four mph. No injuries were reported.

- Waymo was also involved in 14 simulated crashes in which two vehicles collided at an intersection or while turning. There was also one actual collision. These types of crashes, called "angled" collisions, are important because they account for over a quarter of all vehicle collisions in the U.S., and nearly a quarter of all vehicle fatalities, according to Waymo.

153

- The one actual, non-simulated, angled collision occurred when a vehicle ran a red light at 36 mph, smashing into the side of a Waymo vehicle traveling through the intersection at 38 mph.

- Fortunately, the "most severe" collision only took place in simulation. The Waymo vehicle was traveling at 41 mph when another vehicle suddenly crossed in front of it. In real life, the safety driver took control, braking in time to avoid a collision; in the simulation, Waymo's AV system didn't stop in time to prevent the crash. Waymo determined it could have reduced its speed to 29 mph before colliding with the other vehicle.

Waymo's ARS Roll-Out Strategy

As previously stated, Waymo has the first-to-market advantage in ARS. It launched an Early Rider program in April 2017 for 400 people in Arizona.

In late 2018, it launched Waymo One, the first autonomous ride service. Initially, it was available in four Phoenix suburbs: Chandler, Mesa, Tempe, and Gilbert. Combined, this is approximately a 100-square-mile area. Riders use the Waymo One app to request a ride. On Oct. 8, 2020, Waymo One was made available to anyone in Chandler, Southeast Tempe, and Southwest Mesa through Waymo's app. Waymo will gradually increase the area severed and the number of eligible riders. Then it will launch its ARS in other metropolitan areas.

In February 2021, Waymo announced that it also began limited rider testing of its ARS with employee volunteers in San Francisco to gather feedback and improve its ARS technology. It also applied for a license for charging passengers in San Francisco for autonomous rides. This is the first expansion of its ARS service beyond the Phoenix Metropolitan Area and provides new opportunities and challenges in a more urban area. In preparation, Waymo had 238 AVs that drove autonomously 629,000 miles in California in 2020. Waymo claimed that it optimized its autonomous planning, perception, and navigation system, to handle the complexities of San Francisco, including using cameras that can identify jaywalkers.

In addition to the roll-out in those two locations, Waymo is actively mapping Los Angeles to study congestion and expanding its testing in Miami, as well as highways in Florida between Orlando, Tampa, Fort Myers, and Miami. It's also conducting pilots in Death Valley, California; El Paso, Dallas, and Houston in Texas; and various cities in Michigan, Arizona, Georgia, and Ohio, as well as along Interstates 10, 20, and 45.

The Waymo One app verifies a rider's pickup and drop-off locations and gives them an estimated arrival. The app is available for iOS and Android.

The company is trying to manage demand so riders would never be forced to wait more than a few minutes. Occasionally, a blue-and-green "W" may appear on the map to indicate a more accessible pickup or drop-off location. That means riders may be prompted to walk a little bit, so Waymo's vehicles have an easier time locating them. Much like Uber or Lyft, Waymo One riders can rate the quality of their trip on a scale of one to five stars. They can also elaborate on what made the ride great by selecting from a list of canned responses like "route choice," "driving," and "car condition." A support function allows riders to get an immediate phone call from a Waymo representative or engage in an in-app chat with them. This is meant to better prepare riders for when the cars arrive without a trained driver in them. Waymo says it is continuing to experiment with pricing, but it will be using fares that are based on the time and distance of the trip's route.

Waymo has recently started letting its riders plan for stops along the way, so they can pick up food or cleaning, or do some shopping. The ARS vehicle will park nearby for longer stops and then come back to pick up the rider. Unlike taxis, the meter isn't running during these stops since there is no driver worried about time.

Waymo Overall Strategy Assessment

Waymo is the leader in autonomous ride services and the first to market. It has done more development and testing than any other competitor. It has made the largest investment in AVs. Most importantly, it has already deployed its ARS to paying customers in vehicles without a safety driver. It has a factory to retrofit AVs, and it has a commitment to purchase 80,000 vehicles for that factory.

Waymo has an aggressive roll-out strategy that could see it providing ARS in several metropolitan areas by late 2023. I forecast that Waymo could have 100,000 ARS vehicles by late 2023 or early 2024, and potentially 250,000, which would be more than $35 billion in revenue by 2025 or 2026. These assumptions give Waymo a potential value of $150-$300 billion later in 2022 based on proving the feasibility and 2023 projected revenue. By 2024, based on a revenue projection of $35 billion for 2025, it could be valued at $350-$700 billion as an independent business.

The 100,000-vehicle level is already feasible for Waymo. Its AV technology is proven and in service. It has the ride request and dispatch service, Waymo One, for the offering. It has purchase commitments for 80,000 additional vehicles to be retrofitted and has a factory set up to do this. Finally, it has already opened one large metropolitan market in the Phoenix area and is opening several others. I expect that Waymo, as the leader in the market, could have as much as half of the market share in the next few years.

The vulnerability of this strategy, as previously stated, is that the delay in launching its ARS has given competitors an advantage of bringing custom-designed second-generation ARS AVs to market before Waymo. Second-generation ARS AVs may provide these competitors with some significant cost and attractiveness advantages. The recent leadership change at Waymo, whether related or not to this, is also a sign of some setbacks in its launch.

Cruise

Cruise is second behind Waymo in autonomous ride services and also has an aggressive strategy. GM (GM) originally acquired Cruise Automation for more than $1 billion in May 2016. Since then, GM has built its autonomous vehicle efforts, mainly its autonomous ride services, around Cruise. It spun off the company for its ARS business (GM Cruise LLC) in 2018 as an autonomous ride services business with the investment of $2.25 billion by SoftBank. By May of 2021, Cruise raised approximately $8 billion in investments. Its latest investment of $2.75 billion came January-April 2021from Microsoft, institutional investors, and $750 million from Walmart at the tail end of the round. Walmart's investment followed five months of a pilot program in Scottsdale. The estimated valuation of Cruise is $30 billion following these investments. Cruise disclosed that it had $2.3 billion in cash at the end of 2019, most likely much more than that by the middle of 2021, and that it spends about $1 billion per year with 1,750 employees. In June 2021, Cruise secured a $5 billion line of credit from GM's financing business to fund the purchase of Origin autonomous vehicles. In the middle of 2021, Cruise began to build 100 of its second-generation Origin AVs for validation testing. It has a permit from California to remove its backup drivers from its autonomous vehicles.

Most likely, GM will spin off Cruise as an independent company. There are rumors that in 2021 it was in early discussions with investment banks about strategic options. These options include a public offering of shares, listing a separate tracking stock to reflect its value, or spinning off the unit to shareholders.

In March 2021, Cruise acquired Voyage, an autonomous vehicle startup that spun out of Udacity, illustrating the consolidation in this industry. The majority of Voyage's 60-person team moved over to Cruise, and the company's co-founder and CEO Oliver Cameron has a new role as vice president of product. Voyage, which was founded in 2017, was a relatively small startup compared to other well-funded operations. The company was best known for its autonomous operations in two senior-living communities. Voyage tested and gave rides to people within a 4,000-resident retirement community in San Jose, California, and The Villages, a 40-square-mile, 125,000-resident retirement city in Florida. It wasn't clear if Cruise would focus more attention on providing ARS to retirement communities or just acquiring the technology and people. The Cruise Origin vehicle would work well in retirement communities.

Cruise Autonomous Ride Services

Cruise Automation is second behind Waymo, as it plans to launch its ARS service in San Francisco. To support that growth, Cruise is building a large vehicle charging station in San Francisco's Dogpatch neighborhood. It is also expanding its public outreach efforts. Cruise took out a full-page ad in the San Francisco Chronicle and is "expanding and deepening partnerships with the city, first responders and other organizations that matter to San Franciscans, such as MADD and the Coalition for Clean Air."

Cruise has a test fleet of specially designed all-electric GM cars, modified with lidar sensors, cameras, and radar logging thousands of miles every day, all with a safety driver ready to take control of the car if a complex or dangerous situation arises. In 2019, it had 228 AVs that drove 831,000 miles. In 2020, its San Francisco fleet drove 730,000 miles. Over the last five years, Cruise has driven more than 2 million autonomous miles in San Francisco. Each week it claims to experience: 8,500 unprotected left turns, 3,200 cut-ins by other drivers, and 3,000 complex double-parked vehicles.

Its ridesharing app, called Cruise Anywhere, enables riders to request a ride from its ARS vehicles. It is also developing an ARS dispatch platform to manage a fleet of AVs in each metropolitan area. The ARS dispatch platform will send AVs to pick up passengers and then direct the vehicles to the next location. It will also monitor the status of each AV, respond to passenger requests, and even take control of the AV if needed.

Cruise ARS Autonomous Vehicles

Cruise developed multiple iterations of an autonomous first-generation ARS vehicle. Based on the Chevrolet Bolt EV, it is a dedicated self-driving, pure electric sedan, and some versions have no steering wheel or pedals. This is the primary vehicle used to develop and test its autonomous driving in San Francisco. Most likely, Cruise was initially planning to launch Cruise Anywhere with this fleet of first-generation vehicles but changed its plans once launch delays enabled it to use a second-generation autonomous vehicle.

So, Cruise shifted its focus to a second-generation AV, the Origin, explicitly designed for ARS. This is a boxy six-passenger ride-sharing van. The all-electric Origin looks similar to an autonomous shuttle, but it doesn't have any manual controls that would allow a human to take control, such as pedals or a steering wheel. GM has sought clearance from federal safety regulators for self-driving cars that do not have conventional controls, such as a steering wheel.

A box shape is the most efficient design for as much interior space as possible for passengers and cargo. The Origin will operate mostly in the city and on airport runs, so the design can be inviting to passengers rather than sleek for an owner.

The Origin has two big sliding doors that open from the center like a tram, creating an opening that's three times the size of a conventional door, and the low load floor makes it easier to get in and out, even with luggage or packages. The doors are fully automated with sensors that tell them when to open and close. They can also be opened manually or through an app. Sensors in the side panels also know if there is ever any contact, for example, a bump from a cyclist pedaling by.

Origin was designed by Cruise, GM, and Honda, which is a minority owner in Cruise. GM has confirmed it will start building the Origin at its Detroit-Hamtramck plant in early 2023. Cruise is working on a cargo-hauling version of the Origin as well, something more like a van than a shuttle. The delivery version of the Origin is expected to appear at the same time.

Cruise ARS Roll-Out Plans

Cruise will launch its ARS first in San Francisco. In addition to San Francisco, Cruise is also testing in Milford, Michigan, with approximately 40 AVs using the test team as riders and in-vehicle safety operators. And like Waymo, it is also testing in the Phoenix metropolitan area with 12 AVs using employee riders and in-vehicle safety drivers. Cruise is expected to continue testing its ARS in San Francisco with a commercial launch in 2022. In 2023, it plans to introduce tens of thousands of Origin autonomous vehicles in San Francisco and other cities. The $5 billion in financing it received to fund the costs of these AVs will pay for the approximately 100,000 ARS vehicles, depending on the final costs.

It has aggressive plans to roll out its ARS, Cruise Anywhere, across the U.S. Its engineering VP responded to the following question: "How many self-driving vehicles will you have on the road in five years?" He replied that "This race is about getting us into tens of cities with hundreds of thousands of vehicles. We're definitely [going] after launching this on a large scale." That implies multiple vast fleets of ARS vehicles by 2025, making Cruise one of the leading competitors in ARS.

Cruise also has plans to expand outside of the U.S. It has an agreement with Dubai to provide ARS starting in early 2023. Cruise has an exclusive arrangement with Dubai until 2029. The agreement is expected to provide only a 4,000-vehicle fleet, but these would make 25% of the trips in Dubai autonomous. Honda will collaborate with Cruise and General Motors on autonomous vehicles for its autonomous vehicle mobility service business in Japan. Cruise will be sending the first of its autonomous test vehicles to Japan for testing in 2021. Honda aims to launch its autonomous ride services business using the Cruise Origin. Honda Mobility Solutions Co., Ltd., established in February 2020, will be the operator of this service.

Cruise Overall Assessment

As an incumbent car manufacturer, GM faces the unique challenge of dealing with a decline in retail sales of cars. It expects ARS to drain transportation miles from private car ownership and reduce sales. However, instead of just downsizing, GM has chosen a more aggressive strategy to transform itself, at least in part, into an autonomous ride services company. This makes its ARS strategy critical.

So far, GM's progress appears to be sound. It has reallocated resources to developing AVs and created a separate company for the ARS business. Although it is behind Waymo, it is making good progress on testing its ARS AVs in San Francisco, even though that city may not be the easiest for initial success. With a population of almost 900,000 people, and many more working there, San Francisco could be a large initial ARS market for Cruise. It will then follow this up by rapidly launching its Cruise Anywhere service to other cities over the next few years.

Ford Autonomous Vehicles LLC

Argo/Ford

Ford intends to launch its ARS sometime in 2022. This is a little bit later than Waymo and GM, but still early enough to gain significant market share, if executed properly. Like GM, in July 2018, Ford created a subsidiary, Ford Autonomous Vehicles LLC, to launch its ride services. Its intent is that the new business will develop a better strategy and business model because it will have less concern about Ford's legacy business. The new organization is charged with accelerating its AV business to capitalize on market opportunities. Ford Autonomous Vehicles LLC includes: (1) Ford's self-driving systems integration, (2) autonomous vehicle research and advanced engineering, and (3) AV transportation-as-a-service (ARS) network development, user experience, business strategy. and business development teams. It also holds Ford's investment in Argo AI.

Ford originally invested $1 billion to acquire a majority share of Argo AI. In its second-quarter 2020 financial results, Ford announced a gain of $3.5 billion from selling part of its ownership in Argo to the VW Group. With this sale, Ford and VW each owned 40% of Argo, and Argo was valued at approximately $7.5 billion. Ford said Volkswagen would join in its investment in Argo AI to improve "cost and capital efficiencies." Ford and Volkswagen plan to spend more than $4 billion through 2023 to develop autonomous ride services. In 2021, Argo had more than 1,300 employees and was testing more than 150 prototype autonomous vehicles. Most likely, Ford just didn't have enough cash to invest in developing an ARS business on its own, so it needed VW as a partner. In addition, this partnership may give Argo AI a foothold in Europe as Volkswagen's Autonomous Intelligent Driving Group became part of Argo.

Ford made it clear that its initial strategy for AVs is focused on ARS and autonomous home delivery:

Our self-driving vehicles won't initially be sold to customers in the way that cars are today. You'll be able to experience these vehicles through multiple means, including commercial fleets in mobility services such as ride-hailing and goods delivery. We believe we can offer the best value to our customers by providing the technology through a fleet service, similar to the way Ford currently offers specially-engineered vehicles for taxi and police fleets.

Just like GM Cruise, Ford's Autonomous Vehicle LLC is structured to take on third-party investment, and it will hold Ford's ownership stake in Argo AI. Additional development and testing will probably cost $3-$5 billion or more and building the first 100,000 autonomous ARS vehicles will cost as much as $7-$10 billion. Ford doesn't have these financial resources of its own.

There is also a possibility that Ford, and VW may spin-off Ford Autonomous Vehicles LLC or Argo AI. Argo disclosed its intention to raise additional financing privately in 2021 and go public by the end of 2022. Argo AI needs to work out the details with both automakers, and it's not currently clear if it will choose to do a traditional IPO or merge with a SPAC.

Ford AV LLC hasn't demonstrated much yet on how it plans to have riders request ARS and dispatch vehicles. The applications may be still under development, or possibly it may be intending to partner with a ridesharing company like Lyft.

Argo AI/Ford Technology and Vehicles

Like Waymo, Ford AV LLC intends to launch its ARS using a first-generation AV, a retrofitted version of the Ford Escape Hybrid crossover, when it launches its ARS commercial business in 2022. This is the fourth version of self-driving test vehicle developed in partnership with Argo AI. The new vehicles will be used with its current fleet of roughly 100 autonomous test vehicles that are based on the Fusion Hybrid sedan, which the company is no longer producing. The  newest ARS vehicles include "launch-intent" technologies that are needed to support the commercialization of its ARS.

The new autonomous vehicle features the latest advancements in sensing and computing technology. It upgraded the sensing suite with more advanced lidar, higher resolution cameras, and more capable radar sensors. The all-new long-range lidar with the higher resolution has 128-beam sensing to help provide a 360-degree field of view. It added new near-field cameras and short-range lidar that provide surrounding views. Powering these sensors, as well as the state-of-the-art computing systems, is the increased electrification capability of the Escape Hybrid. The AV has hidden forced-air cleaning chambers that surround the camera lenses and lidar sensors to ensure their field of view is clear while providing 360-degree cleaning coverage.

Ford's AV will use lidar as a primary sensor. Four years ago, Argo AI acquired lidar company Princeton Lightwave, which developed lidar technology to help it deliver autonomous vehicles that can operate commercially on highways and in dense urban areas. The lidar sensor was developed to be cost-effective and manufactured at scale. It claims the lidar sensor can see 400 meters away with high-resolution photorealistic quality and the ability to detect dark and distant objects with low reflectivity. While Waymo had developed its own lidar sensors with long-range capabilities, it was not available for other developers to buy. Initially, Ford planned on using lidar from Velodyne, but when it developed its own version, it canceled that relationship and sold its 7.6% stake in Velodyne.

Ford continues to plan on using hybrid AVs for its ARS. It doesn't see vehicle cost as very important in the ARS market. It believes, correctly I think, that revenue per mile is most critical, which is why it believes a hybrid is best because it won't be out of service as long charging its battery. There are some estimates that Ford plans to build 100,000 ARS autonomous vehicles, starting in 2022. It will also use these vehicles for its ARS and autonomous home delivery businesses.

Argo ARS Roll-Out Plan

Ford plans to launch its ARS in Austin, Miami, and Washington, DC. In addition to these three primary areas, it also tests AVs in Detroit, Palo Alto, and Pittsburgh. In Miami, it plans to establish a command center that will serve as the epicenter of its self-driving business and daily operations. The command center is estimated be 140,000-square-feet of mixed-used space west of Miami International Airport. It will include customer relations, public engagement, business development, research, safety evaluations, and testing. It has been testing its AVs in Miami since 2018.

Argo also has a partnership with Lyft. Argo and Ford plan to launch at least 1,000 self-driving vehicles on Lyft's ride-hailing network in several cities, starting with Miami and Austin. According to Lyft, the first Ford AVs, equipped with Argo's autonomous vehicle technology, are expected in Miami by the end of 2021. It plans to launch the service in Austin in 2022. Additional U.S. cities will follow in 2023 and beyond.

Lyft will also provide access to driving data from its entire network in exchange for a 2.5% stake in Argo AI. This agreement increased Argo's valuation to $12.4 billion. Lyft captures information such as hard-braking events and collisions. Argo will use safety information about human drivers and trip movements in a city.

In Austin, Ford and Argo have begun mapping the downtown and east Austin with manually driven vehicles. It will gradually increase the size of the coverage area, as well as its fleet of self-driving cars, with a view towards launching its ARS there in 2022. It purchased property near Austin-Bergstrom International Airport to serve as a command center for its ARS fleet and is leasing space in east Austin that will function as a terminal for the fleet.

Ford initially planned to launch its ARS business in 2021 but delayed it until 2022, citing delays due to the coronavirus pandemic.

Overall Assessment

It's clear that Argo AI, Ford Autonomous Vehicles LLC, and Ford are committed to ARS and autonomous home delivery as their primary AV strategy. This makes a lot of sense. The concern is how it will be able to execute that strategy. It is behind Waymo, and a little behind Cruise in its execution. Its original strategy was to provide autonomous vehicles to companies providing ARS, but most likely changed as major players in the industry wanted to have control over the customers and the largest share of the revenue.

There are a few risks to its strategy. Its use of a first-generation AV, and a hybrid at that, may be short-lived as it may need to provide a second-generation electric vehicle in the next few years. While it has been testing its ARS and autonomous delivery services, it's not clear that it has a proven ride request and scheduling app, so it may need to use a partner. Finally, its corporate structure with Ford, VW Group, Ford Autonomous Vehicles LLS, and Argo AI may be too complex and slow it from executing quickly.

Its plan to enter the market in 2022 is still appropriate, but any setback could delay them from being sufficiently competitive. However, it could choose to enter markets not yet occupied by competition, and its choice of test markets supports this possibility.

Motional (Aptiv and Hyundai) and Lyft

Motional is a joint venture between Aptiv and Hyundai formed in 2020. It has a broad and aggressive partnership with Lyft to deploy its ARS to multiple cities by 2023. If you look back at Figure 7-1 on ARS Industry Structure, you can see how this partnership fits together. Lyft is providing the ride request and dispatch services. Aptiv is providing the autonomous driving technology, and

Hyundai is providing base vehicles. There are no disclosures yet on how the revenue from ARS trips will be distributed, and this could determine which of the three businesses will be most successful. Of the three, however, Aptiv has the defining autonomous driving technology.

Aptiv, Delphi at the time, originally purchased NuTonomy for its autonomous driving technology in October 2017 for $450 million. Last September, Hyundai invested $2 billion to create this 50/50 joint venture, which valued Motional at $4 billion. It has approximately 1,000 employees.

By February 2020, Motional, working with Lyft, provided more than 100,000 autonomous rides (with a safety driver) to 3,400 destinations in Las Vegas. Nevada granted permission for Motional to remove the safety driver from its AVs.

Hyundai will provide the vehicle platform for the Motional ARS AVs. It has deep pockets for developing autonomous technology because it receives financial support from the government of South Korea to develop autonomous technology.

Lyft was also developing its own autonomous driving technology, but it was well behind others and didn't have sufficient financial resources to bring its own ARS vehicles to market. In April 2021, Lyft sold its self-driving division to Toyota Motor Corp. for $550 million. Toyota had previously invested $500 million in Uber's autonomous driving business and is now partnering with Aurora after it acquired Uber's self-driving business.

Motional Autonomous Technology and Vehicles

The Hyundai IONIQ 5 will be the vehicle platform for Motional's new ARS. It is an all-electric, midsize crossover utility vehicle designed for a passenger experience. With a unique and luxurious living space and a sleek, modern exterior, Motional and Lyft claim riders will experience their fully autonomous rides in comfort and style. Built on Hyundai's dedicated battery electric vehicle (BEV) platform, the IONIQ 5 is expected to deliver innovation in both mobility and sustainability.

This isn't the Hyundai IONIQ 5 consumer model. Motional's IONIQ 5 will be equipped with Level 4 autonomous driving capabilities, and it will be the first ARS AV under the Motional name. It is the product of collaboration between Hyundai's manufacturing and design teams and Motional's auton-

omy, robotics, and software teams. Motional's first IONIQ 5 vehicles are already training for their fully-driverless future.

The IONIQ 5s are being fully integrated with Motional's driverless system. This integration is critical for the transformation of the IONIQ 5 into an ARS vehicle. Motional's autonomy experts are adding technology that will allow the AV to see and respond faster and more safely than a human. Lidar, radar, and cameras sense a full 360 degrees around the AV, seeing up to 300 meters away, and enable Motional's driverless system to see, understand, and react to dynamic driving environments.

Motional's IONIQ 5 ARS AVs will then be put through many months of rigorous testing, racking up real-world experience, and navigating challenging and unpredictable road scenarios. This is conducted across simulation, closed courses, and public roads.

The IONIQ 5 is Motional's fifth platform, and the second to go driverless on public roads. The IONIQ 5 benefits from the experience of previous testing on 1.5 million miles of diverse road environments and hundreds of thousands of hours of testing and assessment.

Motional ARS Roll-Out Plans

Motional and Lyft have operated what they claim is the world's longest-standing commercial autonomous ride service in Las Vegas. This has been a public, revenue-generating, autonomous fleet, gaining experience in integrating autonomous cars and ride-sharing networks, operating a commercial autonomous ride service at scale, and building consumer trust in self-driving cars. The service has now delivered well over 100,000 rides, with 98 percent of passengers reportedly awarding their rides a five-star rating.

Motional and Lyft plan to launch autonomous ride services in major U.S. cities beginning in 2023. There is no insight on how fast it will roll out to multiple cities beyond Las Vegas. While it remains unclear where Motional and Lyft will expand their autonomous ride service, Motional has teams in several municipal markets, including Boston, Pittsburgh, and Santa Monica, CA.

Motional – Overall Assessment

Motional, along with Lyft, appears to be preparing for an aggressive rollout, not just incremental expansion. The objective to launch autonomous ride services in multiple cities beginning in 2023 appears ambitious, although this depends on how many cities and how fast. The autonomous technology has been well-proven in Las Vegas.

Motional's fleets will use Motional's autonomous driving capabilities, the Hyundai IONIQ 5, and Lyft's ride request and dispatch capabilities. The partners claim they are joining forces to create "a clear, scalable path to market for robotaxis." Each of the partners is providing a valuable layer of ARS, and this could prove to be very successful.

Aurora/Uber

For years, Aurora was developing self-driving technology but struggled to figure out a successful business model. Initially, its plan was to supply self-driving software and sensors to auto manufacturers. The company had a partnership with Volkswagen that was supposed to lead to Aurora's technology being incorporated into Volkswagen's vehicles, but the two companies parted ways in 2019, putting Aurora at risk.

In 2019, Aurora pivoted to long-haul trucking as the first application for its self-driving technology. That now appears to be a successful strategy, and it will be discussed later in this book. In December 2020, Aurora seized on an opportunity to get back into the ARS business by purchasing Uber's struggling self-driving technology division and selling a large ownership share to Uber. However, autonomous trucking is still Aurora's primary strategy. It plans to launch its autonomous trucking service in 2023 prior to autonomous ride services in 2024.

After spending several billion dollars trying to develop its own autonomous driving technology, Uber finally gave up. It wasn't very successful, had a very serious accident, and needed a lot more capital to complete development. Its autonomous vehicle development was done in its Advanced Technology Group (ATG) subsidiary, which was valued at $7.25 billion following a $1 billion in investments from Toyota, DENSO, and SoftBank's Vision Fund. Uber held approximately 86% ownership of ATG. It "sold" ATG to Aurora along with a $400 million investment for 26% ownership of

Aurora. Aurora raised more than $1 billion of funding, including investments from Amazon and Hyundai. In July 2021, Aurora announced that it was going public through a SPAC, raising almost $2 billion at an equity value of $13 billion.

It appears that Uber will provide the ride request and dispatch layer of the ARS platform for Aurora and that Uber will use Aurora for its ARS vehicles. However, it isn't clear that the partnership is exclusive to either party. Uber will have some advantages in competing in the ARS market. It has a very large customer base, a recognized brand name, and a popular app. It's not entirely clear that it has significant enough customer loyalty to withstand competition in the new ARS market.

Uber intends to follow a hybrid strategy, using both autonomous ride services and driver-based ridesharing in the same markets. The location of some trips and some driving conditions may limit ARS. In those cases, Uber can offer other alternatives that pure ARS competitors won't be able to offer. Uber can include ARS (Uber AV) in its menu of services with UberX, UberXL, and UberSelect. This will enable riders to see if ARS is available for their trip and compare prices.

However, like previous companies making similar transitions, it will have legacy issues. It will have a hybrid business with two very different business models. This is always a challenge. I expect that Uber drivers will fight the introduction of ARS by Uber since their livelihood is at risk. They may not want to take the "leftover" trips after Uber ARS takes all the easier and more profitable trips.

However, its autonomous technology is behind, and it has the lingering shadow of a highly-publicized fatal accident. Uber recognizes this risk, as it stated in its IPO:

If we fail to develop and successfully commercialize autonomous vehicle technologies or fail to develop such technologies before our competitors, or if such technologies fail to perform as expected, are inferior to those of our competitors, or are perceived as less safe than those of our competitors or non-autonomous vehicles, our financial performance and prospects would be adversely impacted.

Aurora Technology and Vehicles

Aurora has developed a complete set of technologies for autonomous driving. Like others, it's developing its own lidar system. In January 2021, it acquired OURS Technology, the second lidar startup it has acquired in less than two years. Aurora acquired Blackmore, a Montana-based lidar startup, in May 2019. OURS adds expertise in developing lidar chips.

The first model that will be equipped with the Aurora Driver (its hardware, software, and sensor suite) is the Toyota Sienna minivan. Testing of an initial fleet is scheduled to begin in late 2021 or early 2022. Toyota was also an investor in Uber Technologies Inc. and therefore is an investor now in Aurora. Aurora stated that: "By the end of 2021, we expect to have designed, built, and begun testing an initial fleet of Siennas near our areas of development." Toyota Motor Corp. and its supplier Denso Corp. aim to mass-produce autonomous vehicles and launch them on ARS networks, including Uber's, over the next few years.

According to its presentation, Aurora plans to provide its autonomous technology to external fleet owners/operators as a driver-as-a-service model. It will provide the aurora Driver hardware and software, maintain these systems, and provide teleassist. The fleet will be owned and operated by a by a third party. In its financial plan it intends to charge $0.30 to $0.50 per mile.

Besides putting Aurora's technology in Toyota vehicles, the partnership also includes a comprehensive services solution for financing, insurance, maintenance, and more. These are some of the other elements of the ARS platform.

Aurora/Uber Rollout Plans

Aurora projects launching its autonomous ride service in 2024. Its forecasts are conservative. It projects only about 1 million miles and $1 million of revenue in 2024, and this increases to 249 million miles and $137 million in revenue by 2027. Its projections for autonomous trucking are much more aggressive.

Aurora – Overall Assessment

Aurora has been developing significant autonomous driving technology that it expects to apply to multiple markets. Before the acquisition of Uber's Advanced Technology Group, it had shifted its focus to long-haul trucking. That may continue to be its initial focus, but with the addition of Uber's technical team and influence from Uber as a major shareholder, it may give ARS a higher priority. The partnership between Aurora and Uber does not appear to be exclusive, but it has significant advantages for both.

Uber's installed base provides an important competitive advantage. A ride can use the trusted Uber app to request an Uber ARS trip. If one isn't available, then a traditional Uber trip will substitute. For Uber, the decision will be how fast it wants to cannibalize its unprofitable ridesharing business with new ARS technology.

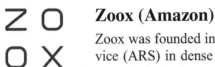

Zoox (Amazon)

Zoox was founded in 2014 to provide mobility-as-a-service (ARS) in dense urban environments. It is building autonomous, symmetrical, bidirectional, battery-electric vehicles for ARS riders, not drivers. The company raised nearly $1 billion in its first few years, but its founder was unexpectedly replaced in 2018, and the company struggled to raise sufficient money to continue to fund development.

In July 2020, Amazon confirmed it was purchasing Zoox and declared its intentions to become a competitor in autonomous ride services. The significance of this strategic move cannot be underestimated. It positions Amazon to become a significant competitor in what will be an enormous market opportunity, providing it with another strategic expansion, following AWS, beyond its online retail business.

Some reactions to this acquisition erroneously concluded that the acquisition of Zoox was intended to procure technology for autonomous delivery. It's not. Amazon made its intentions clear. Amazon said the deal would help bring Zoox's "vision of autonomous ride-hailing to reality," and Zoox will continue to operate as a standalone business within Amazon. Autonomous package delivery isn't practical for the foreseeable future because someone needs to drop off the package since most people are not at home to come out and get delivery from an autonomous vehicle. Autonomous home delivery of groceries from Amazon is a potential secondary use, however.

It is rumored that Amazon paid $1.2 billion for Zoox, which is almost as much as Zoox had already invested in developing its autonomous vehicles. Amazon has very deep pockets and will need to invest several billion dollars more to bring an ARS vehicle to market. So, the expected investment is much greater. Zoox had almost 1,000 employees prior to being acquired.

Zoox has a unique strategy for autonomous driving, one that has proven to be more expensive than others but also has some exciting potential. Most of the early competitors in autonomous ride services, such as Waymo, focused on developing an autonomous driving platform of sensors, software, and computing. They retrofit this technology platform to existing commercial vehicles to create the first generation of autonomous ride services vehicles. Retrofitting existing vehicles makes sense early in the market because it lowers the cost of development and introduction. Following the initial success of autonomous ride services, competitors will develop second-generation vehicles designed exclusively for autonomous driving without the need for human controls. Zoox's strategy, similar to Cruise, is to skip first-generation autonomous vehicles and develop second-generation vehicles purpose-built for autonomous ride services. This bold strategy is also more expensive and takes more time. In addition to developing and testing autonomous driving and building autonomous ridesharing services, it also needs to design and build unique vehicles. This strategy proved to be its downfall because it simply could not raise the amount of capital required. That's why it needed to be acquired, and Amazon was the best fit because it has deep pockets.

Zoox had previously raised almost $1 billion with a reported market valuation of approximately $3 billion in its last round, yet it sold to Amazon for $1.2 billion. This gets back to the problem that Zoox's bold strategy was just too expensive. Most likely, it would need another $1 - $2 billion to complete its autonomous technology and second-generation vehicle. It then would need as much as $8 - $10 billion to contract to build its initial fleet of 100,000 autonomous vehicles, although debt financing would most likely be available for that.

Zoox Autonomous Vehicle

Zoox is developing a unique autonomous ride services vehicle, which I refer to as a second-generation vehicle, without any driver controls and the capability to drive multi-directionally. It drives backward just as it does forward because sensors are all around. This is expected to be an excellent autonomous ride services vehicle, but it may take another couple of years to complete development, so I don't see it as a competitor in the ARS market until 2023.

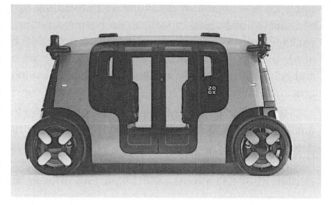

Zoox is the first in the industry to showcase a driving, purpose-built ARS vehicle capable of operating up to 75 miles per hour. Since its inception in 2014, Zoox has combined artificial intelligence, robotics, vehicle design, and sustainable energy to bring its vision of reinventing personal transportation to life — claiming to make the future safer, cleaner, and more enjoyable for everyone.

Designed and manufactured in the U.S., Zoox is the only vehicle to offer bidirectional driving capabilities and four-wheel steering, which enables maneuvering through compact spaces and changing directions without the need to reverse. At 3.63m long, the vehicle has one of the smallest footprints in the automotive industry. The vehicle features a four-seat, face-to-face symmetrical seating configuration that eliminates the steering wheel and bench

170

seating seen in conventional car designs. The vehicle also features a 133-kWh battery, allowing it to operate for up to 16 continuous hours on a single charge. Designed for everyday urban mobility, the vehicle is powered by a NVIDIA computer.

But whereas Cruise can rely on GM to supply its fleet and Waymo is buying tens of thousands of vehicles from automotive partners that it modifies for its fleet, Zoox is keeping vehicle production in-house. Zoox claims its manufacturing factory is capable of producing 10,000 to 15,000 vehicles annually. It receives drive units, body, battery pack, and other essential components from the suppliers.

Zoox ARS Rollout

Zoox has been testing its autonomous driving technology in first-generation test vehicles (retrofitted Toyota SUVs) in Las Vegas and San Francisco. According to reports filed with the state of California, Zoox drove approximately 67,000 autonomous miles in the state in 2019, which was more than many, but it was much less than the leaders.

Zoox plans to initiate its operations first in San Francisco and Las Vegas. The California Department of Motor Vehicles, in September 2020, issued a permit to Zoox, Inc., authorizing the company to test driverless vehicles on public roads within a designated part of Foster City (San Mateo County). While Zoox has had state authority to test autonomous vehicles with safety drivers since 2016, the new permit allows the company to test two autonomous vehicles without a driver behind the wheel on specified streets near its Foster City headquarters. The vehicles are approved to operate in fair weather conditions (light rain/fog) on streets with a speed limit of no more than 45 mph.

Apple

 Apple is the wildcard in the ARS market. It has not yet declared any intention to enter the market, but it is investing heavily in autonomous vehicle technology, and the ARS market is the one that makes primary sense for Apple. Apple has the technological skills, the strategic acumen, and the financial resources to be a strong competitor in ARS.

Rumors in early 2021 that Apple planned to introduce an autonomous electric vehicle caused a lot of excitement. Most people speculated and wondered why Apple would go into the business of building and selling cars. They are missing the major strategic point that autonomous vehicles will redefine the transportation market and create new market opportunities different from selling cars. It's unlikely that Apple will enter the retail market for autonomous EVs. Most likely, Apple will enter the ARS market with third-generation autonomous vehicles explicitly designed to provide passengers with an exceptional autonomous ride experience.

Apple CEO Tim Cook indicated an interest in ARS when he said specifically that he thinks the "intersection of electric vehicles, autonomous vehicles, and ridesharing was an interesting place to be." He intentionally included ridesharing in this statement. This intersection is autonomous ride services.

Apple has been secretive about its plans for autonomous vehicles. Still, it provided several clear indications that it has been investing billions of dollars in autonomous driving technology (Project Titan) for many years. Although it hasn't disclosed its intentions (and never does), legal filings in 2019 indicated that it had 2,700 core employees involved in this project. It also revealed testing in California and filed for more than 100 patents on autonomous driving. Most likely, it has invested more than a few billion dollars in this technology.

Reuters wrote that based on people it talked with that Apple would release an Apple Car in 2024. Others have speculated on a sooner time frame. Apple's general strategy is to enter new markets later with a superior product, and I expect this to be the case here too. For Apple, there is a difference in keeping an autonomous vehicle secret from what it does for other products. An autonomous vehicle needs testing on public roads, so it's difficult to keep it completely under wraps. Most likely, it will need to disclose its intentions in advance of release.

Apple is always secretive about its product development strategy, but in June of 2017, Apple CEO Tim Cook spoke publicly about Apple's work on autonomous driving software, confirming the company's work. "We're focusing on autonomous systems. It's a core technology that we view as very important. We sort of see it (referring to autonomous vehicles) as the mother of all AI projects. It's probably one of the most difficult AI projects actually to work on." "There is a major disruption looming there," Cook later said on Bloomberg Television, citing self-driving technology, electric vehicles, and ride-hailing. "You've got, kind of three vectors of change generally happening in the same time frame." In the interview, Cook was hesitant to disclose whether Apple will ultimately manufacture its own car. "We'll see where it takes us," Cook said. "We're not saying from a product point of view what we will do."

Apple's AV Technology

Because of its penchant for secrecy, Apple's efforts on developing an AV and the extent of its investment must be inferred from rumors and other evidence.

By 2014, Apple reportedly was working on "Project Titan," with upwards of 1,000 employees developing an electric AV at a secret location near its Cupertino headquarters. A few years later, Apple refocused the project under new leadership, laying off hundreds of employees who were working on the project. Apple reportedly transitioned to building an autonomous driving system rather than a full car.

Apple has been very aggressive in hiring technical talent and executives from the auto industry, including Tesla. Several rumors included details suggesting Apple employees were working on the project at a top-secret location in the Bay Area. Apple is also rumored to be operating a secret vehicle research and development lab in Berlin, with people from the German automotive industry, all with backgrounds in engineering, software, and hardware.

In early 2017, Apple was granted a permit from the California DMV to test AVS on public roads using Lexus RX450h SUVs. In the spring of 2018, Apple increased the number of authorized test vehicles in California to 62, along with 83 permitted AV drivers. The California DMV reported that Apple did more than 80,000 miles of testing with its AVs in 2018, third behind Waymo and Cruise. Apple is continuing to increase the number of AV test drivers in California. According to 2019 data from the California DMV, Apple reduced the number of test miles driven but had 70 AVs and 143 certified drivers. It had a similar number of vehicles and miles tested in 2020.

Perhaps the most convincing indication came at the end of 2018 when the FBI arrested a Chinese national accused of stealing Apple's Project Titan trade secrets. Jizhong Chen was arrested prior to flying to China after another Apple employee caught him photographing Apple-classified information. What's important about this arrest is the disclosure around it provides insight into the degree of Apple's investment in AV technology. They found over two thousand files containing confidential and proprietary Apple material on his computer, including manuals, schematics, and diagrams. According to the complaint Apple filed, about 5,000 Apple employees were "disclosed on the Project," and of those employees, 2,700 were designated as "core employees" on the project, giving them access to certain databases. The term disclosed refers to people working on or knowledgeable of the company's efforts in autonomous driving and related technology.

Another strong indication of Apple's investment in autonomous vehicles can be seen in its patent filings. Apple has filed more than 100 patents for autonomous vehicle technologies and has been increasing its rate of filings. Patently Apple tracks these filings, and some of these are very interesting:[vi]

- Guidance of autonomous vehicles using intent signals where a passenger could use something like an iPhone to identify a particular stopping point in the vicinity of a destination.

- A sensor system for gestures of a traffic director to be interpreted and understood by an autonomous vehicle as commands to perform maneuvers related to the traffic diversion, including stopping, slowing, or turning onto a detour route.

- A system for improving the detectability of road signs and vehicles on the road in low-visibility conditions like fog or snow with a plurality of retroreflectors.

- A remote driving control that can be engaged based on the determination, via processing vehicle sensor data, of a health emergency associated with one or more occupants of the vehicle, and the remote-control system can generate remote driving commands which cause the vehicle to be navigated to a particular location without requiring the occupant associated with the health emergency to manually navigate the vehicle.

- A system for communicating actions of an autonomous vehicle to the public, such as in a crosswalk or vehicles behind them.

- A stability control system that may be implemented in vehicles that are operated in autonomous and semi-autonomous modes, and in which a vehicle motion control system uses environment sensors to determine a desired path and a desired vehicle response over that path.

- Doors with adaptive positioning where a vehicle may have left and right front doors for allowing passengers in the front of the vehicle to enter and exit and left and right rear doors for allowing passengers in the rear of the vehicle to enter and exit.

- An augmented reality device to provide next-generation navigation for maps that could be built into future vehicles or an AR device that could be a pair of smart glasses or an iPhone sitting on the vehicle's dashboard.

- A battery in an electric vehicle that can be charged by transferring power wirelessly from a charging pad located on the ground and a corresponding wireless power receiver mounted to the underside of a vehicle.

- An extensible power bumper that is able to crush longitudinally in response to the application of force in a longitudinal direction.

- A system for a car in autonomous mode to effectively communicate its intentions to both the driver and passengers.

- A seating system for vehicles that controls occupant motion, reducing or removing the effects of vibration and discordant stimuli to improve the overall comfort of vehicle occupants.

- A wide range of new systems that include an optical fiber illumination system, how headlight and tail lights will house cameras that's a part of a Vehicle Navigation System, and a nighttime sensing system that's 3X the power of traditional headlights.

- A highly advanced and secured vehicle entry system.

- A system for allowing users to make payments at drive-in services without ever pulling out a credit card or even use Apple Pay in the manner used today.

- A system to allow users to call up their vehicle in a parking lot and have it come to them.

- A system for taking a single function safety belt and turning it into a device that can control various aspects of the vehicle by using gestures on the belt.

Based on the significant increase in R&D investment and the rumor of more than 1,000 engineers, Apple has most likely invested several billion dollars in autonomous driving, and it is probably investing more than half a billion annually.

Overall Assessment

I don't have any inside information on Apple's intentions in this market, but I think there is enough evidence and strategic logic to deduce its potential strategy. While Apple hasn't confirmed its intention to create an autonomous vehicle, I believe that Apple realizes that this market opportunity is too big to ignore. Moreover, there have been sufficient hints contained in information in the public domain to conclude that Apple is investing billions of dollars in AV technology. Apple's autonomous vehicle strategy can be deduced by understanding what it does well and what it tends to avoid.

It's unlikely that Apple would enter the AV retail market or sell directly to end customers. It is just too difficult to build a sales, distribution, and service organization. Instead, it will enter the ARS market. Apple has a significant advantage by being able to automatically download an Apple ARS app to hundreds of millions of iPhones in the U.S. and letting customers use their existing iTunes account for charges. It also has the capital to finance a new ARS business.

I expect that Apple will bring to market a unique and exciting autonomous vehicle based on a proprietary autonomous-driving platform. Apple will design a third-generation ARS vehicle with a passenger-entertainment-focused interior. It will create a proprietary platform of sensors, computing, and software. Eventually, it will subcontract vehicle manufacturing, just as it does today with its iPhones and iPads. Apple will also leverage its video and music resources to provide entertainment in its ARS vehicles. Passengers will automatically have access to all their purchased and streaming Apple content

175

Apple has some competitive advantages in entering the ARS market. It has excellent skills in designing new user-friendly products, and an autonomous ride service vehicle is the ultimate new technology product. It has a broad base of software development technology, and a huge software development staff. It can make the Apple ARS app a standard iPhone app, immediately available to hundreds of millions of customers. Finally, ARS will require enormous capital investment, and Apple has plenty of cash to finance this.

Tesla Network

Tesla Network

No discussion of this type is complete without including Tesla. In 2019, Elon Musk claimed that by 2020, owners of Tesla cars could provide their vehicles for autonomous rides through the Tesla Network and make $30,000 per year. Didn't happen. Not going to happen.

I don't see Tesla as a viable competitor in the ARS market. Questions about its autonomous driving technology aside (and there are serious concerns), Tesla's focus is on retail sales of electric vehicles with a high level of automation. A fleet of autonomous vehicles for ride services is a very different business that it probably won't enter. I say this even though I have a Tesla lease that requires me to return my car (which I love) at the end of the lease to be used its Tesla Network.

The Tesla Network planned to be a fleet of Tesla AVs for ARS. Tesla owners would be able to add their cars to a shared fleet to make money from their cars. "The fundamental utility of your vehicle will increase by a factor of 5," Musk told an audience during Tesla's Investor Autonomy Day early in 2019. Then, during an investor call in May, he said that self-driving would "give Tesla a $500 billion-dollar market cap with vehicles worth up to $250,000 in the next few years thanks to their robotaxi capabilities. Each car will be capable of doing about 100 hours of self-driving hours of work per week to their owners' benefit." Musk's even more astounding prediction was that Tesla's Full Self-Driving chip and real-time development data being fed by current vehicles on the road would lead to some 1 million robotaxi-capable Tesla cars by 2020.

A slide from Musk's presentation promotes the potential value to Tesla owners. Elon Musk estimated that these cars would have a value of $200,000 because of the expected revenue and projected profit of $30,000 per year for a model 3. His estimate is based on assumptions of a gross profit of $0.65 per mile and 90,000 miles per year. And of course, this assumes that these cars will become autonomous.

The service would allow Tesla owners to include their vehicles in a network that will resemble a hybrid of car-sharing and ride-hailing. As with Uber and Lyft, owners who include their vehicles in the network will be able to make money from rides and set restrictions over who can use their vehicles. When an owner needs the vehicle for personal use, it could be recalled from the network. Tesla also planned to add a fleet of company-owned cars to the network. Its current lease program prohibits customers from buying the vehicle at the end of their lease term, so that the company can add these 3-year-old vehicles to its fleet.

Overall Assessment

I doubt the success, or even the launch, of the Tesla Network for several reasons, and I own a Tesla (or rather I lease a Tesla). ARS will be based on managed fleets, as previously explained in this chapter, and a "fleet" of thousands of individually-owned AVs spread throughout the country won't work. Also, it's doubtful that Tesla owners will want to send their cars away during times when they need them.

All this is moot, however, if Tesla vehicles can't become fully autonomous. I love driving my Tesla, but I don't think it will become fully autonomous. Its camera-based system will not work as well as lidar, and it doesn't use detailed HD maps that other AVs use to guide them in geofenced areas. Finally, as envisioned, Tesla Networks will require fully-autonomous, not just sufficiently-autonomous, vehicles. They won't be restricted to geofenced areas and will be directed to go anyplace, even road systems they can't handle.

Projected Size and Timing of ARS Market

There is always a lot of interest in the projected timing of the ARS market. When will it start, how big will it be, and how fast will it develop? Here are two estimates to consider. The first is based on ARK Invest projections, and the second is my projections based on the economic models previously described.

ARK Invest ARS Projections

ARK is an investment company that does extensive research on emerging technologies and has a series of funds that invest in companies developing these technologies. One area of research is mobility as a service and autonomous ride-hailing, which I define as Autonomous Ride Services (ARS). ARK has made some interesting and bold projections for this market.

Figure 7-7 shows its forecast for autonomous ride-hailing operating income in 2025 and 2030. It breaks down the forecast for each of three levels of ARS: the ARS platform provider, auto manufacturers building the ARS vehicles, and the fleet owners. It projects operating income for the global ARS market of approximately $235 billion in 2025 and more than $1.5 trillion in 2030. This is operating income, so revenue would be approximately twice that much or more.

ARK assumes a price per mile of $1.00, compared to $1.85 for ridesharing. It estimates that the 2021 global ridesharing market generates roughly $150 billion in revenue. For autonomous ride-hailing, it estimates expansion of this market to $6-7 trillion by 2030, because of the lower price point. It believes that autonomous ride-hailing will undercut the cost of human-driven ride-hailing by roughly 90% in the U.S. and 50% in China. As a result of all of this, ARK forecasts that the enterprise value for autonomous platform operators could scale to $3.8 trillion by 2025.

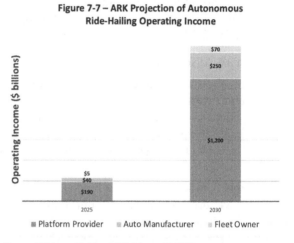

Figure 7-7 – ARK Projection of Autonomous Ride-Hailing Operating Income

Source: ARK Invest Big Ideas 2021, January 26, 2021

My ARS Projections

COVID-19 caused some delays in the roll-out of ARS, and I have shifted some of my earlier projections. Most ARS companies suspended testing on public roads for the remainder of 2020 once the pandemic started, and many project development teams were forced to work from home, slowing progress. Even more importantly, the demand for ridesharing, which ARS is replacing, dropped precipitously, as most people worked from home, stopped traveling, and activities such as eating out and entertainment were suspended. In all, this probably set back the launch of ARS by approximately a year, but it did give the companies more time to refine their autonomous driving technology. I don't think this will shift the market out a year in later years because it looks like market growth may increase even faster after a few years.

The ARS market will grow geometrically. It will grow when more companies enter the market. As was described in the previous section of this chapter, 5-6 major companies will enter the market over the next few years. Each of these will launch its ARS service in its first metropolitan area and

178

then rapidly increase the number of ARS vehicles to grow that metropolitan area. Subsequently, each company will then expand into new metropolitan areas, most likely adding multiple ones as it gets more experience: open one first, then two others, then the next four, etc. So simultaneously, growth will come from more competitors, an increasing number of vehicles within a metropolitan area, and extension into new metropolitan areas. And for the next five years or so, the market won't even need to expand to the more challenging areas of the country.

There are also significant motivations for rapid growth. The development and capital investment in ARS are extremely large, and companies will need to gain access to more capital, most likely by going public after proving the technology and business model. There are even specific incentives, such as the reported incentive Cruise has for an additional $1.3 billion investment from one of its investors when it deploys commercially.

Figure 7-8 summarizes the projected growth of the ARS market. It measures the growth of the ARS market by the number of ARS autonomous vehicles on the vertical axis. It also identifies the expected go-to-market plans for the significant competitors that will drive market growth. As previously discussed, Waymo has already launched its ARS in Scottsdale, initiating paid autonomous rides in late 2020. It will continue to increase the number of autonomous vehicles providing these rides. In 2022 and continuing into 2023, it will greatly expand in the greater Phoenix area to cover Scottsdale, Mesa, Glendale, and Phoenix. This metropolitan area alone serves 4.6 million people over 14,000 square miles and has the capacity to support more than 10,000 ARS vehicles over that time frame. In 2023 and the following years, Waymo will expand by adding Fleets in Mountain View, Southern Florida, Austin, Kirkland, Los Angeles, and other cities.

GM Cruise will launch its ARS in San Francisco in 2022, possibly a little earlier. Cruise and Waymo have applied for permits needed to start charging for rides and delivery using autonomous vehicles in San Francisco. It will also launch in at least one other city by 2023. Cruise's current test fleet is comprised of hundreds of custom Chevrolet Bolt EVs equipped with driverless technology. It plans to launch operations by expanding that fleet, but it really starts to scale up is when the Cruise Origin begins production in 2023. The Origin is the company's first vehicle specifically designed to operate without a driver. It doesn't have manual controls such as pedals or a steering wheel. By 2023, Cruise may have more than 20,000 Origins in its ARS fleet.

Argo is expected to launch its ARS in Austin by 2022 and then rapidly expand the size of its fleet there. Austin provides a significant market opportunity. Argo is then expected to add fleets in Miami and Washington DC by 2023.

179

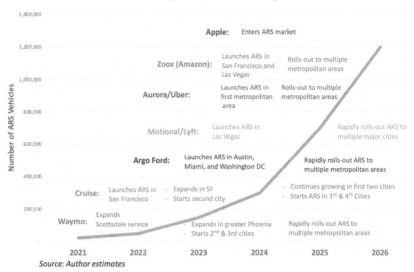

Figure 7 -8 – Estimated Growth in ARS Market As More Companies Enter and Expand-

Source: Author estimates

Motional/Lyft are focusing on Las Vegas as their initial market and have already provided more than 100,000 autonomous rides there. It has stated that it intends a rapid roll-out of fleets to multiple major cities soon following that. So, it could add two more cities in 2023 and more in the following years.

Aurora/Uber and Zoox (Amazon) probably won't launch their ARS fleets until later in 2023 or early 2024. By that time, the first four competitors will be aggressively expanding their fleets, so they will need to catch up quickly to be competitive. By the end of 2024, more than 500,000 ARS vehicles from these six competitors will be active in 20 or more major metropolitan markets.

I expect Apple to enter the market as the last major competitor in 2024. It will have a second-generation ARS vehicle that most likely will be superior to the others. It will enter a market already developed by competitors and try to attract customers that want the superior Apple experience.

By 2026, The ARS market will grow to approximately 1.2 million vehicles in the U.S. That is still a very small share of the total number of vehicles in the country but a very large market size of more than $150 billion. These estimates are not as aggressive as ARK's. ARK considers a big impact from the Tesla Network, which these estimates don't incorporate.

180

Chapter 8
Autonomous Long-Haul Trucking

Autonomous long-haul trucking will be another early market for autonomous driving. It has unique characteristics favorable to autonomous driving and significant benefits. A half-dozen companies are investing billions to capture a share of this new market, and many are following different strategies. Several companies plan to start providing autonomous trucking by 2024.

In this chapter, we will look at the long-haul trucking market, the benefits of autonomous trucking for this market, and the different approaches to autonomous trucking. Following this, we will then explore the expected company strategies for this market.

Long-Haul Trucking Market

The global truck freight market is massive – approximately $4 trillion in annual revenue. In the U.S., the truck freight market is roughly $800 billion, 80% of the total freight market. The truck freight market can be divided into long-haul (middle-mile) and short-haul (last-mile), even though these are now frequently served by the same trucks. Long-haul trucking in the U.S. is approximately $670 billion of that $800 billion market involving about 2.5 million trucks. The long-haul trucking market in China will also be an early target for autonomous trucking. It is approximately a $530 billion market with 6 million trucks. Both markets represent a significant opportunity for autonomous driving.

The long-haul trucking industry has some unique characteristics. To start with, it is highly fragmented. The U.S. Department of Transportation estimates that 500,000 trucking carriers are operating Class-8 trucks. 95% of them operate fewer than 20 semi-trucks, and the top-10 represent less than 10% of the total market. In large part, this is due to the labor-intensive nature of this industry. Labor (truck drivers) is the highest cost at approximately 42%-46% of the total cost and increasing significantly. Autonomous trucking will most likely drive significant consolidation of this industry as it changes from labor-intensive to capital/technology-intensive.

Here are some other facts about long-haul trucking. Trucks for hire provide about 55% of the shipping, and captive fleet owners do 45%. Truck freight can be full truckload or less than truckload (LTL). In long-haul trucking, a semi-truck pulls various types of trailers that contain freight. The focus here is solely on semi-trucks, not trailers. The EPA classifies Class 8 trucks as weighing more than 33,000 pounds. A semi-truck's total cost is approximately $100,000 to $160,000, translating to 15%-20% of the operating cost.

As mentioned, labor is the highest cost, and on top of that, there is a shortage of drivers. The American Trucking Association found that the Class 8 semi-truck shortage tripled from 2005 to approximately 60,000 drivers, and it is forecasted to almost triple by 2028. So, besides significant cost savings, autonomous technologies may also be the answer to an industry struggling to meet demand.

Autonomous trucking will go through a progression of levels like other autonomous vehicles: semi-autonomous, sufficiently-autonomous, and fully-autonomous. However, there are some differences in these classifications for autonomous trucking. Semi-autonomous mode still requires a driver behind the wheel, but it enables the driver to let the autonomous system do much of the driving. There are two modes of sufficiently-autonomous trucking. The first still has a driver on board, but the driver will be able to rest and sleep while the tuck is driving itself. The second doesn't have a driver on board, and the autonomous truck drives itself to and from a depot located near a highway. With fully-autonomous trucking, the truck would drive by itself to and from any loading dock.

Benefits of Autonomous Long-Haul Trucking

Autonomous long-haul trucking has such significant benefits that it is likely to be introduced early and expand quickly. Increased safety is the primary benefit to society, which will also be reflected in reduced insurance costs for carriers. Eliminating the cost of drivers is the primary cost savings, but there are also others like fuel savings and improved truck utilization. Carriers utilizing autonomous trucks will be able to charge 30%-40% lower freight costs, make deliveries up to 40% faster, and utilize their fleets 25% more. Together these will provide insurmountable competitive advantages. Let's look more closely at these benefits.

Increased Safety

On average, there are more than 3,000 fatal accidents and more than 75,000 accidents with major injures annually involving large trucks. Additionally, on average, there are over 275,000 property-damage-only crashes per year involving heavy trucks. Tucking accidents, like all accidents, are caused primarily by human error.

Truck accidents are more likely to result in death or serious injury than a collision between two passenger cars. A "big rig" tractor-trailer or semi-truck can weigh more than 30,000 pounds, and an accident with the average passenger vehicle that weighs only around 4,000 pounds can be disastrous. Truck accidents are usually caused by driver error, either by the truck driver or the driver of another vehicle. These are the most common causes of truck accidents:

1. **Driver Fatigue** - Driving a truck is a high-pressure, high-stress job. Often, trucking companies will require drivers to deliver goods within a short time. That means they're driving long distances with few breaks and little rest. Sometimes, it requires several days on the road, and the drivers have too few hours of sleep (and even less quality sleep). As a  result, they lose concentration and coordination, are slower to react to dangerous road situations, or fall asleep while driving. There are laws and regulations requiring how many hours a trucker can drive in one shift, how much sleep is required, and when rest breaks must be taken. However, driver fatigue remains a big problem. Autonomous trucks won't get tired.

2. **Distracted Driving** - Distracted driving is an increasing problem for all types of driving. Driving long distances can be incredibly dull. That boredom might lead a trucker to risk texting, looking at their phone to find a podcast or playlist, eating, or doing something else to stay occupied. The National Safety Council reports that cell phone use while driving leads to 1.6 million crashes each year. Nearly 390,000 injuries occur each year from accidents caused by texting while driving. 1 out of every 4 car accidents in the United States is caused by texting and driving. Autonomous trucks are not going to be distracted.

3. **Alcohol and Drugs** - Unfortunately, truck drivers have a high rate of alcohol and drug abuse. Some truckers use amphetamines and cocaine to stimulate themselves to stay awake while driving. One study

showed that 30% of truck drivers admitted to taking amphetamines on the job. A reported 20% used marijuana, and 3% used cocaine. These drugs keep the drivers awake unnaturally, but they also induce them to take more risks like faster driving, unsafe lane changes, and using risky maneuvers in bad weather. Trucking employers are legally mandated to test all drivers before allowing them to operate a commercial vehicle. They also must administer random drug tests to 10% or more of the company's average number of drivers each year. An average of 4,700 truck drivers failed these tests every month in 2020 and early 2021. Autonomous trucks won't have alcohol or drug issues.

4. **Speeding and Overtaking** - When you drive on any highway for a while, you will notice some trucks speeding excessively and changing lanes frequently. Excessive speed and frequent lane changes can cause accidents. There are several reasons underlying this. Truck drivers may be anxious to get to their destination or next stop. Sometimes they want to make up for lost time because of delays. Or maybe they just want to drive more aggressively. A driver might go faster than what's appropriate for a vehicle that size, or maybe faster than is suitable for the road conditions. Autonomous trucks will obey all speed limits and drive carefully.

Fewer accidents, injuries, and fatalities will be a benefit for society. For individual trucking companies, lower accident rates will be reflected in much lower insurance premiums. Insurance premiums have been escalating recently, causing some trucking companies to go out of business.

Cost Savings

Labor is the most significant cost in long-haul trucking, approximately 42%-47% of the total cost per mile. This typically equates, on average, to roughly $0.94 per mile on revenue of $1.98 per mile. To put this into perspective, operating profit is only about $0.16 per mile. Autonomous trucks will eventually reduce most of the labor cost by eliminating drivers. In addition to the significant labor cost reduction, autonomous trucks should reduce fuel costs through more efficient driving by using optimal cruising speeds.

Reducing overall costs by more than 40% will upend the industry and most likely cause the consolidation of this relatively fragmented industry. Traditional high labor cost trucking companies will no longer be competitive and will eventually be phased out by more efficient autonomous trucking fleets.

Capital Utilization

Expensive long-haul semi-trucks now sit idle much of the time as drivers need to rest and take legally mandated breaks. For every 11 hours of driving, a truck driver must take an 8-hour break. Autonomous trucks won't need to sit idle for those breaks. This could increase the utilization of each semi-truck by as much as 40%, which will significantly reduce capital investment and increase utilization. Faster delivery times of up to 30% are a very significant related benefit.

The cost of an autonomous semi-truck will be higher than a traditional one, but the additional cost for the autonomous technology will decrease over time. Plus.ai estimates that the cost of the sensors and computing needed for autonomous trucking was $100,000 in 2019 for early prototypes, but this has been reduced to $9,000 in 2021 and projected to drop to $7,000 in 2023. Cleary these additional costs are offset by higher truck utilization.

Driver Shortage

There is currently a driver shortage, which is expected to worsen with the anticipated increase in shipping. According to the American Trucking Association (ATA), in 2018, the trucking industry was short 60,800 drivers, up nearly 20% from 2017's figure of 50,700. Over the next decade, the trucking industry will need to hire approximately 1.1 million new drivers or an average of nearly 110,000 per year. Replacing retiring truck drivers will be the most prominent factor, accounting for over half of new driver hires (54%). The second-largest factor will be industry growth, accounting for 25% of new driver hires. If current trends hold, the shortage could swell to over 160,000 by 2028. This would likely cause severe supply-chain disruptions resulting in significant shipping delays, higher inventory carrying costs, and perhaps shortages at stores.

There are several reasons for the driver shortage, including demographics such as a higher percentage of older drivers retiring and only about 6% of truck drivers are female. Many drivers are on the road for extended periods before returning home, typically a week or two. Therefore, it is not a career but a lifestyle that does not fit everyone's desires or needs. Some also claim that drug testing requirements limit the number of drivers.

Autonomous trucking will eliminate this shortage. Since autonomous trucking will first replace the need for additional drivers, for the time being, it will have a limited impact on current truck drivers. For most of the next decade, current truck drivers will be able to keep their jobs.

Overall Competitive Impact

Why will autonomous long-haul trucking become widespread? A shipper choosing to use autonomous trucking will pay as much as 40% less and have their goods delivered as much as a third faster. These advantages are enough to force a transition to autonomous long-haul trucking. Shorter distance trucking and delivery are very different markets that won't have the same benefits.

Different Approaches to Autonomous Trucking

Like other forms of autonomous driving, autonomous trucking, there will be several different approaches to autonomous trucking based on different levels of autonomy.

Semi-Autonomous Trucks

Semi-autonomous trucking, like semi-autonomous driving, enables the truck to drive itself on highways, while the truck driver is still behind the wheel. In this mode, benefits will be limited to more efficient fuel use since the driver is still in the truck. However, there may be significant safety benefits from a reduction in accidents. Truck drivers must deal with the dangers of the monotony of full days behind the wheel staring at pavement. Autonomous systems don't get bored or mind if the landscape doesn't change, hour after hour.

The challenge of more autonomous driving is pairing the long stretches of nothing with the short bursts of activity: driving through a major city, navigating a construction zone, dealing with bad weather. Semi-autonomous trucking addresses this. Drivers stay in control as usual until they hit the highway. At that point, semi-autonomous driving would be activated.

Sufficiently-Autonomous with a Driver On-Board

In this sufficiently-autonomous version, the truck driver remains in the truck but can be classified as off-duty or in a sleeping berth when the truck is driving autonomously on the highway. When needed, the truck driver will take control of the truck, although not immediately. These situations include where a detour is required, driving to/from the loading dock, off-highway driving, refueling, etc. The truck will need to alert the truck driver in sufficient time to take control. In this mode,  it's expected that the driver would take control of the truck in 20-30 minutes, not in a few seconds. The truck may need to pull over until the driver takes control.

This method will provide a significant portion of the benefits by making deliveries faster without the need to stop the truck for driver-rest periods, significantly increase truck utilization, and reduce shipping costs. Let's take a typical 2,600-mile trip that requires 55 hours of driving. With four required 8-hour breaks and time for bathroom and food stops, the total delivery time would be approximately four days (96 hours). A sufficiently-autonomous truck could make the same trip in less than 60 hours, assuming refueling stops, and that is almost 40% less time. Delivery time is critical in long-haul shipments, and 2½ days is a significant competitive advantage over four days. Another considerable advantage is truck utilization. With shorter delivery times, an autonomous truck fleet could be 40% smaller and make the same deliveries.

The Federal Motor Carrier Safety Administration (FMCSA) publishes the rules that limit the maximum amount of time truck drivers can work and drive before taking a required break. The Hours of Service (HOS) rules identify a truck driver's time in four categories:

- Off-Duty –Time when a truck driver is free from any work-related responsibility.

- Sleeper Berth – Time spent physically in the sleeping compartment of a commercial truck for sleep and rest.

- Driving – All time spent at the driving controls of a commercial motor vehicle in operation.

- On Duty–Not Driving – All time from the time a driver begins to work or is required to be in readiness to work until the time the driver is relieved from work and all responsibilities for performing work.

"Driving" and "On Duty–Not Driving" time combine to determine the total hours a truck driver can work. Truck drivers must log their time, activity, and location in a logbook. In its simplest form, the FMCSA mandates:

- Once reporting on duty, truck drivers can drive/work a maximum 14-hour shift before they are required to go off duty or into the sleeper berth for 10 hours.

- During that 14-hour shift, truck drivers can drive a maximum of 11 hours.

- Truck drivers may not drive once they reach 60 hours of work/driving in 7 days, or 70 hours in 8 days.

Modifying the FMCSA regulations, which are currently being considered, will be required to achieve these advantages. They will need to permit a truck driver onboard an autonomous truck, but not driving, to count these hours as off-duty, or add another category that doesn't count fully against driving time.

Sufficiently-Autonomous with a Transfer Hub

In this sufficiently-autonomous version, transfer hubs near major highways will be used to initiate and complete autonomous truck driving. For example, a trailer could be loaded and driven to a transfer hub near a highway by a traditional semi-truck. Then the trailer would be connected to an autonomous semi-truck to drive autonomously to the destination transfer hub. Refueling or recharging would be done using designated locations on the way with either automated charging or human assistance. There are variations of this model.

The transfer hub model requires a new transfer hub infrastructure, but several companies are already working on this.

Fully-Autonomous Trucking

With fully autonomous trucking, an autonomous truck can drive itself from a loading dock, through city streets, and on and off the highway. No driver will be needed in the truck at any time other than for maintenance and testing. Like the previous mode, refueling or recharging would be done at a designated location on the way with either automated charging or human assistance.

The benefits of fully-autonomous driving are the complete elimination of truck drivers and the costs associated with them. This will ultimately emerge but will take much longer. Given the significant benefits of sufficiently-autonomous trucking, fully-autonomous trucking may not be worth the extra cost for small incremental benefits for some time.

Platooning

Some trucking industry experts see the potential to utilize platooning systems to achieve more efficiency in freight hauling. One autonomous truck can lead a platoon with two or more trucks following close behind, taking advantage of the aerodynamic efficiency.

While truck platooning has some potential benefits, I don't see these as significant as the other cost-reduction opportunities in long-haul trucking. I also anticipate pushback from passenger-car drivers who may be intimidated by long platoons of trucks speeding down highways. In 2019, Daimler said that it would stop working on platooning. While having trucks electronically linked to reduce drag made sense on paper and worked in the lab, in the real world, platooning never lived up to the efficiency hype. If the following truck had lost the link with the truck in front of it, it took more fuel to catch up to the leader truck.

Autonomous Trucking Technology

Autonomous trucking has unique challenges. Long-haul trucks are much larger than passenger vehicles. They are 75% wider, five times longer, and 20 times heavier. This increases their stopping distance by 65%, so they need to see further ahead and react faster. They also require more time and space to make turns.

Sensor systems on autonomous trucks need to see further ahead, up to 1,000 meters. These systems will also require more cameras and lidar, and these need to be placed differently around the truck than on a passenger vehicle. For example, Waymo increased the number of sensors on its autonomous trucks. Their trucks use two perception domes versus the single one on its passenger cars. The dual perception domes help increase rear visibility by reducing blind spots caused by the trailer. Increased and faster computing capacity may also be required for autonomous trucking.

On the software side, autonomous trucks won't need the same level of complexity, at least initially. Autonomous trucks will be driven primarily on highways that are relatively straight lines. Since most freight is carried on a small number of highways, early autonomous trucking will only focus on mapping these few highways.

Autonomous Trucking Company Strategies

More than a half-dozen companies are currently working on autonomous trucking. Some of these are traditional truck manufacturers, and others are startups. One of the most notable, Uber/Otto, has already failed and closed.

Several self-driving technology firms have announced partnerships with major truck manufacturers to co-develop autonomous trucks in North America and other markets, primarily China. In general, these partnerships focus on closely integrating self-driving sensors and software with vehicle platforms at the factory level while introducing new components that developers deem necessary to enable driverless operation safely. These are the most prominent partnerships.

- TuSimple is teaming with Navistar to produce purpose-built autonomous trucks, which the companies aim to build starting in 2024. U.S. Xpress has placed a reservation for "a couple thousand" of those vehicles to supplement its existing fleet. TuSimple has a similar agreement in place with the Traton Group to develop self-driving trucks in Europe, including plans for an autonomous hub-to-hub route in Sweden using Scania brand trucks.

- Daimler Trucks North America and Waymo are partnering to develop a Freightliner Cascadia model piloted by the Waymo Driver. Daimler also is actively developing Level 4 trucks with its subsidiary Torc Robotics, another autonomous vehicle pioneer. Waymo also announced that it would be the exclusive global L4 partner for Volvo Car Group, including its strategic affiliates Polestar and Lynk & Co. International.

- Aurora has partnerships with Paccar Inc. and Volvo Group. Paccar said it intends to deploy Kenworth T680 and Peterbilt Model 579 trucks utilizing the Aurora Driver by 2024. Volvo Autonomous Solutions also is working with Aurora to develop on-highway autonomous trucks, starting with hub-to-hub applications in North America.

- Embark has taken a different approach than some of its competitors by designing its autonomous platform to be compatible with trucks produced by all four of North America's foremost original equipment manufacturers.

The U.S. Southwest has become the premier area for testing autonomous trucking in North America and arguably the world. Although many of the companies developing this technology are based in Silicon Valley, they conduct much of their testing and development work on interstate highways in Arizona, New Mexico, and Texas. In addition to ideal weather conditions and geography, there is also a favorable regulatory and political environment that makes those states conducive for Level 4 truck testing and eventual deployment.

The region also encompasses major truck lanes, including freight flowing from the Southern California ports to other locations across the country. Like other developers, Waymo sees autonomous trucking eventually generalizing across the United States and globally, but the company's "beachhead" has been the U.S. Southwest. TuSimple's fleet of about 50 trucks currently operates on interstate routes connecting cities in Arizona and Texas. Still, the company has outlined plans to expand its network across major shipping lanes throughout the country in the next few years. Aurora's initial deployments will be in the Texas Triangle, a central freight hub connecting Dallas, Houston, and San Antonio.

It's interesting to look at how these autonomous trucking companies are developing their technologies and approaching the market differently.

TuSimple

TuSimple was founded in San Diego in 2015 to develop autonomous driving technology. It has more than 800 employees in Beijing, San Diego, and Tucson developing an advanced autonomous driving system specifically designed to meet the unique demands of heavy-duty trucks.

It has attracted significant capital investment. The company raised $215 million in 2019, bringing its capital raised to $298 million and its valuation to more than $1 billion. In April 2021, TuSimple completed an IPO, raising $1.35 billion on a valuation of about $8 billion.

Starting in 2019, it performed multiple autonomous, revenue-generating trips daily (with safety drivers on board) for over a dozen customers covering four different routes in Arizona. In June 2019, it expanded the size of its U.S. fleet from 11 to 50 trucks. The company has a contract from USPS to complete trips between Arizona and Dallas distribution centers. It is also working with UPS to conduct daily testing between Phoenix and Tucson. The freight flowing along those shipping corridors accounts for 60% of the U.S. total economic activity, and TuSimple expects it to become a central route for its autonomous vehicles in the years ahead.

TuSimple's Class 8 semi-trucks can carry loads exceeding 33,000 pounds and are Level 4 under SAE guidelines, meaning they are capable of full autonomy in controlled (geofenced) highways and local streets. Unlike most other autonomous platforms, TuSimple is camera-based. It uses an eight-camera array and other sensors to detect cars, pedestrians, and other obstacles up to 1,000 meters away.

TuSimple says its approach enables it to achieve three-centimeter precision for truck positioning even in inclement weather and at night, and that it allows for plenty of leeway in real-time decision-making. It also claims better efficiency than its competitors. By keeping aware of traffic flow far ahead, TuSimple asserts that its trucks can maintain a given speed more consistently than human drivers, cutting fuel consumption by as much as 15%.

TuSimple has a unique strategy. It is not just offering autonomous technology; it's providing a complete solution with its Autonomous Freight Network (AFN), including autonomous freight capacity as a service. AFN provides services to freight companies that purchase its autonomous semi-trucks, and it also plans to offer the use of autonomous trucks as a service.

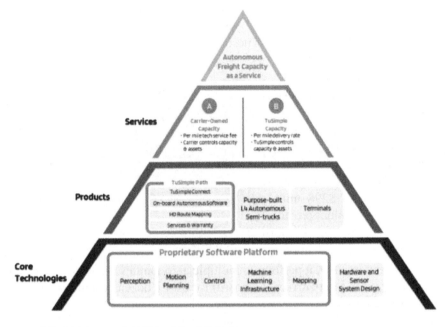

TuSimple's Autonomous Freight Network. Source: TuSimple

Its AFN platform combines three layers: core autonomous technology, products, and service offerings. The core autonomous technology, comprised of its proprietary autonomous software platform and custom sensor system, forms the defining technology of its AFN. Typical of autonomous driving software, its proprietary software includes perception, motion planning, control, machine learning, and mapping. The sensors for autonomous trucking are different from typical autonomous driving because they need to see further ahead to stop a heavy truck at high speeds safely.

These core technologies are the building blocks for its purpose-built L4 autonomous semi-trucks and TuSimple Path, its primary user products. TuSimple Path is a service that includes TuSimple Connect, onboard autonomous software, HD route mapping, and services/warranty. This service enables a customer to continuously update its software, including updates to the HD route mapping.

TuSimple connect provides continuous oversight that monitors a customer's fleet. Continuous monitoring is essential for early autonomous vehicles, including trucks. Without a driver onboard, there is no human to coordinate activities or notify someone if there is a problem. Continuous monitoring is also necessary for autonomous ride services. This service also enables TuSimple to improve driving efficiency by making route changes based on real-time route data.

Another element of TuSimple's strategy is to provide autonomous driving from terminal to terminal, where the terminals are conveniently located just off major highways. This limits the complexity of autonomous software while achieving most benefits. As part of its strategy, TuSimple is building many of these terminals. Its strategic terminal network is the third element of its product offering, providing a valuable and accessible infrastructure.

Notably, combining its core technologies and product platform layers enables two different service models: Carrier-Owned Capacity and TuSimple Capacity. With the Carrier-Owned model, customers acquire an autonomous truck from TuSimple and its partners, and they operate it themselves, but they pay a per-mile service fee for a TuSimple Path subscription. TuSimple estimates a service fee of $0.35 per mile for TuSimple Path. This includes its onboard software with updates, TuSimple Connect to monitor each autonomous truck, and continuously updated HD maps. This can be a valuable and necessary service, providing a cost reduction of $0.40-$0.50 per mile for customers. TuSimple appears to be trying to split the cost-benefit equally with its customers.

TuSimple has a partnership with Navistar to manufacture its trucks under the International and IC brands. It also collaborates with TRATON to develop purpose-built L4 autonomous semi-trucks for the European and Chinese markets. TuSimple claims to have 5,700 reservations for new autonomous semi-trucks, although these are cancellable, and many are from its investors.

TuSimple Capacity is its second service offering. It provides autonomous freight capacity as a service, so customers don't need to purchase autonomous trucks. Customers pay per mile as they do now from third-party freight companies. TuSimple plans on providing this freight service at approximately a 15% lower cost than traditional rates today. It intends to finance its autonomous delivery fleet through third parties.

Overall, TuSimple has an excellent strategy for entering the autonomous trucking market. Like others, it focuses on terminal-to-terminal autonomous trucking, but it is building out its proprietary terminals to make this work easier. TuSimple Path is a valuable service offering that will be necessary for its early customers. Finally, TuSimple Capacity provides an excellent early market strategy. Potential customers can test autonomous trucking before making a commitment, and they can also use this service for additional capacity as they ramp up autonomous trucking. TuSimple plans to launch its autonomous trucking by 2024.

Plus.ai

Based in Silicon Valley, Plus.ai was founded in 2016 by a group of Stanford Ph.D. classmates who saw the potential of artificial intelligence. With trucking being the primary means of shipping in America, the founders decided to focus on autonomous technology to transform the trillion-dollar commercial trucking industry. Plus went public in the summer of 2021 through the SPAC, HCIC, raising almost $500 million at a valuation of $3.3 billion.

Plus.ai specializes in developing full-stack self-driving technology to enable large-scale autonomous commercial fleets. It was the first to obtain California's Autonomous Testing License. The company has since been working on improving the robustness and safety of its fully functional Level-4 autonomous trucks.

Plus.ai collaborates with the largest OEMs to build self-driving trucks that are safer than human-operated vehicles. The company operates a fleet of autonomous trucks in pilot programs with some leading freight shipping companies.

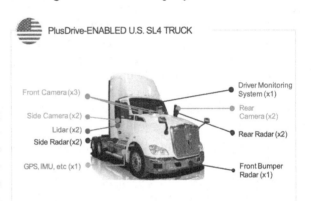

It will launch its autonomous software on Class 8 trucks in the U.S. and China, progressing to complete Level 4 operation.

The Plus autonomous driving system includes 360-degree sensing and ultra-long-range stereo 3D vision with 8X range and 100X resolution. It addresses adverse weather conditions, as well as long-range camera drift problems due to vibration. Its autonomous software includes tractor and trailer dynamic models, fuel efficiency optimization, online dynamic calibration, and other essential functions.

The Plus strategy is to progressively introduce different levels of autonomous driving with three different versions.

- **PlusDrive (SL4)** provides semi-autonomous driving with the driver able to do hands and feet off driving on highways. The autonomous system will be retrofit into existing trucks in the U.S., with initial version available in 2021. Fuel savings are the primary benefit since there will still be a driver in the truck. Plus.ai estimates fuel savings between 10%-20%, and it forecasts selling more than 300 semi-trucks of this version in 2021.

- **PlusDrive Navigate (SL4)** will expand functionality to drive autonomously from ramp-to-ramp, plus highway driving, but it will still be semi-autonomous. It will start installing this semi-autonomous system with OEMs in the U.S. and China. This version is expected to be available in 2022 and 2023, and Plus plans to sell more than 20,000 of these semi-trucks, almost equally between China and the U.S.

- **PlusDrive Full Autonomy (L4)** is the sufficiently-autonomous version that will eliminate the need for a truck driver. It will be capable of driving from hub to hub but not on all roadways. This will provide the full cost-benefit of autonomous trucking. Plus.ai plans to make this version available in 2024, and it forecasts selling more than 56,000 semi-trucks in 2024, about 60% in China, for revenue of more than $100 million.

Plus.ai will upgrade its technology as it progresses through these versions. The PlusDrive will use the Nvidia Xavier 30-TOPS (trillion operations per second) computers, which will be upgraded to the Nvidia Orin-X 254-TOPS system in the Navigate version. The Full Autonomy version will use the Nvidia Quad Orin-X 508-TOPS computer. It will also upgrade its radar from 5 to 7 and then add 4D radar for the Full Autonomy version. Similarly, it will increase the number of lidar sensors from 1 to 5 and introduce HD maps in the full Autonomy version.

The Plus strategy appears to be sound. It will start developing the market with a semi-autonomous version because there are some perceived benefits from fuel savings. Its joint venture with FAW, one of the largest truck OEMs, will help achieve production capacity. Simultaneously introducing its trucks in China and the U.S. may be challenging but will open more market opportunities. However, its forecasts may be a little optimistic.

Embark Trucks

San Francisco-based Embark was founded in 2016. Embark changed its initial strategy and decided in early 2020 to pursue a different approach to OEM integration. Trucking OEMs traditionally build semi-trucks with key components sourced from multiple suppliers, including engines, transmissions, and braking systems, in response to carrier demand. By developing a solid technology platform that can be rapidly integrated on all major OEM trucks, Embark will provide OEMs with autonomous technology that is most responsive to their carrier customers' needs.

Embark went public in the middle of 2021through a SPAC. It raised more than $600 million in this financing and had an initial valuation of $5.2 billion. In its original investor presentation, it projects 2024 revenue of $867 million and 2025 of $2.7 billion. Embark's strategy is to lease its technology on a per mile basis of approximately $0.44 per mile. This essentially splits the costs savings equally with the freight companies.

The Embark Universal Interface (EUI) uses standardized self-driving components and flexible interfaces to integrate Embark's autonomous technology into varied vehicle platforms, including Freightliner, Volvo, Peterbilt, and International trucks. The EUI achieves its universality through a two-part design. Part one is a standardized components package, including sensors and computing system. Between these standardized components and the truck is part two of the EUI design, which is a set of physical, electrical, and software interfaces that enable the standardized components package to connect to and communicate with any OEM platform's steering, braking, throttle, telematics, power, chassis, and HVAC. At the center of the interface package is the Embark Gateway, an automotive-grade ECU developed by Embark to enable API communication between Embark's technology and any OEM platform.

Embark's long-term vision is for OEMs to integrate Embark's technology with their truck platforms. The OEMs will then sell the Level 4 autonomous semi-trucks with maintenance and warranty support to carriers. It is making its AV stack into an accessible option that any carrier or fleet will be able to request, like a telematics component or any one of the other dozen technologies that OEMs integrate with their core platform.

Like others, Embark is pursuing a "middle mile" approach to automated trucking, operating only on limited-access highways and short off-highway segments to reach distribution centers. This operating model is the most likely initial deployment of automated vehicles because it restricts the vehicle's Operating Design Domain to an environment more confined and predictable than the urban environments that automated passenger vehicles must navigate.

Embark's development roadmap is aggressive. By 2020, it had already incorporated night driving, surface streets, stop-and-go, vehicle on shoulder, cut-ins, lane changes, inclement weather (other than snow), construction, and remote monitoring. By 2022 it plans to add pull over to safety, emergency vehicle interactions, evasive & emergency maneuvers, inspections, blown tires and other mechanical failures. By the end of 2023, it plans to have complete enough functionality to safely remove drivers from its trucks.

Embark's strategy to sell its autonomous system to truck OEMs is obvious, but its success depends on the acceptance of major companies in that market, many of which have their own partnerships.

DAIMLER

Daimler Trucks

Daimler has been in the autonomous truck race for longer than most others, first demonstrating a self-driving vehicle back in 2014, and its revolutionary Inspiration autonomous concept truck drove itself across a Nevada dam in 2015.

Daimler has a two-pillar strategy to: accelerate technology and provide options to customers. Currently, the company focuses more on driver safety and freight efficiency as the main drivers of its R&D efforts on the autonomous front.

It has what it refers to as a dual-track strategy for developing autonomous trucking. One track is its use of Torc's autonomous technology. In May 2019, Daimler Trucks acquired a majority interest in Torc Robotics, to help improve and commercialize SAE Level 4 automated trucks. Torc had been developing autonomous vehicle technology for over a decade. Torc was pioneer in heavy-duty autonomous truck technology and now operates as an independent sub-  sidiary of Daimler Truck AG. Its virtual driver optimizes the use of hub-to-hub trucking. It is also developing a new offering of services related to autonomous driving beyond vehicle sales.

Daimler Trucks' and Torc's integrated self-driving product will be designed for on-highway hub-to-hub applications, especially for long-distance, monotonous transport between distribution centers. Daimler's goal is to refine a truck chassis ideally suited for highly automated driving that includes the redundancy of systems needed to achieve safe, reliable driving. Torc is working on the virtual driver, the software that makes the driving decisions.

Daimler Trucks also works with Waymo Via as its second track to develop autonomous driving for the fifth-generation software package for its Cascadia flagship. Daimler Trucks is developing a customized Freightliner Cascadia truck chassis with redundant systems for Waymo. This chassis will enable the integration of the Waymo Driver with its custom, scalable combination of hardware, software, and compute. The goal is to deploy SAE level 4 trucks, which can operate without a human driver behind the wheel but only within a specific geographic location, on a certain type of roadway, or under specific conditions.

The deal between Waymo and Daimler isn't exclusive. Daimler is the fifth automaker to commit to integrating Waymo's AV technology in its vehicles. Waymo also has preexisting agreements with Nissan-Renault, Fiat Chrysler, Jaguar Land Rover, and Volvo. Waymo Via is discussed more later in this chapter.

A year into their autonomous truck collaboration, Daimler Trucks and Torc Robotics cautioned that it's too early to nail down a definitive timeline for when self-driving trucks will become a part of trucking operations – but do predict significant progress within the next decade.

Daimler Trucks appears to be following a cautious approach to introducing autonomous trucks and is not expected to introduce its autonomous semi-truck until after others. It follows a progressive approach to introducing semi-autonomous features to improve safety and efficiency first and then evolve into sufficiently-autonomous trucking.

Waymo Via

WAYMO VIA

Waymo follows an exciting platform strategy with Waymo Driver, which includes the sensors, computing, and software for autonomous driving. The Waymo Driver platform combines advanced laser radars and sensors built into vehicles, plus the software that controls them along with the human and technological infrastructure that works with consumers and governments to bring services to market. The same way that a common software and hardware platform enables both smartphones and tablets, the Waymo Driver is the foundation for all Waymo vehicles, whether it's Waymo One navigating busy city streets, a van delivering packages to a local neighborhood, or a semi-truck driving down the highway. Using the same core technology and infrastructure platform leverages each type of vehicle, enabling them to benefit from 20 million self-driven miles on public roads and over 15 billion miles in simulation. Google's autonomous driving division announced in March 2018 that it planned to automate trucks in addition to cars. That month, the company launched a pilot in Atlanta where Waymo-branded trucks carried freight bound for Google.

Waymo Via is a very different type of business from Waymo One, its autonomous ride services business. Instead of developing a fleet of autonomous vehicles as it is doing with Waymo One, Waymo Via is partnering with OEMs and Tier 1 suppliers to have its driverless technology integrated onto their trucks. In addition, Waymo Via will work with fleets to provide its software services and offer support for things like mapping and remote fleet assistance. As Waymo transitions to this model, it does intend to own and offer its own fleet of trucks in the short term. This will help it develop and improve its autonomous trucking technology. Like others, it will primarily focus on the transfer-hub model. Autonomous trucks will do the highway driving to and from transfer hubs close to highways, and then human drivers would handle the switch-off and surface street driving.

There are differences between autonomous trucking and autonomous passenger vehicles. Waymo said its software is learning to drive semi-trucks in much the same way a human driver would after years of driving passenger cars. The principles are the same, but braking, turning, and blind spots are different with a fully loaded truck and trailer.

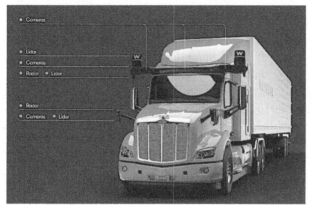

Compared to passenger vehicles, trucks spend a lot more time on freeways, which are higher-speed environments. They also have a lot more mass, are slower to accelerate and brake than passenger cars, requiring nearly two football fields to come to a stop, and have trailers that can move independently from the tractor. Therefore, when configuring the self-driving system for its trucks, it considers that its trucks require more time and space to maneuver and have different blind spots than cars. To accommodate these differences, it increased the number of sensors on the trucks, featuring two perception domes versus the single perception dome on passenger cars. The dual perception domes help increase rear visibility by reducing blind spots caused by the trailer.

Waymo Via is testing on roads in New Mexico, Arizona, and Texas along the I-10 corridor between Phoenix and Tucson. It also mapped routes between Phoenix, El Paso, Dallas, and Houston and ramped up testing in California on freeways in Mountain View. In August 2020, the company added a new trucking hub in Dallas, Texas, to test their fleet of Peterbilt trucks in various commercial settings.

Waymo has already established a couple of significant partnerships with truck manufacturers. In October 2020, it announced a partnership to enable fully autonomous driving with Daimler's Freightliner Cascadia. These fully autonomous trucks, equipped with the Waymo Driver, will be available to U.S. customers first, and the companies will consider expansion into other geographies and brands. In June 2020, Waymo announced that it would be the exclusive global L4 partner for Volvo Car Group, including its strategic affiliates Polestar and Lynk & Co. International. The partnership is not exclusive for Waymo.

Overall, Waymo's strategy to leverage the Waymo Driver platform into multiple markets is vital. It recognizes the differences between the autonomous long-haul trucking market and the autonomous ride services market, and it has a very different strategy. Working with selected truck manufacturers and then providing services to fleets is the right way to succeed in this market.

Tesla Semi

The Tesla Semi is, first and foremost, an electric truck. It will use Tesla's autopilot software to drive autonomously, although this will primarily be semi-autonomous. The Tesla Semi was first mentioned in the Tesla 2016 Master Plan. It was unveiled at a press conference on November 16, 2017, where Musk claimed that the electric Semi would cost 20¢/mi less to operate than a diesel truck if charged at a Megacharger. In March 2018, Tesla announced that the Semi was being tested with actual cargo, hauling battery packs from Nevada to California. In August 2018, a Tesla Semi prototype traveled from California alone, without escort or accompanying vehicles, for a week to arrive at the J. B. Hunt headquarters in Arkansas. In June 2019, Tesla projected that production would begin by the end of 2020. In January 2021, Musk announced that Semi production would be delayed until the end of the year, as the company ramped up high-volume production of its tabless 4680 batteries to meet the demand for the Semi and other vehicles.

The Tesla Semi is an all-electric truck. It will have a significant acceleration of 0 to 60 in 20 seconds and a speed of 60 MPH on a 5% grade. It will be capable of going up to 500 miles on a fully charged battery. The expected base price is $180,000.

A battery-operated truck presents some challenges because it requires a very large battery. Batteries are in short supply, and the necessary volume reduces availability for other Tesla vehicles. In addition, the battery increases the weight of the semi-truck, and this may impose some limitations.

Like Tesla cars, Autopilot for trucks will provide a semi-autonomous system. Musk stated that he thought that Tesla Semi could be the first Tesla vehicle to achieve full autonomy. On top of this, Musk said this version of Autopilot would have truck-specific features like an anti-jackknifing system. He also discussed a platooning feature for Tesla trucks to autonomously follow each other and have only the lead truck controlled entirely by a human driver.

Unlike the other competitors in this market, Tesla will manufacture its semi-trucks. It plans volume production at its massive new Gigafactory in Austin once it can also ramp up battery cell production there. In the interim, Tesla is building a Tesla Semi production line in a new building near its Gigafactory Nevada plant, where it plans

to produce five electric trucks per week. Tesla intends to use the first few units to carry its freight, mostly between Fremont and Reno. Musk mentioned that Tesla could eventually produce 100,000 electric semi-trucks per year. Tesla has several hundred pre-orders for its new semi.

Overall, Tesla's semi-truck strategy is aimed primarily at providing an electric semi-truck. It will enable semi-autonomous driving but will still require a driver to be at the wheel, so initially, it won't achieve the benefits of eliminating driver costs. Its primary appeal may be to customers that want to introduce electric trucks into their fleets. Its manufacturing strategy is different from the other autonomous trucking companies that are partnering with truck manufacturers. This presents some significant risks.

Aurora

Aurora, founded in 2017 by self-driving vehicle pioneers from Google, Tesla, and Uber, has offices in the Bay Area, Pittsburgh, Dallas, and Bozeman, Mont. For years, Aurora was developing self-driving technology but struggled to figure out a successful business model. Initially, it planned to supply self-driving software and sensors to auto manufacturers. The company had a partnership with Volkswagen that was supposed to lead to Aurora's technology being incorporated into Volkswagen's vehicles, but the two companies parted ways in 2019, putting Aurora at risk. In 2019, Aurora pivoted to long-haul trucking as the first application for its self-driving technology.

Aurora decided to focus first on autonomous trucking because it could have the biggest and fastest impact. Driverless trucks can help the trucking industry address pressing business concerns such as the driver shortage and high turnover. Autonomous trucking also will make it possible for fleet operators to haul freight without being constrained by driver hours-of--service limits and benefit from better, more predictable fuel efficiency.

In December 2020, Aurora seized on an opportunity to get back into the ARS business by purchasing Uber's struggling self-driving technology division and selling a large ownership share to Uber.

Aurora is working with Volvo Trucks and PACCAR Inc. PACCAR and Volvo together account for more than 40% of the heavy-duty trucks sold in North America every year.

As mentioned in the previous chapter, Aurora is going public through a SPAC and has disclosed its plans in the process. According to its financial presentation, Aurora plans to charge a fee per mile for its autonomous technology and let others own the truck fleets and manage fleet operations. It forecasts being able to charge $0.45 to $0.65 per mile to autonomous fleet operators.

It expects to launch its first autonomous trucks in 2024, achieving 20 million miles and $30 million in revenue. By 2027, it forecasts providing its autonomous system for trucks driven 3.3 billion miles, generating $1.875 billion in revenue. It estimates that it would have a 2.5% share of the total market (194 billion miles), including all trucking miles driven by traditional trucks.

Others

There are also others developing autonomous trucking. Kodiak Robotics was founded in April 2018 with a focus that on long-haul trucking. At the end of 2020, it made disengage-free customer deliveries on the middle mile. It received approximately $40 million of funding in 2018. Locomation was founded in 2018 and received more than $11 million in funding. Its Autonomous Relay Convoy system will be available commercially as an aftermarket retrofit, with sensors (cameras, lidars, and radars), vehicle interface, and compute power with steering and braking systems optimized for autonomy. It is working on relationships with commercial vehicle retailers and a network of post-delivery installation organizations for sales, distribution, and maintenance of Locomation technology.

Chapter 9
Autonomous Home Delivery

Autonomous home delivery is like ARS in that an autonomous version will replace a driver-based version, and like ARS, the economic advantages of the autonomous version will be substantial. However, there are some significant differences between these, as we will see in this chapter.

Autonomous home delivery is the local delivery of a product to a customer by an autonomous vehicle without a driver. Generally, this is same-day delivery. It includes same-day delivery to offices and similar locations, such as schools and other work locations. It also includes local business-to-business delivery of small amounts of goods such as spare parts or transfers from warehouses to stores. Most notably, it doesn't include long-haul trucking.

According to the Bureau of Transportation Statistics, Americans make roughly 1.1 billion car trips per day, and nearly 45% of those trips are made running errands. This defines a significant opportunity for autonomous home delivery. It can dramatically reduce the number of miles driven and reduce the need for passenger cars. Since autonomous home delivery vehicles will be smaller and lighter, there can be substantial energy and cost savings.

There are several categories of autonomous home delivery, including different types of food delivery, the delivery of groceries and similar products, and package delivery. Each of these categories presents very different opportunities and challenges.

The market characteristics of autonomous delivery are different than ARS. The current economic model for home delivery is different from ridesharing, and the economic model for autonomous home delivery will be a little different. The vehicles used for autonomous home delivery eventually will be different from those used for ARS.

Autonomous home delivery will provide early opportunities for autonomous vehicles, and there are several reasons for this. First, delivery routes can be more predictable and limited, so *sufficiently* autonomous delivery initially can be defined based on a restricted set of delivery locations. Second, delivery vehicles won't have the variety of human interactions that ARS vehicles will encounter. Third, these vehicles can travel at lower speeds, requiring less complex AV software. Finally, autonomous delivery vehicles can be smaller and less costly, although this may take a second generation of vehicles to get there.

Early opportunities for autonomous home delivery leverage four characteristics:

1. Delivery of products where home delivery is already well established, such as pizza delivery,

2. Delivery of products by large national chains that can afford the investment in autonomous delivery. Smaller businesses will be served by third-party autonomous delivery services,

3. Delivery of products with a beneficial price point. Products whose prices are too low can't afford driver-based delivery and may not benefit sufficiently autonomous delivery. Autonomous delivery of very expensive products doesn't provide as much benefit over driver-based delivery, and

4. Delivery of products where the customer is at home to receive the delivery.

These characteristics vary for different categories of delivery. Some categories, such as pizza delivery, have all four of these characteristics: well-established home delivery, national chains, an attractive price point, and someone at home to receive the food. That is why pizza delivery will be an early opportunity for autonomous home delivery. Other opportunities may take longer to emerge. Some categories of delivery face the problem of not having a customer there to receive the products. Package delivery to homes, such as from FedEx and UPS, has this problem.

The development of autonomous home delivery will follow roughly the same path as autonomous ride services (ARS). Initially, home delivery is being established with human drivers, like the evolution of ridesharing. Subsequently, driver-based delivery will be replaced by autonomous delivery, just like ARS will replace ridesharing.

There are three major autonomous home delivery categories: food delivery, grocery (and related items) delivery, and package delivery. The first two categories provide the primary opportunities for autonomous home delivery. Food delivery is best understood by segmenting this category: pizza, fast food, and restaurants. Each has different characteristics. The grocery and related category is best understood by looking at the major competitors in this category.

COVID-19 created a surge in home-delivery across all categories, and more people became comfortable with its benefits. Much of this increase could become a permanent change in lifestyle for many people. Autonomous home delivery was not yet sufficiently developed to take advantage of this surge, but it would have been successful because many people prefer contactless delivery now.

Benefits

The application of autonomous driving technology requires sufficient benefits to get rapid adoption. Autonomous home delivery has very significant benefits. Some of these, such as increased safety and lower energy consumption, benefit society, but they don't necessarily motivate the adoption of autonomous delivery. Cost savings are the primary driver for the adoption of the new technology.

Cost Savings

Autonomous delivery is much cheaper than driver-based delivery because it eliminates the cost of human drivers. Home delivery pricing is very complicated. Part of it is a delivery fee. Part of it is paid for by the company selling the products. Part of it comes from tips.

A rough estimated delivery-driver cost per delivery is approximately $10.00 per delivery. This is based on drivers getting approximately $15-$20 per hour depending on the number of deliveries, 2-3 deliveries per hour, and an average $3 tip per delivery. A savings of $10 can be very significant for lower-priced orders. For example, it's a 50% cost savings on a $20 order. This will give companies using autonomous delivery a significant competitive advantage.

Even though autonomous vehicles will have the additional cost of sensors, computing, and software, they will be less expensive to operate than traditional passenger vehicles. They will be much smaller, lighter, and use much less energy.

Autonomous delivery will require remote monitoring of the delivery fleets. This will be an additional cost but not significant compared to the cost reduction. It will be easier for companies to have a more extensive fleet of autonomous vehicles than it is to have the right number of delivery drivers on hand, so there will be more delivery capacity.

Eventually, people will be saying: "remember when you would order a pizza, and some guy driving a 2,500-pound car with a pizza box in the passenger seat would drive it to you?"

Increased Safety

We have already discussed the reduction in accidents from autonomous driving. Autonomous delivery vehicles have some additional benefits because they are smaller and don't need to protect passengers. The Virginia Tech Transportation Institute (VTTI) quantified the safety benefits of zero-occupant vehicle designs, over and above the substantial safety gains from autonomy software. A team of VTTI researchers analyzed historical crash data to assess what would have happened with a different vehicle design, holding the driver's behavior constant. They estimate that, for every mile of driving replaced by a zero-occupant design vehicle, the risk of fatality or injury can be reduced by approximately 60%.

Central to this reduction is the lack of passengers and drivers in zero-occupant vehicles. By making it convenient and affordable for goods to come to you, these vehicles take people out of harm's way. The innovative design of these new vehicles also substantially improved safety metrics, according to the study. The study showed that a front end designed to absorb energy–rather than protect occupants–could reduce pedestrian risks by 20% or more in some crashes. Researchers also found that a narrower vehicle could avoid 5% of crashes by giving everyone on the road more space to maneuver.

Autonomous Food Delivery

Home delivery of prepared foods, including pizza, fast food, and restaurant meals, will provide early opportunities for autonomous delivery. Each of these categories has some different characteristics, and I see pizza delivery as being the earliest opportunity.

Pizza Delivery

Pizza is a large market, and home delivery is already well established. Pizzerias represent more than 15% of all restaurants. Approximately 3 billion pizzas are sold each year in the U.S., and most of these are delivered. Domino's, for example, discloses that it delivers 2 million pizzas every day, and its drivers travel more than 1.5 million miles daily.

The pizza delivery market in the U.S. is controlled by four large companies that have about two-thirds of this $30+ billion market: Domino's Pizza, Pizza Hut, Little Caesars, and Papa John's. These four chains collectively have more than 20,000 stores providing home delivery. This concentration of a few large companies makes it more likely that they will invest in developing and deploying autonomous pizza delivery.

The price point and cost savings for pizza delivery are also favorable, so with autonomous delivery, the cost of pizza delivery will drop significantly. The estimated cost for pizza delivery is approximately a $6 to $7 cost to the pizzeria, plus a tip of $3 on average as an additional cost to the customer, or roughly a total delivery cost of $9-$10 for typical $15-$18 pizza delivery. This equates to an average order cost of $24-$28 with tips. The cost of buying an autonomously delivered pizza would be 20%-40% lower. Delivered pizza is a very price-sensitive market, so a cost-saving of this magnitude will become a significant competitive advantage, which will drive the rapid adoption of autonomous delivery by these four large companies.

Companies such as Domino's Pizza will be able to replace its delivery drivers with autonomous delivery vehicles for many of the three-quarters of a billion pizzas it delivers each year. The four large national chains will find it profitable to invest in a fleet of autonomous delivery vehicles. If each of them eventually used 3-4 autonomous delivery vehicles per location, collectively, they would have fleets of approximately 60,000 to 80,000 pizza delivery vehicles. This creates some excellent opportunities for autonomous delivery vehicle manufacturers.

In April 2021, Domino's Pizza started pilot tests to deliver pizzas using the Nuro 2 in Houston. Select customers who place a prepaid order on dominos.com on certain days and times from Domino's in Woodland Heights can choose to have their pizza delivered by Nuro's R2 robot. Nuro's R2 is the first completely autonomous, occupant-less on-road delivery vehicle with regulatory approval by the U.S. Department of Transportation. Here's how it works: select customers who place a prepaid website order from the participating Domino's store can opt to have their order delivered by R2. Customers who are selected will receive text alerts, which will update them on R2's location and provide them with a unique PIN to retrieve their order. Customers may also track the vehicle via GPS on their order confirmation page. Once R2 arrives, customers will be prompted to enter their PIN on the bot's touchscreen. R2's doors will then gently open upward, revealing the customer's hot Domino's order.

Domino's Pizza believes that there is still so much to learn about autonomous delivery. This pilot program will allow them to better understand how customers respond to the deliveries, how they interact with the robot, and how it affects store operations. Domino's Pizza also partnered with Ford to test the way delivery customers would interface with autonomous vehicles in Miami and Ann Arbor.

Pizza Hut is partnering with Toyota, and it plans to test automated delivery in 2021. The company stated that it is "dedicating real resources to this effort."

There is also some discussion underway about putting a pizza oven in the autonomous delivery vehicle, so the pizza can be cooked while on route. I'm skeptical of the advantages of this compared to its challenges.

Autonomous pizza delivery will work very much like the current model of driver delivery. A customer will use an app or go online to order a pizza, plus other items. The system will process payment and schedule food preparation. Customers will be informed of the estimated delivery time. The pizzeria will place the food in the appropriate autonomous delivery vehicle and send it on its way. When the order is on route, the automated delivery vehicle will notify customers ahead of arriving, and they will be able to track delivery along the way. The food will be kept warm and the drinks cold along the way. On the downside, autonomous delivery vehicles won't be able to carry the food upstairs or to the door; customers will need to come out to get it.

During the early phase in the evolution of autonomous pizza delivery, some customers will still need to use or prefer driver-based delivery, even at a higher price. Pizza companies will use a hybrid of autonomous and driver-based delivery during the evolution period.

Fast-Food Restaurant Delivery

What about autonomous delivery from fast-food restaurants such as McDonald's and Burger King? While these are large chains, they don't do much home delivery yet, although they increased it during the pandemic. Most of their business is drive-through pickup or eating-in. Their customers are used to picking up a burger as they travel home or to work, or they stop in for a quick meal. That is the advantage of fast food over other alternatives.

Fast-food restaurants currently use third-party delivery services such as Uber Eats, but the cost of delivery is expensive relative to the cost of a meal. Currently, the average McDonald's order is somewhere in the range of $4-$5, so delivery costs can be prohibitive, but autonomous delivery *may* open some new opportunities for McDonald's and its fast-food competitors.

McDonald's executives have called home delivery "the most significant disruption in the restaurant industry in our lifetime." McDonald's uses Uber Eats for delivery. However, Uber charges about 30% of the order, which is most of the profit McDonald's makes. 60% of McDonald's home delivery orders are in the evening, so they tend to be group orders with twice the average purchase of in-store orders. This is the opportunity. McDonald's also estimates that 75% of its customers live within 3 miles of a McDonald's location, making home delivery more cost-effective. A 2-3-mile autonomous delivery could cost as low as $1-$1.50, which could make home delivery feasible for an order of $10 or more.

Home delivery will be an expansion strategy for fast-food companies. They would be giving up some of the advantages of fast food since home delivery takes longer. They would be expanding into market segments for a more substantial group evening home delivery or group lunch delivery to offices. They would probably need to require a minimum order size, which could limit the market. Moreover, they would need to invest in their own autonomous delivery fleet.

In the United States, there are approximately 75,000-85,000 fast-food locations, not including pizzerias. There are more than 25,000 Subway locations, more than 13,000 McDonald's, and approximately 6,000-7,000 locations each for Burger King, Dunkin Donuts, Taco Bell, Wendy's, and KFC. If half to three-quarters of these locations eventually provide autonomous home delivery, that could equate to 80,000-100,000 autonomous delivery vehicles. Like pizza delivery, I expect each of the major chains to use custom-designed autonomous vehicles that promote their businesses.

I expect fast-food companies will aggressively experiment with home delivery, but it's not clear how successful they will be and how fast the opportunity will develop.

Restaurant Delivery

There are over 620,000 restaurants in the U.S., providing a significant opportunity for autonomous home delivery. Most of these restaurants are not major chains, are new to delivery, and use third-party delivery services if they are doing delivery. Restaurant delivery still is in its infancy, in part because it is expensive. However, it is growing rapidly. COVID-19 forced almost all restaurants in the U.S. to close dining facilities. Many of these turned to pickup and delivery as an alternative. Some of these would continue to continue to offer home delivery even if they didn't in the past.

The cost of restaurant delivery is relatively high. Most third-party food delivery services charge a delivery fee of approximately $5, plus take a significant portion of the sale. Amazon's charges to restaurants are high, reportedly to be close to 30%. Early entrants such as Grubhub and Seamless charged somewhere between 12% and 24%, while upstarts such as DoorDash and Postmates have a rate in the range of 15% to 23%. Uber Eats charges a restaurant 30% of their listed prices for delivering their food. Also, Uber Eats does not permit restaurants to increase their prices to "cover" Uber's cost.

Even the best restaurants only make 15-30% profit, so they lose money on this service, but see it as incremental revenue.

Restaurant delivery is more expensive than other types of delivery. The meal needs to be picked up when it is ready and delivered quickly, so driver utilization is lower. Restaurant delivery costs can range from $10-$20 per delivery, which can be very expensive on typical orders of $30-$50.

With autonomous home delivery, mainstream restaurants will be able to add affordable delivery options. The cost of delivery will be greatly reduced. I expect delivery costs to be only a few dollars.

Virtual Restaurants and Cloud Kitchens

With home delivery, restaurants no longer need to prepare food in a real restaurant kitchen where food is served to customers in a dining room. They don't even need to rent space for a dining room. All they need is a kitchen. These virtual restaurants can hang a shingle inside a meal-delivery app and market their food to the app's customers without the hassle and expense of hiring waiters or paying for furniture and tablecloths. Diners who order from the apps may have no idea that the restaurant doesn't physically exist.

Some virtual restaurants are affiliated with real-life restaurants but make different cuisines specifically for the delivery apps. Others, sometimes called "ghost kitchens," have no retail presence and essentially serve as a meal preparation hub for delivery orders. Ghost kitchens can be set up by an individual and may even use a home kitchen, in a way like Airbnb. In some cases, a city's health department may not have inspected them, and they don't have a license to operate a commercial kitchen.

Virtual restaurants offer some significant advantages to incumbent restaurants, including the ability to fulfill a far greater demand of delivery orders. They can also be in lower-cost facilities, such as abandoned warehouses. The New York Times reported Uber has helped start 4,000 of these virtual restaurants. In the realm of delivery, new virtual restaurants and ghost kitchens have significant cost advantages over already-in-place restaurants with large physical footprints and decade-long leases, which means just as leading restaurants are raising prices to offset the margin hit, these virtual restaurants are well-positioned to lower theirs to win market share.

Virtual restaurants have created another innovation: "cloud kitchens." Cloud kitchens offer shareable cooking facilities to support food delivery. Like co-working spaces, such as We Work, cloud kitchens can be rented by an existing restaurant to better juggle walk-ins and delivery during peak times. The bigger opportunity, however, is seen to be for entrepreneurs launching online-only restaurants and avoiding the front-of-house labor and other overhead of walk-in restaurants. Centralized cooking spaces gain efficiencies by being side-by-side, assembly-like. Shared labor costs and equipment reduce recruiting and training costs with access to specialized labor that is shared across multiple restaurants.

Cloud kitchens offer rent savings as well because they can be housed in industrial buildings versus pricey street-facing locales. The rental kitchens come fully equipped with cooking equipment and utilities, and they provide on-demand delivery services as well as apps to take orders and manage the process. The healthier margins versus eat-in restaurants can offset delivery fees. Los Angeles based CloudKitchens estimates that rather than a $1 million upfront investment required to build out a restaurant, cloud kitchen rentals can start at $20,000 and a two-month deposit.

Uber co-founder Kalanick invested $150 million in a startup called City Storage Systems that focused on repurposing distressed real estate assets and turning them into spaces for new industries, like food delivery. That company owns CloudKitchens, which invites food chains — as well as independent restaurant and food truck owners — to lease space in one of its facilities for a monthly fee, charging additional fees for data analytics.

Autonomous Grocery Delivery

Autonomous grocery delivery is another major opportunity. Like pizza delivery and ridesharing, same-day delivery of groceries and related merchandise is increasing, even with the high labor cost for delivery. The strategy behind this is like the strategy behind ridesharing: create a customer base (in this case for home delivery), even at a loss, then switch this over to very profitable autonomous delivery in a few years.

Online grocery shopping is growing. Nearly half of Americans now buy at least some groceries online, according to research from the Food Marketing Institute (FMI) and Nielsen. The organizations conducted a survey in 2018 that found that 49% of U.S. consumers had purchased consumer packaged goods (CPG) online in the past three months. However, because shoppers tend to make online grocery purchases less frequently than they make in-store grocery purchases, these numbers do not yet translate into a major share of the grocery market.

Convenience is the primary benefit of home delivery. Home delivery of groceries can save consumers a lot of time. The average person goes to the grocery store 1.5 times per week and spends more than a half-hour there. Another newly recognized advantage is the reduction in viral risk that comes from having to go inside a grocery store during a pandemic or even during flu season.

Online grocery ordering with 3-day delivery is very different from same-day grocery delivery, which is the focus of autonomous grocery delivery. With both, the customer places an order online or through an app, but with same-day delivery, products are picked from a local grocery store and delivered by car using a driver. When ordered online, same-day grocery delivery is scheduled for a window of time, such as 10 AM-noon or 5 PM – 7 PM.

Home delivery is not yet sufficiently established by all grocery stores, so they need first to develop the basic elements of the home-delivery chain. This starts with consumers ordering online or through an app and then picking up their orders at the store. This saves the customer the time of shopping in the store and enables the grocery store to develop and test online ordering. Then the grocery stores start driver-based home delivery and get this working. Finally, they will switch driver-based delivery to autonomous delivery.

Most likely, these companies are losing money on home delivery, but they need to provide this service to be competitive and to get a foothold in the market for autonomous grocery delivery, where the costs will be much lower. Eliminating the cost of a delivery driver will reduce delivery fees, and delivery could possibly become free without costing the company much. Let's look at what some of the major grocery chains are doing.

Amazon Same-Day Home Delivery

Amazon is the delivery giant, and it certainly has same-day home delivery in its sights. Amazon's acquisition of Whole Foods allowed it to roll out a two-hour grocery delivery service in selected areas. Delivery is free to Amazon Prime members who pay $119 a year for that service. Other grocery stores providing same-day delivery charge for delivery; for example, Safeway charges $9.95, and Walmart charges $9 for delivery plus $1.50 per bag.

Amazon is testing a variety of grocery delivery alternatives, including Whole Foods, AmazonFresh, and delivery from other grocery stores using Prime Now. Prime Fresh delivers groceries for a $299 per year membership and orders over $50 have free delivery. Anything less has a charge of $9.99. Amazon's acquisition of Whole Foods got everyone's attention. Its rapid move to use this for home delivery has accelerated the development of home delivery by competitors.

Walmart

Walmart began testing grocery delivery in different ways. In 2018 it used a variety of delivery services, including Deliv, Postmates, and DoorDash. It initiated and then terminated trials with Uber and Lyft delivery. It subsequently stopped using Deliv. It also tried to use Walmart employees to deliver groceries when their shifts ended, but that failed.

Walmart rolled out an unlimited grocery delivery subscription service starting in 2019, as it raced to gain an advantage in the competitive fresh-food business. The service charges an annual membership fee of $98 for unlimited same-day delivery. Walmart will also offer a monthly subscription option for $12.95; customers will still be able to pay a per-delivery fee of $7.95 or $9.95

for same-day delivery if they decide against the subscription service. About 100,000 items, which include fresh foods and pantry staples as well as select general merchandise like light bulbs and basic toys, qualify for both grocery pickup and delivery. By the end of 2019, this delivery service was available in 1,600 stores – or more than 50% of the country.

The move allows the nation's largest grocer to further serve time-starved shoppers who are looking for convenience. For Walmart, this is an emerging competitive area with Amazon and others to expand fresh-food delivery, which is one of the fastest-growing opportunities.

The grocery services are fulfilled by local stores and require a minimum order of $30. With same-day delivery, there's a four-hour minimum wait between placing an order and having it delivered. Grocery delivery builds on Walmart's grocery pickup service that allows customers to order their groceries online and pick them up in stores without ever getting out of their cars. Grocery pickup is available in nearly 3,000 stores.

Walmart uses more than 45,000 personal shoppers to pick products off store shelves to fulfill orders. These associates must complete a three-week training program learning how to select the freshest produce and the best cuts of meat for online grocery customers.

Walmart is doing several autonomous delivery pilot tests. In 2021, it started pilot tests with Cruise in Scottsdale. As part of the pilot, customers can place an order from their local store and have it delivered, contact-free, via one of Cruise's all-electric self-driving cars. Cruise isn't the only autonomous vehicle company to team up with Walmart. The retail giant also has partnerships with Nuro, Udelv, Ford, and Waymo

Kroger

Kroger acquired Shipt to begin the delivery of grocery and household items. Previously Kroger developed a customer pickup service called Click-List. Kroger illustrates the evolution of home delivery: first, develop the capability for customers to order online and put together that order for them to pick up, then master home delivery using drivers, and finally replace these with lower-cost autonomous home delivery.

With its delivery service, customers can order from a list of more than 50,000 items, including 4,500 items that aren't currently available on Kroger.com. The minimum order for free delivery is $35. The delivery charge for orders less than that is $4.99. This is most likely less than Kroger's delivery cost.

Nuro is partnering with Kroger. Starting in late 2018, Kroger tested delivering groceries to customers using Nuro's autonomous vehicles in Arizona. In 2019, it tested autonomous home delivery from two stores in Houston to residents in four zip codes. Initial deliveries were done using a Prius modified to be autonomous, then deliveries were done with its first-generation R1 autonomous delivery vehicle.

Nuro's goal is to eventually provide service across Kroger's entire retail footprint. In addition to Kroger stores, the company also owns the Dillon's, Harris Teeter, QFC, Ralphs, Roundy's, and Smith's supermarket chains, among others. In total, Kroger says it owns 2,800 stores in 35 states.

CVS

Over 76% of people in the United States live within five miles of a CVS Pharmacy today. Every day, CVS serves 4.5 million customers across the country. That's more people than the entire population of Los Angeles, the nation's second-largest city. CVS has been at the forefront of delivery innovation; it was the first company to make prescription home delivery a nationwide option in 2018. It has continually invested in delivery. That investment is even more critical now, as more Americans opt for home delivery over store visits. CVS is working on pilot tests with Nuro.

How Walmart and Target Can Use Autonomous Delivery to Beat Amazon

Amazon has achieved dominance in online ordering, displacing many retail stores in the process. But is it possible that autonomous home delivery can replace Amazon's advantages in certain retail categories, enabling large retailers such as Walmart and Target to achieve an advantage over Amazon?

A customer can order almost any product from Amazon online and get it delivered in a couple of days. Amazon has a supply-chain infrastructure of approximately 150 warehouses throughout the U.S., enabling relatively rapid delivery using various delivery companies such as Federal Express, UPS, and the U.S. Post Office, and increasingly it is using its own delivery vehicles. This makes it unbeatable in 2-3-day delivery, but what if same-day delivery became even cheaper with autonomous delivery?

Walmart, Target, and other large retail stores are expanding same-day home delivery, but the cost is high because of the need for a delivery driver.

They are providing this service at a loss to establish a position in this new market. However, with autonomous delivery, the delivery cost is significantly reduced, making same-day home delivery affordable.

Same-day delivery requires a different supply-chain infrastructure. Even with 150 warehouses, same-day delivery is not feasible for most customers. In 2018, Walmart had more than 5,000 stores (including Sam's Club) in the U.S. It has a store within less than 20 miles of 90% of the population. This makes same-day autonomous home delivery feasible for Walmart. It can use its stores effectively as mini-warehouses. A customer can place an order online from the Walmart app or website, and the local store can confirm availability and then fulfill the order in a couple of hours using a fleet of autonomous delivery vehicles.

This won't take away all of Amazon's market as it still has some other advantages, but it can siphon off a large segment of the market. Some people will prefer to order a variety of food and other merchandise that Walmart sells, and if they are home, they can receive delivery in a couple of hours.

Amazon is aware of this threat and has initiated its own strategic initiative. It is investing very heavily in next-day home delivery, hiring more than 100,000 people, and incurring heavy losses to achieve this. It shrinks the competitive differentiation to same-day delivery from two days to one day. Amazon also sees the eventual switch to autonomous delivery as the way to reduce its increased costs of two-day delivery.

Third-Party Autonomous Delivery

Third-party delivery companies allow consumers to compare offerings and order meals from a variety of restaurants through a single website or app. Crucially, the third-party delivery companies also provide the delivery logistics for the restaurant. This allows them to open a new segment of the restaurant market to home delivery: higher-end restaurants that traditionally did not deliver. Third-party home delivery companies are compensated by the restaurant with a fixed margin of the order, as well as with a small flat fee from the customer.

Third-party delivery is used primarily for smaller restaurants. These companies have tried to form partnerships with large chains, but these haven't always worked out. As Uber Eats and Grubhub public filings show, these partnerships don't always lead to revenue. Often, partners pay the delivery services lower fees, decreasing their take rates or even causing them to lose money. But the partners often have huge customer pools, thousands of locations, and impressive advertising reach, all of which have delivery services betting that joining forces will pay off in the long term. In addition to other third-party operators, delivery companies also compete against restaurants that offer their own delivery (like Domino's), grocery delivery companies, meal kit deliveries, and even Amazon and Walmart.

These rivalries have contributed to the industry's poor economics, resulting in consolidation. DoorDash acquired Caviar, Amazon invested in Deliveroo, Uber acquired Postmates, and Just Eat Takeaway bought Grubhub. In addition, delivery companies have had to operate under fee caps that numerous localities enacted during the pandemic, limiting their ability to profit. Domino's CEO said he has "struggled a little bit understanding the long-term economics in some of the aggregator businesses. In 60 years, we've never made a dollar delivering a pizza. We make money on the product, but we don't make money on the delivery."

DoorDash is by far the largest third-party delivery company. In October 2020, four third-party delivery companies dominated the market: DoorDash (50%), Uber Eats (26%), GrubHub (16%), and Postmates (7%). This changed to only three a month later when Uber acquired Postmates after failing to acquire GrubHub.

Just like ridesharing, third-party delivery services provide home delivery for a range of businesses. And just like autonomous ride services (ARS) will replace ridesharing, autonomous home delivery will replace driver-based delivery. Even though many large retail and restaurant chains currently are using third-party delivery services, I expect that they will eventually use their own autonomous delivery fleets. The scale advantages and the opportunity to customize and promote their own delivery vehicles are significant. Most smaller businesses will utilize third parties to provide autonomous delivery.

DoorDash

DoorDash Inc. is a San Francisco–based company founded in 2013 by Stanford students. DoorDash has raised a lot of money in its aggressive efforts to capture market share. It added $400 million in capital at the beginning of 2019 from SoftBank and then added $600 million a few months later. DoorDash went public in November 2000. In mid-2021, it had a valuation of $57 billion. A little lower than its IPO price.

In 2020 it claimed to have 18 million consumers, 390,000 merchants, and more than a million Dashers (delivery people). It has the largest market share, which jumped from 17% of the market to 50%, twice the share of the next largest competitor Uber Eats. In 2020, it had 816 million orders for a gross order value of $24.6 billion, which generated $2.8 billion in revenue but ended in a loss of $461 million. This demonstrates how difficult it is to make money in this business.

Even though autonomous delivery could have a meaningful impact on the food-delivery industry, DoorDash hasn't done very much to develop these technologies. In 2019, it partnered with GM's Cruise Automation to test food delivery with autonomous vehicles in San Francisco. It also made a few relatively small investments in autonomous technology. It acquired Scotty Labs, a teleoperations company that is working on technology to enable people to remotely control AVs. The startup had previously worked with Voyage for its self-driving cars in retirement communities. Scotty believes that autonomy combined with remote assistance is a viable solution. DoorDash also brought on the two co-founders from another company that had built technology to create high-resolution maps for autonomous driving using crowdsourced imagery.

DoorDash recognized the threat of autonomous delivery as a risk in its S-1:

> *Certain competitors may commercialize autonomous (and drone) delivery technologies at scale before we or our partners do. In the event that our competitors bring autonomous or drone delivery to market before we do, or their technology is or is perceived to be superior to our or our partners' technology, they may be able to leverage such technology to compete more effectively with us, which would adversely affect our business, financial condition, and results of operations. For example, if competitors develop autonomous and drone delivery technologies that successfully reduce the cost of facilitating delivery logistics services, these competitors could offer their services at lower prices as compared to the price available to consumers on our platform. If a significant number of consumers choose to use our competitors' offerings over ours, our business, financial condition, and results of operations could be adversely affected.*

Grubhub

Grubhub's online and mobile ordering platforms allow diners to order from more than 125,000 takeout restaurants in over 2,400 U.S. cities and London. In 2006, Grubhub founders won first place in the University of Chicago Booth School of Business's Edward L. Kaplan New Venture Challenge with the business plan for Grubhub. In 2013, Grubhub and Seamless merged and acquired other similar companies along the way. Grubhub went public in 2014. GrubHub was acquired by Europe's Just Eat Takeaway for $7.3 billion in June 2020.

Uber Eats

Uber Eats' parent company Uber was founded in 2009. It started food delivery in August 2014 with the launch of the UberFRESH service in Santa Monica, California. In 2015, the platform was renamed to Uber Eats.

Uber Eats is poised to become a bigger part of Uber's business, but it will need to continue leveraging the popularity of its mobility service. Uber's ride-hailing app has a growing user base, and direct integration gives its Uber Eats business more exposure. In June 2019, Uber began to embed Uber Eats directly into its core app in select markets. Embedding Uber Eats in the app instead of requiring a separate app raises its profile significantly, as it places it in front of more of the company's growing base of monthly active platform consumers. Uber Eats changed its flat $4.99 delivery fee to a rate that is determined by distances, ranging from a $2 minimum to an $8 maximum.

During the COVID-19 pandemic, Uber's ridesharing business saw a precipitous decline in riders, but Uber Eats had a significant increase in food deliveries. In November 2020, Uber acquired Postmates for $2.65 billion. Postmates delivers more than just food. It can pick up a variety of items from many stores and deliver them. It charges a fee that varies based on the order and time of day, and it has a monthly subscription that provides free delivery from some select stores.

The Economic Business Model of Home Delivery

The economic model for home delivery is somewhat different than it is for ridesharing, and I expect the model for autonomous home delivery will also be different.

Let's look at Grubhub's pricing to restaurants for delivery and the delivery fees paid to its delivery drivers. Grubhub charges restaurants a marketing commission, delivery fee, and a processing fee. The marketing commission doesn't relate so much to home delivery as it does to promoting a restaurant on the Grubhub website. Promotion on the Grubhub website is optional; a restaurant can take orders itself and have Grubhub fulfill them. 20% is a typical marketing commission charged by Grubhub, although it can vary if a restaurant wants a better promotion.

For delivery, Grubhub charges restaurants a delivery fee of 10% of the order, and a processing fee of $0.30 plus 3.05% of the order. In an example used by Grubhub, delivery for a typical $41.00 order would cost the restaurant $5.75. The restaurant can charge the customer a delivery fee if they want, and the customer is also expected to tip the driver. A 15% delivery tip is typical.

Grubhub pays its delivery drivers $0.22 per mile for both pickup and delivery, plus $0.13 per minute of driving and waiting time. It uses a typical delivery payment of $5.00 (2 miles for pickup and 3 for delivery, and 30 minutes of time). For the example $41.00 order with a 15% tip, a driver would get $11.15. The total cost of delivery for this typical $41.00 would then be $11.15 (including tip) plus the $1.65 processing fee, or $12.80. This is more than 30% of the price of an order.

With autonomous home delivery, this $12.80 would be significantly reduced. Assuming the elimination of the driver time cost and tip, the delivery cost would be reduced by $10.50 to $2.75. This is the $1.65 processing fee to cover overhead and $1.10 for the vehicle cost. The $0.22 per mile is a reasonable charge for an autonomous delivery vehicle. This equates to a cost of

$15,000 - $20,000 per year, depending on miles driven. Since autonomous delivery vehicles are expected to be small, lightweight, and driven at low speeds, they should not cost more than $30,000 to build.

This will make home delivery much more affordable, and price competition will accelerate its introduction. At a typical cost of $2.75 per delivery, autonomous home delivery could become very popular. It most likely will eventually put driver-based delivery out of business.

Autonomous Package Delivery

Package delivery, sometimes referred to as the last-mile delivery, will benefit from autonomous vehicles, but the benefits won't be as significant as they are in the previous categories. The reason is that the recipient is not always there to receive a package, so someone needs to hand-deliver the package from the truck to the recipient or place it correctly by the door. There are two methods under consideration for using autonomous vehicles for package delivery.

Using a semi-autonomous ground vehicle, a delivery person is still required but could replace driving time to take care of sorting packages or smaller administrative tasks more efficiently, e.g., scanning or announcing arrival while the vehicle does the driving. These advantages need to compensate for higher investment costs, as autonomous ground vehicles are likely to be more expensive than regular trucks, at least initially.

DHL is planning to test autonomous delivery trucks that follow a delivery person along the route to deliver packages. The person wouldn't need to get back into the truck between dropping off packages; they would remove packages from the rear of the truck. The company has not revealed how the truck will identify and accurately follow its delivery people.

There may also be efficiencies in better routing and deployment of delivery vehicles. A recently loaded truck could drive itself to the delivery person and replace a truck that is empty, for example. UPS estimates that being able to cut a single mile from drivers' daily route saves the company up to $50 million each year. On any given day, UPS has around 66,000 drivers out on the road.

Autonomous vehicles with lockers could deliver parcels without any human intervention. In this case, the customer receiving delivery would be notified to come out to the truck and retrieve the package. Upon arrival at their door, customers would take the parcel from the specified locker mounted on the truck, using a passcode sent to the recipient or using a Bluetooth connection to the recipient's phone.

The Autonomous Delivery Customer Interface

Autonomous home delivery requires a new type of customer interface. It starts with the online order process, but then there are additional requirements. With autonomous home delivery, customers must be present to receive the delivery and unload it from the autonomous vehicle. In cases where a delivery vehicle has more than one order on it, there needs to be separately locked compartments using a code for the appropriate customer to unlock the compartment.

In general, autonomous home delivery will require the following functions to interface with customers:

1. **Delivery window**. Once the order is placed, there needs to be an agreed-upon window of time for the delivery so that the customer will be home for the delivery. There also needs to be communications with the customer if the delivery window needs to change or if the customer is no longer going to be home to accept the delivery.

2. **Notification of approaching delivery**. When the delivery vehicle is approaching the home for a delivery, it must notify the customer that it will be there in a few minutes, so the customer can come out to get it. Once the vehicle is at the delivery location, it needs to notify the customer that it is there.

3. **Code to unlock compartment**. The delivery service needs to provide the customer with the appropriate delivery code to unlock the proper compartment on the vehicle.

4. **Confirmation of receipt**. The customer needs to provide some sort of confirmation that the delivery was received. Then the vehicle will continue its route or return to its home base.

5. **Customer service contact**. In many cases, there will also be a direct contact capability to deal with problems and issues. This could either be a voice or text service.

6. **Specific delivery location options**. Eventually, autonomous delivery services will provide options for specific delivery locations, such as having the autonomous vehicle go up a driveway, stop at a specifically designated curb location, etc. This capability will take some time to develop.

Ford and Domino's conducted early studies aimed at trying to understand how customers might interact with an autonomous delivery vehicle. The companies conducted a month-long trial in Ann Arbor, and the big questions revolved around whether customers would be put off by the idea of having to walk outside and collect a pizza from the back of a car. Customers who ordered pizza using the chain's online app were asked if they wanted to be part of the test. About 100 trips were conducted. For this test, all cars had a driver on board, but the driver was instructed not to take part in delivering the pizzas or interact with customers. The customers were surveyed afterward about the experience. They liked it, the companies said. They liked not having to talk with a human or feeling required to tip.

But the test also showed some logistical issues, such as the cars having trouble finding a place to park or navigating to the correct entrance of an apartment complex. And while customers liked the lack of human contact, many still wanted some interaction. It also highlighted a problem to be worked out: Parents would order a pizza for their children before leaving for a night out in the town. However, the delivery vehicle was programmed to contact the phone that ordered the pizza to alert the customer that dinner had arrived, a hitch that could result in some failed deliveries.

Autonomous Home Delivery Vehicles

Again, drawing on the comparison with autonomous ride services (ARS), autonomous home delivery vehicles will be developed in two generations. The first will use modified versions of autonomous vehicles based on standard production vehicles or designed for ARS. Basically, an autonomous vehicle is further modified for delivery. There may be storage compartments instead of doors, but the vehicle will use the same production vehicle chassis. These vehicles will be used to pilot test and prove autonomous delivery.

Companies primarily focusing on autonomous ride services intend to use the same vehicles, or modified versions, for autonomous delivery. For example, in January 2020, Waymo partnered with UPS to launch a package delivery pilot program. The Waymo Driver shuttles packages from UPS Stores in the Phoenix area to the company's Tempe hub. The goal is to get packages to UPS sorting facilities quicker and more frequently and allow for later drop-offs for next-day service. The autonomous vehicles are accompanied by a trained operator who monitors transportation operations. Waymo also expanded its partnership with AutoNation. They launched an autonomous parts delivery program, through which AutoNation uses the Waymo Driver to transport automotive parts directly to its business partners. For example, AutoNation staff members at a Tempe dealership can hail the Waymo Driver, place the ordered parts in the vehicle, and start the ride.

Walmart has a pilot program with General Motors' Cruise. Starting in 2021, some of Walmart's deliveries of groceries and other items will be dropped off at customers' homes by a small fleet of cruise AVs. Subsequently, Walmart invested an undisclosed sum in autonomous driving company Cruise. Walmart's investment is part of a larger $2.75 billion round of funding being raised by Cruise. Cruise plans to launch a delivery version of its Origin autonomous vehicle in 2022.

Ford/Argo has been testing autonomous delivery in Miami for several years. Ford has announced a new Self-Driving Vehicle Research Program designed to help businesses in Europe understand how autonomous vehicles can benefit their operations. One of the UK's leading consumer delivery specialists, Hermes, was the first business to partner with Ford on the program. Using a customized Ford commercial vehicle, the research aims to better understand how other road users would interact with an apparently driverless delivery van.

Second-generation autonomous delivery vehicles are designed specifically for home delivery. They will be smaller, cheaper vehicles with compartments for food, groceries, or packages. There won't be seats for a driver, other than possibly a way for a mechanic or service person to control the vehicle. They will most likely be colorful vehicles with advertising promoting the company that owns them and whose products they are delivering. They will most likely have some signage on the outside instructing customers what to do to remove the products.

Autonomous home delivery vehicles will be safer. They are smaller, generally about half the width and shorter than a normal car because they don't need to have room for a driver or passengers. They travel at lower speeds, generally a maximum of 25 to 35 miles per hour. And they can be designed to collapse upon impact in the event of a collision because there is no need to protect a human.

There will be two types of companies using these autonomous delivery vehicle fleets: large companies and third-party delivery companies. Large companies like Walmart, Domino's Pizza, or McDonalds will work with autonomous vehicle manufacturers to design a customized fleet of autonomous vehicles. These companies will most likely order 10,000 to 40,000 autonomous delivery vehicles over time. Third-party delivery companies like Grubhub and DoorDash will have more flexible customer-designed autonomous delivery vehicles.

Let's look at two companies developing these new vehicles. Nuro is the leader with its new small R2 vehicle. Udelv has a larger autonomous delivery vehicle designed for multiple deliveries.

Nuro

Nuro was started in 2016 by founders who previously worked at Waymo. As of the middle of 2021, Nuro had raised more than $1.5 billion in financing. It initially raised approximately $92 million in capital, and in 2019 it received another $940 million from SoftBank Group and others. In November 2020, it raised another $500 million Series C funding round, led by T. Rowe Price, with participation from new investors including Chipotle.

Existing investors SoftBank and Greylock also invested in the round. In December 2020, Nuro acquired self-driving trucking startup Ike Robotics, and Ike's 55 employees joined Nuro's staff after acquisition

The R1 was Nuro's initial autonomous delivery vehicle, which launched in Scottsdale, Arizona, in December 2018 with Kroger. Nuro claimed it was the first-ever unmanned delivery service for the public. It was about half the width of a typical car sedan and weighed less than half. There wasn't any passenger-designated space in the R1. Instead, the interior space was used to carry cargo. Nuro tested the R1 in several different markets. In 2018, Nuro started testing with Kroger, delivering groceries in the R1. Initially, self-driving Toyota Prius cars were used for the pilot.

In February 2020, Nuro announced its plans to test R2, its second generation-autonomous delivery vehicle, in Houston, Texas. In April 2020, Nuro announced that the R2 prototype was being used to transport medical supplies around medical facilities in California. The R2 retained the unique design and the key characteristics that made R1 a success, but it extends the vehicle's lifespan, adds more cargo space, and handles more varied conditions.

Rather than custom-making each individual vehicle, as it had with R1, it is partnering with Roush, based in Michigan, to design and assemble its vehicles in the United States. The R2 has a more durable vehicle body, enabling it to handle inclement weather. It also has an updated sensor array with both supplier-provided and custom in-house sensors. Storage space was increased by two-thirds without increasing vehicle width, and the R2 has temperature control to help keep food fresh. It uses a custom battery solution that nearly doubled the battery size, enabling all-day operation. The R2 has a maximum speed of 25 MPH, a gross vehicle weight of 1,150kg, and a carrying capacity of 22 square feet. It has curbside delivery doors that enable customers to retrieve goods without stepping into traffic. The R2 also features safety innovations designed to keep what's outside the vehicle safer than what's inside.

In December 2020, California's Department of Motor Vehicles approved a license for Nuro to deploy its autonomous vehicles on public streets to make commercial deliveries. Nuro was the first company to be granted a commercial deployment permit by the State of California.

It applied for a regulatory exemption from NHTSA and received one in February 2020. It was the first-ever autonomous vehicle to receive an approved exemption from the National Highway Traffic Safety Administration. Federal vehicle standards were written for traditional passenger cars and trucks, all for passenger safety. But Nuro has a zero-occupant vehicle. The DOT exemption process was designed to accommodate unforeseen technologies like R2 that can enhance safety.

The exemption allows Nuro to replace the mirrors relied on by human drivers with cameras and other sensors. It could round the edges of the vehicle body to take up less road space and make it safer for others. It could remove the windshield meant to let human drivers see out and instead use a specially designed panel at the vehicle's front that absorbs energy and better protects pedestrians. And it doesn't need to turn off the rearview cameras (meant to avoid distracting human drivers), providing a constant 360-degree view with no blind spots.

However, there are limits to the exemption granted to Nuro. The exemption lasts two years on a conditional basis. Nuro must submit reports on the performance of its vehicles, and it must notify communities where the R2 will be operating. Finally, Nuro can't produce and deploy more than 5,000 R2 vehicles during the two-year exemption period.

Nuro is developing some strong partnerships with some significant companies such as Domino's, Kroger, Walmart, CVS, and FedEx.

In May 2020, Nuro started partnering with CVS Pharmacy. This brought Nuro into the health space, delivering prescriptions and essentials across three zip codes in Houston. CVS customers in the Houston pilot area can place prescription orders along with their non-prescription items on CVS.com or via the CVS Mobile Pharmacy app. If they select the autonomous delivery option, one of Nuro's autonomous vehicles (Prius at that time) will deliver the purchase curbside at the customer's address within three hours. To ensure the security of their prescriptions, customers will need to confirm their identity to unlock their delivery when Nuro's autonomous vehicle arrives curbside at their preferred location.

In April 2021, Domino's Pizza started delivering pizzas via Nuro autonomous vehicles in Houston as part of a pilot program. Selected customers in

Houston who make a prepaid delivery order from its store in the Woodland Heights neighborhood during certain dates and times can have their pizza brought to them by a Nuro R2 robot. Here's how the pizza deliveries will work: a customer places and pays for an order online from the Woodland Heights store and opts in to have the order brought by the R2. The customer receives a unique PIN via text alert along with updates on the vehicle's location. When the robot car arrives, the customer enters the PIN on its touch screen, which opens the R2's doors to get the pizza. Given the importance of autonomous pizza delivery as one of the first markets, this is an important step for Nuro.

In June 2021, FedEx Corp. and Nuro announce a multi-year, multi-phase agreement to test Nuro's next-generation autonomous delivery vehicle within FedEx operations. The collaboration between FedEx and Nuro launched in April with a pilot program across the Houston area. This pilot provides Nuro with expansion into parcel logistics and allows FedEx the opportunity to explore various use cases for on-road autonomous vehicle logistics, including multi-stop and appointment-based deliveries.

Nuro has an excellent strategy, little competition, and is highly funded, so its chance of success is very high.

Udelv

Udelv is a California company that created the world's first custom-made public road self-driving delivery vehicle. In January 2018, Udelv successfully accomplished the first autonomous delivery made on public roads. Since then, Udelv has completed hundreds of deliveries for multiple clients in the San Francisco Bay Area. Its focus is autonomous last- and middle-mile delivery.

Udelv announced in April 2021 that it shifted its technical strategy from using Baidu's Apollo software to using Mobileye Drive. At the same time is developing a new delivery vehicle called the Transporter. It's an upgrade in concept from its previous vehicle. The Transporters can be more affordable since they don't require systems for a human occupant, such as seat belts,  airbags, windshield wipers, mirrors, and a steering wheel or pedals. The first order for 1,000 of the Mobileye-powered Transporters was made by Donlen, one of America's largest commercial fleet management companies.

Mobileye's Road Experience Management is a crowd-sourced mapping scheme. Mobileye claims that it is mapping more than 8 million kilometers of roads daily and has mapped nearly a billion kilometers of roads thus far. The company expects to be mapping one billion kilometers daily by 2024.

The Mobileye Drive self-driving system that will be the brain behind the Transporters is built around the company's EyeQ system-on-chip (SoC). It's combined with the company's proprietary Road Experience Management AV mapping solution and Responsibility-Sensitive Safety (RSS), which uses a mathematical model to always keep a safe distance from other vehicles. Intel purchased Mobileye in 2017 for $15.3 billion to gain a foothold in the automotive industry.

Mobileye takes a unique approach by separating the sensors in two channels – one for cameras and another for radar and lidar. The idea is to have each channel independently prove safety and fuse the two channels later. In contrast, the rivals' approach deploys complementary sensors, fuse them together from the very beginning to create a single world model.

The Transporter will be deployed in conjunction with Udelv-developed, proprietary teleoperator system. Teleoperation may be essential for goods delivery because sometimes delivery vehicles must navigate complex areas that are not mapped or loading zones are not clear. Teleoperators also must troubleshoot to guide self-driving vans to a safe state.

Udelv said it has already performed extensive deployment trials with customers across various industries, so the Transporters have been fully tested and are ready for deployment. Udelv has completed over 20,000 deliveries for multiple shipping customers in California, Arizona, and Texas and is preparing for expansion to other states.

Udelv describes its autonomous delivery process as follow:

1. The Merchant loads the vehicle. As a Merchant, you'll see all orders appear in the Udelv Merchant app (available for iPhone and Android). Tap to open a compartment, load an order, and move on to the next one. Client order matching is automated on the back end, and loading takes a few seconds per order.

2. Customers receive a precise ETA, track the vehicle, and get notified when it arrives.

3. The Customer retrieves their order. Customers can use the Udelv app (available for iPhone and Android) or respond to the text notifications to open their compartment.

4. Udelv offers users a paradigm shift in the way deliveries are completed: instead of a large delivery window, customers will be able to name a precise delivery time and location. If the customer misses the delivery, Udelv's back-end system will check availabilities in real-

time and reschedule the delivery for another time of the user's choosing.

Udelv intends to offer monthly subscriptions to its clients instead of selling the Transporters. An early market opportunity may be business-to-business goods delivery because these are fixed, repeatable routes. The Transporter van, running at 65 miles per hour, is expected to do 250 to 300 miles a day, and it is expected to have a sizeable EV battery. Udelv plans to produce more than 35,000 Transporters by 2028, with commercial operation beginning in 2023.

Small Autonomous Delivery Vehicles

A lesser market segment for autonomous delivery is small delivery vehicles. These vehicles are suitcase sized and drive autonomously at low speeds using sidewalks and walkways instead of streets. College campuses are the primary market for these small delivery vehicles since they are not as effective in traveling on public streets. The Russian company, Yandex, is one company making these small delivery vehicles. They have tested them extensively in Russia, and in 2021, Grubhub will start using these on college campuses.

Chapter 10
Autonomous Vehicles - Retail

Eventually, autonomous vehicles will be sold to individuals at retail as most cars are today. However, this market will take longer to evolve than others like ARS, long-haul trucking, and autonomous home delivery. This chapter covers the market for autonomous vehicles sold at retail that will be individually owned.

There are some significant differences between an ARS autonomous vehicle (AV) and an individually-owned autonomous vehicle.

- Retail sales of vehicles with autonomous capabilities to individuals will follow a progression of increasing autonomy. This is different from ARS AVs, which must be autonomous enough to drive themselves in most instances.

- ARS AVs operate in geofenced areas, which is not a problem since that will define their service area. Individually owned AVs can't be restricted to these boundaries, so they will still require human driver controls.

- So, individually-owned AVs will still need a driver's seat, steering wheel, brakes, etc. ARS AVs won't need those and can have more open designs. Drivers can choose to turn over driving control to the vehicle or drive it themselves.

We have already seen the addition of ADAS (Advanced Driver Assistance Systems) and basic semi-autonomous capabilities on many new high-end vehicles. Basic semi-autonomous capabilities include adaptive cruise control combined with lane-keeping or preferably lane-centering, as well as some form of automatic braking. Early experiences show that some drivers use these capabilities extensively, while others have them but choose to ignore them.

These basic semi-autonomous capabilities are extended with additional autonomous functions, such as automatic lane changing, automated parking, traffic jam control, etc. Vehicles will get progressively autonomous as new capabilities are introduced, initially as options, and then as standard equipment in higher-end models. As the costs of these technologies are reduced, they will begin to appear in medium- and lower-end vehicles.

At some point in the progression of becoming increasingly autonomous, individually-owned autonomous vehicles will be considered sufficiently-autonomous. The driver can then let the vehicle drive for long periods and not pay attention. However, there will be unmapped roads and areas where the driver will need to take over the driving.

Auto manufacturers are not oblivious to the impending changes in their markets, and they are aggressively shifting their business strategies and even their business models. In general, they are all following variations of a similar strategic sequence.

- They are reducing manufacturing capacity and costs to adjust to the coming reduction in traditional auto sales.

- They are investing heavily in shifting to develop electric vehicles. These newly designed electric vehicles will most likely be the primary platforms for the progression of autonomous capabilities in AVs sold at retail.

- Many are creating autonomous ride services businesses for the early introduction of autonomous driving. All auto manufacturers adjusted their strategies to focus on autonomous ride services ahead of retail sales of AVs.

- Finally, they are increasing the number of autonomous functions that they offer in new models, with the expectation that they will eventually offer sufficiently-autonomous driving capabilities.

This chapter will first look at the progression of autonomous capabilities in vehicles sold at retail: semi-autonomous, to sufficiently-autonomous, and eventually to fully-autonomous. We will see how the application of sufficiently-autonomous is a little different in this market. Then we will conclude with an overview of the autonomous vehicle strategies of auto manufacturers and Tesla.

Progression of Autonomous Capabilities

Autonomous capabilities in individually-owned vehicles will progress over time. This progression is best illustrated by looking again at the SAE definitions for Levels of Driving Automation.

SAE **J3016**™ LEVELS OF DRIVING AUTOMATION™

Learn more here: sae.org/standards/content/j3016_202104

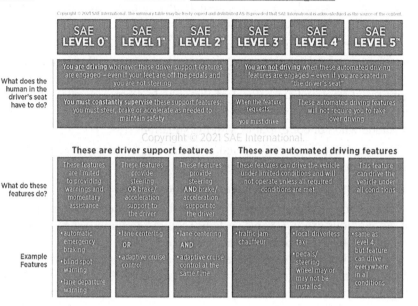

	SAE LEVEL 0"	SAE LEVEL 1"	SAE LEVEL 2"	SAE LEVEL 3"	SAE LEVEL 4"	SAE LEVEL 5"
What does the human in the driver's seat have to do?	You are driving whenever these driver support features are engaged – even if your feet are off the pedals and you are not steering			You are not driving when these automated driving features are engaged – even if you are seated in "the driver's seat"		
	You must constantly supervise these support features; you must steer, brake or accelerate as needed to maintain safety			When the feature requests, you must drive	These automated driving features will not require you to take over driving	
	These are driver support features			These are automated driving features		
What do these features do?	These features are limited to providing warnings and momentary assistance	These features provide steering OR brake/ acceleration support to the driver	These features provide steering AND brake/ acceleration support to the driver	These features can drive the vehicle under limited conditions and will not operate unless all required conditions are met		This feature can drive the vehicle under all conditions
Example Features	• automatic emergency braking • blind spot warning • lane departure warning	• lane centering OR • adaptive cruise control	• lane centering AND • adaptive cruise control at the same time	• traffic jam chauffeur	• local driverless taxi • pedals/ steering wheel may or may not be installed	• same as level 4 but feature can drive everywhere in all conditions

Semi-autonomous is SAE Level 2 driving. It requires lane centering, adaptive cruise control, and automatic braking. Sufficiently-autonomous driving is SAE Level 3 for individually-owned vehicles and Level 4 for ARS vehicles. The primary distinction is the comment: "when requested: you must drive." ARS vehicles are limited to geofenced routes and boundaries, so they never need to ask a driver to take control. Let's look at these more closely. As you can see, there is a big difference between the two because Level 4 does not require driver control such as a steering wheel, brakes, or pedals.

Semi-Autonomous Vehicles

Semi-autonomous capabilities are becoming increasingly popular. These capabilities include: (1) the ability of the vehicle to determine and set its speed based on a driver-requested maximum, adjusted for the speed of cars ahead (adaptive cruise control), and recently speed can be automatically adjusted based on speed limits, (2) the ability of the vehicle to steer within lane markings on the road (lane centering), and (3) the ability to brake automatically if traffic stops quickly, or an object crosses the path of the vehicle. Drivers increasingly use these semi-autonomous features, especially for highway driving.

Semi-autonomous functions are growing beyond these three minimum capabilities. A Tesla vehicle, for example, has several more advanced capabilities: (1) it can use navigation to steer the vehicle onto a highway exit automatically and slow its speed, (2) it can automatically set the speed based on speed-limit signs, (3) it can automatically change lanes when the driver engages the turn signal, (4) it can automatically stop at traffic lights and stop signs, and (5) it can be summoned to come to the driver.

I've used semi-autonomous capabilities to drive thousands of miles in both a Tesla and a Mercedes, and they work very well. Semi-autonomous driving mode is equivalent to SAE Level 2, and drivers must be attentive enough to take immediate control of the vehicle when requested. Also, the driver must continuously monitor conditions and disable the semi-autonomous mode when uncomfortable with the situation.

Let's look closer at semi-autonomous driving, including how it is implemented, its adoption rate, and its benefits and risks.

Different Approaches to Semi-Autonomous Driving

Vehicle manufacturers use several different approaches to implementing semi-autonomous driving. Some systems require a minimum speed to engage semi-autonomous capabilities because they may not operate sufficiently at lower speeds. Likewise, some systems have maximum speeds, and others restrict speeds based on posted speed limits below certain speeds. My Tesla, for example, is set to a maximum speed of 5 MPH above posted speed limits when they are 45 MPH or lower.

All semi-autonomous driving systems use some method of monitoring driving awareness because drivers must be ready to take immediate control. Most require the driver to slightly turn the steering wheel regularly, or it issues a warning and eventually stops the vehicle if there is no response. Some use an internal camera to monitor driver awareness.

All systems require lane markings, but there are differences in how strict they are, with Tesla being the most flexible. There are also differences in the turning degree of lane centering, again with Tesla being the broadest. Remember that lane centering is not turning a corner.

Traffic-jam assistance capabilities function a little differently. They can take over steering at speeds of up to 40 MPH on well-developed roads when traffic is congested. They require a low speed and the presence of cars on both sides.

GM uses a unique approach to semi-autonomous driving. Instead of making it available wherever road markings allow, it maps and pre-approves certain highways for its use. GM's hands-free driver assistance system, Super Cruise, has been lauded for its capabilities, but it's also been criticized because it is limited to certain highways. So far, use is restricted to certain divided highways, more than 270,000 miles of highways by the middle of 2021. GM will start rolling Super Cruise out across brands other than Cadillac. The system should be on 22 vehicles by 2023. Super Cruise is somewhat like what is expected of more advanced sufficiently-autonomous vehicles. It uses a combination of lidar-generated map data with a scan accuracy of 5 centimeters (which is why it authorizes only routes that are mapped), high-precision GPS, cameras, and radar sensors, as well as a driver attention system, which monitors the person behind the wheel to ensure they're paying attention. Users of Super Cruise do not need to have their hands on the wheel. However, their eyes must remain directed straight ahead.

Rapid Adoption

The increase in vehicle sales with semi-autonomous driving capabilities is striking, both in the U.S. and Europe. In Q2/19, more than 250,000 vehicles were sold with level 2 capabilities, an increase of 322% over Q1/18. This represented 7% of new car sales up from less than 2% a year earlier.[vii] Similarly in Europe, the sales of semi-autonomous (Level 2) cars in Q2/19 was 8% (325,000 cars) of all sales, compared to just 3% in the same period in 2018.[viii] I expect that the percentage of vehicles sold with semi-autonomous capabilities will continue to increase.

There is a caveat, however. Some people who purchase these semi-autonomous capabilities don't use them very often. Some drivers are even irritated by simple driver assistance functions like lane warnings, but I expect this will change with time. The proportion of new cars sold with semi-autonomous capabilities will continue to increase rapidly. By 2025, I expect that more than half of all new vehicles will have semi-autonomous capabilities.

Lower price is one reason for more rapid adoption. Generally, these capabilities are sold as options, but the cost of those options is declining.

Increased Convenience

Semi-autonomous vehicles are already providing benefits to those who use them. It makes driving on highways and in traffic less stressful and safer. Here is one person's example:[ix]

Southern California, like many parts of the country, has terrible traffic. With almost 13 million Californians alone driving into work each day, it's no wonder. When I have a long commute, the waves of traffic every few miles are enough to make me loathe driving.

An overlooked aspect to the increased automation of our vehicles is the potential productivity boost American workers could get from expending less mental energy on all that effort getting to and from work. Certainly, if I'm any gauge, I've found driving less taxing since I started driving my Tesla with its Autopilot option on. The car starts and stops when traffic starts moving, so I don't have people laying on their horns if I'm not paying close enough attention to the traffic flow. I don't need to keep my foot on the gas pedal, and I'm probably delaying some future visits to the mechanic because I don't ride the brake anymore. The car basically does the thinking for me. My Tesla has radar and sensors that cover my blind spots -- it recognizes motorcycles between lanes as well as pedestrians walking. It doesn't follow too closely to traffic in front and slows automatically as it senses traffic slowing, too. These take some of the burdens off my brain. And thus, I have more mental energy when I get to where I'm going.

Increased Safety

Semi-autonomous driving is safer than purely human driving. The vehicle maintains a safe speed and distance behind cars in front. It automatically brakes even before the human driver can physically react to a danger. It keeps the vehicle from veering out of its lane.

There is already sufficient data proving that the use of ADAS systems improves safety. For example, The Insurance Institute for Highway Safety, Highway Loss Data Institute, estimates a 50% reduction in 2020 of front-to-rear crashes with forward collision warning combined with auto braking.

Tesla reports accident data every quarter based on the data it collects from all its vehicles. Vehicles using autopilot consistently have much lower accident rates than others. It presented the following safety statistics in its Tesla Vehicle Safety Report for the first quarter of 2021:

In the 1st quarter (2021), we registered one accident for every 4.19 million miles driven in which drivers had Autopilot engaged. For those driving without Autopilot but with our active safety features, we registered one accident for every 2.05 million miles driven. For those driving without Autopilot and without our active safety features, we registered one accident for every 978 thousand miles driven. By comparison, NHTSA's most recent data shows that in the United States there is an automobile crash every 484,000 miles.

Risks of Semi-Autonomous Driving

Although capable of being safer, semi-autonomous driving has its risks. These are primarily related to drivers not being attentive enough to take control of the vehicle immediately when needed.

There have been several accidents involving vehicles operating in semi-autonomous mode, including three fatal Tesla accidents. In these cases, the driver did not take control of the vehicle when needed, and in at least one of these cases, the driver fooled the car controls into thinking he was paying attention.

- On March 23, 2018, a Tesla Model X crashed into a freeway divider, killing the driver. According to the NTSB, the vehicle accelerated from 62 to 71 MPH before the crash with no braking or evasive steering. Autopilot was engaged, and the speed was set for 75, but the driver's hands were not on the steering wheel for the last 6 seconds. The driver had  before his accident that the Autopilot system would malfunction in the area where the crash happened. The barrier was also a location of frequent accidents. In the three years before the Tesla crash, it was struck at least five times, including one crash that resulted in fatalities. It was previously damaged and not repaired prior to the Tesla accident. In reviewing a video by a subsequent Tesla driver who drove the exact location, it is possible that the vehicle misread irregularly painted lines that veered off to the left and moved the vehicle in that direction, accelerating as the car in front was no longer in its path.

- On March 1, 2019, a 2018 Tesla Model 3 in Delray Beach struck a semi-truck with a trailer. As the Tesla approached a private driveway, the truck pulled from the driveway. The truck driver was trying to cross the highway's southbound lanes and turn left into the northbound lanes, blocking the Tesla's path. The Tesla struck the left side of the semitrailer. The driver engaged the Autopilot about 10 seconds before the collision. From less than 8 seconds before the crash to the time of impact, the vehicle did not detect the driver's hands on the steering wheel. Preliminary vehicle data indicates that the Tesla was traveling about 68 mph when it struck the semitrailer. Neither the preliminary data nor the videos suggest that the driver or Autopilot executed evasive maneuvers.

- In May 2016, a Tesla driver was killed in a crash while his car was on Autopilot. Like the previous accident, the Model S "passed under" a semitrailer that had been making a left turn across traffic on a Florida freeway. The National Transportation Safety Board report disclosed that the driver had been using Autopilot for 37 minutes, out of which he had placed his hands on the wheel for a total of just 25 seconds, despite seven separate visual warnings from the system flashed the message: "Hands required not detected." They do not know what the Model S driver was paying attention to instead of the road at the time of his fatal accident, but he took no evasive action. The NTSB report says he had set the software to a cruising speed of 74 mph shortly before the crash, and it was still going that speed when the car hit the truck's trailer broadside. The report suggests the truck driver could have foreseen the crash. A witness said the Model S was visible to the truck over the crest of a rise in the freeway for "several seconds" before the truck began its left turn. The implication is that the truck driver either didn't see the Model S coming or assumed, given the truck's size and visibility, that the Tesla's driver would stop to avoid the collision. That seems like a safe assumption when the driver is human but perhaps less so when the driver is an automated system. This accident, as well as the previous one, also raise the issue of the reliability of monochrome camera-based systems.

- In April 2021, two men were killed in Texas after a Tesla they were in crashed and burned. Based on physical evidence and witness interviews, investigators claimed that neither of them was behind the wheel at the time of the crash, but this was subsequently disputed. According to police reports, the vehicle, a 2019 Model S, was going at a "high rate of speed" around a curve at 11:25 p.m. local time when it went off the road about 100 feet and hit a tree. The crash occurred in a residential area in the Woodlands, north of Houston. It was reported that minutes before the crash, the men's wives watched them leave in the Tesla after they said they wanted to go for a drive and were talking about the vehicle's Autopilot feature.

- In May 2021, a 35-year-old man was killed when his Tesla Model 3 struck an overturned semi on a freeway at about 2:30 a.m. crash in Fontana, 50 miles east of Los Angeles. Another man was seriously injured when the Tesla hit him as he was helping the semi's driver out of the wreck. The California Highway Patrol said that the car had been operating on Autopilot, Tesla's partially automated driving system.

These tragic accidents illustrate how semi-autonomous driving can be dangerous when misused as fully-autonomous, but do not illustrate a heightened risk from autonomous driving capabilities. There are numerous stories and videos demonstrating how Tesla vehicles in Autopilot (semi-autonomous) mode have avoided accidents and saved lives. It has taken over from drivers who have unintentionally fallen asleep or had sudden medical issues. It has abruptly stopped the vehicle when a car ahead stopped suddenly, or an accident occurred. It has automatically stopped (before a human could) when an animal suddenly appeared on the road directly in front. It has stopped or swerved the car when another vehicle veered or moved into a driver's lane.

The correct conclusions are that Tesla's misnamed Autopilot is semi-autonomous, and there are risks if it is used as autonomous. There is no basis to conclude that these accidents are an indictment of autonomous driving.

Sufficiently-Autonomous for Individually-Owned Vehicles

The definition of sufficiently-autonomous is that AVs can drive on their own from location to location, which are generally restricted to geofenced routes and locations. These AVs will generally be deployed in fleets. For individually owned AVs, instead of fleets, sufficiently-autonomous is a little different. Eventually, individuals will be able to use autonomous driving capabilities for most, if not all, of their driving, but they will still need to take control in some driving conditions. For example, they may still need to control driving up their driveway and into their garage, into parking garages, on unmapped areas, and similar situations. Sufficiently-autonomous fleets for ARS, autonomous home delivery, and autonomous long-haul trucking simply avoid these unmapped areas.

Individually-owned sufficiently-autonomous vehicles will still require driver controls, including a steering wheel, brakes, etc. It would be unacceptable for an AV to be unable to go everywhere it needs to go, either autonomously or manually driven. These vehicles will have different configurations than today's cars. Drivers will be able to turn around and face others when the car is driving autonomously. They will be able to do other tasks such as reading, watching movies, video conferencing, etc., while the vehicle is driving itself. Unlike in semi-autonomous mode, drivers won't need to take control immediately.

Sufficiently-autonomous individually-owned vehicles will be able to drive themselves most of the time, including all city and metropolitan roads, highways, etc. They will make all necessary turns, stop at traffic signs and lights, determine the routes to follow, follow speed limits, and avoid all obstacles. When they approach something that they can't navigate automatically, such as coming up a driveway, they will notify the driver to take control well in advance. If the driver doesn't take control, the vehicle will pull over and stop.

These vehicles will be different from semi-autonomous vehicles, just as semi-autonomous vehicles were different from those with no autonomous capabilities. Semi-autonomous vehicles added sensors such as radar and cameras to the vehicle and used more advanced computing.

Sufficiently-autonomous individually-owned vehicles most likely will add lidar and HD mapping. Initially, these capabilities may be limited to high-end vehicles and expensive options, but eventually they will become more standard as the costs decline and the advantages are recognized. A few years ago, these technologies were prohibitively expensive, but costs have come down significantly and will continue to decline.

Sufficiently-autonomous driving may work entirely for people who don't drive to any unmapped locations. Their driveways and garages may be mapped through custom mapping capabilities or a memory function in their AV. They may be able to easily park on mapped locations at work, and all the places they drive may be on the HD maps. They won't need to use the driver controls.

It's also expected that these vehicles will be able to drive themselves for many tasks without any driver. For example, they could drive themselves autonomously to a soccer field to pick up the children from practice and then return home with them, even if the vehicle couldn't yet park in the garage.

Fully-Autonomous Individually-Owned Vehicles

Fully-autonomous vehicles for individuals will take much longer to be deployed. It will require much more precise mapping, such as pull my car into the second garage bay. It will also require more advanced technology. However, the benefits for complete automation of individually-owned vehicles compared to sufficiently-autonomous are not that significant, so the development of fully-autonomous vehicles is not critical.

Auto Manufacturer Strategies

Auto manufacturers are the nucleus of a well-established industry for manufacturing, selling, delivering, and servicing cars. They manufacture almost 17 million cars sold in the U.S. They sell these through dealers across the country who arrange delivery and registration, and they provide after-sales customer service. Tesla, which manufactures its cars and sells them online, operates differently.

Auto manufacturers will be the most important competitors selling AVs at retail to individuals. In addition, Tesla will try to accomplish this in its own way. I don't expect that any technology companies like Waymo and Apple will find the retail market worth investing in the manufacturing and distribution required. There are also some small start-ups developing this technology, but most won't be able to scale sufficiently to provide the necessary manufacturing and distribution.

New companies with disruptive technologies have historically replaced established companies. Auto manufacturers know this, and they plan to avoid it by generally following a four-pronged strategy: (1) aggressively reducing costs and manufacturing capacity for traditional vehicles, (2) aggressively investing in new EV platforms, (3) introducing autonomous ride services as the early application of autonomous technology, and (4) progressively upgrading their retail customers to AVs. This strategy is the successful playbook for managing a disruptive platform shift like this. Disinvest in the platform being phased out and invest in the new platform. While it sounds logical and perhaps deceptively simple, the history of success in executing this change is not good. You can look to examples in the photography platform life-cycle with Kodak, Polaroid, and even Xerox, or the computer market with Digital Equipment and, to a lesser extent, IBM. Let's look a little more closely at the elements of this strategy.

Reduce Costs and Investment in Traditional ICE Vehicles

Auto manufacturers started aggressively reducing costs in 2018 and 2019. They cut manufacturing capacity and investment in traditional internal combustion engine (ICE) vehicles. This accelerated even further in 2020 with the pandemic.

GM acted early with cost reductions to adjust for declining sales. In 2018, it ended production at five plants in the U.S. and Canada, killing off several passenger-car models, and cutting 15% of its salaried workforce. As part of this cost reduction, it discontinued the Chevrolet Impala, Chevrolet Cruze and Volt in North America as well as the Buick LaCrosse. GM shrank the company globally to focus on regions where it was most profitable.

Ford made major cost reductions too. In 2017, it announced plans to reduce spending by $14 billion over the 2018-2022 period. In April 2018, Ford increased this cost-cutting target to $25.5 billion. Ford is shifting capital investment away from sedans and internal combustion engines to develop more trucks and electric vehicles. Ford plans to stop selling all sedans in North America. The only cars it will keep in North America beyond their current generations are the Mustang and the Focus Active. Most of the Ford portfolio in the North American market will be trucks, utilities, and commercial vehicles. It also intends to weed out slow-selling models and potentially close factories in Europe.

The reduction in investment in the previous auto platform, ICE, enables them to shift investment to two critical new technologies.

Invest in New EV Platforms

The sale of electric vehicles is expected to proliferate. Approximately 2 million EVs were sold in 2019. Although the number declined along with all auto sales in 2020, it is forecasted to increase in 2021 and reach 8-10 million by 2025. Some forecast that EV sales will be greater than that of internal combustion engine (ICE) vehicles by 2030 or even earlier. Hundreds of new EV models are expected to be released by 2025, which will drive rapid growth in EV sales. However, the expected sales from these new models and the increasing expectations from Tesla will most likely exceed the total projected market. Dealer networks may provide a competitive advantage for legacy automakers. Will new EV customers prefer to continue going to their regular auto dealer to buy their new EV?

GM is committed to introducing 20 new electric vehicles by 2023, including EVs across Chevrolet, Cadillac, GMC, and Buick. It has already sold out the first-year production of its Hummer electric pickup. By mid-decade, it expects to sell a million EVs per year in its two largest markets: North America and China. As a reference point, Tesla reported deliveries of 367,500 vehicles globally in 2019.

GM has a solid platform strategy for its EVs. It plans on building them using five interchangeable drive units and three different motors from its Ultium Drive System platform. Ultium energy options range from 50 to 200 kWh, enabling an estimated range of up to 400 miles. Most of its EVs will have 400-volt battery packs and up to 200 kW fast-charging capabilities, while the truck platform will have 800-volt battery packs and 350 kW fast-charging capabilities.

The fundamental building blocks of the Ultium battery system are large-scale, high-energy cells. Engineered in partnership with LG Energy Solutions, they use both advanced chemistry and an intelligent cell design that's optimized for a broad portfolio of EVs. GM engineers and scientists are actively researching and testing new elements in battery chemistry to lower costs and improve charge times. Ultium can contain either vertically- or horizontally-stacked cells to integrate into vehicle design: vertically for trucks, SUVs, and crossovers, or horizontally for cars and performance vehicles. As new chemistry is developed and becomes available, the battery management system could digitally update the modules.

GM also has other EV opportunities with its BrightDrop commercial EV service. BrightDrop will not just sell delivery EVs. It will provide an entire service platform for commercial delivery customers. It includes the EV600 and the BrightDrop EP1, a pod-like electric pallet

Likewise, Ford is investing heavily in EVs. It introduced the Mustang Mach-E, a battery-powered crossover with sports car styling, as well as an all-electric version of its best-selling F-150 pickup. Also planned is an electric edition of the full-size Transit van, popular in the commercial delivery market. Ford has confirmed plans to build a luxury Lincoln crossover on a battery-powered platform provided by Rivian. The automaker also plans to introduce two new midsize electric crossovers for the Ford and Lincoln brands by 2023. Volkswagen has also committed billions to develop new EVs.

Invest in ARS

U.S. auto manufacturers now realize that ARS will be the initial market for autonomous vehicles. The retail market will follow later by 4-5 years. They chose not to wait until the retail market comes about. Instead, they are aggressively entering the ARS market for mobility-as-a-service. They know that waiting for the retail market will put them at a considerable disadvantage. The auto manufacturers' strategies for autonomous ride services were detailed in a previous chapter.

Progressively Upgrade Customers to More Autonomous Capabilities

As was previously described, auto manufacturers will gradually introduce more autonomous driving capabilities. Semi-autonomous features will be increasingly integrated into all new cars, and the number of features will continue to increase. Drivers will be able to drive more autonomously as they upgrade to more autonomous features. Eventually, vehicles purchased at retail will cross the threshold to be considered sufficiently-autonomous. Most likely, they will incorporate lidar and HD maps at this point.

Tesla Strategy

Tesla first gained widespread attention following its production of the Tesla Roadster, the first electric sports car, in 2008. The company's second vehicle, the Model S, an electric luxury sedan, debuted in 2012 and was built at the Tesla Factory in California. The Model S was then followed in September 2015 by the Model X, a crossover SUV. Tesla introduced the Model 3 for a starting base price of around $35,000 in 2018.

Tesla's product strategy emulates other successful technology companies. It created a unique technology platform with its battery, powertrain, and semi-autonomous driving technology. It initially entered the market with an expensive, high-end product, targeted at affluent buyers. Then, as the cost of the platform was reduced, it moved into larger, more competitive markets at lower price points.

Tesla's Retail Sales/Service Infrastructure

Because Tesla doesn't have auto dealers to sell its cars, it created a unique sales, service, and distribution channel. It owns and operates more than 200 stores and galleries in the United States (although it announced that it intended to close many of its stores as a cost reduction). However, it must sell directly to customers online because 48 states have laws to protect auto dealers that restrict manufacturers from selling vehicles directly to consumers. Dealership associations in multiple states have filed numerous lawsuits against Tesla to prevent the company from selling cars directly. The Federal Trade Commission recommends allowing direct manufacturer sales, so those restrictions eventually may be lifted.

Tesla is struggling to have enough service centers as it expands its customer base. Because of the proprietary nature of its cars, most major services must be done by Tesla. Tesla previously used a valet service to pick up cars but now sends technicians to the owner's home to do much of the maintenance.

To make its electric cars feasible for longer-range driving, Tesla created a network of high-powered Superchargers located across North America, Europe, and Asia. It also operates a Destination Charging program, under which shops, restaurants, and other venues provide fast-charging stations for their customers.

Tesla's biggest challenge is manufacturing cars in sufficient volume. It has had to build auto manufacturing plants, purchase and implement the necessary equipment, and recruit and train a team of car manufacturing people. But its infrastructure problems extend beyond just making and servicing its cars. It struggles to get its cars delivered to customers even long after they have bought or leased them. Cars already sold just sit at distribution points because they can't be delivered to customers. Tesla employees don't know how to handle the paperwork for selling and leasing cars. I know this from personal experience. It took Tesla 3 weeks to deliver my car that was sitting at a distribution point, and then they told me that it would take them 4-6 weeks to process the registration for a leased car.

Tesla AV Development

Tesla invests almost $1 billion in R&D annually and has invested more than $5 billion since its inception. It's difficult to determine how much of this is invested in autonomous driving since it also invests in electric car and battery technologies. Tesla worked with Advanced Micro Devices to develop its own artificial intelligence processor to replace the Nvidia processor it previously used.

Tesla initially worked with Mobileye (subsequently acquired by Intel), but in September 2016, Tesla and Mobileye dissolved their partnership, leaving Tesla to develop its own driving-assist Autopilot technology. Musk claims that engineers at Tesla recreated the technology powering the Mobileye chip in just six months.

Tesla offers two levels of autonomous technology: Tesla Autopilot for semi-autonomous driving, and a full self-driving capability that has yet to be fully released.

Tesla Autopilot

Tesla Autopilot is a suite of driver-assistance features, making driving safer and less stressful. It includes Traffic-Aware Cruise Control and Auto-Steer. Traffic-Aware Cruise Control matches the speed of the car to that of the surrounding traffic. Autosteer assists in steering within clearly marked lanes while using cruise control.

Navigate on Autopilot actively guides the car from a highway's on-ramp to off-ramp, including suggesting lane changes, navigating interchanges, automatically engaging the turn signal, and taking the correct exit. Auto Lane Change assists in moving to an adjacent lane on the highway when Autosteer is engaged. Autopark helps automatically parallel or perpendicularly park the car with a single touch. Summon moves the vehicle in and out of a tight space using the mobile app or key. Tesla is moving some of these features to its full self-driving capability.

Full Self-Driving Capability

Tesla is promising that all its new vehicles can eventually drive autonomously. It plans to gradually update these features through software updates. According to Tesla:

All new Tesla cars are expected to have the hardware needed in the future for full self-driving. The system is designed to be able to conduct short and long-distance trips with no action required by the person in the driver's seat.

All you will need to do is get in and tell your car where to go. If you don't say anything, the car will look at your calendar and take you there as the assumed destination or just home if nothing is on the calendar. Your Tesla will figure out the optimal route, navigate urban streets (even without lane markings), manage complex intersections with traffic lights, stop signs, and roundabouts, and handle densely packed freeways with cars moving at high speed. When you arrive at your destination, simply step out at the entrance and your car will enter park seek mode, automatically search for a spot, and park itself. A tap on your phone summons it back to you.

The future use of these features without supervision depends on achieving reliability far over human drivers as demonstrated by billions of miles of experience and regulatory approval, which may take longer in some jurisdictions. As these self-driving capabilities are introduced, your car will be continuously upgraded through over-the-air software updates.

These full self-driving capabilities will be released progressively through software updates. Those expected soon include recognizing and responding to traffic lights and stop signs. Automatic driving on city streets is promised in the future but will require a significant leap in technology to do it safely without lidar and detailed HD maps. Tesla uses GPS and its mapping to position the vehicle within a particular lane, but it has yet to prove that this will work sufficiently for full self-driving.

In the middle of 2019, Elon Musk shook up Tesla's software development group by replacing much of its leadership. His unhappiness with the Autopilot group appears to stem from difficulties it has had in adapting the software to work with city driving. The software was initially designed to automatically steer Tesla vehicles on highways. The Autopilot team had been trying to get the software to work in cities as part of the broader goal of achieving full self-driving. This may be the fundamental flaw in Tesla's goal for full self-driving. Autonomous driving on a highway is very different from making turns in cities. It requires a different software architecture, detailed maps with geofencing, and most likely lidar. This is very different from Tesla's platform.

Reliance on Vision Technology

The importance of lidar is one of the controversial technical issues for AVs. Tesla's AVs rely on vision systems, while most other companies additionally utilize lidar systems. Musk has reiterated Tesla's vision-based approach to reassure current owners that autonomy can be achieved using just cameras: "Once you solve cameras for vision, autonomy is solved; if you don't solve vision, it's not solved … You can absolutely be superhuman with just cameras." Tesla has yet to prove that it can have a full self-driving capability without lidar.

Tesla's Assessment

Tesla was one of the early pioneers in introducing semi-autonomous driving and promoting fully-autonomous possibilities. Tesla's stated objective is to be the leader in selling autonomous (Level 4-5) cars to the end customer. Its strategy is to progressively build autonomous capabilities into vehicle software. Certainly, the high valuation of its stock price indicates that many investors believe it will, although some of this confidence started to erode.

I expect that Tesla will have sold more than a million cars by 2021 that it claims will be capable of autonomous driving. If it can make them autonomous, and if half of the owners turn their cars into autonomous vehicles, and if its autonomous technology works (a big IF), Tesla could have 250,000 autonomous vehicles on the road by 2022. That "if" however, is a primary unproven assumption that I currently don't think will be valid.

I am a fan of Tesla (and own one), but there are major risks to its strategy. Tesla may have conflicting core strategic visions: Is its objective to build electric vehicles for the masses or to be a pioneer in autonomous driving? These may be inconsistent objectives. The introduction of the Model 3 creates a more affordable electric vehicle, but the evolution of autonomous driving initially may require more expensive vehicles. This dual strategy has forced Tesla to adopt a lower-cost strategy for its autonomous driving capabilities, particularly not using lidar. It also needs to overcome the sales, distribution, and service network challenges to sell at retail successfully. Scaling the service organization will be a challenge. Tesla needs to build quality cars in volume. Finally, Tesla will require an enormous amount of capital.

Overall, my assessment is that Tesla's strategy has enabled it to pioneer electric vehicles and semi-autonomous driving. This has been no small accomplishment. However, I question its ability to succeed with autonomous vehicles. Most of the early growth and success with autonomous vehicles will be in autonomous ride services, and I don't see the Tesla Network as being successful. Its technical approach to autonomous driving may not work.

Traditional car manufacturers are also catching up fast with Tesla. Once they have viable EVs, they will be capable of manufacturing them in volume and providing proven sales and service capabilities. Some of these companies may also be successful in the first AV market, ARS, where Tesla won't participate. Nevertheless, I hesitate to bet against Elon Musk and Tesla.

Chapter 11
Global AV Development

So far, I have focused almost exclusively on the U.S. Still, opportunities for autonomous vehicles (AVs) are not just restricted to the U.S. AV development is taking place throughout the world. In this chapter, we will look at the progress of AVs in other countries. This global view provides some interesting insights. Each country has unique dynamics such as government structure, population size, age, available technology, economic strength, etc., that will shape its future in AVs. Keep in mind an important point: AVs will initially provide autonomous ride services, which will be a local – not global – market, so the rate of introduction of AVs will be very different in each regional market.

The countries reviewed here are mostly the larger developed countries. This is where the introduction of AVs will come earlier, although there are a few exceptions. It will be a very long time before underdeveloped countries like those in Africa or Central America become viable markets for autonomous vehicles.

There are several published rankings of how prepared countries are for autonomous vehicles. I haven't tried to undertake such a classification. However, it appears clear that the U.S. and China are the two most prominent leaders in developing, testing, and introducing autonomous vehicle technologies.

China

China has the potential to be the largest global market for autonomous vehicles, and recently it has become much more aggressive in developing both electric and autonomous vehicles. China is now the world's largest and most important automotive market. The explosive growth in automobiles is overtaxing the country's infrastructure, increasing traffic congestion, and creating significant pollution. Electric and autonomous vehicles offer a solution to these problems in China. Moreover, autonomous vehicles are a target industry where China wants to lead the world by being the first to bring this technology to market. This sets up a global competition with other countries, particularly the U.S.

China's AV strategy[x] is aggressive. China is making a strong effort to be a leader in AV technology development, testing, and deployment. In addition to improving its auto industry, it wants to increase its auto-export potential as AV technology becomes a significant part of the automotive industry.

China has a unique situation in the automotive industry. Its position in the existing combustion engine and related technologies is relatively weak. It relies on joint ventures with European, American, Japanese, and Korean auto manufacturers. China believes that EV and AV technologies will be significant factors in better control of its automotive industry and becoming a significant exporter of AV vehicles and technology.

China has an aggressive national strategy to become a leader in AVs. Eleven Chinese governmental departments jointly issued their "Strategy for Innovation and Development of Intelligent Vehicles." in February 2020. The term intelligent vehicle is used interchangeably with an autonomous vehicle. The document is a proposal of how China plans to develop AVs over the next 30 years.

China's AV strategy focuses on developing technologies, but it also includes regulation, standards, and the need for disrupting existing transportation segments. The China AV strategy document covers technologies, infrastructure, cybersecurity, regulation, and international cooperation. A centralized government, like China's, can encourage and proactively promote technological disruption if it chooses.

China's AV strategy encourages the creation of open systems to gain rapid innovation. The Baidu Apollo AV platform is an example of creating a large ecosystem for many companies to accelerate innovation. The strategy also includes other technologies such as AV system architecture, AV and AI chips, AV software, software platforms (including operating systems), high-definition maps, and accurate location technologies.

China plans on using several technologies as infrastructure for AVs. High-definition maps are already used by most AV companies, including those in China. However, China has more restrictions on maps, and only a few Chinese companies have the necessary permits for developing HD maps within China. Most likely, this is one way to lockout foreign competition for autonomous ride services. China is also emphasizing its commitment to deploy 5G communication quickly as part of its AV infrastructure, although this may not be as critical as it thinks.

The China AV strategy document encourages domestic and international companies to cooperate on AV technology development in China. It also supports commercialization by global AV companies in China but requires the adoption of standards, certification, and accreditation. China's AV strategy emphasizes the importance of updating laws and standards for AVs. The AV strategy report has limited information on the AV timeline. However, the report includes several goals for 2025. China is poised to be the biggest AV competitor for the U.S.

Autonomous vehicle development is also a crucial part of its "Made in China 2025" plan. The government announced it would introduce strict regulations on foreign automobile companies' operations in China.

China showcased its autonomous vehicle expertise at the 2019 Spring Festival Gala, which by some estimates was the most watched television broadcast in the world with more than 800 million viewers. The segment, as part of the five-hour Gala featured more than 100 of BYD's AVs using Baidu's Apollo autonomous driving technology. The AVs drove themselves on the Hong Kong-Zhuhai-Macau bridge, making figure-8's as they drove on the bridge. This number is auspicious for many Chinese.

China also has unique market conditions making it an opportunity for faster adoption of autonomous ride services. Chinese people aren't as deeply rooted in car ownership. China's rate of vehicle ownership pales compared to Europe and the U.S. World Health Organization data shows that there were 830 vehicles per 1,000 people in the U.S. in 2015, six times higher than in China. In the European Union, that number totaled just over 500 per 1,000. With lower rates of car ownership and a higher demand for mobility, China is the largest ridesharing market in the world.

However, China's unique environment could also hinder the introduction of AVs. Its complex traffic situations will force autonomous vehicles to adapt to road conditions and aggressive driving behaviors. The country has highly complicated signage, with traffic lights and road signs not yet fully standardized. Likewise, right-of-way issues resulting from the failure of Chinese drivers to follow road rules add a significant element of uncertainty for autonomous vehicles.

As an alternative to AVs conquering the chaotic Chinese city streets, some companies are trying an alternative strategy. They are installing sensors on selected roads to guide AVs. This requires input from companies beyond AV developers. Mobile-network operators, such as China Mobile, and telecom-equipment manufacturers, like Huawei, are building technology into their systems to help AVs along the road. Huawei wants to use its 5G mobile antennas to play an important role in the processing required to run an AV, as well as take much of the AV profit. Lowering the cost per autonomous vehicle could accelerate the roll-out.

The Chinese government is also writing and enforcing rules about how humans move around, designing (or redesigning) urban landscapes to be AV-friendly, and limit AVs' legal liability. All this is easier in authoritarian China.

In addition, the authorities promote AV-friendly standards and regulations. They can build national test roads within an urban environment.

There are distinct AV passenger markets in China, just as there are in the U.S.: autonomous ride services, autonomous trucking, and retail sales of AVs. Autonomous trucking covered in a previous chapter included a couple of companies developing autonomous trucks simultaneously for both the U.S. and China.

Autonomous Ride Services

As in the U.S., autonomous ride services is expected to be the initial market for AVs in China. China has unique market conditions giving it an opportunity for faster adoption of autonomous ride services. As mentioned, with lower rates of car ownership and a higher demand for mobility, China is the largest ridesharing market in the world. This makes it a more significant opportunity for ARS.

According to DiDi, in China, shared mobility costs less than traditional private car ownership. It is estimated that the cost of ride-hailing for a rider in China in 2020 is RMB2.9 ($0.45) per kilometer compared to RMB4.1 ($0.63) per kilometer for someone who owns and operates a fossil fuel-powered vehicle. DiDi claims that in contrast to China, the cost of shared mobility in the U.S. is 2.2 times higher than the cost of private car ownership.

Chinese cities are competing to get a head start on ARS. Several major cities, including Beijing, Shanghai, and Guangzhou, have designated areas for testing autonomous vehicles. 2018 saw the start of government-approved testing of AVs on public roads, with tests held by Chinese startups Jingchi and Pony.ai in the southern city of Guangzhou. Although companies, including Baidu, ran such tests as early as 2015, the move represents a regularization of the process. Beijing became the first city in China to allow testing on public roads in late 2017.

And while many of these players are also conducting research and testing overseas, particularly in the U.S., their best bet for early commercialization may be in China, which offers dense urban populations and friendly government policies.

A coming regulatory overhaul could provide a further boost for the industry. Until recently, China has relied on AV standards compiled by SAE International, a U.S. body, but starting in 2021, the country will adopt its own Automotive Driving Automation Classifications, paving the way for domestically set guidelines that industry players hope will drive large-scale development of autonomous driving technology and mass production of vehicles.

Let's look at some of the leading companies developing autonomous ride services in China.

Baidu Inc.

Baidu is called the "Google of China," and like Google, Baidu has been actively developing AV software. Baidu is developing Apollo, an open-source autonomous vehicle technology platform. Apollo Enterprise is designed for mass production vehicles. More than 130 partners around the world already use the company's Apollo system.

Baidu Apollo is the leader in AV testing in China. As of July 2020, Baidu Apollo had received 150 AV licenses for autonomous testing in China, including 120 permits that allow the AVs to carry passengers. Baidu has completed over 100K passenger-carrying trips as of June 2020. Apollo Go is Baidu's autonomous ride service.

Baidu was the first company to provide autonomous ride services in Beijing. It started testing in December 2019, and as of July 2020, it surpassed 6 million kilometers (3.73 million miles) in road testing with a fleet of over 500 AVs. Baidu has tested in 27 cities worldwide, including cities in California.

Baidu opened its Apollo Go services to the public in Changsha in April 2020 with 45 AVs. Apollo Go service has 55 pickup and drop-off points and covers an area of 70 square kilometers. Baidu started its Apollo Go services for the public in Cangzhou in August 2020 with 30 AVs. It also has 55 pickup and drop-off points and covers an area of 130 square kilometers. In March 2020, Baidu won a project in Chongqing worth over $7 million to develop an AV testing area with 5G and C-V2X network capabilities.

Baidu's Apollo Park in Beijing, among the largest autonomous driving test sites in the world, was completed in May 2020. The test area supports the development of autonomous vehicles, as well as C-V2X and 5G technology. The 13,500 square meter (145,300 square ft) Apollo Park contains more than 200 AVs and can support all aspects of AV development and testing.

At the Baidu World Conference in September 2020, Baidu demoed AVs without safety drivers but using teleoperation for safety. Baidu has developed its teleoperation using 5G cellular networks and C-V2X. Tele-operation allows remote control of Baidu AVs instead of safety drivers.

Apollo Lite is a vision-based framework that leverages multiple cameras to achieve Level 4 autonomous driving. Baidu claims that Apollo Lite can process vast amounts of data generated by ten cameras to detect objects up to 700 feet away while delivering real-time, 360-degree sensing of the environment. In tests on public roads in Beijing, vehicles relying on Apollo Lite managed to drive without lidar sensors.

Baidu is extending its car ambitions from mere software to production. In January 2021, it announced that it would set up a company to produce AVs with the help of Chinese automaker Geely. Baidu will provide smart driving technologies while Geely, which has an impending merger with Sweden's Volvo, will oversee car design and manufacturing. The new venture will operate as a Baidu subsidiary where Geely will serve as a strategic partner, and Baidu units like Apollo and Baidu Maps will contribute capabilities. The firm will cover the entire industrial chain, including vehicle design, research and development, manufacturing, sales, and service. The collaboration will be based on Geely's EV-focused platform, Sustainable Experience Architecture (SEA).

Baidu operates the autonomous taxi service Go Robotaxi with safety drivers on board in Beijing, Changsha, and Cangzhou and plans to expand to 30 cities in three years. In early 2021, Baidu got permission to test fully autonomous vehicles on the streets of Sunnyvale, California. While Baidu has had approval from California regulators to test autonomous vehicles with safety drivers since 2016, the new permit allows the company to test three autonomous vehicles without a driver behind the wheel on specified streets within Sunnyvale, located in Santa Clara County. The vehicles are only allowed on roads with speed limits of 45 mph, and they can operate day or night but not during inclement weather like fog or rain.

Pony.ai

Pony.ai is co-located in China and the U.S. It makes software to power AVs but does not make the vehicle itself. Instead, it partners with automakers, including China's BYD and GAC. The startup has offices in Guangzhou, China, and Fremont, California, and raised over $1 billion in February 2021 at a valuation of more than $5.3 billion (up from $3 billion as of February 2020).

Pony's full-stack hardware platform, PonyAlpha, leverages lidars, radars, and cameras to keep tabs on obstacles up to 200 meters from its AVs. PonyAlpha is the foundation for the company's fully autonomous trucks and freight delivery solution, which commenced testing in April 2019 and is deployed in test cars within the city limits of Fremont and Beijing (in addition to Guangzhou).

Pony.ai is one of the few companies to have secured an autonomous vehicle testing license in Beijing. In California, it has obtained an autonomous vehicle operations permit from the California Public Utilities Commission.

Pony.ai partnered with Via and Hyundai to launch BotRide, Pony.ai's second public autonomous ride service after a pilot program in Nansha, China. BotRide allowed riders and carpoolers to hail autonomous Hyundai Kona electric SUVs through apps developed with Via, sourcing from a fleet of 10 cars with human safety drivers behind the wheel.

Since late 2018, Pony.ai has been testing its autonomous ride services with passengers in Guangzhou within a geofenced area in Guangzhou, China. Since establishing its China HQ in Guangzhou in October 2017, Pony.ai has been consistently testing and expanding its autonomous vehicle operations in the city's Nansha district.

It is one of the first Chinese companies to use an app that allows users to hail an autonomous ride. The app enables a user to order an AV from a preset location in Nansha. The AV can travel to specific areas that have been set by the company, such as its offices or residential areas. Pony.ai autonomous ride service with passengers started in May 2020 in Beijing. In July 2020, Pony.ai announced it would begin testing AVs in Shanghai.

The Pony.ai AV fleet of 100+ vehicles have traveled more than 2.5 million kilometers (1.6 million miles) in China, and the U.S. combined.

Pony.ai has secured a license from the Guangzhou municipal government to test self-driving trucks on the city's public roads, a sign that it is aiming to apply its technology to autonomous logistics. The public road tests in Guangzhou will accelerate the validation of its autonomous truck technology. During the third China International Import Expo, Pony.ai showcased its Level 4 autonomous hardware and software system specially designed for heavy trucks.

AutoX

AutoX was founded in 2016 by Dr. Jianxiong Xiao (a.k.a. Professor X), a self-driving technologist from MIT and Princeton University. The company's AV platform is designed to handle the densest and most dynamic traffic conditions in urban cities worldwide. AutoX is the second permit holder for California DMV's completely driverless AV permit. AutoX has deployed more than 100 ARS vehicles in Shanghai, Shenzhen, Wuhan, and many other cities in China. Headquartered in Shenzhen, AutoX has eight offices and five R&D centers globally. It raised more than $160 million from investors, including Shanghai Auto (China's largest car manufacturer), Dongfeng Motor (China's second-largest car manufacturer), Alibaba AEF, MediaTek MTK, and leading financial institutions.

In December 2020, the company became the first company to deploy completely driverless vehicles on the streets of Shenzhen, China, and now, it has launched a fully autonomous ride service. AutoX has removed backup drivers or any remote operators for its local fleet of 25 AVs. Although there's no safety driver involved, customer support agents are available for questions during the ride. The government isn't restricting where in the city AutoX operates, though the company said it is focusing on the downtown area.

The AutoX Fiat Chrysler Pacifica minivan is integrated with an array of advanced sensors built seamlessly onto the vehicle: 360 degrees of solid-state lidar sensors, along with numerous high-definition cameras, blind-spot lidar sensors, and radar sensors housed in a package that flows with the design of Chrysler Pacifica. Its sensing capability is advantageous in urban scenarios. Its AV is also equipped with AutoX's proprietary Level-4 vehicle control unit for urban driving environments in China, meaning faster processing speed and higher computation capability.

AutoX also collaborates with Letzgo, a taxi fleet operator with 16,000 taxis in 18 cities in China. In April 2020, AutoX opened its Operations Center in Shanghai to manage the data from its AV operation. The center will also provide extensive AV driving simulation to test complex driving scenarios and improve its driving software.

AutoX has one foot in its home market, and one in the U.S., but its priorities are clear cut. "Our goal is to win the China market first," Jewel Li, the chief operating officer, told the Nikkei Asian Review in an interview. The company has also signed an AV partnership with China's largest EV maker, BYD. Alibaba is a leading investor and supporter of AutoX.

AutoX is also looking into the logistics and delivery business in China. AutoX has strategic partnerships with courier company ZTO Express and food delivery giant Meituan-Dianping.

DiDi Autonomous Driving (Didi Chuxing)

Didi is China's largest ridesharing company and the largest ridesharing company in the world. In 2016, Apple announced it had invested $1 billion in the ridesharing service. At the time, Didi was locked in intense competition with Uber for China's rapidly growing ridesharing market. Eventually, the battle grew too costly for Uber, which was reportedly burning through $1 billion a year to compete with Didi. In August 2016, Uber sold its Chinese business to Didi for a 17.7% stake in Didi and a seat on the company's board. In exchange, Didi also invested $1 billion in Uber.

DiDi went public on the NYSE at an initial valuation of more than $60 billion. With its dominance of the enormous Chinese ridesharing market and continued aggressive interest in autonomous driving technology, DiDi projects to become a significant competitor, perhaps the dominant competitor, in the Chinese ARS market. However, two days after its public offering, the Chinese government announced restrictions on DiDi relating to cyber security and other practices.

Like other companies entering autonomous ride services, DiDi spun off its ARS business in August 2019 and started raising external funding. DiDi Autonomous Driving is an independent company with majority ownership by DiDi. Didi Autonomous Driving has received outside funding of $800 million: $300 million in January 2021 and $500 million in May 2020, led by Softbank. There are rumors that it is raising billions more.

Didi originally announced its AV project in 2017. Within a year, it obtained a certificate for HD mapping in China. In February 2018, Didi started testing its self-driving fleet in three cities in both the U.S. and China. The local government in Shanghai awarded Didi a permit to test its autonomous vehicles on public roads in Jiading District of Shanghai. However, the company says it plans to expand beyond that district starting in 2021. The company says it will deploy 30 different models of Level 4 autonomous vehicles. Similar projects are set to follow across the country.

Customers can use Didi's app to summon an autonomous vehicle to pick them up, but initially, the AVs will include a human driver behind the wheel. Didi began the program with a mixed dispatching model, combining autonomous vehicles and human-driven vehicles.

DiDi Autonomous Driving acquired public road-testing licenses in Beijing, Shanghai, Suzhou, and California, along with one of the first Intelligent connected vehicle demonstration licenses in China issued by Shanghai. In June 2020, Meng Xing, chief operating officer of Didi Autonomous Driving, said the company plans to operate more than 1 million autonomous ride services vehicles through its platform by 2030 as part of ongoing efforts to build an intelligent transport system.

DiDi's 2021 initial public offering document provides some insights into its intentions and strategies for ARS. It believes that autonomous driving offers the opportunity to reshape the cost structure of mobility, which would significantly lower the overall operating costs of vehicles and pass those cost savings along to riders and mobility platforms. It also helps to increase the supply and availability of shared mobility vehicles. For Didi, autonomous driving  is the key to the future of mobility. It has the potential to improve safety by significantly reducing the risk of accidents meaningfully. Autonomous driving also improves vehicle utilization by allowing cars to operate throughout the day, therefore increasing supply and lowering transportation costs. It is building a full-suite autonomous solution that combines world-leading technology with commercial operations for mobility and shared mobility deployment.

It is developing Level 4 autonomous driving technology and the operating system for an autonomous fleet with our team of over 500 members. It claims to have the world's largest repository of real-world traffic data from its shared mobility fleet. Additionally, its high-definition mapping capabilities allow it to create and update digital city landscapes close to real-time.

In 2021, Didi operated a fleet of over 100 autonomous vehicles and partnered with multiple leading global automakers. It intends to deploy our autonomous fleet alongside driver-operated vehicles to offer shared mobility with hybrid-dispatching based on specific trip conditions. It was among the first companies to obtain a passenger-carrying service license for an autonomous fleet in Shanghai.

It plans to adopt a hybrid dispatching model, where autonomous vehicles would be dispatched for common or only slightly complex scenarios under non-extreme weather conditions. Human drivers would be dispatched for particularly complex trips or extreme weather conditions. It began testing this model in Shanghai in June 2020 through the launch of a commercial pilot that, upon sign-up through the main DiDi app, allows passengers to request on-demand rides for free on autonomous vehicles within a designated open-traffic area in downtown Shanghai. It has a safety command center for real-time monitoring of vehicle and road conditions and enhanced remote command assistance designed to handle larger-scale autonomous fleet operations in the future.

DiDi is one of a limited number of companies in China that have been granted a Class-A mapping qualification concerning the production of electronic maps for navigation systems, giving them an edge in navigation and route research. Its HD maps have centimeter-level precision, an accuracy exceeding that of most competitors.

WeRide

WeRide, headquartered in Guangzhou, China, was founded in 2017 and has R&D and operations centers in Beijing, Shanghai, and Silicon Valley. It aims to develop level 4 autonomous vehicles that can handle most driving situations independently. WeRide has raised more than $500 million in funding, with the most recent round in January 2021

WeRide operates AVs primarily in Guangzhou. It started ARS testing in November 2018. In November 2019, it deployed an ARS pilot program in a joint venture with Baiyun Taxi Group, the largest taxi company in South China. As of September 2020, WeRide had done over 900 days of AV testing. It has accumulated 2.8 million kilometers of AV testing and has served 90,000 passengers.

WeRide launched a publicly accessible ARS service in Guangzhou in November 2019, covering roughly 89 square miles in the Huangpu and Guangzhou Development districts. It received a permit in July 2020 to launch China's first AV tests on public roads in Guangzhou without a safety driver. However, these driverless AVs can be controlled via teleoperation by a remote operator, if needed. WeRide has 10 AVs that are tested without a safety driver. WeRide's goal is to start its ARS service without a safety driver in late 2021 in a designated area in Guangzhou.

WeRide resumed services in December 2020, after a brief interruption during the coronavirus outbreak. It recorded ARS 8,396 rides in December

2020 alone, carrying 4,683 passengers who hailed its ARS through a mobile app. The trial in partnership with state-owned Baiyun Taxi Group, the largest taxi company in southern China, involved a fleet of 40 vehicles that covered 100 fixed pickup and drop-off spots within a 144.6 sq. km area of designated public roads.

WeRide buys vehicles from auto OEMs, including Nissan, Lincoln, and GAC, and adds its suite of AV technology. WeRide has 120 AVs with 40 AVs used in ARS operations and the remaining AVs used for testing.

Autonomous Vehicle Retail Sales

Retail sales of autonomous vehicles in China are expected to be slightly different from in the U.S. In the U.S. market, the incumbent car companies, like GM and Ford, are positioning themselves, along with Tesla, to penetrate this market. China doesn't have significant incumbent auto companies, so AVs for use by consumers are expected to come from some of the new Chines EV companies.

XPeng

Xiaopeng (XPeng) Motors is a Chinese electric vehicle and technology company that designs and manufactures smart cars. It was founded in 2015 and went public on August 27th, 2020, using American depository shares, raising about $1 billion. By 2021, it raised about $2.6 billion.

XPeng aims its EVs at technology-savvy middle-class Chinese consumers, with prices ranging from $22,000 to $45,000 after government subsidies. In some ways, it is a Tesla knock-off at a much lower price. XPeng is interesting because it has a platform strategy and is moving aggressively into autonomous driving. It uses a platform strategy to expand product offerings by launching one Smart EV model each year to broaden the addressable market. It also adopted a platform approach for software systems.

In November 2020, it announced its next-generation autonomous driving architecture that will include Lidar technology. It also announced significant upgrades to its autonomous driving software and hardware systems for the 2021 production models. XPeng is the first car manufacturer globally to integrate lidar technology into its production of electric vehicles.

Its next-generation autonomous driving architecture will deliver significant enhancements. XPeng claims this will achieve an advanced level of navigation-guided autonomous driving, with comprehensive coverage of different road conditions, low manual takeover rates, and longer continuous autonomous driving times. It will cover multiple weather conditions and city and highway driving situations, including urban congestion, expressways, underground parking lots, toll gates, tunnels, and night driving conditions. The lidar systems will improve its next-generation autonomous driving architecture, specifically by enhancing the vehicle's high-precision object recognition performance.

Li Auto

Lixiang, formerly known as Chehejia ("Car and Home"), was founded in 2015 and went public on July 30th, 2020, raising $1.1 billion. It is a Beijing-based electric vehicle startup that plans to integrate manufacturing vertically. It designs, researches, manufactures, sells, and offers services featuring a few models of electric vehicles.

The company's SUVs are hybrids of a sort. They use electric motors (one on the front axle and one on the rear). Still, those motors are powered by a combination of a 40.5kWh battery pack and a 1.2-liter turbocharged engine paired to a 45-liter fuel tank and a 100kW electric generator, which generates power for the battery pack in real-time. The idea is that the car can be driven for about 100 miles on battery power alone, but it has a total range of nearly 500 miles when leveraging the combustion engine generator.

Li Auto is teaming up with Nvidia, and its Chinese partner Desay SV Automotive, to develop an AV platform based on the Orin chipset and software stack for its next large-sized premium SUV, which will launch in 2022. Li Auto will be the first automaker to use Nvidia's newest processor to facilitate upgradeable autonomous driving functions for its EVs, ranging from assisted driving functions and, eventually, vehicle autonomy. Nvidia's Orin is a next-generation system-on-a-chip (SOC) for automobiles, capable of performing 200 trillion operations per second (TOPS) using just 45 watts.

NIO

NIO Inc. is a pioneer in China's premium electric vehicle market. It designs, jointly manufactures, and sells smart and connected premium electric vehicles, and develops driving innovations in next-generation technologies in connectivity, autonomous driving, and artificial intelligence. Joint manufacturing means that it uses a state-owned contract manufacturer to build its cars.

NIO's Chinese name is Weilai, which means Blue Sky Coming. Nio has been a public company for some time. It originally went public in the US back in September of 2018, selling IPO shares at $6.26 and raising $1 billion. NIO's North American headquarters and advanced research and development center is in the heart of Silicon Valley.

January 9, 2021, NIO launched its first autonomous driving model, NIO ET7, a smart electric flagship sedan. The ET7 has a pre-subsidy price starting from RMB 448,000 or RMB 378,000 with BaaS (Battery as a Service). The ET7 features NIO's latest NAD (NIO Autonomous Driving) technology, including NIO Aquila Super Sensing and NIO Adam Super Computing. Nio claims that its NAD brings a safer and more relaxing experience of autonomous driving from point A to point B, gradually covering use cases from expressways, urban streets, parking, and battery swapping.

NIO has built up the NAD full-stack autonomous driving capability, including perception algorithm, localization, control strategy, and platform software. NIO Aquila Super Sensing features 33 high-performance sensing units, including ultralong-range high-resolution lidar. Five millimeter-wave radars, 12 ultrasonic sensors, two high-precision positioning units, V2X and ADMS. NIO's Adam features 4 NVIDIA DRIVE Orin SoCs with a total computing power of 1,016 TOPS.

The interior of ET7 is a further interpretation of the second living room concept: a sophisticated and cozy mobile living space. NIO's second-generation digital cockpit on the ET7 has enhanced its in-car mobile connectivity and communication capabilities powered by the 3rd Generation Qualcomm® Snapdragon™ Automotive Cockpit Platform.

Tencent

Tencent, which owns China's largest mobile messaging platform and the largest gaming portfolio in the world, is also investing in developing AVs. Tencent owns stakes in electric vehicle makers NIO and Tesla, as well as the ridesharing platforms Didi Chuxing and T3. It launched an autonomous driving lab in 2016 as part of its broader expansion into AI-related fields. The following year, Tencent started testing AVs and formed a new alliance for developing driverless AI technologies.

China's Tencent has teamed up with automaker Geely on various car technologies as traditional vehicle manufacturers continue to partner with technology giants. The deal will see the two companies work on areas "in the fields of digitalization, intelligent cockpits, autonomous drive, and low carbon development."

BYD

BYD is the leader in new energy vehicle sales in China. BYD primary expertise is in hardware, not autonomous vehicle software. So, its primary AV focus is on partnering with companies developing AV technology.

Germany

Germany's powerful automotive industry gives the country a strong base for AV development. Germany is famous for such big names as Audi, BMW, Mercedes (Daimler), and Volkswagen. Automotive is one of the most significant industrial sectors in the country. German OEMs serve all global markets, producing more than 70% of all premium vehicles manufactured worldwide. Approximately one million employees work for small and midsized businesses in the automotive sector, as well as for world-known OEMs and global suppliers.

U.S. and Chinese companies are implementing ADAS and semi-autonomous driving functionality into some cars, but German OEMs are providing driving assistance systems in most mass-produced vehicles.

Germany was the first country to legalize fully-autonomous driving systems. This will help to strengthen its leading positions in the fields of automated and connected driving. Previously, only a licensed driver could operate a vehicle, but in December 2016, the government announced it aims to create self-driving infrastructure in Germany. The parliament introduced an amendment to the German Road Traffic Act that allows drivers to pass off control to a vehicle.

Autonomous vehicle technology companies in Germany recently got the approval to test autonomous vehicles on public roadways. Some cities have adopted pilot fleets that recreate regular traffic on public roads in isolated areas to test the technology. Berlin has an autonomous shuttle service that works in the enclosed areas of The Charité University.

Since 2015, the German government has followed a national AV strategy and recently started working to ensure that AVs are used ethically. However, the highly devolved nature of the German government, with more than 11,000 municipalities, makes it challenging to set national standards and strategies.

Fully-autonomous vehicles with no steering wheel or pedals were not included in the national AV strategy since driverless cars are not allowed under the United Nation's 1968 Vienna Convention on Road Traffic, a treaty that Germany both signed and ratified. (The U.S. and China are non-signatories to that agreement.) Driverless cars can, however, be tested on public roads just like any other vehicle prototype if the authorities provide an exemption. One of the fundamental principles of the Convention has been the concept that a driver is always fully in control and responsible for the behavior of a vehicle in traffic. This requirement is challenged by the development of technology for collision avoidance systems and autonomous driving. Countries that have subscribed to the Convention will need to agree on a new Convention or find other ways of accommodating the concept for autonomous driving.

United Kingdom

In August 2018, the UK Parliament passed the Automated and Electric Vehicles Act, which adapts the existing motor insurance framework by extending compulsory insurance to AVs as well as the driver. In November 2018, the government announced support for three public trials in 2021, including AV buses across the Forth Bridge in Scotland and ARS in London. A statement issued by the Department for Transport says that the UK is "on track to meet its commitment to have fully self-driving vehicles on UK roads by 2021."

The UK faces challenges concerning digital and physical infrastructure. It lags other countries in 4G coverage, global connectivity, quality of roads (especially smaller roads), and logistics infrastructure. However, physical infrastructure is expected to improve as the UK government delivers increased investment across the road network and critical infrastructure operators collaborate with central government and industry to support the deployment of AVs.

Brexit is another significant roadblock that may hamper the UK's AV development. Several car manufacturers have already announced the closure of their British-based factories, and the U.K.'s withdrawal has left many automotive companies questioning whether Britain is where they want to place future investments.

There are a couple of notable British companies developing AVs.

FiveAI

FiveAI raised $35 million in investment capital by 2019, making it one of the best-funded AV cars start-ups in Europe. But this is a low amount compared to international competition. The company is specializing in Europe, especially the UK, where it is collecting data on city layouts that are slightly less uniform than similarly populated areas in the U.S. Environmental factors are also different in Europe than in the U.S. London gets more rain, for example, affecting driving conditions. FiveAI has been testing its AVs in two London boroughs, Croydon, and Bromley, since 2018. Initial testing has been conducted by FiveAI employees.

Jaguar/Land Rover

Jaguar and Land Rover have been crucial to the UK car industry since they merged in 2008. The company has invested and expanded into a wide range of automotive technologies. In 2018, the company announced it had completed the first-ever autonomous driving lap of one of the U.K.'s most challenging road layouts, Coventry Ring Road, in a prototype autonomous Range Rover Sport. The trial saw the vehicle successfully change lanes, merge with traffic, and exit junctions at the speed limit of 40 mph. Jaguar Land Rover also has plans to create a fleet of more than 100 research vehicles to develop and test a wide range of AV technologies

Russia

Russia issued a resolution allowing testing of AVs on public roads in Moscow and Tatarstan from December 2018 to March 2022, to confirm that they can operate on roads to develop technical requirements. This builds on a more general resolution passed in 2016 to cut barriers to technology innovation. Several major organizations, including Yandex and Kamaz, are engaged in the development of highly-automated and fully-automated vehicles. This interaction between the state and commercial organizations creates a friendly environment for the introduction of AVs.

Yandex

Yandex is the largest technology company in Russia, and it is the largest internet search engine in Russia, with a market share of over 50%. It also has the largest market share of any search engine in the Commonwealth of Independent States, and it is the 5th largest search engine worldwide after Google, Baidu, Bing, and Yahoo!. Like Google and Baidu, Yandex is investing in autonomous vehicles.

Yandex first started its limited public trial in the small town of Innopolis in August 2018, racking up over 1,000 trips just two months later. It also expanded to Moscow and Skolkovo that same quarter. The cars are hailed through a smartphone app. There have been safety drivers on board. However, it plans to eliminate them on some of its trips. Yandex is starting small, initially with one car, but it is aiming to put 10 AVs on the road by the end of 2019 and expanding to cover the city over the next five years.

Hyundai will jointly develop autonomous vehicles with Yandex based on the South Korean automotive company's cars. The two companies will initially work on developing a prototype AV. The deal will also build an autonomous control system to be marketed to rival car manufacturers and ARS start-ups.

Japan

Japan is lagging in the development of AVs, but some start-ups and big companies are becoming increasingly interested. Japanese Prime Minister, Shinzō Abe, announced that the country would begin testing AVs on public roads with the goal of launching an ARS service for the 2020 Tokyo Olympics before they were rescheduled because of the pandemic. The government plans to commercialize this system as early as 2022.

The Japanese government is also trying to enable AVs. A new law offers a slight loosening of the current restrictions on autonomous vehicles, although it is intended for semi-autonomous vehicles. It would allow drivers in traffic to use a smartphone behind the wheel as their vehicle drives itself, so long as they can switch to manual driving immediately in case of emergency. 2018 saw AV proofs of concept by public and private-sector organizations focused on taxis and buses within defined areas, including airports.

AVs in Japan are influenced by its rapidly aging society, where a quarter of the population is older than 65. Yet, the problems of out-of-date public infrastructure in roads, tunnels and bridges, and their maintenance costs are also serious.

Partnerships are driving innovation to explore the potential of autonomous vehicles in Japan. Baidu, Nissan, General Motors have collaborated to test autonomous vehicles in Japan. In February 2019, Nissan and Japanese gaming software maker DeNA, announced the launch of Easy Ride, an autonomous vehicle mobility service developed by both companies. Honda invested $2.75 Billion in GM's Cruise. It will work jointly with Cruise and General Motors to fund and develop a purpose-built autonomous vehicle for Cruise that can serve a wide variety of use cases and be manufactured at high volume for global deployment. In addition, Cruise, General Motors, and Honda will explore global opportunities for commercial deployment of the Cruise network. Waymo has signed a deal with Nissan to develop AVs and autonomous trucks for use in Japan and possibly other countries throughout much of Asia.

Toyota Motor set up a strategic partnership and joint venture called Monet Technologies Corporation with SoftBank to facilitate new mobility services. Monet added investment from Honda Motor Co. and Toyota's truck-making subsidiary, Hino Motors, leaving SoftBank Corp the largest shareholder with a 40.2% share and Toyota owning 39.8%. When Honda and Hino joined in March 2019, the total investment in Monet was 2.5 billion yen ($23.20 million). This is not a significant amount compared to initiatives in other countries. Mazda Motor Corp, Suzuki Motor Corp, Subaru Corp, Isuzu Motors, and Toyota unit Daihatsu will each take a stake of a few percent in the venture

Singapore

The city-state is a testbed for AVs. The government of Singapore is determined to make the small country a global pioneer in autonomous vehicles. In February 2017, the Ministry of Transport introduced a series of Autonomous Vehicle Rules for prospective trials. With the amendment to the Road Traffic Act, Singaporean law now recognizes that motor vehicles don't require human drivers, making it the first country to widely adopt autonomous driving.

Singapore has long been a leader in several different technology fields, and it wants to continue this with autonomous technology. The first autonomous vehicle test center was opened in 2017 in the Jurong Innovation District. The center was built to support the Centre of Excellence for Testing & Research of AVs.

In Singapore, a country that has the third-highest population density in the world, AVs would reduce the number of private vehicles and reduce congestion and air pollution, which affect the country. Implementation of Autonomous Vehicle Rules could dramatically reduce the cost of transportation and could improve access for people who have been neglected by the transport authorities, such as people with disabilities or the elderly.

Many autonomous vehicle start-ups are testing in Singapore. NuTonomy is one of the most prominent examples of this, launching its autonomous ride service in the city in 2016. Operated through the Grab app, the company took its autonomous vehicles onto a designated 2.6 sq. mile area of Singaporean streets. Since then, the company has expanded its routes and now has permission to operate in several regions in Singapore.

Singapore has another interesting factor that will promote the use of AVs, particularly ARS, as well. It taxes private cars heavily to discourage people from driving. Approximately two-thirds of the price of a car in Singapore is tax. This excessive tax changes the economics of the trade-off between owned vehicles and autonomous ride services. In addition, the population of Singapore is aging at a faster rate than anywhere else in the world, so ARS can also provide mobility for seniors.

Netherlands

The Netherlands leads the KPMG Autonomous Vehicles Readiness Index (AVRI) by being rated as one of the readiest countries in the world for the introduction of driverless vehicles. The 2019 KPMG Autonomous Vehicles Readiness Index evaluates countries based on 25 factors, which are divided into four categories: policy and legislation, technology and innovation, infrastructure, and consumer acceptance.

The Dutch ministry announced a legal framework for autonomous driving. It allows experiments on public roads without drivers, although the AVs must be monitored remotely. The Netherlands is also preparing a Driving License for a Vehicle. This is being developed in cooperation with the Dutch Vehicle Authority, the primary road authority, and the central office for driving exams. The approach focuses on the extent to which a vehicle can produce safe and predictable automated driving behavior that aligns as closely as possible to human performance in an open traffic system. Finally, it is working on a Vehicle Safety & Security Framework (VSSF) to be able to assess the robustness of in-vehicle software.

Canada

Canada has a three-level government structure regulating transportation. Like the U.S., motor vehicle transportation is a shared responsibility between federal, provincial, and territorial governments. Transport Canada, under the Motor Vehicle Safety Act (MVSA), establishes safety regulations for the manufacture and importation of motor vehicles, as well as designated motor vehicle equipment and the shipment of newly manufactured vehicles and equipment across provincial/territorial boundaries. The objective of these regulations is to reduce the risk of death, injury, and damage to property and the environment.

Provinces and territories are responsible for the licensing of drivers, vehicle registration, and insurance, as well as laws and regulations regarding the safe operation of vehicles on public roads. As such, provinces and territories are also responsible for approving and overseeing trials of automated vehicles within their jurisdiction. These jurisdictions are encouraged to engage Transport Canada in this process to seek their input and views on applications and trial practices.

Falling under the jurisdiction of provinces and territories, municipal governments, to varying degrees, are responsible for: the enactment and enforcement of laws concerning vehicle movement, the use of local infrastructure, and the provision of public transportation in their respective jurisdictions. In conjunction with the relevant provincial/territorial road transport agency, trial organizations are encouraged to engage municipal authorities to ensure local traffic and infrastructure considerations are addressed and that local law enforcement and emergency response personnel are appropriately informed about trial operations.

An example is Ontario, home to more than a third of the population and many vehicle and technology companies. The province has lifted some regulations on AVs, meaning that from January 2019, completely driverless vehicles can be tested on its roads. The changes are a development of Ontario's 10-year Automated Vehicle Pilot Program, started in 2016 and involving Uber, Canadian technology company BlackBerry, and the University of Waterloo. The province has established an Autonomous Vehicle Innovation Network and an Automotive Supplier Competitiveness Improvement Program. The latter providing matched funding for innovation by smaller suppliers.

France

Driverless minibuses already move passengers around otherwise pedestrianized areas of La Défense, an office complex in the west of Paris. Through legal changes, the French government hopes to see more services of this kind. The changes will allow drivers of AVs to be outside vehicles and will release them from responsibility for accidents that take place when the software is activated. There are already more than 50 AV pilots taking place across France, with many around Paris and others in cities including Rouen and Lyon, the latter claiming the world's first autonomous public transport service from September 2016. The changes are part of a national strategy for AVs published in May 2018, which also considers safety, public support, the development of digital infrastructure, how data is exchanged, and the overall transport ecosystem

There are reasons why France may not become a leader in AVs. Its road systems, especially in larger cities, are not conducive to AVs. (It's not even conducive to human-driven cars in many cases.) France also has strong labor practices, and I expect that there will be many protests to replacing taxi and truck drivers with autonomous vehicles.

India

Having the second largest population in the world with 1.3 billion people, India would appear on the surface to provide a major market opportunity for autonomous vehicles. But it isn't. Indian road conditions are not conducive to autonomous driving. Creating an AV ecosystem in India would require a massive investment in new and dedicated physical infrastructure, given the geographical expanse, density, and population of the country. And this investment is not a priority.

Even more importantly, government policy is against autonomous vehicles. A government minister stated it very succinctly: "We have decided not to allow driverless cars in India. I am sorry." He went on to say, "Presently, there are 30 lakh (hundred thousand) people who are getting employment through the automotive and related industries. And in our economy, the most important thing is how to create more employment potential as our country's population is very high. In a country where the population is very less, it can be a good idea for them."

South Korea

South Korea's government is funding autonomous vehicle technology, with President Moon Jae-in declaring that he expected AVs to account for half of the new cars on the country's roads by 2030. The government intends to spend 1.7 trillion won between 2021 and 2027 on self-driving technology. It expects Hyundai to launch Level 4, or fully autonomous, cars for fleet customers in 2024 and for the public by 2027. This time frame would put it about three years behind the U.S.

South Korea's government said it would prepare a regulatory and legal framework for autonomous cars and the safety questions they pose by 2024. The government acknowledged South Korea lags in some key areas necessary for self-driving cars, such artificial-intelligence, sensors, and logic chips.

Hyundai Motor Group said it plans to invest 41 trillion won ($35 billion) in mobility and other auto technologies by 2025, part of which will be directed to an ambitious effort to become more competitive in AVs. The plan, which Hyundai said encompasses autonomous, connected and electric cars, as well as technology for ridesharing, comes after the automaker and two of its affiliates announced an investment of $1.6 billion in a venture with U.S. AV tech firm Aptiv.

Part III
Disruptions and Regulations

Chapter 12
Disruptions Caused
by Autonomous Vehicles

Autonomous Vehicles (AVs) will be a hugely disruptive innovation. In general, disruptive innovation refers to an innovation that creates a new market and value network, which eventually disrupts an existing market and value network, typically displacing established market-leading firms. The theory of disruptive innovation was first coined by the late Harvard professor Clayton M. Christensen (one of the best thinkers on business concepts) in his research on the disk-drive industry and later popularized by his book *The Innovator's Dilemma*, published in 1997.

This theory explains the phenomenon by which an innovation transforms an existing market or sector by introducing simplicity, convenience, accessibility, and affordability where complication and high cost are the status quo. Initially, disruptive innovation is formed in a niche market that may appear unattractive or inconsequential to industry incumbents, but eventually, the new product or idea completely redefines the industry.

A classic example of Christensen's theory is the personal computer. Before its introduction, mainframe computers and minicomputers were the prevailing products in the computing industry. At a minimum, they were priced around $200,000 and required engineering experience to operate. Apple, one of the pioneers in personal computing, began selling its early computers in the late 1970s and early 1980s — initially as something for hobbyists. At that point, the product wasn't good enough to compete with the minicomputers, but Apple's customers didn't care because they couldn't afford or use expensive minicomputers. Entrenched competitors dismissed this innovation, just as many are dismissing AVs today. Ken Olsen, the founder of Digital Equipment, said that "There is no reason for any individual to have a computer in his home" in a talk given to a 1977 World Future Society meeting in Boston. The inferior computer was much better than their alternative: nothing at all. Little by little, the innovation improved. Within a few years, the smaller, more affordable personal computer became good enough to do the work that previously required minicomputers. This created a vast new market and ultimately reduced the market for large computers.

The original theory behind disruptive technology begins at a low-quality or low-usage level, so it is perceived as being a non-threat by established competitors who take it for granted until it is too late. Ironically, there is a difference with autonomous vehicles, though. Executives at the significant established competitors, such as the auto manufactures, have all read Christensen's theories on disruptive innovation, and they know what is going to happen. So, they are moving deliberately to disrupt themselves.

Like other disruptive technologies, AV technology will initially have limited use. For some time, it will serve only small market segments, and its disruptions will be limited. AVs will provide ride services or home delivery only on restricted routes that are easy to drive and clearly mapped with HD maps. However, relatively quickly, they will become more competent, and more routes will be mastered until they can serve an entire metropolitan area. Then, more metropolitan areas will be mastered. Eventually, but not too far in the future, AV technology will serve personal driving needs.

There are degrees of disruptive innovation. Smartphones, for example, weren't a significant disruption. Cell phones, before smartphones, disrupted land-line phone services, but smartphones were an innovation that added vast new capabilities that previously weren't available. Also, to some extent, the original automobile wasn't very disruptive because it provided transportation to most people who didn't have alternative transportation. It did displace using stagecoaches and horses to some degree, but most people didn't own those.

Autonomous vehicles will create an extreme degree of disruption, perhaps, more than any other disruptive innovation in history. The primary reason is that it will displace a huge existing industry, transportation, along with all its supporting industries. When we look at the benefits of AVs to virtually eliminate auto accidents, significantly reduce the cost of transportation, etc., we need to realize that there is a corresponding offset. In other words, these savings need to come from some place.

In this chapter, we will look at disruptions in terms of entire industries that will be reduced or eliminated, as well as the millions of jobs replaced. Before getting into the disruptions, though, it's worth repeating the fundamental causes of these disruptions:

1. Autonomous Ride Services (ARS) will provide more convenient transportation at a much lower cost than ridesharing, taxies, and even individual car ownership. The higher utilization of ARS vehicles, expected to be 40%-50%, will require many fewer vehicles than cars that are only used only 5% of the time on average. This

will result in a significant reduction in the number of cars manufactured and diminish related industries.

2. Accidents will be reduced because AVs will be safer. While this is an essential benefit for society, it will cause significant disruptions in all the businesses that make money from auto accidents.

3. Autonomous home delivery will enable the delivery of food and other goods at a much lower cost than driver-based delivery. Of course, this will eliminate the jobs of those who make these deliveries today, and it will also cause other unexpected disruptions.

4. Autonomous trucking, and related, will reduce the need for truck drivers, although this will happen gradually.

Let's look at these disruptions by industry. To get a sense of the timing of these disruptions, refer to the final chapter, which summarizes the timeframe for the adoption of autonomous vehicles, along with the timetable for these disruptions.

Disruptions to Taxi and Ridesharing

ARS will replace ridesharing, taxis, and limos. However, this will take many years, and more importantly, it won't happen uniformly across the country.

There are approximately 200,000 taxi drivers in the United States (depending on different estimates). While not a high-paying job, for many drivers, it is their primary source of income. Even worse, many drivers in large cities invested a lot of money in their taxi medallions, giving them the right to own a taxi. Some paid as much as $500,000 to $800,000 and will be bankrupt with the elimination of the taxi industry. Ridesharing is already eroding the taxi industry in many locations.

There is another estimated 50,000-100,00 limo and car service drivers in the United States, with most of those working part-time. This is also being eroded by ridesharing, and ARS will eventually displace most of these jobs.

The number of ridesharing drivers is exceptionally high. Uber claimed to have 2 million drivers worldwide in 2017, and the number is increasing every year. In the United States, it estimates a million drivers. This would place the total estimate for ridesharing drivers at approximately 4-5 million worldwide and about 1.5 million in the U.S. Many of these drivers are part-time.

Initially, autonomous ride services will only be offered in selected metropolitan regions, so ridesharing in other metropolitan areas will be unaffected. Also, in the areas where it is introduced, ARS will coexist with ridesharing for some time. When first introduced, ARS will provide transportation only on selected routes, such as the easier and higher-volume ones.

Ridesharing will continue to serve the other routes, but gradually ridesharing will be displaced almost entirely by ARS because it is much less expensive.

In some cities, such as New York, I expect there will be legal barriers for some time limiting ARS to protect the taxi industry. There are barriers now protecting the taxi industry by limiting ridesharing.

Disruptions to Home Delivery

Home delivery of food and other products is a rapidly growing industry. I estimate that there are more than a half-million home-delivery drivers. This is based on the home-delivery volume estimates from DoorDash, Grub Hub, and Domino's Pizza. Home delivery is a rapidly growing market, and the number of drivers may increase to close to a million in the next few years.

Autonomous home delivery will displace home delivery drivers because the cost is much lower. When this begins to happen, autonomous delivery will occur quickly because the major companies will create fleets of thousands of delivery vehicles throughout the country. For a while, though, there will still be human-driver delivery in locations particularly challenging to reach.

Package delivery won't be much affected by autonomous home delivery because there wouldn't be anyone at home to take the package from the autonomous delivery vehicle.

Disruptions to the Auto Industry

Let's start with some basic facts about the auto industry in the United States. There are approximately 250 million registered vehicles (excluding trucks) in the United States, with around 16 million new cars sold annually. Globally, there are roughly a billion vehicles, with nearly 60 million new cars produced annually. More than 3 trillion miles are driven in the United States annually.

The most significant disruption to the auto industry will initially come from ARS. ARS will provide more transportation per vehicle than current cars that sit idle 95% of the time. Let's assume that an autonomous ride services (ARS) vehicle is utilized 40%-50% of the time. Every ARS vehicle will eventually displace 8-10 individually-owned vehicles. For example, a million ARS vehicles will replace the need for 8-10 million individually-owned vehicles.

As I stated earlier, ARS will become a significant new industry in the United States and most developed countries. The extent of the disruption to the auto industry from ARS will depend on what percentage of miles driven shifts from individually-owned vehicles to ARS. For the sake of illustration, let's create one potential scenario and assume that this shift is 30% at some time in the future. Then, the remaining 70% of miles traveled will be done by individually-owned human-driven or autonomous vehicles. This would translate into the need for 30% fewer individually-owned cars or approximately 75 million fewer cars. As a note, this would only require about 7-8 million ARS vehicles, given a displacement ratio of 8-10 to 1.

It remains to be seen if the bulk of this reduction will be seen initially in used cars or new cars, although inevitably, it will impact new car sales.

New Car Manufacturers

This decline in individually-owned cars would significantly impact new car manufacturers over time. Assuming 10-12-year average car ownership, the reduction would eventually be approximately 5 million cars annually from 16 million. This 30%, or higher, drop in new car sales would create enormous disruption to the auto industry, both in the United States and globally. See chapter 8 for long-term projections of this decline in sales.

The auto industry relies on manufacturing economies of scale, and any reduction to this extent would threaten the viability of many manufacturing facilities. I expect that there would be a significant reduction in auto brands and considerable consolidation of companies. These estimates are for the United States alone. On a global basis, the drop to the 60 million cars manufactured annually would be much higher.

Of course, these estimates rely on some assumptions, particularly the penetration rate of ARS. If the penetration is only half of the 30% in the base scenario, then the reduction would be 2.5 million cars, but still a significant reduction. If it were twice that estimate, then the reduction would be closer to 10 million cars annually.

The other factor determining the impact on new car manufacturing is how fast this reduction comes from new cars instead of used cars. The conservative assumption is that it would be proportional. Most likely, though, people will stop buying new cars faster, so the impact would come more quickly to new car manufacturers.

Fleet sales of ARS vehicles may be a source of new sales for a few car manufacturers but remember the displacement ratio of 8–10 to 1, so it won't replace the loss. There will also be a reduction in other fleet sales, especially those to rental car companies.

More than 900,000 people work for automobile manufacturers in the United States. Still, since this is such a global industry, it's impossible to predict how many job reductions will occur in this country.

Most auto manufacturers recognize this coming disruption, which is why they are racing to have a leading role in autonomous ride services.

Used Car Sales

Autonomous vehicles will also disrupt the used-car market. Edmunds estimates that almost 40 million used cars are sold annually from the approximately 250 million cars in use. I expect that AVs and ARS will significantly reduce the demand for used cars and depress pricing. The overall reduction in individually-owned cars will lessen the demand for used cars as much as new cars. Additionally, cars without at least semi-autonomous capabilities will have much less value in the future than they have today. This reduction will create an excess of supply over demand for used cars, driving prices lower.

The reductions in demand and value have several other implications as well. Lower resale values will force some people to hold onto their cars longer when trade-in values decline. The reduction in resale value will also have an impact on leasing, where the expected residual values could be much lower. As an additional note, the residual values for AVs will also be lower because of the expected rapid change in technology.

Disruption to Industries Supporting the Auto Industry

Many industries support the auto industry. There will also be a disruption in most of these. These industries include auto dealerships, auto repair shops, gas stations, lease financing companies, retail auto parts suppliers, driver training, and many others. Let's look more closely at some of these.

Auto Dealers

A 30% or higher decline in new car sales will significantly disrupt auto dealerships. Even a 20% decline will affect the viability of many dealers who rely on a minimum volume of sales to cover operating costs such as rent and overhead. I expect that many dealerships will consolidate or go out of business until there is a new equilibrium with fewer dealers. Also, the reduction in residual values may delay new car sales, and the decrease in individually-owned cars will reduce service revenue.

Some dealerships will shift to focus on selling autonomous vehicles. Doing this will require some significant investments and retraining, but it will provide them with future opportunities. Since dealerships are based on a franchise to sell specific brands, it will be interesting to see if the auto manufacturers create new brands for AVs and try to sign-up new dealerships. Approximately 1.3 million people work for automobile dealers in the United States.

Gas Stations

There are approximately 150,000 gas stations in the United States, but this number is declining already. Fewer gas stations will be needed because of the decline in the number of individually-owned vehicles. Still, even more broadly, the demand for gasoline sales will be reduced by the switch to electric vehicles. The increase in autonomous vehicles will accelerate the number of electric vehicles. Within a decade, the demand at the gas pump will significantly diminish.

Even a 30% reduction in individually-owned cars will drive a significant reduction in volume at gas stations. There won't be any offsetting business from ARS vehicles because they will be primarily electric (or hybrid) and will be in fleets, so that they won't use gas stations. Over time, I expect most vehicles will be autonomous and electric, so gas stations as we know them today will mostly disappear. Some newer gas stations will provide electric charging capabilities to offset the loss of gasoline sales. Some stations, like many of the RaceTrac locations, have additional space for charging stations where multiple vehicles could sit for an hour or more, and they also offer food service and tables for customers to eat while waiting for their vehicle to charge. However, unlike gasoline cars, electric vehicles can be charged at home. It's likely that by 2035, most gas stations, at least as we know them today, will be a thing of the past.

Oil Industry

Autonomous vehicles will predominately be electric, which, as predicted earlier, will reduce the need for gas stations. It also will reduce gasoline and oil consumption. The International Energy Agency estimates that the worldwide oil demand used for road transport is approximately 42 million barrels per day. Under current conditions, this would increase to about 54 million barrels per day by 2040. With a moderate change to electric vehicles, demand would be relatively flat at 45 million barrels per day by 2040. However, with more aggressive change and the adoption of electric vehicles, the demand could reduce significantly to only 23 million barrels per day by 2040.

Retail Auto Part Suppliers

Retail auto part companies may see a massive drop in business as car ownership goes down and autonomous ride services maintain their own fleets. Approximately 500,000 people work in retail auto parts stores and related businesses, such as tire stores.

Driver Education Companies

More people of all ages, especially young people, aren't getting their driver's licenses. A study by the University of Michigan Transportation Research Institute indicates that the percentage of people aged 16 to 44 with driver's licenses in 1983, 2008, 2011, and 2014 declined in each period. The need for driver education will be even less with ARS and AVs, as more new driving-age teenagers realize that they won't need a license. By some reports, driver education teachers can make $60,000 to as much as $100,000 per year. In some states, driver's education is state-funded.

Correspondingly, there will be a reduction in the need for state motor vehicle registrations and licenses. Driver's licenses will slowly disappear, and the Department of Motor Vehicles in most states will shrink. Other forms of ID may emerge as people no longer carry driver's licenses.

Auto Financing

With lower automobile ownership because of ARS, there will be a reduction in auto financing and leasing. The jobs of people who arrange the leases and financing will be significantly cut, as will the amount of capital invested in auto financing.

Disruptions to the "Auto Accident Industry"

The reduction of auto accidents will severely disrupt one group of industries. These are the companies and people whose work supports auto accidents, even those who are helpful in times of accidents. This includes auto insurance companies, trial lawyers, and auto repair shops. Even though there will be a significant loss of jobs, it's challenging to make the argument that it's not worth the benefit. It will also reduce the need for emergency services and the jobs it provides.

Auto Insurance Companies

Insurers such as State Farm Insurance, Allstate Corp., Liberty Mutual Group, GEICO, Citigroup Inc., and Travelers Group could lose most of the $200 billion paid in personal auto premiums. Initially, the expected decline in auto accidents from AVs may benefit their claims expense, but this will quickly reflect lower premiums and revenues.

These top five companies for direct premiums written in 2018 (NAIC data, sourced from S&P Global Market Intelligence, Insurance Information Institute) will be impacted significantly:

- State Farm Mutual Automobile Insurance: $41 billion
- Berkshire Hathaway Inc.: $33 billion
- Progressive Corp.: $27 billion
- Allstate Corp.: $22 billion
- USAA Insurance Group: $14 billion

On top of this, ARS will reduce the number of individually-owned vehicles, further eroding the market. ARS vehicles will be primarily in fleets with lower premiums, and many of these may be self-insured by the companies operating the fleets. The impact on auto insurance companies will be severe. Auto insurance premiums will be reduced by 50%, and possibly a lot more.

Insurance Agents

Corresponding to the reduction in auto insurance, those agencies that rely on selling auto insurance policies will be significantly affected. The reduction of 50% or more in insurance premiums will substantially reduce property and casualty insurance premium revenues.

About 35,000 insurance agencies employ approximately 1 million people in the United States. Auto insurance makes up about 40% of the property and casualty sector of the insurance industry and about 15%-20% of the total insurance industry of more than $1 trillion. The anticipated reduction in auto insurance premiums will probably drive consolidation in the number of agencies.

Auto Repair Shops

There are approximately 225,000 auto repair facilities in the United States, employing nearly 850,00 people. Many of these are small independent auto repair shops. The reduction in the number of vehicles will significantly shrink this business, but this will be amplified. AVs will be too sophisticated for most of these to repair. Also, as the value of used cars declines, fewer will be repaired. A 50% reduction over time is probably conservative.

Trial Lawyers

In the U.S., legal costs are a high cost of accidents. The estimated legal cost of traffic accident litigation is more than $11 billion.[xi] The bulk of this goes to personal injury lawyers, who are typically paid a contingency fee of 33% to 45%, depending on whether the lawsuit settles or goes to trial.

With the reduction in accidents from the increased use of AVs, this source of income for trial lawyers will be significantly decreased. Also, trial lawyers who defend those accused of traffic violations, including serious ones, will see a decline in work. Some law firms are almost entirely reliant on this type of income and will go out of business. It should be no surprise that trial lawyers are lobbying against autonomous vehicles.

Emergency Services

As accidents are reduced by 90%, ambulances and other emergency vehicles will be needed less. Hospital emergency rooms will see a reduction in accident patients. One unintended consequence may be the reduction in the number of organs available for organ transplants.

Disruptions to Truck Drivers

There are approximately 3.5 million professional truck drivers in the United States, based on American Trucking Association estimates. The total number of people employed in the industry, including those in positions that do not entail driving, exceeds 8.7 million. At the current time, the need for truck drivers is increasing by an estimated 100,000 per year, and the industry is challenged to meet increasing demands. The truck driver shortage in the U.S. is significant and getting worse.

Autonomous trucks will slowly replace drivers. At first, autonomous driving will supplement drivers in a truck by allowing them to rest and sleep when they are driving autonomously. This productivity improvement will reduce the need for 10% - 20% of the drivers, but this reduction will probably come out of the need for more drivers, so the early impact on truck drivers will be minor.

Eventually, probably in the 2030s, autonomous trucks will reduce the need for 3.5 million truck drivers. Those related trucking positions who are not drivers most likely will not be affected as much.

Disruption to Rental Car Companies

The rental car industry will be upended as autonomous ride services become cheaper and ubiquitous. Why would a consumer rent a car if the cost of ordering a ride service from Uber or Apple was 80%-90% cheaper? Car rental is a $75 billion industry that will need to change as it shrinks. A few of these companies may be able to innovate to survive.

JP Morgan's analysts stated a belief in 2017 that the advent of fully autonomous driving will level the playing field for rental car companies and rideshare solutions, making them the same, additionally necessitating investments in fleet management services by rideshare companies. There is already some rotation from car rentals toward ridesharing for short rental periods with low utilization. Both Hertz and Avis estimate that such substitution is feasible only in less than 10% of their transactions. Still, using technology to further lower cost-per-mile and improved convenience will increasingly cause overlap and competition for the same customer between ride services and car-rental businesses.

I disagree with the view that rental car companies will be successful participants in autonomous ride services. It's too far-fetched for rental car companies to develop autonomous vehicles. Still, they are experts at managing and maintaining large fleets of cars spread out across a variety of geographies. They have a model for buying cars in volume, managing them, and then selling them from their fleets. They also can service and maintain large fleets, which includes a broad geographical footprint. A few rental car companies may be able to transform themselves by servicing autonomous fleets of cars for ARS companies such as Apple, Waymo, Uber, Lyft, etc. But they won't control the ride services businesses; it will be more like a low-margin building-maintenance type of business.

There also may be an opportunity for car rental companies to provide autonomous vehicles for medium-distance rentals, say from Boston to New York. They have facilities throughout the United States to offer pick-up in one location and drop-off in another. ARS primarily will be focused on fleets based in designated metropolitan areas. But this opportunity remains to be seen.

Auto rental is a large industry that is at risk. Enterprise has $14 billion in revenue. Hertz has a revenue of almost $9 billion. Avis has $6 billion in revenue. Rental car companies were already losing business to ridesharing. Hertz, for example, lost money for the previous five years, and then COVID-19 brought its business almost to a halt, with most of its 700,000 cars sitting idle. In May 2020, it filed for bankruptcy.

Avis

Waymo's ARS service in Phoenix, Arizona, uses a fleet of adapted Chrysler Pacifica hybrid minivans with its autonomous-driving technology. The company announced a deal with Avis to service and store the vehicles. Waymo will own the autonomous test fleet and will pay Avis to look after the vehicles.

Under a multi-year agreement, Avis will service and store 600 of Waymo's self-driving cars. The arrangement solves a fundamental problem faced by companies working to incorporate autonomous vehicles into ridesharing services. The vehicles need standard maintenance and cleaning, so they are ready for passengers. While it's too early to project that this will be a broader partnership, it is the start of an interesting relationship that may, in fact, blossom into something much bigger.

Hertz

Apple is leasing a small fleet of cars from Hertz Global Holdings Inc. to test autonomous technology. The agreement may be part of a more significant deal. It is leasing Lexus RX450h sport-utility vehicles from Hertz's Donlen fleet-management unit, according to documents released by the California Department of Motor Vehicles.

Disruption to Parking Lot Companies

There are more than a billion parking spaces in the United States -- that's correct, a billion. And parking is a $100 billion industry. The parking industry segments into on-street parking and off-street parking. On-street parking (i.e., parking meters) represents about a third of parking-related revenue in the U.S. and is typically controlled by cities and municipalities. Off-street parking (i.e., garages and surface lots), representing about two-thirds of all parking-related revenue in the U.S., is primarily owned by private enterprises.

In the U.S., there are more than 40,000 garages and surface parking lots. Owners of these facilities rarely manage them; instead, they rely on parking operators and equipment providers (that provide access and revenue control solutions) to maximize parking revenue. The number of parking lot attendants is probably well over 100,000.

While ARS and individually-owned AVs won't eliminate parking lots, it may significantly reduce that need. In many cities, a significant reduction in parking will make garages and parking lots unprofitable and force them to close.

Disruption to Short/Medium-Distance Air Travel

Disruptions will not be limited to auto industries. Airlines with short- and medium-distance flights also may see disruptions. Let's look at short trips of 200 miles or so. These include flights such as Boston to/from New York, New York to/from DC, or Austin to/from Dallas. Airfare each way ranges from $175-$300, but the total cost could be much higher when you include parking and taxi costs. Parking could add $30-$50, depending on the length of time. A taxi on the other end could add $25-$50, although ARS will reduce this cost. In any case, the total cost for the flight, including parking and taxi, ranges from $225 to $400. The cost for an autonomous ride service for longer trips such as this would be initially similar and eventually lower.

The time required and convenience are also considerations. In traveling some of these routes, I know that I would fly for several trips until I got delayed or missed a flight. Then I would drive for a while until I got stuck in traffic or got drowsy driving. With AVs, driving will become more convenient. Depending on the distance to and from the airport, it can take less time. For example, let's assume someone is 45 minutes from the departure airport and 30 minutes from the arrival airport to the destination. They arrive at the airport an hour before the flight, providing just enough time to park, go through security, and board. There is another 30 minutes to get off the plane and get to the taxi. The flight itself is probably an hour and 15 minutes. That's a total of four hours, approximately the same or less than the travel time for an AV from your home to your destination without the hassle of delayed flights. You can also leave on your own schedule without worrying about your flight.

Disruptions to Municipal Revenue

Municipalities (cities, towns, and counties) will see a decline in some revenue sources. In some municipalities, this will be significant.

Loss of Traffic Ticket Revenue

The money from fines for speeding, cruising through stop signs, and lesser infractions like parking violations generate hundreds of millions of dollars for cities, helping to pay for infrastructure and even court budgets. But a city of autonomous, law-abiding cars and trucks could spell the end of moving violations and traffic tickets.

The total municipal revenue from traffic tickets is difficult to estimate accurately, but it is considerable. One estimate from 2007 is that somewhere between 25 and 50 million traffic tickets are issued each year. Assuming an average ticket cost of $150.00, the total revenue from tickets ranges from $3.75 to $7.5 billion. I think the estimates may be a little high, but even at a more conservative estimate of $2.5 billion, a 70%-80% reduction would significantly impact many municipalities. New York City, for example, collected $569 million in parking and traffic fines in the 2016 fiscal year.

A decline in revenue from tickets could be more painful in cities and towns that rely more on fines. A 2015 investigation found five Colorado towns relied on traffic fines for at least 30% of their budgets. These fines comprised almost the entire budget of one town. The Nevada Supreme Court complained in 2015 that a decline in traffic tickets was crimping the court's budget. States will be forced to come up with other ways to bridge the gap when AVs become commonplace.

DUI/OUI

There will be no more DUI/OUI offenses with AVs, eliminating the associated fines and court costs. The social benefit of eliminating DUIs is significant, but reducing revenue related to processing these cases will be a disruption for some municipalities. It's not likely to be one that they try to prevent.

Gasoline Tax

Federal fuel taxes raised $36.4 billion in 2016, with $26.1 billion raised from gasoline taxes. The states get approximately the same tax revenue in total. Most of this is used to pay for road infrastructure. More than $50 billion in gasoline tax revenue is at risk as AVs drive an increase in the percentage of electric vehicles. The municipalities will have to come up with other ways of raising the tax to offset this decline.

Overall Disruption

The advent of autonomous vehicles will bring tremendous benefits, but it will also spell the loss of millions of jobs in the United States alone. Historically, when technology wipes out jobs, these jobs are replaced by other jobs in new areas. That pattern continues, of course, until it doesn't. Eventually, technology will eliminate so many jobs that they can't be replaced, and society will need to react in some, preferably orderly, way.

AVs and autonomous ride services will create new jobs too. For the most part, those jobs involved in developing autonomous technology have already been created, but there will be some increase. Other jobs will be created in the deployment stage of AVs and ARS. However, these won't offset the sheer number of jobs lost.

Many of the businesses discussed here will be diminished or go away. This is part of the natural evolution of an industry. Billions of dollars are made with the creation of new industries, while billions are lost in the industries they replace.

In the concluding chapter, I try to estimate the timing of how these disruptions will occur. I'm hopeful that the transitions resulting from autonomous vehicles can be managed orderly, and I encourage government leaders to consider constructive solutions.

Chapter 13
Government Regulation & Support

G overnment regulation of autonomous vehicles is a much-debated topic, but my current opinion is that it won't stop or significantly delay the advent of autonomous driving. In the longer term, the significant reductions in death and injuries from accidents, meaningful decreases in the cost of transportation, and the opportunity to provide mobility to millions who are currently deprived of it will outweigh the disruptions described in the previous chapter. In the shorter term, autonomous driving will be focused primarily on autonomous ride services (ARS). State and local regulations control ARS, so companies can launch their ARS services first in areas that support autonomous vehicles.

As always, there will be some vocal Luddites who are afraid of this new technology, and there will be some reasonable-sounding arguments they will make in lobbying for restrictions. There will be lobbying against AVs from groups, such as trial lawyers, insurance companies, and truck drivers. They can raise unfounded fears that software bugs in cars will kill people and that vehicles shouldn't make moral decisions selecting outcomes in different ways to react to an impending accident. There will be concerns about hacking the software running AVs, and I expect there will be some best-selling novels on this theme (probably by Steven King). Finally, there will be very well-justified arguments about the loss of jobs, as was discussed in the previous chapter. However, I don't think that the trade-off of jobs for lives and injuries will prevail. Nevertheless, there is now and will continue to be lobbying to restrict or delay autonomous vehicles through government regulation.

There will also be lobbying for AVs. For example, Waymo launched a public campaign called "Let's Talk Self-Driving" along with the National Safety Council, Mothers Against Drunk Driving, and the Foundation for Senior Living, among other organizations.

Some governments, particularly at the local and state levels, will encourage and cultivate autonomous vehicles. It could even become a way for a metropolitan area to compete in attracting new residents and travelers.

Eventually, the availability of autonomous ride services and being AV-friendly may become essential factors in the rankings of the best places to live.

Since the focus of this book is on autonomous vehicles in the United States, I'll only focus here on American government regulations. Foreign regulations of AVs are extraordinarily complex and varied. Chapter 11 touched on how some foreign governments regulate and support autonomous driving.

Government regulation in the United States has three levels: national (federal), state, and local (municipal). Each level of government has a different focus on the regulation and support of autonomous vehicles.

Federal Regulation of AVs

At a national level, regulation focuses on making AVs legal to produce and sell. In 2017, the U.S. House overwhelmingly passed a bill providing the federal government with a framework for developing new rules for driverless cars. However, the Senate failed to consider the legislation before its session ended in 2018.

The House bill was called the Safely Ensuring Lives Future Deployment and Research In Vehicle Evolution, or the SELF-DRIVE Act. The Senate's bill was named the American Vision for Safer Transportation Through Advancement of Revolutionary Technologies, or the AV START Act. Cute acronyms, aren't they? Both bills would have given the National Highway Traffic Safety Administration the authority to regulate the design, construction, and performance of self-driving cars. There are some differences in the directives to the Department of Transportation in the two bills, generally involving timing for new rules and the need for safety evaluation reports.

The most important part of the proposed regulations was an increase in the number of exemptions for car manufacturers before complying with comprehensive Federal Motor Vehicle Safety Standards. The current number is 2,500 vehicles. Under the House bill, exemptions would begin at 25,000 for the first year and then increase to 100,000 for the third and fourth years. The Senate bill, by comparison, allowed the National Highway Traffic Safety Administration to grant up to 15,000 exemptions in the first year. The cap increased to 40,000 self-driving vehicles per manufacturer in the second year and ramps up to 80,000 for subsequent years. To receive an exemption, manufacturers were required to prove to the National Highway Traffic Safety Administration that the car was as safe or safer than cars already on the road.

Congressional legislation may not even be necessary because the NHTSA could revise its regulations on its own. The agency could issue interpretive guidance to clarify different requirements for AVs from human-driven vehicles. It can also use waivers, exemptions, and pilot program authority to address safety issues for AVs while it gathers real-world information about how AVs can operate safely.

The federal highway system can also be improved to provide an AV-compatible infrastructure, including requiring visible highway lane markings, electronically readable signs, and support for vehicle-to-infrastructure communications.

Department of Transportation

The U.S. Department of Transportation has broad authority to oversee transportation systems within the U.S., including auto, trucking, air travel, trains, and water transportation. Three agencies are essential to regulating autonomous vehicles.

Federal Highway Administration

The Federal Highway Administration (FHWA) is responsible for providing stewardship over the construction, maintenance, and preservation of the nation's highways, bridges, and tunnels. Through research and technical assistance, the FHWA supports federal, state, and local agencies to accelerate innovation and improve safety and mobility.

National Highway Traffic Safety Administration

The National Highway Traffic Safety Administration's (NHTSA) mission is to save lives, prevent injuries, and reduce the economic costs of road traffic crashes through education, research, safety standards, and enforcement activity. NHTSA implements highway safety programs by setting and enforcing safety performance standards for motor vehicles and equipment, identifying safety defects, and through the development and delivery of effective highway safety programs for state and local jurisdictions.

Federal Motor Carrier Safety Administration

The Federal Motor Carrier Safety Administration's (FMCSA) mission is to reduce crashes, injuries, and fatalities involving large trucks and buses. FMCSA partners with industry, safety advocates, and state and local governments to keep the nation's roads safe and improve commercial motor vehicle (CMV) safety through regulation, education, enforcement, research, and technology.

DOT Approach to AVs

The United States Department of Transportation (U.S. DOT) has established a straightforward approach to shaping policy for autonomous vehicles, based on the following six principles.[xii]

1. We will prioritize safety.

Automation offers the potential to improve safety for vehicle operators and occupants, pedestrians, bicyclists, motorcyclists, and other travelers sharing the road. However, these technologies may also introduce new safety

285

risks. U.S. DOT will lead efforts to address potential safety risks and advance the life-saving potential of automation, which will strengthen public confidence in these emerging technologies.

2. We will remain technology-neutral.

To respond to the dynamic and rapid development of automated vehicles, the Department will adopt flexible, technology-neutral policies that promote competition and innovation as a means to achieve safety, mobility, and economic goals. This approach will allow the public — not the Federal Government — to choose the most effective transportation and mobility solutions.

3. We will modernize regulations.

U.S. DOT will modernize or eliminate outdated regulations that unnecessarily impede the development of automated vehicles or that do not address critical safety needs. Whenever possible, the Department will support the development of voluntary, consensus-based technical standards and approaches that are flexible and adaptable over time. When regulation is needed, U.S. DOT will seek rules that are as nonprescriptive and performance-based as possible. As a starting point and going forward, the Department will interpret and, consistent with all applicable notice and comment requirements, adapt the definitions of "driver" and "operator" to recognize that such terms do not refer exclusively to a human, but may, in fact, include an automated system.

4. We will encourage a consistent regulatory and operational environment.

Conflicting State and local laws and regulations surrounding automated vehicles create confusion, introduce barriers, and present compliance challenges. U.S. DOT will promote regulatory consistency so that automated vehicles can operate seamlessly across the Nation. The Department will build consensus among State and local transportation agencies and industry stakeholders on technical standards and advance policies to support the integration of automated vehicles throughout the transportation system.

5. We will prepare proactively for automation.

U.S. DOT will provide guidance, best practices, pilot programs, and other assistance to help our partners plan and make the investments needed for a dynamic and flexible automated future. The Department also will prepare for complementary technologies that enhance the benefits of automation, such as communications between vehicles and the surrounding environment, but will not assume universal implementation of any particular approach.

6. We will protect and enhance the freedoms enjoyed by Americans.

U.S. DOT embraces the freedom of the open road, which includes the freedom for Americans to drive their own vehicles. We envision an environment in which automated vehicles operate alongside conventional, manually-driven vehicles and other road users. We will protect the ability of consumers to make the mobility choices that best suit their needs. We will support automation technologies that enhance individual freedom by expanding access to safe and independent mobility to people with disabilities and older Americans.

Comments to the FMCSA

One of the key issues is how federal regulations affect autonomous vehicles since those regulations were put in place for human drivers. In the middle of 2019, the FMCSA requested comments concerning Federal Motor Carrier Safety Regulations (FMCSRs), which could be a barrier to the safe testing and deployment of automated driving systems equipped commercial motor vehicles on public roads. It received many responses, one from Waymo, which is the leader in autonomous vehicles. The following is a summary of some of Waymo's comments that I believe reflect the essential perspectives on this issue:[xiii]

- Geographic limitations are one essential part of the operational design domain (ODD) for any Level 4 vehicle. The geo-fenced territory of a particular system's ODD may span highways, surface streets, or both within a single city, throughout a state, or between many states. In order for a CMV (commercial motor vehicle) equipped with a Level 4 automated driving system (ADS) to continue its trip beyond the geo-fenced ODD, a human driver would have to disengage the ADS and take over the driving and would be subject to all of FMCSA's existing requirements for drivers.

- With respect to the question of "whether the FMCSRs, under certain conditions, could be read to require, or not require, the presence of a trained commercial driver in the driver's seat," Waymo shared its interpretation, referencing a previous independent report. The (Volpe) report analyzing the FMCSRs, speaks to this issue, stating that "the FMCSRs do not appear to contain an explicit requirement that CMVs be operated by a human driver, but instead present requirements that apply to human drivers." Waymo believes that there is no explicit requirement that a driver must be present in a CMV and recommended that the FMCSA issue interpretive guidance to clarify that the FMCSRs do not require that a driver be present in a CMV or that any other natural person be behind the wheel of a CMV, particularly in the case of a CMV equipped with a Level 4 ADS that is operating within its ODD or a Level 5 system.

- Waymo also addresses the issue of Hours of Service for truck drivers. It believes that applying FMCSA definitions in the context of fully autonomous CMVs yields these conclusions: (1) An

287

individual who is operating a CMV (i.e., performing the dynamic driving task) is generally considered a driver, even if the CMV is equipped with an ADS, and (2) An individual who does not operate a CMV (i.e., does not perform the dynamic driving task) is not a driver, even if that person is on board the CMV. Transporting goods with fully autonomous CMVs may involve human roles that will require FMCSA to reconsider how to interpret and apply current rules. In one scenario, a person might be responsible for operating the vehicle only in minimal, planned situations (e.g., moving the vehicle for refueling or through a weigh station). The Agency could, for example, consider such a person a non-driver. Or, even if the person is considered a "driver," the Agency may find that these incidental tasks do not constitute driving time for Hours of Service purposes because, when those tasks are performed, the CMV is not "in operation" as the term is commonly understood. Another scenario might involve a person with no regularly assigned driving responsibilities but who has the capability to operate the vehicle in an emergency situation (e.g., failure of the ADS requiring manual movement of the CMV to a safe place). This person, who may be on board the CMV regularly, should reasonably be considered a driver only in such emergency situations. FMCSA could interpret current rules, for example, to require such a contingent driver be subject to all driver requirements (including physical qualifications and alcohol and drug testing) but only be subject to the Hours of Service rules on the rare occasion when the contingency requiring the person to drive should arise.

- Fleet monitoring of ADS-equipped vehicles is distinct from "remote driving" or "teleoperation," which involves individuals who can actually drive a vehicle from a remote location through a wireless connection to the vehicle. For safety and security reasons, Waymo has chosen to avoid including such technology in its autonomous vehicles because it feels that relying on such features would conflict with its objective of reducing the number of fatalities and injuries caused by crashes on U.S. roads – an overwhelming percentage of which are caused by human error.

- If interpretive guidance cannot resolve all such barriers, the Agency's waiver, exemption, and pilot program authority are well-suited to address safety issues for fully autonomous CMVs. Such tools provide FMCSA with ample flexibility to ensure safety while gathering real-world information about how fully autonomous CMVs operate safely and are expected to be used in the marketplace.

288

Uber also added similar comments. It agrees with Waymo's arguments on the definition of a driver, and it also adds a couple of other points:[xiv]

- Distracted Driving (Prohibition Against Texting and Using Handheld Wireless Phones) and Driver Monitoring should be appropriately confined to SAE Level 3 and below vehicles. When a Level 4 ADS is engaged, any human passengers are not driving and need not be subject to texting or phone use restrictions or driver fatigue monitoring.

- All existing medical qualification requirements apply to the driver of an ADS-equipped vehicle. However, medical qualifications cannot and do not apply to an ADS (i.e., to the vehicle itself).

- Hours of service rules for drivers do not apply to the machinery, including an ADS, and should not apply to persons traveling in a vehicle when a Level 4 or Level 5 ADS is engaged.

There were also comment letters seeking to delay the introduction of AVs. The American Property Casualty Insurers Association (APCIA) believes that for the potential of the technology to be realized, any changes to the FMCSR's should be rare, limited to the highest levels of automation, and maintain the current level of safety. APCIA comprises over 1,200 member companies and 330 insurance groups, who together write 70 percent of the commercial auto insurance in the United States.

State Regulations

State governments regulate vehicle registration, licensing, insurance, as well as safety and emissions inspections. They can impose restrictions on AVs or on the opposite end of the spectrum, enact legislation to promote AVs and prohibit municipalities from restricting AVs, as Florida has done. They also regulate and manage their state highway systems.

By the middle of 2019, more than 25 states had legislation or executive orders related to autonomous vehicles, according to the National Conference of State Legislators. Some of these are restrictive. New York, for example, strictly regulates AV testing by requiring that AVs follow an approved route with a police escort.

Each year, the number of states considering legislation for autonomous vehicles has gradually increased.[xv]

- In 2018, 15 states enacted 18 AV-related bills.
- In 2017, 33 states introduced legislation.
- In 2016, 20 states introduced legislation.
- Sixteen states introduced legislation in 2015, up from 12 states in 2014, nine states and D.C. in 2013, and six states in 2012.

- Since 2012, at least 41 states and D.C. have considered legislation related to autonomous vehicles.

By 2019, 29 states: Alabama, Arkansas, California, Colorado, Connecticut, Florida, Georgia, Illinois, Indiana, Kentucky, Louisiana, Maine, Michigan, Mississippi, Nebraska, New York, Nevada, North Carolina, North Dakota, Oregon, Pennsylvania, South Carolina, Tennessee, Texas, Utah, Virginia, Vermont, Washington, Wisconsin, and Washington D.C. have enacted legislation related to autonomous vehicles. Governors in Arizona, Delaware, Hawaii, Idaho, Illinois, Maine, Massachusetts, Minnesota, Ohio, Washington, and Wisconsin have issued executive orders related to autonomous vehicles.

Some states promote the use of AVs. Michigan, California, Arizona, Pennsylvania, and Florida are examples. Eventually, all states will embrace AVs because they won't want to be left behind.

Let's look at regulations in three different states promoting AVs. Each of these has a somewhat different approach to its regulation.

California

California has regulations to encourage the testing of AVs and issues permits for testing. Under its testing regulations, manufacturers are required to provide the DMV with a Report of Traffic Accident Involving an Autonomous Vehicle within ten business days of the incident. The California Autonomous Vehicle Testing Regulations also require every manufacturer authorized to test autonomous vehicles on public roads to submit an annual report summarizing its activity for the year, including disengagements of the technology during testing.

On October 30, 2018, California's Department of Motor Vehicles (DMV) issued Waymo the state's first permit to test autonomous vehicles on public roads without a human in the driver's seat. It has had permission to test autonomous vehicles with safety drivers since 2014. Waymo's test area under this California permit is limited to the core of Silicon Valley (near Alphabet's headquarters in Mountain View) and the surrounding towns of Sunnyvale, Los Altos, and Palo Alto. The permit allows testing on streets and highways with speed limits of up to 65 miles per hour at any time of day, as well as during inclement weather.

California's regulations qualify AV manufacturers for testing with a safety driver and with no driver in the vehicle. Here is a summary of the significant provisions in its regulations:

Requirements for a Manufacturer's Testing Permit.

A manufacturer may conduct testing of autonomous vehicles on public roads in California provided:

(a) The manufacturer is conducting the testing. The term manufacturer includes anyone who modifies any vehicle by installing autonomous technology.

(b) The vehicle is operated by an autonomous vehicle test driver who is an employee, contractor, or designee of the manufacturer, and who has been certified by the manufacturer as competent to operate the vehicle.

(c) The manufacturer has in place proof of the manufacturer's ability to respond to a judgment or judgments for damages for personal injury, death, or property damage arising from the operation of autonomous vehicles on public roads in the amount of five million dollars ($5,000,000).

(d) The manufacturer has applied for, and the department has issued to the manufacturer a Manufacturer's Testing Permit or a Manufacturer's Testing Permit – Driverless Vehicles to conduct autonomous vehicle testing on public roads in California.

Identification of Autonomous Test Vehicles.

A manufacturer needs to provide complete identification of the autonomous vehicle to be used.

Requirements for Autonomous Vehicle Test Drivers.

Autonomous vehicle test drivers need to meet each of the following requirements:

(a) The autonomous vehicle test driver must be in immediate physical control of the vehicle or actively monitoring the vehicle's operations and capable of taking over immediate physical control.

(b) The autonomous vehicle test driver must be an employee, contractor, or designee of the manufacturer.

(c) The autonomous vehicle test driver must obey all provisions of the Vehicle Code and local regulation applicable to the operation of motor vehicles whether the vehicle is in autonomous mode or conventional mode.

(d) The autonomous vehicle test driver must know the limitations of the vehicle's autonomous technology and be capable of safely operating the vehicle in all conditions under which the vehicle is tested on public roads.

(e) A manufacturer conducting testing of autonomous vehicles on public roads must maintain a training program for its autonomous vehicle test drivers.

Manufacturer's Permit to Test Autonomous Vehicles that do not Require a Driver.

A manufacturer desiring to conduct testing of autonomous vehicles capable of operating without the presence of a driver inside the vehicle on public roads in California must apply for a permit to conduct driverless testing.

(a) The manufacturer must certify that the local authorities, within the jurisdiction where the vehicle will be tested have been provided a written notification that contains all the following:

(1) The operational design domain of the test vehicles.

(2) A list of all public roads in the jurisdiction where the vehicles will be tested.

(3) The date that testing will begin.

(4) The days and times that testing will be conducted on public roads.

(5) The number of vehicles to be tested and the types of vehicles to be tested.

(6) Contact information.

(b) The manufacturer must certify that the autonomous test vehicle complies with the all the following:

(1) There is a communication link between the vehicle and the remote operator to provide information on the vehicle's location and status and allow two-way communication between the remote operator and any passengers if the vehicle experiences any failures that would endanger the safety of the vehicle's passengers or other road users, or otherwise prevent the vehicle from functioning as intended, while operating without a driver.

(2) There is a process to display or communicate vehicle owner or operator information if the vehicle is involved in a collision or if there is a need to provide that information to a law enforcement officer for any reason.

(3) The subject autonomous vehicles must comply with all required Federal Motor Vehicle Safety Standards. Alternatively, the manufacturer shall provide evidence of an exemption that has been approved by the National Highway Traffic Safety Administration.

(c) The manufacturer must certify that the autonomous vehicles can operate without the presence of a driver inside the vehicle and that the autonomous technology meets the description of a Level 4 or level 5 automated driving system under SAE International's Taxonomy.

(d) The manufacturer must inform the department of the intended operational design domains of the autonomous vehicle.

(e) The manufacturer must provide a copy of a law enforcement interaction plan, which includes information that the manufacturer will

make available to the law enforcement agencies and other first responders.

(f) The manufacturer must maintain a training program for its remote operators and certify that each remote operator has completed training sufficient to enable him or her to safely execute the duties of a remote operator and possesses the proper class of license for the type of test vehicle being operated.

(g) Manufacturers that have publicly disclosed an assessment demonstrating their approaches to achieving safety must provide the department with a copy of that assessment.

(h) The manufacturer must disclose to any passenger in the vehicle that is not an employee, contractor, or designee of the manufacturer what personal information, if any, that may be collected about the passenger and how it will be used.

Arizona

Arizona is a hotbed of autonomous vehicle testing. Both Waymo and Intel are testing their autonomous cars in Chandler, while Uber and GM's Cruise have vehicles on the roads in and around Scottsdale. Arizona legalized AVs through an executive order of the governor.

Arizona governor Doug Ducey issued an executive order that fully driverless cars without anyone behind the wheel can operate on public roads. The only caveat is that the vehicles follow all existing traffic laws and rules for cars and drivers, including federal regulations. Here is a summary of that executive order:

- Testing or Operating Autonomous/Self-Driving Vehicles on Arizona Public Roads

Testing or operation of self-driving vehicles equipped with an automated driving system on public roads are required to follow all federal laws, regulations, and guidelines, Arizona State Statutes, Title 28 of the Arizona Revised Statutes, all regulations and policies set forth by the Arizona Department of Transportation and Executive Orders.

- Testing or Operating WITHOUT a person present in the vehicle

Testing or operation of vehicles that do not have a person present in the vehicle is allowed only if such vehicles are fully autonomous, and if prior to commencing testing or operation of the fully autonomous vehicles, an Autonomous Vehicle Testing Statement and Certification has been submitted to the Arizona Department of Transportation acknowledging:

- Unless an exemption or waiver has been granted by the National Highway Traffic Safety Administration, the fully autonomous vehicle is equipped with an automated driving system that follows all applicable federal law and federal motor vehicle safety standards and bears the required certification label(s) including reference to any exemption granted under applicable federal law.

- If a failure of the automated driving system occurs that renders that system unable to perform the entire dynamic driving task relevant to its intended operational design domain, the fully autonomous vehicle will achieve a minimal risk condition.

- The fully autonomous vehicle is capable of complying with all applicable traffic and motor vehicle safety laws and regulations of the State of Arizona, and the person testing or operating the fully autonomous vehicle may be issued a traffic citation or other applicable penalty in the event the vehicle fails to comply with traffic and/or motor vehicle laws.

- The fully autonomous vehicle meets all applicable certificate, title registration, licensing, and insurance requirements.

- Compliance with the Law Enforcement Protocol.

"As technology advances, our policies and priorities must adapt to remain competitive in today's economy," Ducey said in a statement. "This executive order embraces new technologies by creating an environment that supports autonomous vehicle innovation and maintains a focus on public safety."

Duce's move to codify his state's policies on autonomous vehicle testing came shortly after California announced that it would permit fully driverless cars to operate on its roads. Previously, a safety driver was required to be behind the wheel during autonomous testing. There is intense competition between both states for AV development. Arizona has fewer regulations and requires no public disclosures.

Florida

In June 2019, Florida approved a bill removing "unnecessary obstacles that hinder the development of autonomous vehicle technology"—including backup drivers. Unlike California and Arizona, which focus on AV testing, this bill addresses the operation of autonomous vehicles in the state. It promotes autonomous ride services and prohibits any local governments from restricting autonomous ride services.

The new law, which took effect July 1, 2019, allows a self-driving car (meeting all insurance requirements) to run without a human operator. In summary, the bill provides for the following:

- It revises various provisions of law relating to autonomous vehicles. The bill deems an automated driving system to be the operator of an autonomous vehicle while operating in autonomous mode, regardless of whether a person is physically present in the vehicle.

- It authorizes the operation of a fully autonomous vehicle on Florida roads regardless of whether a human operator is physically present in the vehicle. Under the bill, a licensed human operator is not required to operate a fully autonomous vehicle. The bill authorizes an autonomous vehicle, or a fully autonomous vehicle equipped with a teleoperation system, to operate without a human operator physically present in the vehicle when the teleoperation system is engaged. A remote human operator must be physically present in the United States and be licensed to operate a motor vehicle by a United States jurisdiction.

- It exempts fully autonomous vehicles operating with the automated driving system engaged from certain duties, such as the duty to give information and render aid, in the event of an accident. Provisions relating to unattended motor vehicles or property are also deemed inapplicable to such fully autonomous vehicles. The bill amends other provisions related to video displays, wireless communications devices, and other statutes to incorporate exemptions for autonomous vehicles.

- It applies provisions relating to the operation of transportation network companies and on-demand autonomous vehicle networks. The bill requires a fully-autonomous vehicle with the automated driving system engaged while logged on to an on-demand autonomous vehicle network or engaged in a prearranged ride to have specified insurance coverage. The bill also requires proof of financial responsibility to respond to a claim for damages arising out of a motor vehicle accident for owners or registrants of certain fully autonomous vehicles that are not subject to the insurance requirements described above. These requirements are scheduled to be repealed on January 1, 2024.

- It authorizes the Florida Turnpike Enterprise within the FDOT to fund, construct, and operate facilities for the advancement of autonomous and connected innovative transportation technologies for specified purposes.

- It expresses legislative intent to provide for uniformity of laws governing autonomous vehicles throughout the state. It prohibits a local government from imposing any tax, fee, for-hire vehicle requirement, or other requirements on automated driving systems, autonomous vehicles, or on a person who operates an autonomous vehicle.

Municipal (Local) Regulation and Support

Local regulation and support for AVs will be an essential focal point, especially for autonomous ride services (ARS). Autonomous vehicles may be restricted in some places, but they will benefit from local support in most. A local municipality could be a city, metropolitan area, or county. Since most road systems outside of federal and state highways are managed locally, they can promote autonomous vehicles in their area.

ARS is the reason that local support will be favorable. Municipalities that support AVs, particularly ARS, will be priority locations for initial autonomous ride services deployments. ARS companies will merely bypass those municipalities with restrictions or lack of support. The demand for mobility by seniors and the disabled, the convenience of ARS, and the safety improvements from AVs will be overwhelming. All municipalities will eventually come around to support AVs.

There are some relatively simple things that local governments can do to promote AVs in their jurisdictions:

- They can make sure all roads have painted lines sufficient for the cameras on autonomous vehicles to identify.
- There may also be some intersections where painted lines need to be redone to make them easier for AVs to understand.
- It may be helpful to replace four-way stop signs at intersections where drivers need to alternate because this may be difficult for AVs.
- They can replace or repair any traffic signs that are damaged or hidden from sensors.
- In some cities, it would be helpful to provide defined pick-up and drop-off areas for autonomous cars. There will be a need for an increase in these, as the demand for parking spaces and lots decreases.
- It may be helpful to have reserved temporary parking facilities for autonomous vehicles, like defined parking for electric vehicles.
- In some cases, more left-turn traffic signals could be helpful.
- Eventually, it will be helpful to support vehicle-to-infrastructure communications at traffic lights, intersections, etc.

Many of these changes will be helpful for autonomous ride services, which will be the first primary market for autonomous vehicles. Companies planning to introduce ARS will be willing to review the roads and traffic control systems and make recommendations to a local government. The cost of these changes may not be significant. Given the benefits to the local citizens, many local governments will make these to entice autonomous ride service companies to enter their markets. Some local governments may want autonomous ride service companies to fund these improvements, which they might be willing to do in return for an exclusive license in that area for a period, effectively locking out competition from benefitting from their investments.

Summary of Government Regulation and Support

Because of the significant benefits from AVs already discussed, I believe that government regulation will not impede deployment at any of the three levels. There may be some delays to get the regulations completed, but these delays should be minor.

Most state and local governments will be eager to promote autonomous driving, particularly ARS. I expect that there will be competition to secure early ARS operations. The ARS companies will be able to prioritize their deployments based on the support provided by municipal governments.

Part IV
Autonomous Vehicle Adoption Rate

Chapter 14
Stages for The Adoption of Autonomous Vehicles

Proponents of autonomous vehicles claim that AVs are right around the corner. Pessimists argue that it will take decades to replace cars as we know them with autonomous vehicles. Who is correct? They both are. The crucial difference is understanding the adoption rate for autonomous vehicle technology.

In this concluding chapter, I use a stages model to forecast adoption timing in major AV markets. Each stage is 5-6 years long, and it's important to note that every significant AV market will emerge differently in each stage.

This chapter includes an overall forecast of the evolution of AV technology over the next two decades. It is not an extrapolation of current trends since there are none yet. It is not a precise forecast that will be exact. It is a directionally accurate and thoroughly derived forecast considering several dynamics:

- From the top-down, it considers previous similar technology adoption rates.

- It is constructed by major markets because each market has different dynamics.

- It is well-grounded in statistical data as a starting point.

- It considers various factors, including the evolution of technology, expected benefits, anticipated social reluctance, resistance to the disruptions, etc., that were previously described in detail in this book.

- It considers important company strategies and the expected timing of those strategies.

Categorizing the timing for the adoption of AVs into stages enables a more strategic view. The exact timing of what will happen in each year within a stage is difficult to predict. Before looking at each of the stages of AV adoption, let's consider the history of technology adoption rates.

Technology Adoption Rates

Historical adoption rates provide useful insight into how long it takes a new technology to be adopted by consumers in the U.S. Adoption rates are different for different types of products, and new "systems technology" requires a more extended adoption period since it is more complicated. Electricity, the telephone, cell phones, and air travel are examples of these. They need some infrastructure in addition to the new product.

Economic conditions also impact adoption rates throughout the adoption period. In general, adoption rates are faster today than they were 50 years ago. Another factor affecting adoption rates is whether the product is a new product addition or a replacement product. Most new technologies are new product additions.

Figure 14-1 summarizes technology adoption rates for different products. Those based on "systems technologies" are in the first category. Those that are more individual products are in the second. The chart uses data from various studies on technology adoption. Data from multiple studies differ in the starting points they use. Some start when the technology was initially proven. Others start when it was sufficiently available for use. The data in this table starts the adoption period based on the time the technology was sufficiently available for use.

It took autos approximately 15 years to get to a 10% adoption rate and 25 years to get to 25% adoption. Electricity, telephone, and air travel required 20 years to get to 10% adoption. Autos required new road systems. Electricity and telephone required infrastructure to be put in place before consumer adoption.

Cell phones required infrastructure too (cell phone towers), but they got to 10% adoption in 10 years and 75% in 25 years. The investment in building cell phone towers in the 1990s was fast and furious as cell phone operators tried to beat each other to get sufficient coverage. Cell phone infrastructure companies invested billions of dollars every year to build cellphone towers. By 2013, less than 20 years from introduction, more than 55% of the U.S. primarily or exclusively used cell phones, and only about 8% of the homes had only landlines.[xvi]

Television also took 15 years to get to 10% because it required programming broadcasts before people would purchase a TV, but once the programming was in place, adoption jumped to 50% of the households in 25 years.

Figure 14-1 New Technology Adoption Rates

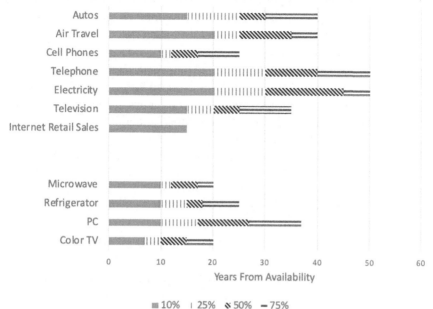

Source: Author estimates from various research and publications

Internet retail sales as a percentage of all retail sales rose to 10% in 15 years. Future adoption remains to be seen, but clearly, it already has had a disruptive effect on in-store retail. It's unlikely that internet retail sales will eliminate all physical retail stores.

Of these examples, the adoption rate for autonomous vehicles will be most like cellphones. Let's look at the stages for adoption and expected adoption rates. The measure that I use for the AV adoption rate is what I believe to be the most correct: the percentage of miles driven.

Stages for the Adoption of Autonomous Vehicles

The best way to understand the adoption rate of autonomous vehicles is to look at it in stages. First, it's important to realize that autonomous vehicles will transform transportation as we know it today. Many people pay lip service to this idea, but they then ask when all cars will be autonomous. The proper perspective is to anticipate how this transformation will create new autonomous-vehicle markets and then look at the potential timing for developing and growing these new markets. Throughout this book, we explored the primary new markets: autonomous ride services (ARS), autonomous home delivery, autonomous long-haul trucking, and individually-owned autonomous vehicles. In this chapter, we will conclude by projecting the timing for the adoption of autonomous technology in these markets, as well as the expected benefits and disruptions. Other types of transportation, such as construction, buses, etc., will also become autonomous, but the focus is on the primary markets.

I see the adoption of autonomous driving as evolving over five stages. Each stage represents an evolution in the major markets for autonomous vehicles. COVID-19 caused delays in the roll-out of ARS, and I have shifted some of my earlier projections. Most ARS companies suspended testing on public roads for the remainder of 2020 once the pandemic started, and many development teams were forced to work from home, slowing progress. Also, the demand for ridesharing, which ARS is replacing, dropped precipitously in 2020, as most people worked from home, stopped traveling, and activities such as eating out and entertainment were suspended. These probably set back the launch of ARS by approximately a year, but it gave the companies more time to refine their autonomous driving technology.

Each stage is discussed in some detail, but Figure 14-2 summarizes the central forecasts. It provides some base data for 2021, which is the conclusion of Stage 0 and the forecasts adoption rates in each of the four primary new markets for the end years of each stage. The first section of Figure 14-2 provides some basic reference data: population and passenger miles. The second section has two parts. The first is ridesharing market forecasts combined with ARS forecasts. While ARS will increase the combined market, it will principally cannibalize ridesharing. The forecast estimates ARS as a share of the combined market and a percentage of total passenger miles. The third section forecasts the adoption of autonomous trucking, and the fourth forecasts autonomous home delivery.

Stage 0 (2016-2021)
AV Initial Development

Stage 0 is the initial development and testing stage for autonomous vehicles. Even though there was research done before 2016, I mark 2016 as when the focus shifted from research to development.

Many attribute the start of AV research to the DARPA Grand Challenge, a prize competition for autonomous vehicles, funded by the Defense Advanced Research Projects Agency, the most prominent research organization of the United States Department of Defense. Congress authorized DARPA to award cash prizes to further DARPA's mission to sponsor revolutionary, high-payoff research.

Figure 14-2 -- Forecasted Adoption of AVs In U.S.

	2021	Stage 1 2025	Stage 2 2030	Stage 3 2035	Stage 4 2040
U.S. Population (millions)	335	347	359	370	380
Passenger Vehicle Miles (billions)	3,100	3,400	3,700	4,000	4,200
Miles per person	9,268	9,790	10,295	10,802	11,047
Ridesharing/ARS					
Ridesharing/Taxi Miles (billions)	120	180	200	150	100
ARS Miles (billions)	0.3	40	400	1,200	1,500
Total Ridesharing/ARS Miles	120	220	600	1,350	1,600
ARS % of Ridesharing/ARS	**0%**	**18.2%**	**66.7%**	**88.9%**	**93.8%**
ARS % of Passenger Miles		**1.2%**	**10.8%**	**30.0%**	**35.7%**
Individually Owned AVs					
AVs Owned (millions)	-	0.7	12.0	40.0	90.0
Total Registered Vehicles (millions)	285	281	258	212	200
Miles per Registered Vehicle	11,000	11,300	12,000	12,500	13,000
AV % of All Registered Vehicles	0%	0.2%	4.6%	18.9%	45.0%
AV Miles (billions)		8	144	500	1,170
AV % of Owner-Driven Miles		**0.2%**	**4.6%**	**18.9%**	**45.0%**
Passenger Adoption Rate		**1.4%**	**14.7%**	**42.5%**	**63.6%**
Autonomous Trucking					
Long-Haul Trucking Miles (billions)	335	370	400	450	500
Long-Haul Trucks (thousands)	3,350	3,700	3,200	3,700	4,000
Autonomous Trucks (thousands)		100	700	1,700	2,500
Miles Driven Autonomously (billions)		20	150	250	350
Autonomous Trucking Adoption Rate		**5.4%**	**37.5%**	**55.6%**	**70.0%**
Autonomous Home Delivery					
Home Deliveries (billions)	4.0	7.0	8.9	11.4	14.6
Home Delivery Miles (billions)	12.0	21.0	26.8	34.2	43.7
Autonomous Home Deliveries (billions)	-	0.15	3.0	6.0	10.0
AV Delivery Vehicles (thousands)		34	685	1,370	2,283
Autonomous Delivery Miles (billions)		0.5	9.0	18.0	30.0
Autonomous Delivery Adoption Rate		**2.1%**	**33.6%**	**52.6%**	**68.7%**

Source: Author Estimates

DARPA ran its Grand Challenge to encourage American ingenuity to accelerate the development of autonomous vehicle technologies that could be applied to military requirements. No team completed the designated DARPA Grand Challenge route from Barstow, CA, to Primm, NV, on March 13, 2004. The event offered a $1 million prize to the winner from the 15 finalists that emerged from a qualifying round at the California Speedway, but the prize went unclaimed as no vehicles could complete the challenging desert route.

A year later, on October 8, 2005, another round of the Grand Challenge was held in the Southwest desert near the California/Nevada state line. The Stanford Racing Team won the $2 million prize with a winning time of 6 hours, 53 minutes. A total of five teams completed the Grand Challenge course, which was 132 miles over desert terrain. These challenges helped to create both a mindset and a research community that a decade later would design autonomous vehicles.

During Stage 0, more than $100 billion was invested in developing and testing AVs. More than a hundred companies are involved in AV development in differing ways. The most significant investment in testing was for ARS. Also, by the end of Stage 0, the valuation of companies developing autonomous technologies exceeded $200 billion.

Autonomous Ride Services

In Stage 0, ARS is reaching completion of initial testing, although testing will continue as the service is expanded and refined. Waymo has made the most progress in Stage 0. By the middle of 2019, Waymo's AVs had driven more than 10 billion autonomous miles in simulation and 20 million real-world autonomous miles in 25 cities. Waymo's continued progress and aggressive expansion demonstrate the viability and attractiveness of ARS.

Waymo launched its ARS ahead of others with an Early Rider program in the later part of 2018 in Arizona. Essentially, it was a pilot program that enabled selected passengers to go places they frequented every day, to work, to school, to the movies, and more. Then, they shared their thoughts and experiences to help shape Waymo's ARS.

In 2019, it tested a fleet of 600 AVs in its autonomous ridesharing service. Waymo expanded its service center in Chandler, Arizona, which housed operations and support teams, including fleet technicians, fleet dispatch, fleet response, and rider support, to 60,000 square feet. The company also plans to open an 85,000-square-foot technical service center in the city of Mesa, Arizona, near Phoenix, which it expects will more than double its capacity to maintain the fleet of cars in Waymo One.

In November 2018, Waymo was issued a permit by the California Department of Motor Vehicles to begin testing its AVs in an autonomous mode, which would not require a safety driver behind the wheel. It allows Waymo to use the vehicle's driverless capabilities in an area between Palo Alto and San Jose. The permit will enable Waymo to operate its autonomous vehicles on the road during both the day and night, so long as weather conditions do not exceed fog and light rain. Vehicle speeds are limited to 65 miles per hour.

Waymo announced it would begin testing AVs in Florida, expanding from its initial test cities of Novi, Kirkland, Washington, San Francisco, and Phoenix. It used its modified Chrysler Pacifica minivans and a Jaguar I-Pace to drive on a closed track in heavy rain, ahead of testing on public Miami roads. Waymo says that its cars will initially be manually driven by trained operators, allowing them to collect real-world driving data in heavy rain. When they venture beyond the closed track, they will drive on highways between Orlando, Tampa, Fort Myers, and Miami.

Waymo also announced it would add up to 62,000 minivans to its fleet, and it had signed a deal with Jaguar Land Rover to equip 20,000 of the automaker's Jaguar I-Pace electric SUVs with its autonomous system by 2020.

Other companies also made progress in Stage 0. Motional launched its pilot test for ARS at the end of 2018 in Las Vegas. Using 30 autonomously modified BMWs, it offered paid autonomous rides with a safety driver to 1,600 stops in Las Vegas. Many of the trips are provided in partnership with Lyft. Lyft claims to have provided 100,000 rides in less than a year with an excellent passenger rating of 4.97 stars. The pilot program operates the AVs for 20 hours per day within a 20-square-mile section of Las Vegas that includes the busy Las Vegas strip area with more than 2,000 hotels, casinos, and restaurants. Passengers are charged the same as standard fare for a driver-based Lyft ride. Apple has been increasingly testing AVs in Northern California.

GM Cruise plans to start testing its ARS in San Francisco in 2021.

Autonomous Trucking

Autonomous trucking, particularly long-haul trucking, came into focus in 2021. By the middle of 2021, three companies developing autonomous trucks went public, raising billions for their development efforts. TuSimple let this group with a valuation of more than $11 billion. They disclosed their strategies and solidified the near-term process of autonomous trucking from one terminal off a highway to another.

During this stage, there was also meaningful testing of autonomous trucking. For example, in May 2019, UPS started testing autonomous tractor-trailers in Arizona with TuSimple. The autonomous trucks are used to transport goods between Phoenix and Tucson. A driver and engineer have been riding in each vehicle because a driver is legally required. The companies monitor the distance and time the trucks drive themselves, plus safety data and transportation time. TuSimple also ran a two-week test for the U.S.

Postal Service in early 2019, transporting mail across three Southwestern states.

Autonomous Home Delivery

Several companies are testing autonomous home delivery in Stage 0, but it lags ARS. The issue with autonomous home delivery is that it is most practical with custom-designed vehicles, and these will take some time to design and build. In the meantime, some companies like Ford are testing home delivery with modified passenger vehicles. Several start-ups are developing and testing small autonomous delivery prototypes.

AV Retail Market

The development of individually owned AVs to be sold at retail has taken a back seat to the development of AVs for ARS, although AVs developed for ARS will be adapted to be sold at retail.

The exception to this is Tesla, which only sells cars at retail. Tesla is working to make its vehicles function as AVs, continually improving their functionality through software releases to its Full Self-Driving function. It claims that it will release these capabilities by the end of Stage 0 in 2021. I own a Tesla with Full Self-Driving, and I'm skeptical about this.

Stage 1 (2022-2025)
Initial Launch of AVs

The era of autonomous vehicles will begin during Stage 1, covering the five-year period from 2022-2026. Autonomous ride services (ARS), autonomous long-haul trucking, and autonomous home delivery will be the first three uses of autonomous driving technology. ARS will start replacing ridesharing in select locations in the southern and western parts of the country at the beginning of this stage and accelerate by the end of it. Long-haul trucking will progressively incorporate autonomous driving. By the end of this stage, most new semi-trucks will be autonomous and use specially designated terminals on primary shipping routes. Autonomous home delivery will start in this stage and proliferate during it, especially in pizza delivery.

Autonomous Ride Services

The ARS market will grow geometrically. Five to six significant companies will enter the market in Stage 1. Each will launch its ARS service in an initial metropolitan area and then rapidly increase the number of ARS vehicles. Subsequently, each company will expand into new metropolitan areas, most likely adding multiple as it gets more experience: open one first, then two others, then the next four, etc. So, simultaneously during this stage, growth will come from more ARS companies, an increasing number of vehicles within the first metropolitan areas, and expansion into new metropolitan areas. During this stage, the market won't even need to expand to the more challenging areas of the country, such as the Northeast.

There are also significant motivations for rapid ARS growth. The development and capital investments in ARS are considerable. Companies will need to gain more capital, most likely by going public after proving the technology and business model.

Waymo already launched its ARS in Scottsdale in Stage 0, initiating paid autonomous rides in late 2020. It will continue to increase the number of autonomous vehicles providing these rides. In 2022 and continuing into 2023, it will significantly expand in the greater Phoenix area to cover Scottsdale, Mesa, Glendale, and Phoenix. This metropolitan area alone serves 4.6 million people over 14,000 square miles, so that it can support more than 10,000 ARS vehicles during this stage. In 2023 and the following years, Waymo will expand by adding ARS fleets in Mountain View, Southern Florida, Austin, Kirkland, Los Angeles, and other cities.

GM Cruise will launch its ARS in San Francisco by 2022. Cruise and Waymo have applied for the permits needed to start charging for rides and delivery using autonomous vehicles in San Francisco. Cruise will also launch in at least one other city by 2023. Cruise's current test fleet is comprised of hundreds of custom Chevrolet Bolt EVs equipped with driverless technology. It plans to launch operations by expanding that fleet, but it starts to scale up is when the Cruise Origin begins production in 2023. The Origin is the company's first vehicle specifically designed to operate without a driver. It doesn't have manual controls such as pedals or a steering wheel. By 2023, Cruise may have more than 20,000 Origins in its ARS fleet.

Argo is expected to launch its ARS in Austin by 2022 and then rapidly expand its fleet size there. Austin provides a significant market opportunity. Argo will add fleets in Miami and Washington DC by 2023.

The Motional/Lyft joint venture focuses on Las Vegas as its initial market, and it has already provided more than 100,000 autonomous rides there. It stated that it intends a rapid roll-out of fleets to multiple large cities soon following that. So, it could add two cities in 2023 and more in the following years.

Aurora/Uber and Zoox (Amazon) probably won't launch their ARS fleets until later in 2023 or early 2024. By that time, the first four competitors will be aggressively expanding their fleets, so these companies will need to catch up quickly to be competitive.

I expect Apple to enter the market as the last major competitor in 2024. It will have a second-generation ARS vehicle that most likely will be superior to the others. It will enter a market already developed by competitors and attract customers who want the exceptional Apple experience.

By the end of Stage 1, in 2025, the ARS market will grow to more than 300,000 vehicles driving approximately 24 billion miles in the U.S. That is still a minimal share of the total number of vehicles in the country. ARS will start cannibalizing ridesharing by the end of this stage, capturing 18% of the combined market.

At this point, ARS will be established as a standard and accepted way of travel.

Autonomous Trucking

In Stage 1, autonomous long-haul trucks without drivers will start carrying freight between specially designed terminals just off major freight highways. This makes autonomous driving much simpler because it only needs to master highway driving. Yet, it also provides significant cost savings by eliminating the driver for 90%+ of the driving.

Autonomous long-haul trucking will start early in the stage with drivers still in the cab, but the truck will mostly drive autonomously. There are some benefits in this with lower accident rates, less driver stress, and fuel savings. The companies developing autonomous trucking expect to implement driverless autonomous trucking by 2023-2024. They forecast rapid adoption of autonomous trucking because of the significant benefits.

Several companies developing autonomous trucks have very aggressive expectations during this stage, which they have publicly disclosed:

- Embark expects to have driverless autonomous tucks in 2023. It forecasts achieving 2.3 billion autonomous miles in 2024, 7.4 billion in 2025, and many times that in 2026.

- Plus expects to have autonomous trucks where the driver does not need to pay attention to driving by 2022-2023. It expects fully autonomous driving by 2024 and forecasts selling 56,000 trucks in that year. By 2025, it forecasts selling 104,000 tucks, with 66,000 of these in the U.S.

- As of May 2021, TuSimple had 6,775 reservations from blue-chip customers.

These three companies represent only half, or fewer, of the competitors for autonomous trucking, so extrapolating these to a Stage 1 adoption rate yields very high expectations. My forecast for autonomous trucking in Stage 1 is much lower. At the end of Stage 1 in 2025, I forecast 100,000 autonomous trucks on the road driving 20 billion autonomous miles. While significant, it is much less than the combined forecasts of the companies developing these technologies. By 2025, autonomous long-haul trucking would be approximately 5.4% of the miles driven.

Autonomous Home Delivery

Same-day autonomous home delivery will begin in Stage 1 but will lag ARS for two reasons. First, most companies are looking initially for ARS to introduce and resolve the issues of autonomous driving technology. Second, the real benefit from autonomous home delivery comes from specially-designed autonomous home delivery vehicles, and there are not enough companies manufacturing these in volume.

There are two categories of customers for autonomous delivery. In the first category are large restaurant and grocery companies such as Dominos and Walmart. Many started doing pilots in Stage 0 and will expand these in Stage 1. When sufficiently proven, they will purchase tens of thousands of autonomous delivery vehicles and roll them out to their stores, mainly focusing on the southern and western parts of the country in this stage. The second category is third-party delivery companies such as Uber Eats and DoorDash. Once they prove that autonomous delivery works, they will move aggressively to replace costly driver-based delivery to achieve a profit.

Autonomous delivery will prove effective in this stage, but the roll-out will be constrained by the availability of second-generation customer-designed autonomous delivery vehicles. By the end of Stage 1, there will be approximately 21,000 autonomous delivery vehicles, making 150 million autonomous deliveries and traveling 500 million miles. AVs will do about 2.5% of same-day home deliveries.

AV Retail Market

The retail AV market, which is the sale of AVs to individuals, will lag the growth of the ARS market. The reasons for this were previously described in detail but include the cost of AVs, limited availability of road systems, and rapid technological obsolescence.

Semi-autonomous technologies will be the dominant trend in the retail market for individually-owned AVs. By the end of Stage 1, I expect that almost half of the cars sold at retail will have semi-autonomous capabilities, although not all drivers will use this functionality.

There are two different technical views on individually-owned sufficiently-autonomous AVs. Each of these uses different autonomous technology platforms. The first is that they will develop progressively from semi-autonomous vehicles as more features are introduced. This is essentially the Tesla strategy. Semi-autonomous vehicles will become sufficiently-autonomous with software upgrades. If this happens, then there will be millions of sufficiently-autonomous vehicles created during Stage 1.

The second technical view is that sufficiently-autonomous vehicles will require a different autonomous vehicle platform with lidar and computers to position the vehicle in an HD map. This will be more expensive and limited, with few AVs available for retail purchase in Stage 1.

My view is the latter will be the most feasible direction. Even though I am a Tesla fan (I own one and drive it regularly in semi-autonomous mode), I don't believe camera-based technology will be viable for sufficiently-autonomous driving.

Premium-priced vehicles will be the initial beneficiaries of autonomous technology in Stage 1. These buyers will be willing to pay more for autonomous features than will other car buyers. I estimate that only about 700,000 sufficiently-autonomous vehicles will be sold at retail in the U.S. during Stage 1, with most of these sold at the very end of the stage. Of course, if my assumption on camera-based platforms is incorrect, there will be many millions of autonomous vehicles enabled by Tesla and sold by others.

The Stage 1 forecasts also show a slight decline in vehicles registered, even as the population grows. The decline goes from 290 million registered vehicles in 2021 to 280 by 2025. This decline is due to ridesharing, and then ARS are fulfilling a more significant part of transportation needs.

Benefits in Stage 1

We will begin to see some benefits from AVs in this Stage, but they will be small at this point because AVs will only account for a small portion of transportation. Most of the benefits will be concentrated in those areas of the country using ARS. They will see immediate mobility for those who can't drive, costs savings for those who can use ARS instead of owning a car, and a slight reduction in accidents. However, the reductions in accidents involving AVs will be enough to demonstrate their increased safety.

Disruptions in Stage 1

There will be minimal disruptions in Stage 1 since most AV technology inroads will be in ARS. The initial disruption will be a shift from ridesharing to ARS in the southern and western areas of the country. Some of this will offset the potential growth of ridesharing, and some will cannibalize ridesharing in Stage 1. This will start to reduce opportunities for Uber, Lyft, and taxi drivers.

Even though autonomous trucking will grow during this stage, it shouldn't impact the number of truck drivers since it will mostly offset the growing need for new truck drivers.

Stage 2 (2026-2030)
Broad Acceptance of AVs

During Stage 2, from 2026-2030, AVs will become broadly accepted in the U.S. More people will become comfortable using ARS, and people will increasingly rely on it as their primary form of transportation. Individuals will start to purchase AVs at retail for their own use.

Other markets will also see rapid growth in this stage. Autonomous home delivery will rapidly begin to replace driver-based delivery as custom-developed vehicles are incorporated into fleets. Autonomous trucking will grow significantly.

Most importantly, the benefits of AVs will become more evident during this stage. The disruptions will also become more apparent.

ARS

ARS will proliferate during Stage 2. The number of ARS vehicles in use in the United States alone will increase to more than a million by 2026 and 5 million in 2030 at the end of Stage 2. It will expand into the northern and northeast parts of the country. ARS will displace ridesharing in this stage, becoming about 2/3 of the combined market.

ARS will continue to grow in metropolitan areas in the southern and western states during this stage. It will also begin to be offered in the northern and eastern states as the capabilities of vehicles are improved. Second-generation ARS autonomous vehicles will be introduced in this stage, making the rides even more appealing to passengers.

The ARS market will grow to be one of the largest markets in the U.S. and the world during Stage 2. The combined revenue of ARS companies in the United States will be greater than $500 billion by 2028 and greater than $750 billion by the end of Stage 2. There will be more than a half-dozen significant companies aggressively competing in this market during Stage 2.

I expect that all ARS companies will be spun off from the companies that initially created them. The largest ARS companies will have more than $100 billion in revenue with substantial profits. Their stock market capitalizations will collectively exceed $2 trillion, making them some of the most successful companies ever. However, the total investment to get there will be staggering. I estimate that $600 - $750 billion will be invested in ARS in Stage 2, including new ARS vehicles, the replacement of first-generation vehicles, and fleet operations centers.

Autonomous Trucking

Stage 2 will see a significant surge in autonomous trucking. Long-haul autonomous trucking will have unbeatable competitive advantages over traditional trucking. It will be 20%-30% less expensive and have 30%+ faster delivery. Terminal-to-terminal will still be the dominant autonomous mode, but autonomous deliveries will be made directly to endpoints by the end of the stage

By the end of Stage 2, approximately 700,000 autonomous trucks in service will provide 37% of the trucking miles. Most trucks manufactured will be autonomous, as manufacturers try to fill the demand for autonomous trucks, and the demand for non-autonomous trucks will dry up. The total number of long-haul trucks needed will start to decline slightly as the increased productivity of autonomous trucks offsets the growth in demand for long-distance trucking.

Autonomous Home Delivery

Autonomous home delivery will proliferate in Stage 2. Designing and building specialized autonomous delivery vehicles will accelerate toward the end of Stage 1. By Stage 2, these will be produced in volume, and major food chains and third-party delivery services will put them quickly into use because the competitive cost advantages are so significant.

Autonomous food delivery will become the norm in Stage 2. More than 400,000 specialized autonomous delivery vehicles will be used to deliver pizza, fast food, and other meals by the end of Stage 2. Everyone will become used to seeing these cute little colorful vehicles buzzing around town. Acquiring these vehicles will require an investment of approximately $20-$25 billion in this stage by the companies providing autonomous delivery. The major pizza chains will lead the way with specially-designed delivery vehicle fleets of AVs that will be much smaller than cars today. Other major companies like McDonald's and Walmart will also have their own fleets. Third-party delivery services will offer an autonomous delivery service for restaurants and others. These services will become so pervasive that individuals and groups will also use these services. Families can have meals delivered to their elderly parents, churches can have meals delivered to shut-ins, and entrepreneurs will create restaurants in their homes with autonomous delivery.

Autonomous deliveries will grow to almost 40% of the total home-delivery market by 2030.

AV Retail Market

The AV retail market will start growing in Stage 2. More vehicles will be designed and manufactured to be sufficiently-autonomous, and the price for these vehicles will come down to more affordable levels. More customers will want the functionality and convenience of sufficiently-autonomous vehicles.

AV sales will grow rapidly beginning in 2026. It will jump to 10%. At the end of Stage 2, there will be 12 million AVs owned by individuals. This is larger than the 5 million AVs operated by autonomous ride services, but ARS AVs will still drive more miles.

Even with the rapid growth of new AV sales, AVs will be less than 5% of all vehicles registered in the U.S. at the end of Stage 2. Used cars are such a significant proportion of the number of registered vehicles that it will take many years for them to be displaced by AVs. I expect that the resale value of used cars will decline because they don't have semi-autonomous capabilities.

Benefits

In Stage 2, we will start to see the full extent of benefits from AVs. Annually, thousands of lives will be saved, and hundreds of thousands of people will avoid serious injuries. The cost of transportation will be dramatically lowered for those who have shifted from owning cars to ARS. Millions of people previously unable to travel will now be mobile. During Stage 2, many of the rapidly growing population of older people will forego driving, replacing it with ARS or their own AVs.

Autonomous home delivery will lower the cost of home delivery significantly, making it a more used service. The cost of shipping by autonomous trucking will rapidly decline. All of these will have a measurable positive impact on productivity and the cost of living.

Disruptions

During Stage 2, the disruptions from AVs will be unmistakable. Millions of jobs will be lost in the United States in this stage, primarily those involved in ridesharing, home delivery, and trucking. This loss of jobs will cause protests and lobbying to slow the progress of autonomous vehicles, but it won't stop what is inevitable. The United States, and the world, will need to figure out how to adjust unless those jobs are replaced elsewhere.

As more people use ARS in this stage, the demand for car sales will begin to decline gradually. I expect this decline will be more in the mid-priced and lower-priced ranges where people primarily use cars for transportation. Families that own more than one vehicle will reduce the number they own and use ARS instead. Some auto segments won't be as affected in Stage 2. The market segment for premium-priced cars will probably not decline as much because reducing the cost of transportation will not be as crucial in this segment. Also, the pick-up truck market will not drop since these are used for more purposes than transportation.

Industries supporting retail car sales will start to see a gradual decline in Stage 2. These industries include auto dealers, car repair, insurance agents, etc. It won't be destructive for most of them in this stage, but they will see their level of business decline, with profits declining faster

Stage 3 (2031-2035)
AV Proliferation

In Stage 3, AVs will become an accepted form of transportation. More than 20% of all passenger vehicle miles will be made with AVs by the beginning of this stage, and it will double by the end of the stage.

The technology of AVs will continue to advance, and during Stage 3, connected vehicles will become more popular. Using post-5G communications technologies, AVs will communicate with other AVs and infrastructure, such as traffic lights. With these technologies, AVs will be able to operate much more safely at higher speeds than traditional cars could even do at lower speeds.

By the end of this stage, combined revenue from ARS, AV retail sales, autonomous trucking, and autonomous home delivery will exceed $2.5 trillion. There will be more than 50 million AVs of different types on the road in the U.S.

ARS

In Stage 3, ARS will become thoroughly entrenched, accounting for as much as 30% of the total miles traveled and generating well over $1 trillion in annual revenue in the United States. Globally, ARS will be a $2 trillion market. During this stage, the cost per mile of ARS will drop well below $1.

Winners and losers will be established in the ARS market. I expect about a half-dozen successful companies dominating this market throughout the country. There will also be some smaller specialized companies.

By Stage 3, ARS AVs will be in their fourth generation with different versions for mobile offices, living rooms, group meetings, and entertainment. There will be luxury options as well as low-cost single-passenger ARS options. Overall, there will be more than 10 million autonomous ARS vehicles in the U.S. Almost all will be third or fourth generation vehicles by the end of Stage 3, requiring additional investment of more than $600 billion during this stage. ARS will be fully integrated into other transit systems providing innovative combined transportation alternatives.

Autonomous Trucking

During Stage 3, almost all new long-haul trucks will be autonomous, and the manufacturing capacity of autonomous trucks will be the limiting factor. The number of autonomous trucks will increase during this stage by one million to more than 1.7 million in 2035. Autonomous trucks produced in this stage will be more advanced than those produced in Stage 2. They will be capable of being fully-autonomous and be able to drive from warehouse to warehouse.

More than 50% of the trucks, carrying most of the shipping, will be at least sufficiently-autonomous. Both fully-autonomous and transfer-hub models will be used. Trucking companies that are not autonomous will find it challenging to compete in this stage because they won't be price competitive. This will cause the trucking market to consolidate with larger trucking fleets.

Autonomous Home Delivery

By the end of this stage, there will be more than 1.3 million autonomous home delivery vehicles. They will be so common that they will cease to be unique. More than half of the same-day home deliveries will be done by autonomous vehicles. Pizza, fast food, and other restaurants that still rely on human-based delivery will find it difficult to compete.

Same-day home delivery will start to become a competitive advantage for groceries and other routine household products. Walmart and Target may use this as an opportunity to displace Amazon in many product categories. The investment in autonomous home delivery will be in the hundreds of billions of dollars.

AV Retail Market

By the end of Stage 3, There will be only about 200 million registered vehicles in the United States, and AVs will represent 20% of these. These 40 million individual-owned AVs still will only provide less than half of the autonomous miles traveled compared to ARS.

With the inroads of ARS, new car sales will be less than 13 million per year, and more than half of them will be autonomous. The remaining auto manufacturers in the U.S will be those that are successful with their AV models.

AVs will still account for less than 20% of the personal-vehicle passenger miles because there will still be a large installed base of more traditional cars. With an average vehicle lifespan of more than 12 years, it will take some time to replace all cars, although these will decline.

This will also be the stage where the containment or possible elimination of traditional human-driven cars will be discussed. Will they be considered too dangerous by the new AV safety standards? Will they be restricted to certain roads?

Benefits

The benefits of autonomous vehicles will be fully recognized in Stage 3. There may still be some doubters, but the momentum will swing in favor of AVs. Some of the benefits that will be measured in this stage include:

- A significant reduction in traffic accidents with tens of thousands of lives saved annually. This will shift attention to the unnecessary risk of human-driven vehicles. ("My son would still be alive if the drunk driver was using an AV.")
- Millions of families will save thousands of dollars a year by not owning a car. They will tell stories about what a waste it was to own a car that sat idle for 95% of the time.

- Millions of people previously unable to travel will have mobility. Most older adults will stop driving altogether and use AVs.

- Same-day home delivery will proliferate even more with the lower cost of autonomous home delivery.

- Air pollution will be reduced as electric vehicles (primarily AVs) replace gasoline cars. Discussions will begin about penalizing gas cars for pollution.

Disruptions

As the benefits materialize, the full consequences of the disruption from AVs will also emerge. Remember the discussion previously in this book that benefits come at a cost to someone. In this stage, some of the following disruptions will begin to emerge:

- The "auto-accident" industry will contract. This includes trial lawyers, insurance companies, auto repair shops, the others. There may even be a measurable reduction in ambulance calls and emergency room visits.

- Gas stations will begin to disappear. With more than half of the vehicles being electric, there will be an overabundance of gas stations with less volume. Correspondingly, the oil industry will see a significant decline in demand. Governments will have found alternatives to gasoline tax to fund road infrastructure.

- The auto industry will see the final stage of disruption, with some succeeding in AVs, some shrinking, and some going out of business entirely.

- Millions of people driving for ridesharing and home delivery companies will lose their jobs. Many of these are part-time jobs, but there will also be a lot of full-time jobs lost.

- There will be a decline in the need for truck drivers in this stage, and more than 100,000 will lose their jobs.

- The airline industry will begin to see competition for short and medium-distance routes.

Stage 4 (2040)
AVs Become the Primary Form of Transportation

Stage 4 goes from 2036 to 2040 and beyond. By 2040, approximately 2/3 of the transportation will be provided by AVs. ARS will provide more than a third of passenger miles and will be a routine mode of travel. The cost of ARS will go down to $.50 per mile. Many more people won't even bother getting a driver's license and owning a car will be something of the past for the new generation coming into adulthood in the 2030s.

All AVs will be connected, and traffic will be synchronized at high speeds with almost no accidents. Driving a car will be considered a hardship for many who don't have other alternatives. However, it will still be a sport or hobby for many who still enjoy driving. Autonomous trucks will be the norm. By 2040, approximately 70% of trucking will be autonomous.

Over the 20 years between the start of Stage 1 and 2040, approximately 60% to 70% of different forms of transportation will be autonomous. This adoption rate is like many of the new technologies discussed at the beginning of this chapter.

At some point during this stage, society will need to deal with the remaining non-autonomous vehicles and decide how to regulate them.

Conclusion

It's clear that autonomous vehicles eventually will replace traditional cars and trucks, and they will transform transportation as we currently know it today. We are now at the end of Stage 0, the AV Initial Development Stage. The launch of autonomous vehicles will begin in 2022, the start of what I refer to as Stage 1. The fastest and most profound change in this first stage will be the advent of autonomous ride services (ARS), which will begin to replace individually-owned cars. ARS will eventually become one of the largest industries in the world. Autonomous trucking and autonomous home delivery will follow closely.

By Stage 2, starting in 2026, autonomous vehicles will become accepted entirely. The benefits of AVs will be realized, but so will the disruptions. Both will be substantial. Stage 3 will usher in even more advanced AVs. By stage 4, 20 years after their introduction, AVs will have a 60%-70% adoption rate, and AVS will have almost completely replaced dumb cars as we know them today.

At that time, the horseless carriage, a little more than a century after its introduction, will pass into history, replaced by the driverless autonomous vehicle.

Index

Footnotes

[i] National Highway Traffic Safety Administration, *Traffic Safety Facts*, April 2019.

[ii] National Highway Traffic Safety Administration, *Traffic Safety Facts*, August 2016.

[iii] INRIX Research July 12, 2017.

[iv] 2018 Annual Disability Statistics, National Institute on Disability, Independent Living, and Rehabilitation Research.

[v] www.ride.guru, July 2019

[vi] Source: Patently Apple

[vii] Canalys (Palo Alto, Singapore) "US Sales of cars with level 2 driving automation features grow 322% in Q1 2019", May 28, 2019

[viii] Canalys (Palo Alto, Singapore) September 9, 2019.

[ix] Mike Montgomery, Forbes, June 5, 2019.

[x] Autonomous Vehicles in China By Egil Juliussen 09.18.2020

[xi] US Department of Transportation: May 2015 (Revised), The Economic and Societal Impact of Motor Vehicle Crashes, 2010 (Revised)

[xii] U.S. Department of Transportation, Preparing for the Future of Transportation Automated Vehicles 3.0

[xiii] Waymo LLC letter to the FMCSA, June 18, 2019.

[xiv] Uber's August 2019 comment letter to the FMCSA

[xv] Autonomous Vehicles | Self-Driving Vehicles Enacted Legislation, National Conference of State Legislators, March 19, 2019.

[xvi] Reid Wilson, New York Times, March 3, 2014.